# Whistleblowing in the Australian Public Sector

Enhancing the theory and practice of
internal witness management in
public sector organisations

# Whistleblowing in the Australian Public Sector

Enhancing the theory and practice of internal witness management in public sector organisations

Edited by A. J. Brown

ANU

THE AUSTRALIAN NATIONAL UNIVERSITY

E PRESS

ANU
E PRESS

the Australia and New Zealand
**School of Government**

Published by ANU E Press
The Australian National University
Canberra ACT 0200, Australia
Email: anuepress@anu.edu.au
This title is also available online at: http://epress.anu.edu.au/whistleblowing_citation.html

---

National Library of Australia
Cataloguing-in-Publication entry

| | |
|---|---|
| Title: | Whistleblowing in the Australian public sector : enhancing the theory and practice of internal witness management in public sector organisations / editor, A J Brown. |
| ISBN: | 9781921536182 (pbk.)<br>9781921536199 (pdf.) |
| Series: | ANZSOG series |
| Notes: | Bibliography. |
| Subjects: | Whistle blowing--Australia<br>Whistle blowing--Law and legislation--Australia<br>Corruption--Australia--Prevention.<br>Ethics--Australia.<br>Responsibility--Australia. |

Other Authors/Contributors:
      Brown, A. J. (Alexander Jonathan), 1966-

Dewey Number:   353.460994

---

Cover design by John Butcher.

Funding for this monograph series has been provided by the Australia and New Zealand School of Government Research Program.

# John Wanna, *Series Editor*

Professor John Wanna is the Sir John Bunting Chair of Public Administration at the Research School of Social Sciences at The Australian National University. He is the director of research for the Australian and New Zealand School of Government (ANZSOG). He is also a joint appointment with the Department of Politics and Public Policy at Griffith University and a principal researcher with two research centres: the Governance and Public Policy Research Centre and the nationally-funded Key Centre in Ethics, Law, Justice and Governance at Griffith University. Professor Wanna has produced around 17 books including two national text books on policy and public management. He has produced a number of research-based studies on budgeting and financial management including: *Budgetary Management and Control* (1990); *Managing Public Expenditure* (2000), *From Accounting to Accountability* (2001) and, most recently, *Controlling Public Expenditure* (2003). He has just completed a study of state level leadership covering all the state and territory leaders — entitled *Yes Premier: Labor leadership in Australia's states and territories* — and has edited a book on Westminster Legacies in Asia and the Pacific — *Westminster Legacies: Democracy and responsible government in Asia and the Pacific*. He was a chief investigator in a major Australian Research Council funded study of the Future of Governance in Australia (1999-2001) involving Griffith and the ANU. His research interests include Australian and comparative politics, public expenditure and budgeting, and government-business relations. He also writes on Australian politics in newspapers such as *The Australian*, *Courier-Mail* and *The Canberra Times* and has been a regular state political commentator on ABC radio and TV.

# Table of Contents

# Foreword

Whistleblowing, or the public interest reporting of wrongdoing by public officials, is a key means for identifying and rectifying wrongdoing in the public sector. The way that whistleblowers are managed is a vital issue—for the individuals and organisations involved and for public accountability and integrity more generally.

Since 2005, the national research project 'Whistling While They Work: Enhancing the theory and practice of internal witness management in the Australian public sector' has investigated this vital process. It is the first comprehensive project of its kind in Australia. Through the participation of numerous partners across many Australian jurisdictions, the project has collected levels of data that also makes it, per capita, the most comprehensive empirical study of whistleblowing conducted worldwide.

This book constitutes the first of two major reports from the project, setting out the lessons from this research. While the findings expressed are those of the authors, the data they report and the issues they highlight provide important new departure points for debate about how whistleblowing can be better managed.

The Whistling While They Work project focused on the less sensational and more practical aspects of how public interest whistleblowing should be managed. The objectives of the project include the development of new standards for internal disclosure procedures in public sector integrity systems; fostering improved coordination between public agencies and integrity bodies in the handling and oversight of disclosures; and supporting improved internal witness management strategies in a range of different types of public sector organisations.

The project has produced a comprehensive picture of the issues faced by those involved in reporting wrongdoing and managing the response. This picture highlights the strengths and weaknesses of current systems. A full cross-section of systems is covered—with data based on agency statistics, the experience of whistleblowers, the views of managers, the assessments of 'case-handlers' involved in managing whistleblowing and the perceptions and experiences of public officials generally, including many who have not seen wrongdoing and many who have seen it, but not reported it.

The research highlights the factors that make the facilitation and management of public interest disclosures so challenging and complex. Findings are made that will help public sector managers improve existing processes, at an individual, organisational and jurisdictional level. The findings range from the steps to be taken by managers to assess the risk of reprisal against a person who has made a disclosure to the need for stronger mechanisms to support staff members who report wrongdoing, and the legislative reforms needed to underpin these processes.

A second report from the Whistling While They Work project will describe in more detail the 'internal witness management systems' of a cross-section of the 304 public agencies studied in this project. The second report will contain new model procedures for managing whistleblowing and provide practical insights on encouraging and managing public interest disclosures.

We congratulate the research team for assembling a rich body of information on current practice in Australia for managing public interest whistleblowing. We also thank the large number of public sector agencies and public employees who participated in the research. The picture presented in this report would be less complete, and the findings less compelling, without their participation and support.

The research collected in this book provides an excellent platform for review and reform. The challenge now lies with public sector agencies, managers and integrity and oversight agencies to build on these research findings to establish—or, where established, improve—our nation's systems for managing public interest whistleblowing.

Professor John McMillan, Commonwealth Ombudsman

Bruce Barbour, NSW Ombudsman

Robert Needham, Chairperson, Crime and Misconduct Commission (Queensland)

David Bevan, Queensland Ombudsman

James Purtill, Public Service Commissioner (Queensland)

Dr Ruth Shean, Commissioner for Public Sector Standards (Western Australia)

The Hon L W Roberts-Smith RFD QC, Commissioner, Corruption and Crime Commission (Western Australia)

Chris Field, Ombudsman, Western Australia

George Brouwer, Ombudsman, Victoria

Frank Costigan, QC, Transparency International Australia

# Acknowledgments

This book forms the first report of the national research project 'Whistling While They Work: Enhancing the theory and practice of internal witness management in the Australian public sector' (see www.griffith.edu.au/whistleblowing). This research was made possible by support from the Australian Research Council (Linkage Project LP0560303) and the partner organisations to the project:

| | |
|---|---|
| *Commonwealth:* | Commonwealth Ombudsman |
| | Australian Public Service Commission |
| *New South Wales:* | Independent Commission Against Corruption |
| | NSW Ombudsman |
| *Queensland:* | Crime and Misconduct Commission |
| | Queensland Ombudsman |
| | Office of the Public Service Commissioner |
| *Western Australia:* | Corruption and Crime Commission |
| | Ombudsman Western Australia |
| | Office of the Public Sector Standards Commissioner |
| *Victoria:* | Ombudsman Victoria |
| *Northern Territory:* | Commissioner for Public Employment |
| *Australian Capital Territory:* | Chief Minister's Department |
| *Non-government partner:* | Transparency International Australia |

The authors thank all project partners and colleagues on the project research team for their support and direct and indirect contributions to these results. Special thanks is given, in addition to the authors listed in this book, to Yasmine Fauzee, Linda Waugh, Susan Johnson, John Boyd, Hilary Fox, Michael Carrel, Lindy Annakin, Glenn Ross, David Solosy, Coral Leary, Laurie Cullinan, Peter Larmour and our international advisors Janet Near, Marcia Miceli, Guy Dehn and David Lewis, for all their major contributions to the project. We also thank the many individuals and organisations who commented on the draft report, released in October 2007 at the inaugural Australian Public Sector Anti-Corruption Conference, Sydney—in particular, Whistleblowers Australia for detailed and constructive criticism of the draft report.

The findings and views expressed are those of the authors and do not necessarily represent the views of the Australian Research Council or the partner organisations in the project.

# Authors and contributors

**Lindy Annakin** is a doctoral scholar with the Whistling While They Work project, Discipline of Government and International Relations, University of Sydney, and an officer of the NSW Government. Email: bann3421@mail.syd.edu.au

**Dr A. J. Brown** is project leader of the Whistling While They Work project, Senior Lecturer, Socio-Legal Research Centre, Griffith Law School, Griffith University. He is also a former Senior Investigation Officer with the Commonwealth Ombudsman. Email: A.J.Brown@griffith.edu.au

**Dr Peter Cassematis** is an organisational psychologist and senior research assistant with the Whistling While They Work project Socio-Legal Research Centre, Griffith Law School, Griffith University. Email: P.Cassematis@griffith.edu.au

**Marika Donkin** is a senior research assistant at the University of New South Wales and former senior research assistant, Discipline of Government and International Relations, University of Sydney, and Research and Prevention Officer, Independent Commission Against Corruption (New South Wales). Email: m.donkin@unsw.edu.au

**Associate Professor Paul Latimer** teaches law in the Faculty of Business and Economics, Monash University. Email: Paul.Latimer@BusEco.monash.edu.au

**Professor Paul Mazerolle** is director of the Key Centre for Ethics, Law, Justice and Governance and director of the Violence Research Program, Griffith University. He is a former Director of Prevention and Research at the Crime and Misconduct Commission (Queensland). Email: P.Mazerolle@griffith.edu.au

**Dr Evalynn Mazurski** is Senior Research Officer, Corruption Prevention, Education and Research, at the Independent Commission Against Corruption (New South Wales). Email: emazurski@icac.nsw.gov.au

**Professor John McMillan** is the Commonwealth Ombudsman. Email: ombudsman@ombudsman.gov.au

**Professor Margaret Mitchell** holds a chair at the University of Western Sydney and was formerly director of the Selinger Centre at Edith Cowan University (Western Australia). Email: m.mitchell@uws.edu.au

**Jane Olsen** is a Research and Prevention Officer of the Crime and Misconduct Commission (Queensland) and former senior research assistant, Socio-Legal Research Centre, Griffith University. Email: jane.olsen@cmc.qld.gov.au

**Peter Roberts** is Senior Lecturer, Centre for Investigative Studies and Crime Reduction, Charles Sturt University, and a former senior executive with the

Commonwealth Attorney-General's Department and the National Crime Authority. Email: peroberts@csu.edu.au

**Dr Rodney Smith** is Senior Lecturer, Discipline of Government and International Relations, University of Sydney. Email: r.smith@econ.usyd.edu.au

**Chris Wheeler** is NSW Deputy Ombudsman and a partner investigator on the Whistling While They Work project research team. Email: CWheeler@ombo.nsw.gov.au

**Professor Richard Wortley** is Head of School, School of Criminology and Criminal Justice, Griffith University. Email: R.Wortley@griffith.edu.au

# Glossary

**ANOVA:** 'Analysis of variance' tests for the difference between the mean score of two or more groups and a single dependent variable measured on a continuous scale. For example, the difference between reporters and non-reporters (groups) and job satisfaction (measured 1–5).

**Case-handler:** A person in a non-managerial role whose duties include dealing with reported wrongdoing. In the present research, case-handlers include officers working in: a) internal audit, fraud, investigation or ethics units; b) human resources/equity and merit units; c) internal support programs for employees who report wrongdoing; d) peer support for employees who report wrongdoing; e) internal staff counselling or welfare services; f) external staff counselling or welfare services; g) external watchdog or investigation agencies; h) unions or professional associations; and i) other specialist units or roles relevant to the reporting of wrongdoing.

**Case-handler and manager surveys:** A matched pair of surveys exploring the experiences and beliefs of employees whose role requires them to deal with reported wrongdoing. The results of the two populations are directly comparable. Limited to the **case study agencies**.

**Case study agencies:** A subset of 15 agencies (from across Australia) that participated in the **agency survey** and **employee survey**, which volunteered to also participate in further research. Results from these agencies can be validly generalised to the wider sample population.

**Commonwealth:** Commonwealth Government, also known as the Australian Government.

**Employee survey:** The workplace experiences and relationships questionnaire, examining attitudinal, organisational and situational reasons for making, or not making, a report. Open to employee samples from 118 participating agencies, with 7663 participants.

**Internal witness:** An alternative, but definitional equivalent (in the present research) to the term 'whistleblower', developed for use in the context of internal and regulatory disclosures. Intended to recognise the many different roles and forms **whistleblowing** can take.

**Internal witness survey:** A questionnaire intended to give a more detailed picture of the whistleblower experience than provided by the **employee survey**. The sample included voluntary participants who reported wrongdoing between July 2002 and June 2004. Limited to the **case study agencies**.

**Logistic regression:** A method of statistical analysis that allows the use of either categorical or continuous predictor variables. The aim of this analysis is to predict group membership (also called an outcome or dependent variable) from a combination of predictor variables (also called independent or explanatory variables). The estimates from a logistical regression model for each predictor variable give an estimate of the effect of that variable on the outcome variable, after adjusting for all other predictors in the model.

**Non-role reporter:** A person who made a report of wrongdoing when it was not within the requirements of their formal position within the organisation to do so, defined in this research as any reporter of wrongdoing who was not a **role reporter**.

**Organisational citizenship behaviour (OCB):** Discretionary extra-role behaviour performed voluntarily by an employee without any formal job requirement to do so, which promotes the effective functioning of the organisation. In the present research, this was measured with an established scale that assessed 'interpersonal helping', 'individual initiative', 'personal industry' and 'loyal boosterism'.

**Pearson's correlation:** Measures the strength of the relationship between two continuous variables. For example, if time spent reading this report increases your knowledge of whistleblowing, there is a positive correlation between reading the report and knowledge gained. Correlation is not causation.

**Personnel and workplace grievances:** A category of wrongdoing types that can impact on individuals in organisations without necessarily reflecting lack of organisational or public integrity generally, or impacting on society at large. These are excluded in this research from analyses of public interest **whistleblowing**. Examples include unfair dismissal, unfair selection processes and bullying (see Appendix 2 for items and categories used in this research).

**Pro-social behaviour:** Behaviour that would generally be perceived within a particular social group as benefiting other people. This behaviour does not have to be purely altruistic in motive because the outcome is the focal point.

**Public interest matters:** All wrongdoing not categorised as a **personnel or workplace grievance** in this research. Major categories include defective administration, misconduct for material gain, perverting justice or accountability (see Appendix 2 for items and categories used in this research).

**Role reporter:** A person who made a report in line with formal job requirements related to their organisational role. In the present research, a role reporter was defined as a reporter who found out about the wrongdoing only because it was reported to them in their official capacity *or* a manager whose report concerned only wrongdoers below them in the organisational hierarchy.

**Statistical significance:** The probability that the result of an analysis indicates a real measure of difference or association and should not be discounted as a chance outcome. Represented by the 'p' value reported in text or tables (for example, $p = 0.01$ indicates that the result would occur by chance only 1 per cent of the time). Significance is not the same as 'importance' in a practical sense, particularly in very large samples.

**Watchdog agency:** Independent government agencies whose role is to ensure other public sector agencies perform their role with due regard to law, policy, procedure and integrity. Their roles can involve research, policy, training and advice as well as investigation.

**Whistleblower:** An organisation member (former or current) who engages in whistleblowing.

**Whistleblowing:** The disclosure by an organisation member (former or current) of illegal, immoral or illegitimate practices under the control of their employers to people or organisations that might be able to effect action. This research focuses on 'public interest' whistleblowing, in which the issues disclosed raise **public interest matters** in addition or as opposed to those that involve simply a personal or private complaint (for example, **personnel or workplace grievances**).

# Summary

## 1. Introduction

### The Whistling While They Work project

This book presents results from a program of empirical and comparative legal research into public interest whistleblowing in Australian public sector agencies, undertaken in 2005–08 through the Australian Research Council-funded Linkage Project 'Whistling While They Work'.

The study was the largest of its kind ever undertaken in Australia, and one of the largest per capita ever undertaken in the world. It has involved six Australian universities, a number of international collaborators and 14 partner organisations, including many Australian public integrity and public sector management agencies.

### What is 'whistleblowing'?

Whistleblowing is the disclosure by organisation members (former or current) of illegal, immoral or illegitimate practices under the control of their employers to people or organisations that might be able to effect action.

In this book, whistleblowing is also taken to mean disclosures by organisation members of matters of 'public interest'—that is, suspected or alleged wrongdoing that affects more than the personal or private interests of the person making the disclosure.

The research encompasses internal whistleblowing, whistleblowing to regulatory or integrity agencies and public whistleblowing.

### What is 'wrongdoing'?

A wide definitional approach was taken in the research in order to better differentiate between different types of perceived wrongdoing (including public and private interest) and to be consistent with the need to encourage an 'if in doubt, report' approach to workplace problems. The project surveys offered a list of 38 different behaviours covering a wide spectrum of wrongdoing types, grouped into seven categories for the purpose of analysis:

- misconduct for material gain
- conflict of interest
- improper or unprofessional behaviour
- defective administration
- waste or mismanagement of resources
- perverting justice or accountability
- personnel or workplace grievances.

In this book, public interest whistleblowing refers to the data from respondents who indicated they reported wrongdoing in the first six of these seven categories.

## Methods and limitations

The empirical research involved Commonwealth, NSW, Queensland and West Australian public agencies.

The major employee survey captured evidence from 7663 public officials from 118 public agencies across these jurisdictions.

Other agency, internal witness, case-handler and manager surveys captured evidence from larger and smaller groups of agencies, including 15 'case study' agencies, also from these jurisdictions.

The bulk of the data reflect the experience of individuals who are still public sector employees, rather than those who might have left the public sector as a result of their experiences.

Extensive comparative analysis was also undertaken into the relevant legislative regimes of the jurisdictions and the content and comprehensiveness of the whistleblowing procedures of public agencies. All this evidence and analysis has been drawn on to produce the lessons and key findings presented in this book.

## Continuing analysis: towards best practice

This book represents the first of two major reports of the Whistling While They Work project.

A second report on current and prospective 'best practice' in agency-level systems for managing whistleblowing will also be published, involving further quantitative analysis and additional qualitative research into how whistleblowing is currently managed, based on experiences in the 15 case study agencies.

## Part 1: A new picture of public sector whistleblowing

Part 1 presents empirical data of the experiences of a wide range of public servants across a wide range of agencies, including those who observe wrongdoing but don't report it, and those who report it and do or don't suffer. These chapters present an aggregate or averaged picture of the experiences of public officials. They also point to the substantial differences in outcomes depending on the circumstances in which wrongdoing is seen and whistleblowing occurs, including substantial differences in the responses of different agencies.

# Chapter 2: The incidence and significance of whistleblowing

## How much reporting goes on in the Australian public sector?

Reporting of wrongdoing, including public interest whistleblowing, is a more common and routine activity in the majority of Australian public sector agencies than previously understood.

In the two years before the employee survey (undertaken in 2006–07), 71 per cent of all respondents had direct evidence of at least one of the wide range of nominated examples of wrongdoing in their organisation.

Sixty-one per cent of respondents rated at least one form of perceived wrongdoing as being at least 'somewhat serious', while 28 per cent of respondents said they had formally reported the wrongdoing that they considered to be the most serious.

## 'Whistleblowing' as opposed to 'reporting'

Twenty per cent of respondents were estimated as having reported the most serious wrongdoing outside their organisational role—that is, as potential 'whistleblowers'.

In the case of 12 per cent of respondents, the reported (most serious) wrongdoing involved 'public interest' wrongdoing such as corruption, defective administration or waste, as opposed to personnel and workplace grievances.

Using this conservative estimate, if 12 per cent of all public servants had also reported some form of public interest wrongdoing outside their role in the two years, this estimate would equate to 197 000 public servants nationally.

## How important is current whistleblowing?

Evidence from public employees who have reported wrongdoing, public employees in general and agency statistics indicates that whistleblowing is widely recognised across the public sector as being important to achieving and maintaining public integrity.

Eighty-one per cent of all employee survey respondents who had reported wrongdoing indicated that they would be either 'very likely' or 'extremely likely' to report again.

In the 15 case study agencies, respondents to a survey of managers and case-handlers rated 'reporting by employees' as the single or equal most important means by which wrongdoing was brought to light in their organisations.

## High and low rates of reporting

At least as many public servants who have directly observed wrongdoing do not report it as currently indicate they report it.

Twenty-nine per cent of employee survey respondents who had observed wrongdoing they considered to be 'very' or 'extremely serious' did not report it or otherwise act on it (the inaction rate).

In some agencies, the inaction rate in response to perceived serious wrongdoing is less than 10 per cent of respondent employees; but in at least one agency in each jurisdiction, the inaction rate rises to more than 50 per cent.

These variable results reinforce the fact that general barriers to reporting exist across the public sector and suggest that differences in approach and management culture have strong, measurable effects at the agency level.

# Chapter 3: Who blows the whistle, who doesn't and why?

## Employee characteristics

Employee survey respondents who reported wrongdoing outside their role (non-role reporters—that is, potential whistleblowers) shared most of the same attitudes to their organisation, job and management as non-reporters.

Non-role reporters were slightly more likely to be female and have spent longer in their organisations than others.

There is little evidence that employees who report wrongdoing are predisposed to conflict or are likely to be disgruntled or embittered employees, driven to report by perverse personal characteristics.

Depending on the circumstances, almost any employee could be expected to speak up about wrongdoing. Similarly, depending on the circumstances, almost any employee might also remain silent.

## Characteristics of the wrongdoing

Public employees' decisions about whether to blow the whistle appear to be influenced much more strongly by their organisational context, perceptions of the seriousness of the wrongdoing and their beliefs about whether reporting the wrongdoing will serve any good purpose.

The likelihood of reporting increases when employees assess wrongdoing to be more serious and frequent, when they have direct evidence of the wrongdoing (as opposed to simply observing it) and when it affects them personally.

The likelihood of reporting decreases when these features are not present, when employees assess that the wrongdoing involves multiple participants or when the participants are at a higher organisational level than the observer.

## Reasons for reporting and not reporting wrongdoing

The most important reasons nominated by employees for reporting wrongdoing, when motivated by the circumstances to do so, were confidence that action would be taken on their report, followed by knowledge and confidence in the process they were meant to follow.

Confidence that they would be supported or protected after their report was a lesser consideration for most employees who reported, and was a less important consideration than generally believed by respondents to the case-handler and manager surveys in the case study agencies.

The main reasons for not reporting, given by respondents who did not report, were a belief that no action would be taken or a fear of reprisal, or that management would not protect them from reprisal, especially in circumstances in which the perceived wrongdoers included managers.

These results show that the best ways to ensure that staff will speak up are by demonstrating that if wrongdoing is reported, something will be done and whistleblowers will be supported.

The results also underscore the responsibility of agencies to provide safe and just processes for employees who blow the whistle, given that many do so notwithstanding logical risks of conflict or reprisal. The prospects for encouraging early and more constructive forms of reporting may well depend on management's larger commitment to organisational justice.

## Chapter 4: How do officials report? Internal and external whistleblowing

### Reporting paths

The bulk of whistleblowing begins and ends as an internal process. Ninety-seven per cent of the public interest whistleblowers identified through the employee survey reported internally in their agency in the first instance. Ninety per cent of all public interest whistleblowing also ended internally within the agency.

Only 2.9 per cent of public interest whistleblowers had reported to an external agency or body in the first instance, and only 9.7 per cent of whistleblowing involved an external agency or body at any stage.

Only an extremely small proportion (less than 1 per cent) of all whistleblowers went outside official channels to the media at any stage—typically as a last resort.

Of the majority of whistleblowers who reported internally in the first instance, most also did so up the management chain (84 per cent of all whistleblowers) rather than through specialist internal units or processes (less than 10 per cent).

Of the 138 whistleblowers surveyed in more depth in the case study agencies (internal witness survey), 80 per cent still chose to report internally in the first instance and, for 70 per cent, their whistleblowing remained internal.

## When do whistleblowers choose internal or external paths?

Internal and external whistleblowers indicated high levels of 'organisational citizenship behaviour' (OCB), further challenging the stereotype of an external whistleblower as a disgruntled, organisationally unhappy employee.

Officials who reported externally at any stage indicated higher levels of initiative and lower levels of loyalty than purely internal whistleblowers. It is possible, however, that slightly lower loyalty is simply a result of the conditions that lead an official to report externally, having first reported internally in most cases.

Overall, the results indicate that internal reporting is—and is likely to remain—the most natural reporting path for the majority of public interest whistleblowers, being the path most consistent with traditional ideals of organisational citizenship and 'pro-social' behaviour.

## Do whistleblowers' choices vary with trust in management?

The employee survey found higher trust in management among employees who only ever reported wrongdoing internally and lower trust in management among those who reported externally at any stage, including after having reported internally in the first instance.

These results indicate that when organisations can engender a higher level of trust, they should be able to encourage more employees to report internally, being also the first and only avenue that most public officials currently use. These results also confirm the importance of organisations' internal disclosure procedures and increase their responsibility to manage reporting well on an internal basis.

Challenges include greater effort in training and equipping managers to handle disclosures appropriately, lifting employee awareness of and confidence in different internal and external reporting paths and a need for closer coordination between 'line' and integrity agencies to ensure disclosures are managed in the most appropriate way as early as possible, rather than simply waiting for whistleblower dissatisfaction to become a trigger for further, external complaints.

## Chapter 5: The good, the bad and the ugly—whistleblowing outcomes

### Substantive outcomes including organisational changes

In response to the employee survey, 63 per cent of public interest whistleblowers reported that their disclosure was investigated, 56 per cent of whom indicated that the investigation resulted in improved organisational outcomes.

## Whistleblower satisfaction

Whistleblowers were most likely to be satisfied with the handling of their disclosure if they were kept informed and the investigation resulted in positive, substantive outcomes.

In the case study agencies, the understanding of most respondents to the manager and case-handler surveys about the issues of greatest importance in the management of whistleblowing did not align well with the expectations and understanding of most whistleblowers, even though the overall value of whistleblowing was strongly acknowledged.

## Overall treatment of whistleblowers

Contrary to some stereotypes, it is not inevitable that a whistleblower will suffer mistreatment from co-workers or management as a result of reporting wrongdoing, even if reporting is frequently a difficult and stressful experience.

In response to the employee survey, 78 per cent of public interest whistleblowers said they were treated either well or the same by management and co-workers in their organisation as a result of reporting. Twenty-two per cent of whistleblowers said they were treated badly by management and/or co-workers.

On average, most public interest whistleblowers (at least 70 per cent) are treated either well or the same by management and co-workers in their organisation. While the employee survey did not sample former employees, even on an excessively pessimistic estimate of the experience of former employees, the total proportion of whistleblowers experiencing mistreatment would be unlikely to exceed 30 per cent.

Contrary to common assumptions, when whistleblowers are treated badly, this mistreatment is more likely to come from management than from colleagues or co-workers. Eighteen per cent of whistleblowers indicated that they were treated badly by management, compared with 9 per cent of whistleblowers who indicated they were treated badly by co-workers (with 5 per cent indicating they were treated badly by both).

Indications of whistleblower mistreatment vary greatly between agencies. The proportion of whistleblowers indicating bad treatment by management fell close to zero in some agencies, but in others rose up to 46 per cent.

While 90 per cent of all reporters said they were at least 'somewhat' likely to report again, this was true of only 59 per cent of reporters who said they were treated badly.

## Deliberate mistreatment and reprisals

In the case study agencies, the internal witness survey confirmed that the bad treatment or harm suffered by whistleblowers was most likely intimidation, harassment, heavy scrutiny of work, ostracism, unsafe or humiliating work or other workplace-based negative behaviour.

The main sources of bad treatment or harm reported by those whistleblowers who suffered were not immediate co-workers or colleagues, but managers themselves.

Results from the case-handler and manager surveys confirm the overall pattern of the most and least common types of reprisals.

Only in very rare cases is the nature of the reprisal such that it could meet the legal thresholds required to prove criminal liability on the part of any individual. These results raise questions about whether reliance on criminalisation and prosecution is a well-founded strategy for addressing the bulk of reprisal risks.

## General impacts on whistleblowers

Even successful whistleblowers often report adverse psychological experiences (for example, increased stress) from whistleblowing, though not as adverse as those treated badly.

Based on relationships between the internal witness and employee surveys, approximately 62 per cent of all whistleblower respondents might be estimated as having suffered increased stress as a result of reporting wrongdoing (the most common form of adverse impact), with about 43 per cent of all whistleblowers estimated as suffering extreme stress.

In the case study agencies, 54 per cent of case-handler and manager respondents indicated a belief that employees who reported wrongdoing in their organisations 'often' or 'always' experienced 'emotional, social, physical or financial' problems as a result.

## Chapter 6: Whistleblower mistreatment—identifying the risks

### Expectations of treatment and support

While different employees and whistleblowers assess the risk of mistreatment differently, results from the employee survey do not suggest that mistreated whistleblowers are any more likely to be troublemakers, disgruntled employees or individuals predisposed to conflict than those treated well or the same.

Mistreated whistleblowers appear to have had higher original expectations about management support than those not mistreated, as well as lower expectations that they would be left exposed to risks. Whistleblowers also appear to usually be relatively accurate in self-assessing the reaction of co-workers to their disclosure, but less accurate in their ability to predict the likely reaction of management.

These results confirm the importance of internal disclosure systems that support employees in navigating the management response to disclosures, given the trust that employees are asked to place in management by reporting and the reality that the responses of individual managers can be adverse.

## Risk factors for mistreatment of whistleblowers

While the proportion of all employee survey whistleblower respondents who reported mistreatment was 22 per cent, this could be much higher in whistleblowing cases in which one or more of a number of risk factors were present.

The key risk factors for reported mistreatment by co-workers are, in order of significance, any public interest whistleblowing case in which:

1.  the wrongdoing is perceived as more serious
2.  there is a lack of any positive outcome from an investigation
3.  more than one person is involved in the alleged wrongdoing
4.  the whistleblower is situated in a work group of less than 20 people.

The key risk factors for reported mistreatment by management are, in order of significance, any public interest whistleblowing case in which:

1.  the investigation is not resolved internally and becomes external (although the perceived mistreatment could itself have led to the external disclosure)
2.  there is a lack of any positive outcome from an investigation
3.  the wrongdoing is directed at the whistleblower personally
4.  some or all of the alleged wrongdoers are employed at a higher organisational level than the whistleblower
5.  the wrongdoing is perceived as more serious and/or frequent.

These risk factors confirm the complexity of many whistleblowing cases and help identify the circumstances to which agencies need to be most alert and prepared to address the strongest efforts, in order to reduce or prevent mistreatment.

## Against-the-odds outcomes

Where a 'high-risk' reporting case (based on the above factors) does not result in the reporter indicating mistreatment, the available evidence indicates the reporter might have been better able to escape or ride out mistreatment by co-workers because he or she was significantly older (mean of 46 years) than reporters who recorded mistreatment (mean of 40 years).

Where a 'low-risk' reporting case did result in the reporter indicating mistreatment, the available evidence indicates three further risk factors that could also identify the likelihood of a negative outcome:

- reports of wrongdoing that went through a larger number of internal stages before leading to positive action
- positive action was taken but not as a result of any formal investigation, or any of which the reporter was aware
- the reporter was employed on a part-time, casual or contract basis, rather than a full-time and/or permanent basis.

These results provide new guidance on the processes that public agencies can use to better assess, anticipate and thereby reduce and manage the risks of whistleblower mistreatment.

## Part 2: Managing whistleblowing—organisational systems and responses

Part 2 shifts to analysis of the different management environments and systems within which reporting and non-reporting occur in public sector agencies. The chapters cover management attitudes, internal investigation standards, internal witness support programs, agency whistleblowing procedures and the legislative context.

## Chapter 7: Support for whistleblowing among managers—exploring job satisfaction and awareness of obligations

### Managers, job satisfaction and support for whistleblowing

In the employee survey, the 21 per cent of all respondents who identified as managers demonstrated even greater levels of support for whistleblowing than non-managers, measured in terms of having a favourable personal attitude towards whistleblowing.

General support for whistleblowing also increases among those managers with higher job satisfaction, which appears to be a salient facilitating factor in managers' support for whistleblowing 'in principle'.

Greater levels of trust in management, job satisfaction and organisational citizenship all significantly increase the probability of any employee supporting whistleblowing, as do age and education. Being a manager, however, also increased the probability of supporting whistleblowing, net of other influences.

### Managers, job satisfaction and knowledge of whistleblowing procedures

Managers with higher job satisfaction also indicated an increased knowledge of, and confidence in, their ability to navigate whistleblowing policies.

These results suggest that the organisational benefits of having highly satisfied managers extend not only to having managers with a more favourable personal attitude towards whistleblowing, but managers who should be able to put this attitude into practice through greater knowledge of relevant procedures.

## Managers and knowledge of whistleblowing legislation

Fifty-four per cent of all employee survey respondents indicated that they did not know whether they were covered by legislation setting out their 'rights and responsibilities associated with reporting alleged wrongdoing' involving their organisation.

While managers were more likely than non-managers to indicate that they knew whether they and their employees were covered by relevant legislation, a large proportion of managers—40 per cent—still did not know.

Most respondents who believed they were covered by legislation also indicated that they felt they needed more information and training about it—with this perceived need being significantly higher among managers than non-managers.

These results reinforce the importance of agency systems and procedures, and senior management leadership, that build on and maximise the general support for whistleblowing that exists among individual managers—especially given the dual role that managers often play as the potential solution to, and potential source of, the problems and conflicts associated with reporting of wrongdoing.

## Chapter 8: Investigations—improving practice and building capacity

## Who conducts investigations?

Based on the agency, employee and case-handler and manager surveys, a wide variety of internal organisational units and individuals and external resources are used to conduct investigations in or on behalf of the agencies studied. With almost all employee disclosures made internally, the responsibility for investigating reports of alleged wrongdoing rests primarily within organisations.

In the case study agencies, most internal witnesses, case-handlers and managers tended to agree that investigations were most often well handled if undertaken by some kind of specialist unit (for example, ethical standards, internal audit unit), rather than by line managers—on whom many agencies currently rely heavily.

Public sector organisations also currently rely heavily on using their chief executive officers (CEOs) to investigate whistleblowing matters—even though, in the assessment of most case-handlers and managers, the CEO is rarely the most appropriate person to conduct investigations.

These results highlight the need for appropriate expertise in investigations, but also the need for more careful consideration of the way in which institutional responsibilities for investigations are configured, given that not all management roles can be considered to be routinely compatible with investigation roles.

In the case study agencies, the results from the internal witness, case-handler and manager surveys also indicated that external watchdog or investigation agencies (that is, integrity agencies) did not enjoy much confidence in respect of the timeliness or effectiveness of their involvement in investigations.

These results indicate the importance and the difficulty of achieving more effective relationships between agencies and integrity agencies to help ensure that, wherever possible, the primary investigation of a disclosure is undertaken properly.

## Training and qualifications of investigators

Only 26 per cent of agencies that responded to the agency survey indicated that they required or provided professional training for any staff involved in the investigation of employee-reported wrongdoing.

While 35 per cent of agencies indicated that they provided 'informal or on-the-job' training, the largest group of agencies—39 per cent—indicated that they did not require or provide any particular training.

In the case study agencies, 33 per cent of case-handler and manager respondents indicated that they had experienced professional training in how to deal with whistleblowing cases, while 43 per cent of respondents indicated that they had received only informal training and 24 per cent confirmed that they had no particular training.

This result was largely repeated in respect of case-handlers from internal audit, fraud, investigation and/or ethics units, 24 per cent of whom also confirmed that they had no particular training.

The amount and quality of training were shown to be positively related to case-handler and manager confidence in their ability to deal with whistleblowing reports, as well as less harsh or stereotypical views about the usefulness of whistleblowing and the feasibility of managing whistleblowing incidents to a positive outcome.

## Comparing investigation practice across agencies

Based on a comparison of 12 of the case study agencies, agencies with 'better-than-average' investigatory capacity were more likely to have a higher proportion of employees who reported the most serious wrongdoing they observed (50 per cent) than agencies with only 'average' investigatory capacity (44 per cent).

In agencies with better-than-average investigatory capacity, employees who had reported wrongdoing were also significantly more likely to indicate that they would be likely to report again (mean = 4.22) than equivalent employees in agencies with only average investigatory capacity (mean = 4.01).

These findings reinforce the crucial importance of good investigation practice and capacity to the process of realising the benefits of whistleblowing, and indicate that the conduct and management of internal investigations represent a major, continuing challenge for public sector agencies.

## Chapter 9: Internal witness support—the unmet challenge

### Internal witness support programs

All the surveys indicate that organised systems for supporting and protecting internal witnesses are in relative infancy. Only 54 per cent of all agencies that responded to the agency survey had procedures for identifying internal witnesses in need of active management support and only 11 per cent of all agencies surveyed had a formal internal witness support system.

Even within the case study agencies, which did have higher levels of informal and formal systems, only a very small proportion of public interest whistleblowers (perhaps 1.3 per cent, or 6.5 per cent of all whistleblowers who indicated mistreatment) were estimated as having been provided with active management support.

The reasons for this low take-up of organised or dedicated support services, even in the case study agencies, are likely to include:

*   the low level of resources dedicated to such programs
*   a previous shortage of data about the overall level of whistleblowing
*   uncertainty or confusion about the types of employees intended to be targeted
*   an absence or inadequacy of procedural guidance on how employees should access the support, including an over-reliance on whistleblowers self-identifying for the purposes of gaining support
*   lack of management information systems for ensuring that all deserving whistleblowing cases can be identified and assessed for support
*   inadequate or misapplied statutory definitions.

### Sources and methods of internal witness support

The main sources of support that currently prevent more whistleblowers from suffering more than they do are not organised support programs, but informal social and professional networks, including family, friends, colleagues, union officials and supervisors.

For those whistleblowers whose experience becomes more difficult, some sources of support, including professional counsellors and more formalised assistance programs, become more important, but supervisors, managers and investigation agencies become increasingly less so.

Case-handlers and managers—while not excessively optimistic about their own success—continue to overestimate the extent to which organised or official sources of support are helping prevent worse outcomes. The extent to which whistleblower support is currently reliant on informal, social and professional networks does not appear to be properly appreciated.

There is a high risk that support will fail in any of the many circumstances in which the dual role of direct supervisors and line managers, described in Chapter 7, can turn from positive to negative. There are also signs that most support strategies are reactive, attuned to bolstering the coping skills of whistleblowers to help them 'tough out' difficult situations, rather than geared to management intervention against the sources of workplace conflict.

## Reprisals, risk assessment and responses

Seventy per cent of agencies that responded to the agency survey did not carry out any assessment of the risks of reprisal when officials blew the whistle. Only 15 per cent of all agencies were able to nominate anyone with specific responsibility for undertaking or coordinating risk assessments and only 2 per cent indicated that their risk-assessment procedures were formal.

Thirty per cent of agencies indicated that they had no staff (including existing line managers) responsible for protecting whistleblowers from reprisals.

Reasons for the reactive and inadequate nature of systems for managing reprisal risks and other problems include a lack of previous data about the real nature of the risks, and a lack of the internal management information systems needed to enable case-handlers to engage supervisors and other managers in an effective risk-management approach.

Where reprisal risks are realised, agency case-handlers and managers do not currently regard themselves as very well equipped or well placed to deal with them. Their evidence confirms that, generally, allegations that whistleblowers have suffered reprisals or other management lapses are not currently handled well.

In case study agencies, 38 per cent of manager and case-handler respondents with experience of reprisal allegations indicated a belief that disciplinary action was 'sometimes' or 'often' used as a cover for reprisals.

According to case-handler and manager respondents, the most common reasons for the fact that reprisal allegations are only rarely substantiated relate to difficulties in investigation, including the fact that most reprisals are not acts for which individuals can be held culpable to a criminal standard of proof, but rather are management reprisals and institutional reactions.

Most case-handler respondents from watchdog or integrity agencies were highly critical of agencies' responses to reprisals, but also quite sceptical—like internal agency case-handlers—about their own agencies' ability to improve the situation under existing circumstances.

These results indicate the need for a fresh approach to the handling of whistleblowing cases in which questions arise about the adequacy of the management response, including a new or different relationship between line agencies and integrity agencies in the reporting, monitoring and handling of reprisal risks.

## Chapter 10: Evaluating agency responses—the comprehensiveness and effectiveness of agency procedures

### Awareness and confidence in legislation

Based on the employee survey, in agencies in which more staff are aware of and confident in whistleblowing legislation, there are more positive attitudes to whistleblowing, higher whistleblowing 'propensity' on the part of staff, higher trust in the anticipated management response to whistleblowing and a higher likelihood that serious wrongdoing will be exposed or 'flushed out' (lower inaction rates).

Agencies with higher levels of staff awareness and confidence in legislation are not experiencing any lower rates of mistreatment of reporters than other agencies—suggesting that while increased awareness of legislation encourages staff to report and to trust management, more is needed to meet these raised expectations.

### Comprehensiveness of policies and procedures

A comparative assessment of the comprehensiveness of the whistleblowing procedures of 175 agencies that responded to the agency survey indicates systemic weaknesses in all jurisdictions in the internal disclosure procedures that guide agencies' formal responses to whistleblowing.

Agency internal disclosure procedures are typically weakest for procedures relating to support and protection of whistleblowers. Formal procedures are frequently skewed more towards encouraging reporting and setting in place investigative responses to those reports than towards protection or management of the welfare of the individual employees involved.

Only five of the 175 agencies were rated as having developed reasonably strong procedures for the management of whistleblowing, measured against the current Australian Standard.

## Impact and effectiveness of procedures

Among the 102 agencies whose procedures were reviewed and that participated in the employee survey, more comprehensive internal disclosure procedures were positively associated with a number of positive outcomes, including:

- higher staff awareness of the procedures
- higher levels of general employee support for whistleblowing
- higher staff trust in management's likely response if they blew the whistle
- higher proportion of staff who observed wrongdoing who also reported it
- fewer whistleblowers indicating mistreatment by management
- somewhat fewer whistleblowers indicating mistreatment by co-workers.

More-senior staff members in most agencies, however, currently appear to have little accurate grasp of the quality and comprehensiveness of their own procedures. More-senior staff members tended to have lower trust in their own management's response in agencies whose procedures were in fact more comprehensive, and higher (but probably misplaced) trust in agencies whose procedures were less comprehensive.

While the general weakness of systems for protection of whistleblowers makes it difficult to trace any positive outcomes to better whistleblower support, these results suggest that more comprehensive approaches do yield better outcomes and provide encouragement for agencies prepared to make an effort to develop better whistleblowing management systems.

The patchiness, generally low comprehensiveness and substantial variability of procedures were found across all jurisdictions, indicating a need for the development of new 'best-practice' or 'model' procedures, clearer statutory requirements and better oversight of the quality of procedures and the adequacy of their implementation.

## Chapter 11: Best-practice whistleblowing legislation for the public sector—key principles

### Organisational systems for encouraging and managing whistleblowing

This research has shown that, among the set of clearer, first principles needed to inform the revision or development of best-practice legislation for the management of public interest whistleblowing, several principles relate to the need for more effective operational systems at agency and jurisdictional levels.

The need for more effective operational systems is underscored by the extent of differences between the agency and employee survey results, indicating that, in practice, the bulk of public interest whistleblowing is currently occurring without being recorded, monitored or reported under public interest disclosure legislation.

Legislative reforms requiring prioritisation include:

- redefinition of legislative coverage—that is, subject matter and jurisdiction—in a more comprehensive or 'inclusive' manner to support an 'if in doubt, report' approach to the encouragement and management of disclosure
- minimum standards for internal disclosure procedures in agencies, particularly for managing the welfare of employees who report
- new frameworks for coordinating the management of public interest disclosures, including the tasking of an appropriate external agency with an oversight role and setting out a new relationship between that agency and public sector organisations.

## Realistic compensation mechanisms

There is also a special need for legislative reform to address the current lack of practical remedies for public officials whose lives and careers suffer as a result of having made a public interest disclosure.

The research results and recent case law combine to show that current legislative settings are insufficiently focused on restitution (including financial compensation) as a response to adverse outcomes, as opposed to criminal remedies that are, in any event, inappropriate for the bulk of cases.

Legislation needs to better define the legal responsibilities of employers for the welfare of employees who report, including by providing incentives for public sector managers to be more diligent in exercising their duty of care to ensure a safe workplace for employees by preventing and minimising adverse outcomes.

## Recognising public whistleblowing

Contrary to widespread public expectations and the larger logic of whistleblower protection, only one Australian jurisdiction (New South Wales) has legislative provisions dealing with circumstances under which a whistleblower may take a public interest disclosure outside official channels. Even in New South Wales, the provisions are inadequate.

While the research has confirmed that public whistleblowing is statistically infrequent in comparison with internal whistleblowing, it nevertheless does arise—legitimately. Recognition of this fact is of continuing importance to the successful management of whistleblowing as a process, including to the confidence of employees and the understanding of agencies that if authorities fail to act, a further disclosure may well be justified and protected .

## Best practice legislation: the key principles

In summary, this chapter presents 13 key principles to form the basis for best-practice whistleblowing legislation, reflecting comparative analysis of existing provisions, feedback on the issues identified through the project, lessons from the empirical research and previous reviews from academic literature.

# Chapter 12: Project findings—an agenda for action

In summary, the lessons from the research show particular need for action in all jurisdictions and most public agencies, in the following priority areas:

1. more comprehensive agency systems for recording and tracking employee reports of wrongdoing
2. agency procedures for assessing and monitoring the risk of reprisals or other conflict for those who report
3. clearer and better advice for employees on the range of avenues available for reporting wrongdoing
4. basic training for public sector managers in how to recognise and respond to possible public interest disclosures
5. a program of training for internal investigators in basic techniques, with special attention to issues of internal witness management
6. adoption and expansion of structured support programs for employees who report wrongdoing
7. improved mechanisms for monitoring the welfare of employees who report wrongdoing, from the point of first report
8. more detailed and flexible agency procedures for the investigation and remediation of reprisals and breaches of duty of care
9. a dedicated oversight agency or unit for the coordination of responses to employee-reported wrongdoing
10. legislative action to provide more effective organisational systems and realistic compensation mechanisms, and to recognise public whistleblowing.

# 1. Introduction

## A. J. Brown and Marika Donkin

## Whistleblowing: shifting the focus

Of the many challenges in modern public sector management, few are as complex as the encouragement and management of whistleblowing. The complexity of the challenge is underscored by a severe lack of knowledge about some of the basic facts regarding this important phenomenon.

Because it can lead to the discovery and rectification of wrongdoing, whistleblowing is widely acknowledged as having potentially positive effects—for organisations and for society at large. It is also, however, widely assumed to be undervalued in organisations and in many situations as a relatively rare event likely to involve something of a 'crisis' for the organisation involved. This is because, almost by definition, whistleblowing is often accompanied by many conflicts, tensions and short-term negative effects—including for whistleblowers—whatever long-term positive outcomes might also emerge. Indeed, the problems often associated with whistleblowing have led to a widespread belief that every whistleblower is destined to suffer for their experience and that nothing can be done to protect them from reprisals. Even if they do it once, a sensible employee is often seen as unlikely to blow the whistle a second time.

This bleak picture provides public sector managers with little hope for, or reason to invest in, strategies for encouraging staff to blow the whistle on perceived wrongdoing within their organisation. In this book, however, this bleak picture is revealed to be substantially inaccurate. Resulting from continuing research involving up to 304 public sector agencies from four Australian jurisdictions, the preliminary analysis presented here shows the management of whistleblowing to be a far more varied and sometimes far more positive area of organisational and administrative practice. Rather than rare or 'special', whistleblowing is a routine activity in the majority of Australian public sector agencies. As Chapter 2 explains, on a conservative estimate, perhaps 12 per cent of all public servants have reported some form of public interest wrongdoing in their organisation in a two-year period—an estimate that would equate to 197 000 public servants nationally. At least as many public servants who have directly observed wrongdoing choose not to report it; nevertheless, on average, the number prepared to do so is high.

The level and frequency of whistleblowing appears to have gone under-recognised, until now, for various reasons. Much of this reporting remains confidential. Legislative requirements and administrative systems for the reporting of whistleblowing are patchy. Many if not most whistleblowers prefer not to be tagged as such. There is confusion and inconsistency in the ways in which whistleblowing is defined and labelled. Finally, until very recently, systematic, independent research has been limited. All these explanations raise different, but soluble problems for public sector management.

Another departure from the previous bleak picture comes in new evidence, set out in Chapter 5, that it is not inevitable that whistleblowers must suffer for their experience. Overall, a substantial majority of officials who reported public interest concerns in recent years—on average, at least 70 per cent—responded that management and colleagues treated them either the same or as well as a result of the incident. Contrary to many stereotypes about the fate of whistleblowers, there are a great many who do not experience deliberately inflicted negative outcomes. These results accord with other evidence that the social and organisational importance of whistleblowing is well recognised in many public agencies. While debate is alive and well about how to manage the complexities of these situations, many agencies have actively grappled with the practical issue of how to encourage staff to disclose perceived wrongdoing, and even with the difficult issue of how to protect staff from reprisals should they do so.

While this research changes the previously bleak picture, it also brings a shift in focus. New questions arise. Previously, concerns centred on whether whistleblowing processes could be made to work at all. Now the question becomes: how is it that some organisations appear to be encouraging and managing whistleblowing more successfully than others? Some of the agencies studied can boast that less than 10 per cent of employees who observed serious wrongdoing did nothing about it. In at least one organisation in each of the four jurisdictions, however, more than 55 per cent of staff in the same position did nothing—they neither reported the wrongdoing nor took any other action. The answers to this lie in the context and culture of these different organisations.

Similarly, in some agencies, the proportion of whistleblowers that claimed mistreatment fell close to zero. In others, however, upwards of 46 per cent claimed to have been mistreated directly by management of the agency as a result. Moreover, even when direct reprisals are not involved, the evidence shows that whistleblowing often involves stress, tension and lasting consequences that prove difficult for whistleblowers and their organisations alike. When whistleblowers survive the experience, this is likely to be despite the formal management systems of their organisations for dealing with such situations, rather than because of them. As Chapter 9 reveals, even when agencies have developed special 'internal witness' management programs to better support their staff, perhaps only 1.3 per cent of all public interest whistleblowers are making it onto the 'radar' of these programs.

This book sets out both sides of this complex reality. Resulting from the world's largest known study of whistleblowing on a per capita basis, it provides the first comprehensive empirical data in Australia on the relative effects—and therefore the strengths and weaknesses—of a decade of legislative and management reform on the issue of public interest whistleblowing. The analysis draws on the results of this empirical research, together with qualitative assessment of the procedures used by agencies to guide their responses and comparative analysis of the different legislative frameworks in place. The conclusions flow from an analysis of all these facets of the way in which public sector whistleblowing is currently managed.

Part 1 of the book presents the empirical data, looking at the experiences of a wide range of public servants across a wide range of agencies, including those who observe wrongdoing but don't report it and those who report it and do or don't suffer. The five chapters in this section examine the results of the project surveys as a whole, typically presenting an aggregate or averaged picture of the experiences of public officials in total. The chapters also, however, point to the substantial differences in outcomes depending on the circumstances in which wrongdoing is seen and whistleblowing occurs, including the substantial differences in the responses of different agencies.

Part 2 begins the major shift in focus that is needed as a result of this research. It presents the empirical data describing, or most relevant to, the different management environments and systems in public sector agencies within which reporting and non-reporting occur. The five chapters in this part cover management attitudes in general, internal investigation standards, internal witness support programs, agency whistleblowing procedures and the legislative context. Through this shift in focus, the research sets out a new basis for evaluating what types of management approaches are making a difference and what types of procedural and legislative reforms are needed to reinforce best-practice approaches.

A second report from the project will help complete this new picture of current and prospective best practice for the management of whistleblowing at an organisational level. The findings reached here, however, already point the way to some of the major reforms needed. Agencies that make more credible efforts to encourage whistleblowing and protect their staff are achieving more positive results and are therefore showing the way for the development of more comprehensive models of best practice in the management of whistleblowing. At the same time, the relative success of these agencies provides the evidence that many more systems are patchy and are therefore missing out on achieving more positive outcomes in a higher proportion of whistleblowing cases. Chapter

10 assesses only five of 175 agencies nationally as having developed reasonably strong procedures for the management of whistleblowing, measured against the current Australian Standard. Legislative regimes for managing whistleblowing are indeed having positive effects, but they contain many problems and gaps, which must be addressed in a more comprehensive and consistent way if the original intent is to be fulfilled. There is some way to go to bring these regimes up to an acceptable overall standard, and a long way to go before a majority of individual public sector agencies are maximising their chances of gaining improved outcomes for themselves and their staff.

This new picture of public sector whistleblowing shows it will be worth the effort to travel these distances. In a field of policy and public management that previously looked wholly bleak, these data show that many more of these complex conflicts are being, and can be, resolved in a positive manner. By managing whistleblowing better, outcomes can be found that are just to individuals, serve the long-term interests of organisations and better discharge our institutions' wider obligations to ensure transparency and integrity in public office.

## The Whistling While They Work project

The analysis presented here is derived from a suite of research activity examining the incidence, outcomes and management of whistleblowing conducted in 2005–07 across a wide cross-section of public agencies from the Commonwealth, NSW, Queensland and West Australian governments. This research was conducted as part of an Australian Research Council-funded Linkage Project, 'Whistling While They Work: Enhancing the theory and practice of internal witness management in public sector organisations', led by Griffith University. The project involves four other Australian universities and 14 partner organisations, including the public integrity and management agencies listed in the Acknowledgments and on the project web site (www.griffith.edu.au/whistleblowing). A steering committee representing the partner organisations oversaw the project. The project team comprised the lead researchers from each participating university plus three partner investigators from the NSW, Queensland and West Australian governments.

The overall aim of the project was to identify and expand current best-practice systems for the management of public interest disclosures in the Australian public sector, including more effective whistleblower protection. Underpinned by empirical research into the performance and potential of existing internal witness management approaches, the project sought to develop new standards for internal disclosure procedures (IDPs) in public sector integrity systems, foster improved coordination between integrity bodies in the handling and oversight of disclosures and support implementation of improved internal witness management strategies in a range of organisational settings. To these ends, the four main objectives, or 'terms of reference', for the research were:

1.  to describe and assess the effects of whistleblower legislative reforms on the Australian public sector in the past decade, including effects on workplace education, willingness to report and reprisal deterrence
2.  to study comparatively what is working well and what is not in public sector internal witness management, to inform best-practice models for the development of formal IDPs and workplace-based strategies for whistleblower management
3.  to identify opportunities for better integration of internal witness responsibilities into values-based governance at organisational levels, including improved coordination between the roles of internal and external agencies, and strategies for embedding internal witness responsibilities in good management
4.  to inform implementation strategies for best-practice procedures in case study agencies, including cost-efficient options for institutionalising and servicing such procedures in a range of organisational, cultural and geographical settings, as well as legislative and regulatory reform where needed.

In late 2005, detailed research questions were developed to guide the empirical research, which are set out in Appendix 1. Table 1.1 sets out the primary questions and indicates which chapters in the book provide the main answers to each question.

This book reports extensive quantitative research results, examining public servants' experience of and attitudes towards whistleblowing. It also presents a wide range of conclusions based on those results, together with qualitative assessment of agency procedures and systems and comparative analysis of legislative frameworks. Findings are made in relation to priority areas for action, for most agencies and all governments. Further results will also be published in combination with a second phase of analysis, supplemented by qualitative research in 15 'case study' agencies, as outlined below.

As can be seen from the project objectives, the major purpose of the quantitative research program is to provide an up-to-date, representative picture of how much whistleblowing goes on in the Australian public sector and how it is being managed. Historically, in Australia and overseas, published accounts of whistleblowing have often been based on anecdotal evidence drawn from high-profile case studies of public whistleblowing (Dempster 1997; Elliston 1985:50–3; Glazer and Glazer 1989; Martin 1997; Senate Select Committee on Public Interest Whistleblowing 1994). As will become clear, however, these accounts provide relatively few insights into how much whistleblowing goes on in total and the full range of outcomes that might befall those who make internal or regulatory, as against public, disclosures.

## Table 1.1 Research questions

| Research questions | Relevant chapters |
|---|---|
| A. The incidence and significance of public sector whistleblowing | |
| 1. How common is whistleblowing in public sector organisations? | Chapters 2 and 4 |
| 2. How important is whistleblowing in public sector organisations? | Chapters 2 and 5 |
| 3. What factors and circumstances give rise to whistleblowing in public sector organisations? | Chapter 3 |
| B. The experiences and perceived experiences of public sector whistleblowers | |
| 4. What do whistleblowers and other internal witnesses experience in the course of this role? | Chapters 5 and 6 |
| 5. How common are reprisals against whistleblowers and what forms do they take? | Chapters 5 and 6 |
| C. The incidence, nature and influence of internal witness management/whistleblower protection programs within and across the public sector | |
| 6. What is the range of internal witness management policies and programs within and across the public sector? | Chapters 9 and 10; further report |
| 7. Are different outcomes of whistleblowing associated with differences in a) legislation, b) procedures/programs and/or c) CEO/senior management commitment and culture? | Chapters 7, 8, 9 and 10 |
| 8. Which external factors have effects (positive or negative) on internal witness management? | Chapter 10 |
| 9. What policies can organisations pursue to most effectively manage and maximise whistleblowing? | Chapters 9, 10 and 12; further report |
| 10. What reforms can governments pursue to most effectively manage and maximise whistleblowing? | Chapters 10–12 |

Early Australian empirical studies provided valuable insights into the range of adverse outcomes that befell a wider range of whistleblowers, but suffered from having access only to limited self-selecting or convenience samples, and certain organisational contexts and jurisdictions (de Maria 1994; de Maria and Jan 1994). Anecdotal case study research and this early quantitative research tended not to provide clear indicators of what might constitute good whistleblowing practices because the outcomes for whistleblowers appeared to be so uniformly bad. The bleak picture described at the outset of this chapter is perhaps best summed up by de Maria's description of his research as a 'tour through the entrails of our society' in which he finds 'nothing to celebrate…except perhaps the valour of the whistleblowers who guide us into the netherworld of corruption, incompetence, cover-ups and organisational vendettas' (de Maria 1999:xiii).

While whistleblowing research has suffered from similar problems internationally, it is clear that some large-scale studies of random samples of organisations, notably in North America, have yielded a more representative picture of whistleblowing incidence and experience, along with awareness and attitudes, than previously available in Australia (for example, US Merit Systems Protection Board 1981, 1993, 2003; Miceli et al. 1991, 1999, 2001; Trevino and

Victor 1992; Sims and Keenan 1998; Pershing 2003; Near et al. 2004; Miceli and Near 2006). In the late 1990s, empirical research was extended to a larger, more representative sample of randomly selected NSW public employees spread across several agencies, conducted by the NSW Independent Commission Against Corruption (ICAC)—but this focused on knowledge of whistleblowing procedures and attitudes towards whistleblowing rather than real experience (Zipparo 1999a, 1999b). This project's first objective was therefore to undertake the first comprehensive, large-scale empirical study in Australia.

The second objective was to study the nature of the management of public interest disclosures, as an organisational process, across a wide cross-section of the Australian public sector. This aim reflected practical experience on the part of many of the researchers and partner organisations to the project that many public agencies were struggling valiantly to operationalise new whistleblowing legislation, encourage disclosure and better manage those involved. The Commonwealth Ombudsman (1997) documented this in the case of the Australian Federal Police. Evaluations of the NSW Police Force Internal Witness Support Program suggested that such a program might help prevent and contain some of the many adverse outcomes that potentially threatened whistleblowers (Freeman and Garnett 1996). Contrary to some of the early Australian empirical research, limited statistics flowing from the introduction of whistleblowing legislation in New South Wales and Queensland indicated that, across a range of agencies, whistleblower disclosures were more likely to be investigated and found substantiated than information about similar matters from other types of sources (Brown et al. 2004).

These indicators meant that even if the management of whistleblowing was known to be problematic, there was a clear need to understand the growing institutional experience in internal witness management across a range of organisations and sectors. It was therefore decided to broaden the empirical research from actual and potential whistleblowers to groups responsible for managing whistleblowing and related conflicts, including line managers, investigators, employee welfare personnel and other forms of case-handlers. This wider focus had not previously been attempted, including in the large American studies. Part 2 of this volume draws particularly on this evidence, along with the other available data relevant to gauging the extent and effectiveness of different agency approaches.

The third and fourth objectives were to assemble the research results in a way that would help identify practical strategies by which organisations might better fulfil their statutory disclosure-management obligations and assist the evaluation and reform of Australia's relatively new statutory regimes for whistleblower protection. The third objective is being met not only through the publication of the present volume, but by further analysis setting out current and potential best practice in agency-level internal witness management systems, as discussed at the end of this chapter.

The lessons of this research for current statutory frameworks become clear in Chapter 11. In November 2006, to help focus debate on the complexities of the legislative issues involved, the project produced an issues paper entitled *Public interest disclosure legislation in Australia: towards the next generation* (Brown 2006). Since that time, many jurisdictions have proceeded with formal reviews of their legislation and the Commonwealth Government has committed to introduce comprehensive legislative reform for the first time. By including multiple jurisdictions and a large number of agencies in the quantitative research program, the project team set out to assemble a body of data capable of supporting a wide range of comparative and multivariate analyses, to help answer some vexed questions about administrative, procedural and legislative approaches to whistleblowing.

## What is 'whistleblowing'?

The essential feature of whistleblowing is the 'disclosure by organisation members (former or current) of illegal, immoral or illegitimate practices under the control of their employers, to persons or organisations that may be able to effect action' (Miceli and Near 1984:689). This definition provides a sound starting point because it allows for the many types of wrongdoing about which such disclosures might arise and the many forms that whistleblowing can take (Miceli et al. 2001). It is also the most commonly accepted and widely used definition in related empirical research (Tavakoli et al. 2003).

In this book, whistleblowing is also taken to mean disclosure by organisation members about matters of 'public interest'—that is, suspected or alleged wrongdoing that affects more than the personal or private interests of the person making the disclosure (Senate Select Committee on Public Interest Whistleblowing 1994:Par.2.2). This qualification aligns with most public and public policy conceptions of the term and with the objectives of the many different legislative regimes for public sector whistleblower protection now in place in Australia. Despite the controversies surrounding policy and legislative responses to whistleblowing, the objectives of this legislation are relatively consistent and clear (NSW Ombudsman 2004a; Brown 2006:5):

1.  to facilitate public interest disclosures—that is, to encourage whistleblowing
2.  to ensure that disclosures by whistleblowers are properly dealt with—that is, properly assessed, investigated and actioned
3.  to ensure the protection of whistleblowers from reprisals taken against them as a result of their having made the disclosure.

In its method, the present research did not use the term 'whistleblowing' itself, just as no existing legislative regime actually makes substantive use of the term.

Instead, our surveys asked respondents about 'wrongdoing' of which they were aware (discussed further below) and whether they or anyone else had formally 'reported' it. Throughout the research, however, there remains an important distinction between wrongdoing that can be considered resolved when an affected individual considers it resolved (personal or private interest) and wrongdoing that threatens wider organisational and/or public integrity, above and beyond any outcomes for affected individuals (public interest). Conventionally, whistleblowing refers to the latter category, and it is used in this sense in this book.

Whistleblowing is an important public policy issue for two major reasons. Integrity in government relies on the effective operation of a range of 'integrity systems' for keeping institutions and their office-holders honest and accountable (Brown et al. 2005; Dobel 1999; Spigelman 2004; Uhr 2005). Within these systems, few individuals are better placed to observe or suspect wrongdoing within an organisation than its very own officers and employees. In Australia, this was brought into sharp relief by the Fitzgerald Inquiry into official corruption in Queensland (1987–89), which established that honest police officers had observed corruption but felt powerless to act. Even so, their honest evidence remained important in finally bringing corrupt officers to justice. Consequently, Queensland became the first Australian jurisdiction to introduce (interim) whistleblower protection legislation (Queensland Electoral and Administrative Review Commission 1991). There is now a substantial consensus in Australian public policy that irrespective of the challenges it might involve, whistleblowing is a crucial resource in modern efforts to pursue public integrity.

The second major reason is that, given natural organisational and peer pressures for employees to stay silent about public interest wrongdoing, whistleblowing is often not something that is likely to happen naturally, especially in a timely fashion. While organisation members might have many incentives to disclose workplace wrongdoing that affects them personally, there are less direct incentives—and many direct disincentives—for them to notice or report wrongdoing that affects only organisational interests or the larger public interest. As recorded in the early Australian research and overseas (Near et al. 2004; Miceli and Near 2006), even the most noble employee is justified in thinking twice about coming forward. Predictably, the wrongdoing exposed might be controversial and damaging and its disclosure could provoke conflicts that involve negative outcomes for all involved. For whistleblowing to be properly encouraged, it is clear that these natural disincentives to reporting must be reduced, removed or overcome.

While simple in theory, the definition of whistleblowing is complex in practice. First and foremost, whistleblowers are understood to be 'organisation members' (for example, employees, volunteer workers or contractors) for both of the above reasons. It is their internal position in the organisation that is most likely to make them aware of internal wrongdoing and also most likely to place them under pressure to stay silent. At times, however, any person who claims to have revealed wrongdoing might also seek to claim this title, even when they are outside the organisation concerned—for example, when they are an aggrieved consumer, client or citizen complainant. The fact that legislation in five Australian jurisdictions currently supports this second concept of a whistleblower—confusing the purpose of whistleblower protection—is a basic issue for reform (see Brown 2006:8; Chapter 11, this volume).

Different conceptions of whistleblowing also stem from the question of 'to whom an official may validly make a disclosure' in expectation of action. For most citizens, the quintessential example of whistleblowing is public—such as a disclosure to the media or one that reaches the public–political domain. Journalist Laurie Oakes (2005) reinforced this perception when he wrote that 'leaks, and whistleblowers, are essential to a proper democratic system', and recent Commonwealth prosecutions of officials for making unauthorised disclosures have increased the focus on this issue (Brown 2007). Some academic commentators even regard public disclosure as the only 'true' form of whistleblowing (for example, Grace and Cohen 1998; Dawson 2000; Truelson 2001). Certainly, in the view of the Whistling While They Work project team, there will always be a legitimate role for some public whistleblowing—a fact that needs to be recognised in any credible whistleblower protection regime. The implications are discussed further in Chapter 11, especially in light of the Commonwealth Government's recent acknowledgment of this issue.

While it is obviously the 'loudest' form, public whistleblowing also easily takes on a prominence that excludes proper attention on other important types of disclosure. Whistleblowing is not always 'public', in the sense of being subject to widespread publicity. Chapter 4 suggests that public whistleblowing is statistically infrequent and usually represents the disclosure avenue of last resort, with the bulk of whistleblowing taking place either internally or as a 'regulatory' disclosure to a government integrity agency. It is also clear that if whistleblowing is handled responsibly by organisations in this first instance, the outcomes are more likely to be positive than if the matter is forced to escalate into a public–political conflict. Consequently, in our research, the crucial element is that the information is communicated 'to those who need to know about it'—that is, it is made 'public' in the sense of being made 'a matter of public record' (see Elliston 1985:8, 15, 21–2), which could be quite confidentially as well as with great publicity.

In practice, assessments of what whistleblowing is can also hinge on issues of motive: why the relevant employee is believed to be making the disclosure. The question of motive is, however, deliberately absent from the definition above.

This is because a valid matter of public interest can be raised without the person who raises it necessarily being driven by altruistic motives. Public interest disclosures made for self-serving reasons or as part of a personal grievance nevertheless remain public interest disclosures. The question of motive has therefore long been regarded by analysts as irrelevant to whether a disclosure amounts to whistleblowing, even though perceptions of motive could be relevant to how a disclosure is then managed.

The best way of understanding the secondary importance of motivations in whistleblowing is by understanding such disclosures as examples of 'pro-social behaviour' (Dozier and Miceli 1985; Brief and Motowidlo 1986). This is behaviour that is 'defined by some significant segment of society and/or one's social group as generally beneficial to other people' (Penner et al. 2005:366), irrespective of what particular benefits, if any, are intended in the individual case. Figure 1.1 outlines the model of whistleblowing as pro-social organisational behaviour (POB) initially presented by Dozier and Miceli (1985) and since revised by Miceli et al. (2001) and Miceli and Near (2006).

**Figure 1.1 Model of whistleblowing as pro-social behaviour**

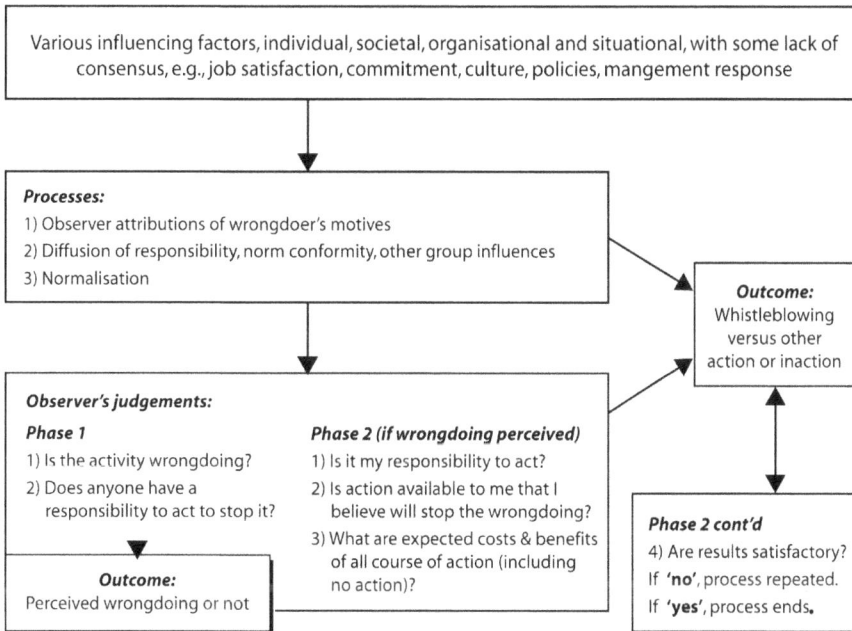

Source: Adapted by M. Donkin from Miceli, M. P., Van Scotter, J. R., Near, J. P. and Rehg, M. 2001, 'Responses to perceived organisational wrongdoing: do perceiver characteristics matter?', in J. M. Darley, D. M. Messick and T. R. Tyler (eds), *Social Influences on Ethical Behaviour*, Lawrence Erlbaum Associates, Mahwah, NJ, pp. 119–35; and Miceli, M. P. and Near, J. P. 2006, Whistle-blowing as constructive deviance: an integration of the prosocial and social information processing models, Manuscript submitted for publication.

The POB model draws on Latané and Darley's (1970) theory of 'bystander effect', which explains why witnesses to a crime might not intervene. It proposes that when employees become aware of wrongdoing, they make decisions in similar ways to these witnesses. What, if anything, a witness hopes or stands to gain by coming forward does not affect the utility of their role or its 'pro-social' value as part of society's system of criminal justice.

The POB model also suggests that blowing the whistle is not a single decision but rather a complex process. Even the assessment that the behaviour in question constitutes wrongdoing, or that a response is warranted, is a subjective judgment. Miceli et al. (1991) found that the final decision regarding whether to act was related to a number of individual, organisational and situational factors, including judgments about the reporting environment and cues about whether reporting was likely to change the behaviour.

Even internationally, however, few empirical studies have attempted to demonstrate the link between whistleblowing and pro-social behaviour more generally, instead simply using it as an explanatory theory, by assuming or observing indirect links (Miceli and Near 2006). For example, Miceli and Near (2005:11–12) advised that prominent American whistleblowing cases 'appeared' to demonstrate pro-social behaviour, but that research was needed to 'clarify relationships'. In the present research, it was therefore decided to look for the combination of factors that gave rise to whistleblowing decisions in Australian public sector settings and for direct evidence that it was accurate to describe whistleblowing as a pro-social process.

Chapters 3 and 4 set out the results. Chapter 3 shows that organisational and situational factors typically prove more distinctive in the mix of decision making than many of the measurable characteristics of individuals. Both chapters confirm the accuracy of the description of whistleblowing as pro-social behaviour in an Australian public sector context, particularly by examining reporting behaviour in terms of established scales of organisational citizenship behaviour: 'individual behaviour that is discretionary, not directly or explicitly recognised by the formal reward system, and that…promotes the effective functioning of the organisation' (Organ 1988:4; see also Graham 1989; Penner et al. 2005).

This approach to issues of motive contrasts with several other approaches, in which the motives of whistleblowers are seen as more central to how whistleblowing is defined and categorised. Because it has positive organisational and social effects, and can indeed sometimes be selfless, whistleblowing is often presented by commentators as being always selfless even though this is unlikely to be the case. Whistleblowing has therefore been described as an example of civil disobedience (Elliston 1985:135–44), ethical resistance (Glazer and Glazer 1989; Martin 1997) and/or principled organisational dissent (Lennane 1993, cf. de Maria 1999:28–9), as if ethical reasoning is always involved. One author has even generalised that whistleblowers should be considered the 'saints of secular culture' (Grant 2002:391). In seeking to emphasise the public interest relevance of whistleblowing, even Australia's Senate Select Committee on Public Interest Whistleblowing suggested, unhelpfully, that whistleblowers should be recognised as always '*motivated* by notions of public interest' (Senate Select Committee on Public Interest Whistleblowing 1994:Par.2.2, emphasis added; see also de Maria and Jan 1994:5–7).

This emphasis raises significant problems. Even if many whistleblowers are altruistic, to make this a defining characteristic and therefore a prerequisite for whistleblower protection is extremely problematic. On this approach, a substantial proportion of whistleblowers will never qualify, simply because they might also have a personal or private interest in the outcome. Whistleblowers who cannot prove that they conform to a stereotype of pure or altruistic motivation—which could be the bulk of them—can be relegated to a different category, including the equal and opposite stereotype of mere 'vengeful troublemakers' (Lewis 2001). Such stereotypes therefore confound the purpose of recognising whistleblowing in the first place.

Another problem is posed by a further definitional variant—that of defining whistleblowers in terms of the outcome of their experience. After his survey of 83 Queensland whistleblowers in 1994–95, de Maria concluded that the definition of a whistleblower should include the feature of suffering, because he recorded no individuals who had not suffered in some way; 'the non-suffering' whistleblower was seen as 'a contradiction in terms' (de Maria 1999:25). There are two major problems with this qualification. First, as already noted, de Maria's sample was limited to respondents recruited by a newspaper advertisement and word-of-mouth, a method naturally more likely to attract aggrieved people than those who had not suffered. Second, the qualification is impossible to reconcile with a major policy rationale of defining whistleblowing in the first place—namely, to protect whistleblowers in a positive or proactive way before they experience bad outcomes. A definition that enables whistleblowing incidents to be recognised only after conflict has arisen and damage is done cannot function to help identify whistleblowing for the purpose of preventing or reducing such damage. In this report, outcomes are an essential issue for analysis, but do not define who is a whistleblower.

Finally, this research also makes use of the term 'internal witness' as an alternative to 'whistleblower' in the context of internal and regulatory disclosures. This term was developed by the NSW Police Force (Freeman 1998; Smith 1996; Wood 1997:408) and is now also in increasing use among other public sector agencies in Australia. It aligns with the pro-social role of whistleblowing, akin to other witness roles, as discussed above. The value of this term also lies in combating a number of problematic stereotypes of whistleblowers, given that, in practice, disclosures can be made not just for a wide variety of motives but in a wide variety of ways, including with differing levels of formality and under different degrees of legal compulsion. It should be noted, however, that this term, as used in this research, is consistent with the definition of whistleblowing given earlier.

## What is 'wrongdoing'?

Whistleblowing can be about a wide spectrum of illegal, immoral or illegitimate practices. In this research, the spectrum is captured by the general term 'wrongdoing', with data collected in terms of a large number of different types of behaviour that could be categorised in a number of different ways—including whether there could be primarily private or public interests involved. A wide definitional approach was necessitated not only by the imprecision of existing categories, but by the inherent dangers of taking too restrictive an approach, whether in research or in legislation. For example, restricting whistleblowing to only 'serious' examples of public interest wrongdoing begs the question of in whose judgment the wrongdoing meets that threshold. An agency wishing to minimise the amount of whistleblowing to which it need respond can simply increase the threshold. In reality, the benefits of whistleblowing are likely to be encouraged only when agencies promote an 'if in doubt, report' approach (Brown et al. 2004). For this reason, the present research sought to establish a comprehensive picture of the breadth of wrongdoing types that public officials observed and might potentially disclose.

Appendix 2 lists the 38 different behaviours that were offered to survey respondents in the present research as examples of wrongdoing. These were then grouped into seven major categories for the purpose of analysis:

- misconduct for material gain (including bribery, corruption and theft)
- conflict of interest
- improper or unprofessional behaviour (including many types of recognised official misconduct)
- defective administration (including incompetence and negligence)
- waste or mismanagement of resources
- perverting justice or accountability
- personnel or workplace grievances.

The first six of these major categories align substantially with the subjects about which statutory public interest disclosures may be made in several jurisdictions (see Brown 2006:16–19). For the same reason, they also align with the jurisdictions of several of the key integrity agencies that were partner organisations to the project. Consistent with the definition discussed in the previous section, when this report refers to 'whistleblowing', it is referring to reports made about wrongdoing in one of these six categories—that is, 'public interest' whistleblowing.

Data about wrongdoing types in the last category—personnel or workplace grievances—were also collected in order to maintain the comprehensive approach. In this report, however, they are presumed to constitute mostly private or personal complaints and they are not included in the results for whistleblowing. At times, where relevant, these grievances are nevertheless included in analyses of reporting behaviour and outcomes as a whole, but when this occurs it is made clear in the relevant sections of the report (primarily in Chapters 2 and 3).

As can already be seen, all attempts to measure and categorise perceptions of wrongdoing are subject to their own limitations and are unlikely to ever be perfect. For example, it can be argued that many of the wrongdoing types included in some of the public interest categories are chiefly issues of organisational integrity and will become matters of public interest only if exceptionally serious. This possibility alone, however, combined with the fact that the under-counting and under-reporting of public interest disclosures is already known to be a problem in many jurisdictions, makes it important to include such items. Similarly, some forms of public interest wrongdoing are clearly more likely than others to be triggered first and foremost by a private interest or personal grievance (for example, several of those wrongdoing types grouped as 'improper behaviour'). As outlined earlier, however, the fact that such disclosures might also involve personal grievances does not detract from their public significance. Indeed, the extent to which these wrongdoing types could also be re-categorised as personal grievances is offset by the likelihood that some 'personnel or workplace grievances' excluded from the analyses of whistleblowing in this report involve entrenched or systemic wrongdoing of sufficient seriousness that they could be reclassified objectively as matters of public interest.

For all these reasons, the results given in this research are best understood as simply an approximation of the numbers of cases falling into the different categories used. While the project team is confident that this is a more comprehensive and useful approximation than previously achieved, it should not be seen as definitive.

## Methods and further limitations

As set out in Table 1.2, eight surveys were used in the project to collect data on individual experiences and institutional practices. Figure 1.2 outlines the relationships between the resulting data sets. While not the only basis for the findings presented in the later chapters, this large body of empirical research has been instrumental in developing a new overview of how public sector whistleblowing is managed.

**Table 1.2 Quantitative research instruments, Whistling While They Work project**

| Short title | Full title | No. of items | No. of participating agencies | | | | | Total surveys | Total responses | Response rate |
|---|---|---|---|---|---|---|---|---|---|---|
| | | | Cth [a] | NSW | Qld | WA | Total | | | |
| 1. Agency survey | Survey of Agency Practices and Procedures (2005) | 42 | 73 | 85 | 83 | 63 | **304** | | | |
| 2. Procedures assessment | Assessment of Comprehensiveness of Agency Procedures (2006–07) | 24 | 56 | 60 | 31 | 28 | **175** | | | |
| 3. Employee survey | Workplace Experiences and Relationships Questionnaire (2006–07) | 50 | 27 | 34 | 32 | 25 | **118** | 23 177 | 7 663 [b] | 33% |
| | Surveys distributed | | 5 545 | 8 324 | 6 343 | 2 965 | -- | | | |
| | Responses | | 2 307 | 2 561 | 1 729 | 1 007 | -- | | | |
| | (Procedures assessment and employee survey) | | (25) | (31) | (29) | (17) | **(102)** | | | |
| 4. Internal witness survey [c] | Internal Witness Questionnaire (2006–07) | 82 | 4 | 4 | 4 | 3 | **15** | 455 | 240 | 53% |
| 5. Case-handler survey [c] | Managing the Internal Reporting of Wrongdoing Questionnaire (2007) | 77 | 4 | 5 | 4 | 3 | **16** | 1 651 | 315 | 19% |
| 6. Manager survey [c] | Managing the Internal Reporting of Wrongdoing Questionnaire (2007) | 77 | 4 | 5 | 4 | 3 | **16** | 3 034 | 513 | 17% |
| 7. Integrity agency survey | Survey of Integrity Agency Practices and Procedures (2007) | 45 | 5 | 5 | 3 | 3 | **16** | | | |
| 8. Integrity case-handler survey | Managing Disclosures by Public Employees Questionnaire (2007) | 75 | 3 | 3 | 3 | 3 | **12** | 304 | 82 | 27% |

[a] Throughout this report, Commonwealth figures include a range of Australian Public Service (APS) and non-APS agencies unless otherwise indicated.
[b] Includes 59 responses for which jurisdiction/agency unknown.
[c] Written questionnaire response to be followed up with qualitative interview in willing cases (case study agencies).

**Figure 1.2 Relationships between data sets**

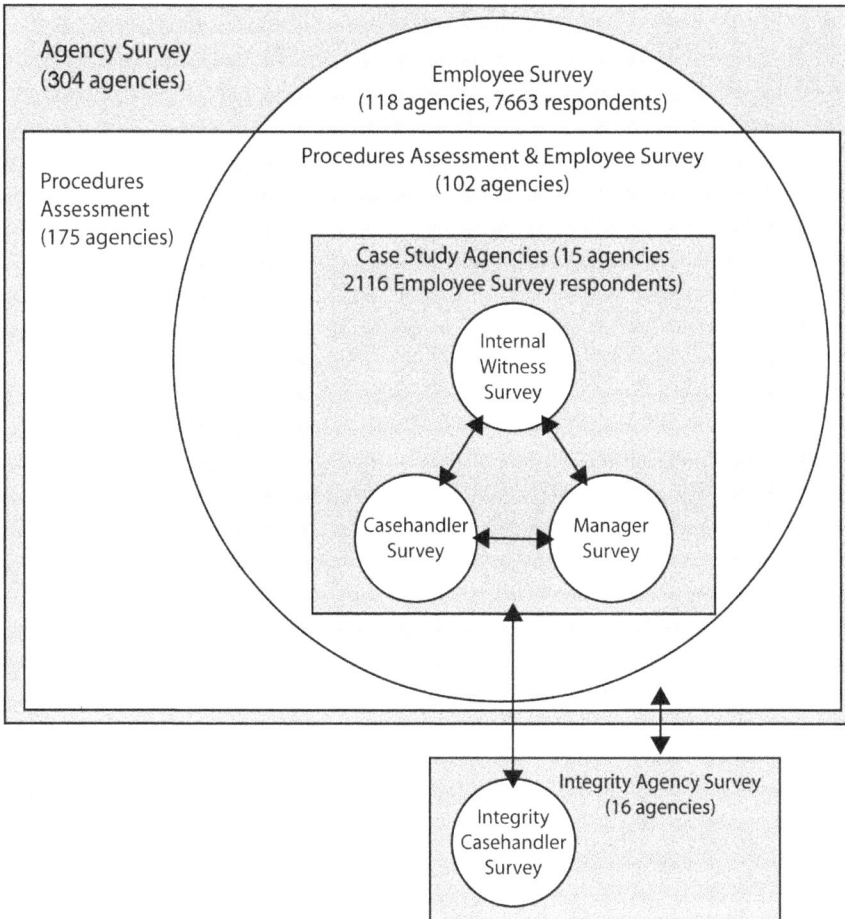

Agency Survey
(304 agencies)

Employee Survey
(118 agencies, 7663 respondents)

Procedures Assessment & Employee Survey
(102 agencies)

Procedures
Assessment
(175 agencies)

Case Study Agencies (15 agencies
2116 Employee Survey respondents)

Internal
Witness
Survey

Casehandler
Survey

Manager
Survey

Integrity Agency Survey
(16 agencies)

Integrity
Casehandler
Survey

Squares indicate surveys of agency-wide systems and procedures.
Circles indicate surveys of individuals.
Arrows indicate surveys designed to give consistent/comparable data.

First, the agency survey sought data on the extent, content and operation of whistleblowing procedures in agencies, as well as participation in further stages of the research. With the support of the partner organisations, this survey was distributed to almost all agencies of the four participating governments (793 agencies in total), resulting in 304 returns. The participating agencies represented a wide cross-section of government organisations in each jurisdiction, from small to large, covering a wide range of functions and portfolios. They included many of the most major departments and statutory authorities in each jurisdiction, government-owned corporations, the military and local governments of varying sizes.

Similar data on practices and procedures were sought from specialist integrity agencies in the jurisdiction—including partner organisations to the project—through a corresponding integrity agency survey.

Of the 304 agencies that answered the agency survey, 175 also supplied their written whistleblowing-related procedures, which were analysed in a separate procedures assessment, comparing their comprehensiveness and completeness using a 24-item rating scale. The research team developed this scale on the basis of existing literature and the Australian Standard, as discussed in Chapter 10.

The largest single research activity was the employee survey, in which 136 agencies initially agreed to participate, with 118 agencies ultimately doing so. This was a confidential, anonymous survey of a random sample of staff from each agency. While much of the survey design was original, it also drew on instruments used in previous research in Australia and internationally (including US Merit Systems Protection Board 1981, 1993, 2003; Zipparo 1999a, 1999b; Keenan 2002; Near et al. 2004). Target sample sizes were varied according to agency size, ranging from 1–2 per cent of all staff in very large agencies (more than 5000 employees) to 50–100 per cent of all staff in very small agencies (150 employees or less). From July to October 2006, printed surveys were distributed by agencies to approximately 23 000 public employees, with responses returned directly to Griffith University via a reply-paid envelope.

A total of 7663 public officials responded to the employee survey, providing the main data analysed throughout this book. It is the largest data set on whistleblowing ever gathered in Australia, and probably the largest per capita in the world. At times, these data are analysed in conjunction with the results of the agency survey (all 118 employee survey agencies also completed this), as well as the results of the procedures assessment (in which 102 of the employee survey agencies also participated).

In addition, 87 of the agencies volunteered to participate in further research as 'case study agencies', with 15 agencies selected by the research team for this role in May 2006. In this report, the further data drawn from these agencies will be reported in aggregate, with differences between organisations to be analysed in later publications. It is significant, however, for the data reported here, that this smaller group of 15 agencies is just as diverse as the larger group of 118 agencies from which the employee survey data set is drawn, with many of the results confirming that as a group, the experiences of the case study agencies remain in many ways typical of those of the total group. In all, 2116 responses to the employee survey were received from the case study agencies, meaning that while these agencies represented only 13 per cent of the larger group, their respondents accounted for 28 per cent of the total employee survey data set. Accordingly, interim results from the three further case study agency surveys are also reported here, not only for their interest in their own right, but because these are likely to be typical of organisational experience more generally.

The purpose of these three surveys was to gather targeted, in-depth information about the whistleblowing arrangements and management practices of these agencies and the experience of particular target groups of staff. In each case, respondents were also invited to volunteer for a confidential interview. Each survey was designed for consistency of approach with the employee survey and with each other.

The internal witness survey was a long, written questionnaire designed to elicit more extensive information from whistleblowers. These were recruited between November 2006 and August 2007 through invitations for individual staff to contact the research team (in confidence), distributed in three ways: by internal advertisement within each agency; by direct contact from agency management to known whistleblowers; and by a number of partner organisations (integrity agencies) to known whistleblowers relevant to the case study agencies. This recruitment strategy produced 455 expressions of interest to participate from these 15 agencies—a far lower number of whistleblowers than are known to exist within these agencies based on the results of the employee survey. This response itself tends to confirm that recruitment strategies that rely heavily on employees self-identifying as a 'whistleblower' are only ever likely to capture quite a small, even if important, proportion of the total whistleblower population. The data set was further limited by seeking information only in relation to reports of wrongdoing made between July 2002 and June 2004, to ensure that respondents' experiences were relatively current and more likely to have been dealt with under current procedures, as well as reflective of a similar two-year period to that studied in the employee survey. Accordingly, only 242 individuals ultimately returned surveys, of whom only 114 fit fully within the requested parameters, but who nevertheless provided detailed, quality information.

The case-handler and manager surveys were slightly shorter questionnaires designed to elicit more extensive, comparable information from these two groups within the case study agencies. Case-handlers were defined as including: internal investigation, audit and ethics staff; human resource management staff; internal and external (for example, contracted) employee welfare and assistance staff; and union staff. Surveys were typically distributed to all, or a large proportion of, the identifiable case-handlers in each case study agency and to a random selection of managers (typically 5 per cent of the total population of managers or 150 individuals, whichever provided the larger figure). Data collection occurred from April to December 2007. This report includes analysis of the 828 responses received from both groups (13 per cent of all surveys distributed): 315 from case-handlers (many of whom also identified as managers) and 513 from managers (who did not necessarily also identify as case-handlers). In addition, a corresponding integrity case-handler survey was distributed to relevant case-handling staff from specialist integrity agencies in each jurisdiction (including partner organisations).

All data were collected in accordance with ethical approvals issued by the Griffith University Human Research Ethics Committee. All instruments were piloted in the final stages of design and refined in light of pilot results. Copies of the instruments are available on the project web site: www.griffith.edu.au/whistleblowing

As with all data sets, there are several limitations in the way in which it should be interpreted, as noted in relevant sections of the report. While care was taken to recruit a large sample size across the four jurisdictions, the study did not provide coverage across the full Australian public sector population, therefore its generalisability was constrained. Although a large number of agencies participated, clearly a great many also elected not to do so. As a result, it is arguable that the results most likely provide a best-case scenario of the ways in which whistleblowing is currently handled in the public sectors concerned, since agencies with poorer systems might have been more likely not to participate. Whether this is the case is obviously unknown; it is known that some agencies with significant integrity challenges did choose to participate, in order to find ways to rectify these problems. Some of the results are also sufficiently concerning to suggest they might well be realistic. Nevertheless, the sample of agencies was not total.

Within agencies, the extent to which the survey samples and respondent groups are representative of the demography of individual agencies has not been established. While participating agencies were requested to draw random, representative samples, whether or not they really did so was not within the researchers' control. By sampling current employees, the major employee survey data set does not include former employees, such as those who might have observed and reported wrongdoing but have since left the organisation. This is a particular issue for Chapter 5, which includes analysis of the incidence of reprisals reported by whistleblowers. An effort is made there to estimate the alternative range of results that might have been expected had former employees been included in the sample.

The study relies on the self-reported perceptions of individual survey respondents, which are inevitably subject to errors in recall and specificity.

The bulk of survey results presented are quantitative, supplemented in several places by additional qualitative accounts provided by survey respondents as free text. It can be argued that quantitative research can only ever be of limited value in understanding the true nature and true lessons of any particular whistleblowing incident, given the complexity of all such incidents. In particular, it has been argued that only detailed case studies of more prominent cases will provide meaningful insights into the challenge of achieving better outcomes. Qualitative data can indeed play a useful role, and interviews with whistleblowers, case-handlers and managers from the case study agencies are providing the basis for further analysis in the second report. Here, however, quantitative research methods are used to paint a larger picture across thousands of individual reporting incidents, in order to help shift attention from whistleblowers as individuals to the performance of organisations in response to whistleblowing as a process. Whatever their limitations, the data reported in this book provide a new and different basis for understanding how whistleblowing is being managed in the Australian public sector.

## Continuing analysis: towards best practice

As already mentioned, the analysis here—combining the quantitative data and evaluations of procedures and legislation—provides a first major output from the present research, but is also subject to a second phase. The overall aim is to use the improved understanding of how whistleblowing is being managed to inform assessments of what might constitute reasonable best-practice systems at the agency level. The final results will be the subject of further publications from this project. These will amplify a new framework for internal witness management systems already developed by the project team, with the participation of representatives of the 15 case study agencies, and revised in light of comments received on the draft report (Appendix 3). The framework sets out the different dimensions and sub-dimensions contained in existing and prospective approaches to the management of whistleblowing in the agencies and jurisdictions studied.

The framework in Appendix 3 has three purposes. First, it sets out the bases on which quantitative and qualitative data about the current performance of agency systems can be compared and analysed. That research involves further analysis of the quantitative evidence for insights into how individual agencies are addressing each of these dimensions and sub-dimensions and lessons as to the measurable effectiveness of these efforts. In addition, the further research involves a more qualitative picture of how systems currently work in practice in the 15 case study agencies, based on confidential interviews with individual survey respondents from those agencies (whistleblowers, case-handlers and managers). The result will be a more detailed picture of how agency procedures work in practice.

The second purpose of the framework, flowing from this, is to set out a new structure for the development of best-practice procedures in a wide range of public sector agencies. While there will be variations between different types of agencies in the precise way in which each of these dimensions is addressed, overall, the framework provides a check list of all the elements that should be present if an agency is seeking to establish a comprehensive approach to the encouragement and productive management of whistleblowing. The further project publications will therefore also use the extra data to present a guide to how better systems might be developed and implemented using this framework.

Finally, it is clear that the effective management of whistleblowing often relies on broad transparency, including the relationship that line agencies have with the central integrity agencies in their jurisdiction. Whistleblowing is a process that also goes beyond integrity agencies to the interests of the public at large. While focused on the procedures and systems needed at the agency level, an effective framework such as that outlined in Appendix 3 is also dependent on support and reinforcement from wider policy settings, including legislative regimes. Such frameworks are likely to command full employee confidence only if supported by the right statutory provisions, placing internal and regulatory whistleblowing in their public context and dealing more effectively with the obligations of employers.

For all the new insights that can be gained from this research, the management of whistleblowing remains a complex and challenging process. The good news is that there could be greater scope than previously appreciated for maximising the positive impacts that whistleblowing can have on organisational and public integrity, and for reducing the negative impacts of the whistleblowing process on organisations and individuals alike. The bad news is that much of this potential continues to go unrealised. Even where statutory frameworks for whistleblowing are strong, and agencies are endeavouring to achieve better outcomes, the new picture of whistleblowing suggests that the effort is often not being directed where it is really needed. This research is intended to help public sector agencies grapple more effectively with the challenges of internal witness management.

# Part 1

## *A new picture of public sector whistleblowing*

# 2. The incidence and significance of whistleblowing

A. J. Brown, Evalynn Mazurski and Jane Olsen

## Introduction

As set out in the first chapter, until now, there has been little comprehensive research to establish the overall frequency or importance of whistleblowing in the Australian public sector. Based on anecdotal accounts, even though cases of public whistleblowing can occasionally gain significant media prominence, the fact is that these cases—taken alone—suggest that whistleblowing is relatively rare. At most, Australian federal, state and local governments might each experience a few such cases each year, with occasional outbreaks of additional cases in the event of a major crisis or inquiry. Given that Australian governments employ approximately 1.66 million people (ABS 2007), this low incidence might also suggest that even if it is necessary to have legislation and procedures for managing whistleblowing, it is only in relatively rare or irregular cases that these will need to be used.

If really as low as this, the incidence of whistleblowing would provide little justification for governments or senior public sector managers to think 'proactively' about how to manage whistleblowing cases. Instead, such an apparently low incidence could suggest that managers need only ever know how to react to such cases if or when they happen, or when they become problematic. It also supports the assumption that whistleblowing spells 'trouble' for an organisation and that, consequently, even when they are correct about what they have observed, whistleblowers are typically still primarily 'troublemakers'. Public discussion about the adverse outcomes suffered by some whistleblowers contributes to assumptions that even if wrongdoing is widespread, few employees will be reckless enough to blow the whistle on it. In some of the limited representative research conducted before this study, 71 per cent of a sample of 800 NSW public sector respondents agreed that 'a lot of people who know about corruption don't report it' (Zipparo 1999b:87). This all becomes the subject of mutually reinforcing stereotypes. Those who blow the whistle are easily presumed to be relatively abnormal—either simply acting out personal grievances or irrevocably predisposed to fall into conflict with the organisation. If this is the case, it might be logical for the typical public sector manager to assume that little can ever be done to protect whistleblowers, even when they might deserve it.

In fact, none of these common assumptions about the incidence of whistleblowing is correct. This chapter seeks to break the vicious circle created by these stereotypes by filling a major gap in our knowledge about how much whistleblowing occurs and how it is regarded in public sector organisations. It presents basic data from all the project surveys, but especially the employee survey. The first part of the chapter reviews the data indicating how many respondents observed wrongdoing in the two years before the survey and how many went on to report the most serious wrongdoing they observed. At least 61 per cent of respondents indicated that they observed serious wrongdoing, with 28 per cent of respondents indicating that they reported the wrongdoing they observed. The second part of the chapter refines these results to arrive at an estimate of how much of this reporting activity can be categorised accurately as 'whistleblowing'. The analysis includes discussion of the types of wrongdoing observed and reported and the different organisational roles that reporters of wrongdoing can occupy, both of which are important definitional issues that inform analyses throughout later chapters of the report. The conclusion is an estimate that perhaps 12 per cent of all respondents satisfy the approximate definition of a public interest whistleblower—a substantial figure when extrapolated to the larger public sector, and one at substantial odds with public stereotypes.

The third part of the chapter goes on to review evidence from the surveys about the significance of this whistleblowing activity. Again, contrary to many stereotypes, it becomes clear that whistleblowing plays a pivotal role in current public sector integrity systems and that its value is typically highly recognised in public sector organisations. Questions logically arise about whether all types of whistleblowing are equally highly valued and whether this level of recognition flows through to the way in which whistleblowing is managed. Nevertheless, the results confirm that few if any public sector agencies have reason to ignore the imperatives that exist to try to manage whistleblowing more productively.

The fourth part of the chapter highlights that, notwithstanding this broadly positive picture, major challenges confront many agencies. It moves beyond the broad averages provided when the results across the four jurisdictions are taken together to present data about the amount of observed wrongdoing reported by staff on an agency-by-agency basis. These results show enormous variability in the degree of success that different agencies appear to be having, in all four jurisdictions, in encouraging employees to speak up about wrongdoing they perceive or observe. The analysis uses the employee survey data to identify not only the 'reporting rate', but an even more significant performance measure, the 'inaction rate', in response to perceived wrongdoing in each agency—a measure against which the success of agency approaches will be judged further in later chapters. Some agencies could boast that less than 10 per cent of employees who observed serious wrongdoing then did nothing about it; but in at least one organisation in each jurisdiction, more than 50 per cent of staff in the same position neither reported the wrongdoing nor took any other action. These indicators of the varying 'reporting climates' in different agencies reinforce that general barriers to reporting exist across the public sector and suggest that differences in approaches and management culture can have strong, measurable effects at the agency level.

## How much whistleblowing goes on in the Australian public sector?

Against stereotypes of whistleblowing as a relatively rare phenomenon, evidence has been emerging that whistleblowing is, in reality, far more frequent or even routine. Since the 1980s, in the United States, studies by the Merit Systems Protection Board have indicated that about half or more of all federal public servants have observed wrongdoing in their organisation, with about 30 per cent of these then going on to report it (see, for example, US Merit Systems Protection Board 1981). While US studies indicate that more observers of wrongdoing tend not to report it than those who do (Miceli and Near 2006), the numbers of those who do report remain substantial.

Recent Australian research has tended in the same direction. An estimate of the number of Queensland public servants reporting serious wrongdoing in any one year, as of 2000–01, was a minimum of 1.8 per cent of all employees based simply on the internal investigation case load of large agencies (Brown et al. 2004). In 2003–04, the Australian Public Service Commission (APSC) first surveyed a cross-section of employees from Australian public service agencies about whether they had 'witnessed another Australian Public Service [APS] employee engaging in…a serious breach' of their statutory code of conduct in the previous 12 months and whether they had then reported it (APSC 2004:111). Examples given of a 'serious breach' were 'fraud, theft, misusing clients' personal information, sexual harassment [and] leaking classified documentation'. In this and the next annual survey (APSC 2005), 11 per cent of respondents indicated that they had witnessed such a breach, with about 50 per cent of these (about 5–6 per cent of all respondents) saying they had also reported it. While these indications were lower than in the US research, they nevertheless amounted to a substantial number.

In the present research, the employee survey was the primary means for establishing a comprehensive picture of the current incidence of whistleblowing in the four jurisdictions studied. This was to learn how this whistleblowing was then managed but also, for the above reasons, to establish a more accurate overall picture to start with. In a manner broadly consistent with the larger US surveys, respondents were asked to indicate which of the 38 types of wrongdoing listed in Appendix 2 they had 'direct evidence of having occurred' in their current organisation in the previous two years. Direct evidence was defined as 'something that you personally observed, experienced or was formally reported to you'. The responses for the four participating jurisdictions are set out in Table 2.1. Overall, 5473 of the 7663 respondents, or 71 per cent, observed at least one of the nominated types of wrongdoing.

This rate of observation was larger than expected based on prior estimates and surveys. For Commonwealth agencies, methodological differences would certainly account for some differences with the APSC survey results. These include the fact that the employee survey included a wide range of Commonwealth agencies not covered by the Commonwealth *Public Service Act 1999* and therefore not covered by the APSC surveys, given that APS agencies employ only a little more than half of all Commonwealth Government employees. Further, the employee survey used different sampling and stratification, asked respondents for experience from the previous two years rather than a single year and offered respondents 38 different examples of wrongdoing from which to choose—compared with the five examples offered by the APSC surveys. In addition, the APSC surveys tested for 'serious' misconduct, whereas not all of the wrongdoing perceived by respondents in the present study would qualify as 'serious'.

Accordingly, the proportion of respondents who observed 'serious' wrongdoing is estimated in Table 2.2. The employee survey asked respondents to nominate which of any observed activities they felt to be the 'most serious' and then how serious they felt it to be on a five-point Likert scale. This time, the table shows how many respondents observed any of the nominated activities, grouped in the broad categories introduced in Chapter 1 and set out in Appendix 2. It also shows how many respondents regarded each activity as the 'most serious' they observed and how many also felt the activity was at least 'somewhat serious'. The result is conservative, given that some respondents might have observed more than one type of wrongdoing that they considered serious. At least 61 per cent of respondents observed wrongdoing that was, in their view, at least somewhat serious in the previous two years.

## Table 2.1 Proportion of public employees with direct evidence of wrongdoing (per cent)

| Wrongdoing type | Cth [a] (n = 2 307) | NSW (n = 2 561) | Qld (n = 1 729) | WA (n = 1 007) | Total [b] (n = 7 663) |
|---|---|---|---|---|---|
| Covering-up poor performance | 30.9 | **30.0** | 30.7 | 24.2 | **29.6** |
| Bullying of staff | 29.0 | 29.6 | **33.4** | 24.0 | 29.5 |
| Favouritism in selection or promotion | **32.0** | 25.7 | 28.5 | **25.6** | 28.3 |
| Incompetent or negligent decision making | 27.7 | 26.4 | 25.6 | 21.4 | 26.0 |
| Improper private use of agency facilities/resources | 27.0 | 22.5 | 24.3 | 23.2 | 24.3 |
| Rorting overtime or leave provisions | 22.2 | 20.7 | 20.3 | 19.2 | 20.9 |
| Inadequate record keeping | 19.5 | 18.7 | 17.6 | 16.2 | 18.4 |
| Failure to follow correct staff-selection procedures | 18.2 | 16.0 | 19.7 | 14.9 | 17.4 |
| Waste of work funds | 17.5 | 16.2 | 18.5 | 16.1 | 17.1 |
| Theft of property | 13.7 | 14.1 | 15.5 | 15.5 | 14.5 |
| Drunk or under the influence of illegal drugs at work | 15.3 | 12.8 | 12.1 | 13.3 | 13.4 |
| Using official position for personal services/favours | 10.1 | 13.4 | 12.4 | 11.1 | 11.9 |
| Failure to correct serious mistakes | 12.3 | 11.3 | 11.7 | 8.9 | 11.4 |
| Misuse of confidential information | 10.1 | 10.9 | 13.4 | 9.1 | 11.0 |
| Acting against organisational policy, regulations or laws | 10.4 | 10.6 | 10.9 | 9.4 | 10.5 |
| Giving unfair advantage to contractor, etc. | 6.8 | 8.7 | 10.5 | 10.3 | 8.8 |
| Allowing dangerous or harmful working conditions | 7.1 | 9.5 | 9.9 | 7.8 | 8.7 |
| Sexual harassment | 10.2 | 7.4 | 8.3 | 8.1 | 8.6 |
| Theft of money | 9.8 | 7.7 | 8.4 | 7.0 | 8.4 |
| Intervening on behalf of friend or relative | 6.1 | 7.7 | 8.2 | 5.7 | 7.1 |
| Downloading pornography on a work computer | 9.1 | 5.9 | 5.5 | 7.7 | 7.0 |
| Racial discrimination against staff member | 6.7 | 7.5 | 5.9 | 6.2 | 6.8 |
| Making false or inflated claims for reimbursement | 5.3 | 5.9 | 4.5 | 6.0 | 5.4 |
| Racial discrimination against member of public | 4.2 | 5.6 | 4.2 | 4.0 | 4.6 |
| Endangering public health or safety | 3.0 | 5.0 | 6.1 | 4.4 | 4.6 |
| Reprisal against whistleblowers | 3.9 | 5.2 | 5.0 | 2.7 | 4.5 |
| Unfair dismissal | 5.5 | 3.7 | 4.9 | 1.9 | 4.3 |
| Negligent purchases or leases | 3.9 | 3.9 | 3.2 | 3.8 | 3.7 |
| Misleading or false reporting of agency activity | 3.7 | 3.6 | 3.5 | 2.9 | 3.5 |
| Stalking (unwanted following or intrusion) | 3.7 | 2.7 | 3.1 | 2.5 | 3.1 |
| Bribes or kickbacks | 2.4 | 2.9 | 3.7 | 3.4 | 3.0 |
| Unlawfully altering or destroying official records | 2.7 | 2.7 | 3.1 | 1.6 | 2.7 |

| Wrongdoing type | Cth [a] (n = 2 307) | NSW (n = 2 561) | Qld (n = 1 729) | WA (n = 1 007) | Total [b] (n = 7 663) |
|---|---|---|---|---|---|
| Covering-up corruption | 1.6 | 3.2 | 2.1 | 1.2 | 2.2 |
| Improper involvement of a family business | 2.1 | 2.1 | 2.0 | 1.0 | 1.9 |
| Producing or using unsafe products | 1.6 | 1.9 | 2.6 | 0.8 | 1.8 |
| Hindering an official investigation | 1.5 | 2.0 | 2.2 | 0.7 | 1.7 |
| Failing to declare financial interest | 1.0 | 1.6 | 1.3 | 1.6 | 1.4 |
| Sexual assault | 1.3 | 1.6 | 1.2 | 0.6 | 1.3 |
| Other | 3.9 | 3.9 | 4.4 | 3.5 | 4.0 |
| At least one of the above | 72.6 | 71.3 | 71.8 | 68.1 | 71.4 |

[a] Throughout this report, Commonwealth figures include a range of APS and non-APS agencies unless otherwise indicated.
[b] Includes 59 respondents for whom jurisdiction and agency unknown.
Source: Employee survey: Q19; see also Appendix 2.

## Table 2.2 Wrongdoing considered most serious by public employees

| Wrongdoing category | Respondents with direct evidence (Table 2.1 grouped) % (n = 7 663) | Percentage who felt this activity was the most serious they observed % (n = 7 663) | Percentage who *also* felt the activity was serious (somewhat, very or extremely) % (n = 7 663) |
|---|---|---|---|
| Personnel and workplace grievances | 48.7 (3 732) | 23.5 (1 801) | 22.2 (1 702) |
| Misconduct for material gain | 46.5 (3 560) | 15.8 (1 213) | 13.3 (1 016) |
| Defective administration | 33.1 (2 536) | 6.9 (530) | 6.2 (477) |
| Perverting justice or accountability | 31.5 (2 413) | 5.2 (400) | 4.7 (363) |
| Waste or mismanagement of resources | 29.2 (2 236) | 3.7 (286) | 2.8 (211) |
| Improper or unprofessional behaviour | 25.1 (1 925) | 9.3 (709) | 8.8 (678) |
| Conflict of interest | 9.1 (696) | 0.9 (72) | 0.9 (70) |
| Reprisals against whistleblowers | 4.5 (346) | 0.5 (35) | 0.5 (35) |
| Other | 4.0 (305) | 1.8 (140) | 1.7 (130) |
| At least one of the above | 71.4 (5 473) | -- | -- |
| Total | -- | 67.7 (5 186) | 61.1 (4 682) |
| Missing | 0.0 (2) | 3.7 (287) | 4.4 (334) |

Source: Employee survey: Q19 (see Appendix 2), Q20, Q22 (n = 7663).

**Table 2.3 Wrongdoing considered most serious by public employees and whether they reported it**

| Wrongdoing category | Respondents with direct evidence (Table 2.1 grouped as per Appendix 2) | Percentage who felt this activity was the most serious they observed, and reported it | Percentage who reported it, who *also* felt the activity was at least somewhat serious |
|---|---|---|---|
| | % (n = 7 663) | % (n = 7 663) | % (n = 7 663) |
| Personnel and workplace grievances | 48.7 (3 732) | 8.7 (669) | 8.7 (665) |
| Misconduct for material gain | 46.5 (3 560) | 6.0 (462) | 5.9 (452) |
| Defective administration | 33.1 (2 536) | 3.1 (237) | 3.0 (227) |
| Perverting justice or accountability | 31.5 (2 413) | 2.3 (174) | 2.2 (171) |
| Waste or mismanagement of resources | 29.2 (2 236) | 1.1 (86) | 1.0 (75) |
| Improper or unprofessional behaviour | 25.1 (1 925) | 4.3 (328) | 4.3 (327) |
| Conflict of interest | 9.1 (696) | 0.4 (33) | 0.4 (32) |
| Reprisals against whistleblowers | 4.5 (346) | 0.3 (23) | 0.3 (23) |
| Other | 4.0 (305) | 1.1 (84) | 1.1 (83) |
| At least one of the above | 71.4 (5 473) | -- | -- |
| Wrongdoing type unknown | -- | 0.7 (50) | 0.6 (49) |
| **Total** | -- | **28.0 (2 146)** | **27.5 (2 104)** |

Source: Employee survey: Q19, Q20, Q22, Q26 (n = 7663).

Table 2.3 indicates how many of those who observed wrongdoing went on to report it. The employee survey asked respondents whether they had 'formally reported' the perceived wrongdoing 'to any individual or group', also explicitly advising them that 'talking about it with your family or with co-workers is *not* a formal report'. Those who reported the wrongdoing amounted to 39 per cent of all those who observed wrongdoing, or 28 per cent of all respondents. As shown, almost all these respondents also regarded the wrongdoing that they reported as being at least somewhat serious; very few said they had reported matters they regarded as trivial. Figure 2.1 shows this result in another way, confirming that, across the data set, as the level of perceived seriousness increased, so did the likelihood that the matter would be reported.

While these results provide a new basis for estimating how many public officials currently report wrongdoing, they are also conservative, not only for reasons given above and below, but because the respondents were limited to those officials who were currently with the organisations surveyed. The non-inclusion of individuals who might have reported wrongdoing but have since left the organisation, which will be further discussed in Chapter 5, means that the total number of individuals who observed and reported wrongdoing is likely to be larger than that indicated.

**Figure 2.1 Proportion of respondents who reported wrongdoing they saw, by level of perceived seriousness (per cent)**

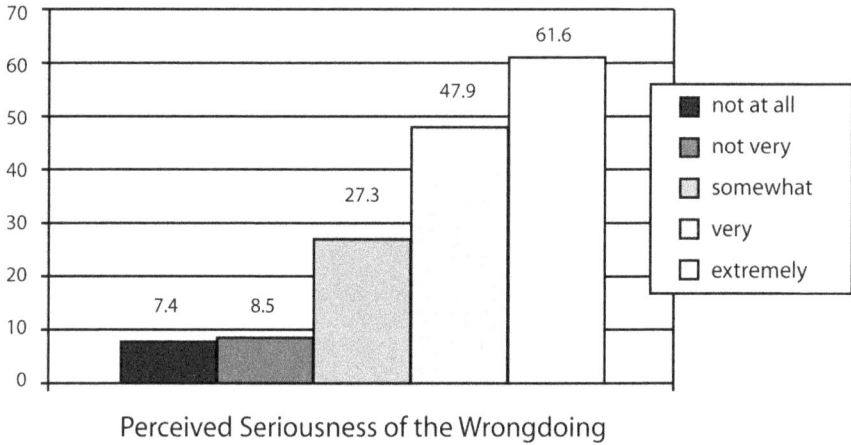

Perceived Seriousness of the Wrongdoing

Source: Employee survey: Q22, Q26.

## 'Whistleblowing' as opposed to 'reporting'

The above results provide an overview of the number of employees who currently perceive and report wrongdoing, but are these all 'whistleblowers'? While all this reporting activity is important for understanding how wrongdoing is detected and how whistleblowing is managed in public sector organisations, it does not all fit the definition of whistleblowing outlined in Chapter 1. There are two major distinctions to be drawn in order to arrive at an estimate of current levels of public interest whistleblowing, which is the core of the present study. These are:

- the type of wrongdoing involved—for example, a 'personnel or workplace grievance' in which the wrongdoing is most likely to concern the employee as an individual employee, and less likely to involve a matter of larger organisational integrity and/or public interest
- the 'organisational role' of the employee—that is, whether reporting the wrongdoing was part of their normal professional job responsibility, rather than a discretionary action.

## Role reporting versus non-role reporting

Taking the second distinction first, of the 28 per cent of respondents who said they reported the most serious form of observed wrongdoing, it can be presumed that some did so because it was part of their professional role, or job, to pass on this information. For example, these respondents likely included at least some supervisors who observed wrongdoing by a member of their own staff and formally reported the matter to their own superior for disciplinary action, or to other internal units for further investigation. Similarly, an internal auditor might have formally reported a matter to the CEO in line with standard procedures. In neither case would the report normally be regarded as an act of 'whistleblowing' because it was part of their usual professional role.

How much reporting is 'role reporting' of this kind and how much is 'non-role reporting', which might fit more closely with conventional concepts of whistleblowing? While the question is simple, the answer is complex and not necessarily definitive. In some contexts, every member of an organisation may be under a legislative or contractual obligation to report perceived wrongdoing of particular kinds. This is the case in most Australian police services, agencies dealing with child safety or welfare and other public health agencies. The reasons why employees report wrongdoing are analysed in Chapter 3, but it is noteworthy that 58 per cent of all respondents who reported wrongdoing indicated they believed they were under a 'legal responsibility to report' and this was very or extremely important in their decision to do so.

Similarly, employees can make their reports in ways that reflect different degrees of 'official' compulsion. The case study and integrity agency surveys confirm that, even when most employee reporting is seen as discretionary, it is not unusual for reports to be made in response to official requests or as part of evidence gathering during an investigation that is not triggered by the 'whistleblower'. In such circumstances, the obligation to report can effectively be 'made' part of the employee's role on at least a one-off basis, even if it is not normally part of their role. Table 2.4 sets out some of this evidence, drawn from the internal witness, case-handler and manager and integrity case-handler surveys. These reporters could have identical management needs to other whistleblowers, as discussed in Chapter 9.

**Table 2.4 How do reporters first provide their information? (per cent, mean)**

|  | Internal witnesses (n = 214) | Case-handlers and managers (n = 712) | Integrity case-handlers (n = 63) |
|---|---|---|---|
|  |  | 1 = never, 2 = rarely, 3 = sometimes, 4 = often, 5 = always | |
| I/they decided to report it, without anyone asking me/them to do so | 86 (184) | 3.41 | 3.57 |
| I/they reported it after being asked to provide information about the matter by a supervisor or manager | 7 (16) | 3.34 | 2.67 |
| I was/employees were approached to assist in an existing investigation into the wrongdoing | 4 (8) | 3.32 | 3.08 |
| I was/employees were formally directed or compelled to provide information in an official investigation or hearing | 2 (4) | 3.10 | 2.89 |
| Missing | 1 (2) | -- | -- |
| **Total** | **100 (214)** | -- | -- |

Sources: Internal witness survey: Q24 ('How did you first come to report or provide information?'); case-handler and manager surveys: Q24; integrity case-handler survey: Q18 ('When employees report wrongdoing, how often do they first provide their information in this way?').

Returning to the employee survey, two variables were used in combination to estimate how many reports could be 'role reports'. The first relates to how the respondent became aware of the perceived wrongdoing. Table 2.5 sets out some key data about how reporters indicated they first became aware of the wrongdoing they reported. Of the 2146 reporters, 651 (30.3 per cent) indicated that it was 'reported to them in their official capacity', of whom 457 (21.3 per cent of all reporters) also indicated that this was the only way in which they became aware of the wrongdoing. This is one indicator that they learned of the wrongdoing, and therefore probably acted on it, only because dealing with this information was part of their role.

**Table 2.5 How reporters become aware of the wrongdoing**

| How did you find out about this activity? <br> Please circle all that apply. | | % (n = 2 146) |
|---|---|---|
| It was directed at me — | only | 16.3 (350) |
| | along with other responses | 9.3 (200) |
| | subtotal | 25.6 (550) |
| I was invited to participate in it — | only | 1.4 (30) |
| | along with other responses | 2.2 (48) |
| | subtotal | 3.6 (78) |
| I observed it — | only | 25.3 (544) |
| | along with other responses | 18.8 (404) |
| | subtotal | 44.2 (948) |
| I came across direct evidence (eg., documents) — | only | 9.4 (201) |
| | along with other responses | 11.6 (248) |
| | subtotal | 20.9 (449) |
| **It was reported to me in my official capacity —** | **only** | 21.3 (457) |
| | along with other responses | 9.0 (194) |
| | subtotal | 30.3 (651) |
| Other | | 5.8 (124) |
| At least one of the above | | 99.3 (2 131) |
| Missing | | 0.7 (15) |

Source: Employee survey: Q21.

The second variable was the organisational relationship between the reporter and those he or she perceived to be involved in the wrongdoing. As already indicated, a manager who becomes aware of wrongdoing by their own employees is normally expected to report it as part of their role. Such cases are also not simple to separate, since a supervisor might find their own employees to be involved in wrongdoing that also involves employees at other levels, or they might become aware of wrongdoing by junior employees for which other managers are responsible. In some circumstances, reporting such wrongdoing could be regarded as part of any manager's role; in others, less so.

Table 2.6 shows the positions held by the perceived wrongdoers relative to: a) all respondents who reported the most serious wrongdoing, and b) reporters who also indicated that they held a managerial role in the organisation. Of the 2146 reporters, 660 indicated that they held a managerial role, of which 376 (57 per cent of all managers) indicated that the only people involved in the wrongdoing that they reported were employees below their level. This is taken as a second indicator of an organisational relationship that means the report is likely to be part of their role.

**Table 2.6 Position of wrongdoers relative to reporters**

| What position did the wrongdoer(s) have in the organisation? Please circle all that apply. | | (a) All reporters % (n = 2 146) | (b) All managers % (n = 660) |
|---|---|---|---|
| **Employee(s) below my level—** | only | 31.4 (674) | **57.0 (376)** |
| | along with others | 5.7 (123) | 5.5 (36) |
| | subtotal | 37.1 (797) | 62.4 (412) |
| Employee(s) at my level— | only | 21.2 (455) | 9.8 (65) |
| | along with others | 9.4 (202) | 5.6 (37) |
| | subtotal | 30.6 (657) | 15.5 (102) |
| My immediate supervisor(s)— | only | 9.6 (207) | 3.6 (24) |
| | along with others | 9.6 (206) | 4.4 (29) |
| | subtotal | 19.2 (413) | 8.0 (53) |
| High-level manager(s)— | only | 17.2 (369) | 15.5 (102) |
| | along with others | 8.8 (188) | 4.8 (32) |
| | subtotal | 26.0 (557) | 20.3 (134) |
| Outside contractor/vendor(s)— | only | 2.9 (63) | 2.6 (17) |
| | along with others | 1.6 (35) | 0.6 (4) |
| | subtotal | 4.6 (98) | 3.2 (21) |
| At least one of the above | | 97.4 (2 091) | 97.4 (643) |
| Missing | | 2.6 (55) | 2.6 (17) |

Source: Employee Survey: Q25, Q44.

Combining these variables, 457 respondents who reported wrongdoing indicated that they became aware of it only because it was reported to them in their official capacity, while 376 indicated that they were a manager who observed wrongdoing that involved only employees below their level. With 214 respondents falling in both categories, the total number of reporters falling into either group was 619—or 28.8 per cent of all reporters. While not perfect, this provides some indication of the proportion of all reporters whose reports are likely to have amounted to role reports. Conversely, after removing missing cases, the remaining 1497 (69.8 per cent) of all employees who reported wrongdoing are likely to have done so outside their normal role, and therefore are more likely to fit the conventional definition of a whistleblower. This figure would place the proportion of potential whistleblowers at 27.3 per cent of all those who observed wrongdoing in the previous two years and 19.5 per cent of all respondents—as depicted in Figure 2.2.

The likelihood that an employee reported wrongdoing as part of their role does not mean they are of less interest for the remaining analysis. For example, if employees in this situation observe wrongdoing and do not report it, this could be of greater concern than whether or not other staff members blow the whistle. Similarly, if employees who make a 'role report' then suffer harassment or reprisals as a consequence, this is likely to be a very strong indicator that an agency has problems with how it responds to information about wrongdoing from any internal source. It does, however, provide a useful indicator of how much reporting of wrongdoing approaches the conventional definition of whistleblowing—that is, reporting that is less likely to occur without official encouragement or policies, and at which most legislative and organisational responses are aimed.

## Whistleblowing as opposed to personnel or workplace grievances

The second threshold distinction is the subject matter of the wrongdoing—in particular, whether it constitutes a matter of potential public interest or involves only matters of personal or private interest to the reporter. As discussed in Chapter 1, if a report is only in the latter category, it is more accurately categorised as a personal grievance than a whistleblowing matter. The distinction can, however, again be difficult to draw in practice. As outlined in Chapter 1, many reports of wrongdoing involve a personal grievance and matters of broader organisational or public integrity. An employee's personal grievance could be indicative of a larger breakdown in organisational procedures (whether or not this is known to them); an employee could be aware of a matter of serious public interest but reveals it only after a personal grievance arises (whether or not related to the public interest matter); or an employee could raise a public interest matter but receive an initial response that immediately gives rise to a personal grievance (causing the two issues thereafter to travel in tandem).

The frequency with which public interest concerns are mixed with personal conflicts is confirmed by responses to the case study and integrity agency surveys. Table 2.7 sets out how often a variety of conflicts appears to precede or accompany the making of reports, even when the wrongdoing observed does not include matters classified in Appendix 2 and the earlier tables as 'personnel or workplace grievances'. The table indicates the frequency with which the specified conflicts were present in the experience or opinion of: a) all those who volunteered for the internal witness survey; b) internal witnesses whose observed wrongdoing did not include 'personnel or workplace grievances'; c) case-handlers and d) managers from the same group of case study agencies; and e) case-handlers from integrity agencies. It shows that in any view of the situation, a range of interpersonal conflicts is sometimes or often likely to be present, in addition to whatever public interest issues might be involved.

Another indication of the complex mix is provided by the opinions of case study and integrity agency case-handlers and managers about the type of information provided by employees who report. Table 2.8 shows how these respondents replied to questions about their experience of the mix of personal and public interest matters to be found in employee reports of wrongdoing. The means show a diversity of opinion as to whether any of the statements accurately summarise the type of information provided in employee reports, with many disinclined to state a view. Those with a view were, however, much more likely to agree than disagree that 'reports are often about [both] personal grievances and matters of public interest' (32 to 21 per cent for case study agency case-handlers and managers, and 55 per cent to 8 per cent for case-handlers in integrity agencies). This is despite the fact that these respondents were twice as likely to disagree than agree with the statement that 'reports are often entirely about matters of public interest' (40 to 17 per cent for case study agency case-handlers and managers; 46 to 20 per cent for integrity agencies) and just as likely to agree as disagree that 'reports are often entirely about personal grievances' (35 to 32 per cent for case study agency case-handlers and managers; 33 to 34 per cent for integrity agencies).

## Table 2.7 Conflicts that accompany reports of wrongdoing

| | Internal witness survey: Q23 | | Case-handler and manager surveys: Q26 | | Integrity case-handler survey: Q22 |
|---|---|---|---|---|---|
| | (a) All respondents (inc. b) [a] % (n = 214) | (b) Respondents whose observed wrongdoing did not include 'personnel or workplace grievances' [a][b] % (n = 74) | (c) Case-handlers (n = 244) | (d) Managers (n = 343) | (e) Integrity case-handlers (n = 65) |
| | | | 1 = never, 2 = rarely, 3 = sometimes, 4 = often, 5 = always | | |
| Dissatisfaction with one or more agency policies | 12.6 (27) | 14.9 (11) | 3.10 | 3.11 | 3.55 |
| A decision about a promotion that affected you (the employee) | 11.2 (24) | 1.4 (1) | 3.10 | 2.77 | 3.18 |
| Failure to renew your (the employee's) contract | 0.5 (1) | 1.4 (1) | 2.44 | 2.27 | 2.60 |
| Dissatisfaction with your work duties | 11.7 (25) | 6.8 (5) | 3.16 | 3.03 | 2.95 |
| Conflict or serious disagreement or another grievance with or against... manager(s) or supervisor(s) | 41.6 (89) | 21.6 (16) | 3.40 | 3.16 | 3.52 |
| Conflict or serious disagreement or another grievance with or against... co-worker(s) | 13.6 (29) | 8.1 (6) | 3.30 | 3.19 | 3.24 |
| At least one of the above | 58.9 (126) | 45.9 (34) | -- | -- | -- |

[a] Total does not add to 100 per cent because multiple responses were permitted.
[b] For items classed as 'personnel or workplace grievances', see Appendix 2.
**Sources:** Internal witness survey: Q23 ('When you first reported or provided information about the wrongdoing, were any of the following already causing you concern?'); case-handler and manager surveys: Q26; integrity case-handler survey: Q22 ('When employees first report wrongdoing, how often do you think any of the following issues are already also causing them concern?').

## Table 2.8 Personal grievances and matters of public interest (mean)

| When employees/public employees report wrongdoing, what type of information do they provide?<br><br>Please indicate your level of agreement with each of the following statements:<br><br>1 = strongly disagree to 5 = strongly agree | Case-handler and manager surveys: Q27 | | Integrity case-handler survey: Q23 |
|---|---|---|---|
| | (a) Case-handlers (n = 291) | (b) Managers (n = 422) | (c) Integrity case-handlers (n = 76) |
| Reports are often entirely about personal grievances | 3.09 | 2.94 | 3.00 |
| Reports are often entirely about matters of public interest | 2.66 | 2.78 | 2.72 |
| Reports are often about personal grievances and matters of public interest | 3.09 | 3.09 | 3.50 |

Sources: Case-handler and manager surveys: Q27g–i; integrity case-handler survey: Q23g–i.

## Figure 2.2 An overview of whistleblowing in the Australian public sector

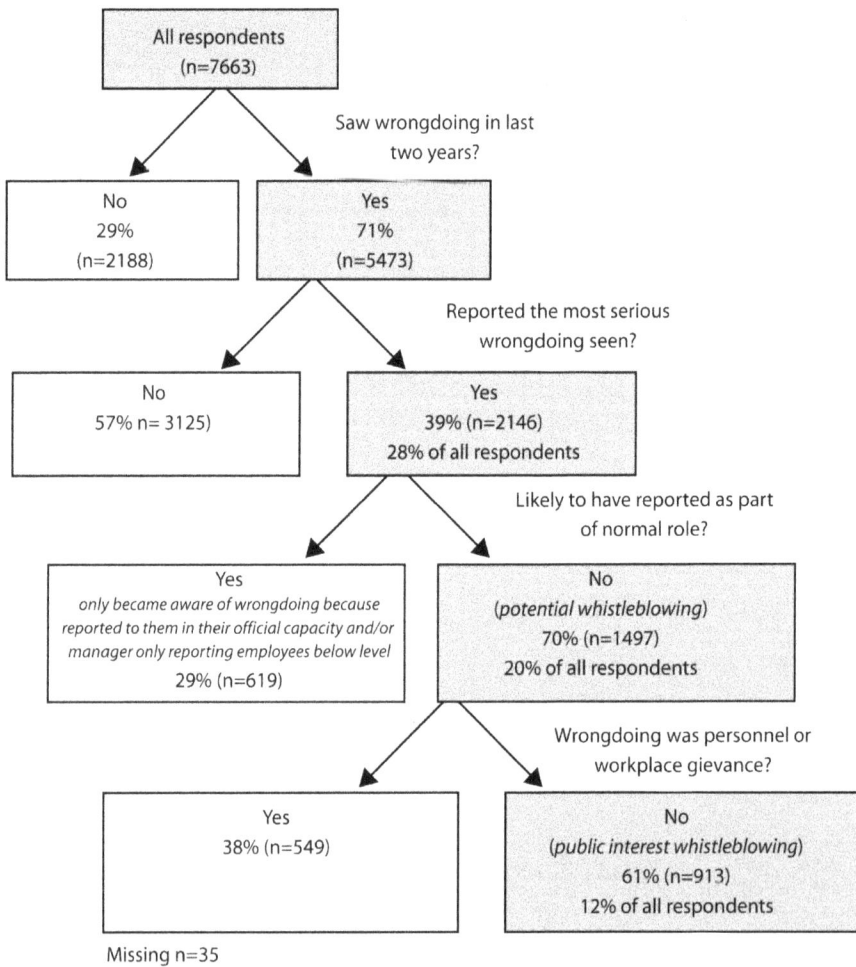

Source: Employee survey.

As will be discussed in later chapters, it is important that organisational systems recognise the degree to which personal and public interest matters are intertwined, otherwise, issues of public interest can go overlooked and employees might be left subject to reprisals simply because personal interests are also involved. The focus of the present research is, however, on ensuring that appropriate organisational and legal consequences flow whenever employee reporting of wrongdoing includes any matters of organisational integrity and/or public interest, even if it also involves personal or private grievances. As explained in Chapter 1, the rationale for this includes the need to encourage organisation members to report perceived wrongdoing, even though it does not impact on them personally, before it becomes sufficiently serious or systemic to affect the functioning of the whole workplace.

As also acknowledged in Chapter 1, a number of the wrongdoing types listed among the public interest categories in Tables 2.1–2.3 above, and in Appendix 2, are more likely than others to frequently be provoked by personal or private grievances. Sometimes the distinction is straightforward—for example, all the wrongdoing types grouped as 'misconduct for material gain' are typically regarded as contrary to the public interest irrespective of whether they also impact on any individual. In other cases, the distinction is less clear. For example, some of the wrongdoing grouped as 'improper or unprofessional behaviour'—such as being drunk or under the influence of illegal drugs at work, or sexual harassment—could have their only direct impacts on fellow employees and therefore seem to be simply workplace-based disputes with no external impact, but they are usually regarded as sufficiently corrosive of public integrity to qualify as official or criminal misconduct.

A final approximation of the extent of public interest whistleblowing is arrived at by excluding the large number of reports about 'personnel or workplace grievances', including dangerous or harmful working conditions, unfair dismissal and bullying of staff within the workplace. The single largest group of employees (48.7 per cent of all employee survey respondents, as shown in Table 2.2) observed wrongdoing types in this category. This result tends to confirm that these types of wrongdoing affected employees most directly, irrespective of their relative seriousness or wider significance for public integrity—a result also confirmed in Chapter 3. In comparison with this major category of wrongdoing, the reporting in the remaining categories can be identified as relatively unlikely to be concerned purely with personal grievances. While this remains only an approximation, it provides a basis for estimating the proportion of reports consistent with a workable definition of whistleblowing.

Figure 2.2 sets out an overview of this current incidence of whistleblowing across the 118 agencies surveyed. Of those respondents whose reporting was probably done outside their normal organisational role, 913 or 60.9 per cent reported wrongdoing other than (or in addition to) a personnel or workplace grievance. This equates to 11.9 per cent of all employee survey respondents. In other words, while about 71 per cent of all respondents observed wrongdoing in the two years and at least 28 per cent of all respondents then reported the most serious instances, perhaps 12 per cent of all respondents would fit a conventional definition of public interest whistleblowing.

This figure remains substantially larger than previous estimates. As only four jurisdictions and not all agencies are represented in the study, this result cannot be reliably generalised across the entire Australian public sector. Nevertheless, the range of agencies and the size of the data set make some notional extrapolation useful. Even if none of the non-respondents to the survey had reported wrongdoing, these whistleblowers would amount to about 4 per cent of the sample—or about 65 000 public officials when extrapolated nationally. If the result held true for the entire Australian public sector, it would suggest that about 197 000 individual public servants might have engaged in public interest whistleblowing in the two years. Assuming each of these officials reported on only one type of relevant wrongdoing once in the two years, these percentages suggest that, on average, each weekday in Australia, at least 125 individual public servants—but more likely about 380—might be expected to blow the whistle on a matter of potential public interest.

## How important is whistleblowing?

As will be seen in Chapter 4, the bulk of the whistleblowing identified in the present research begins internally and is resolved without being made public. Nevertheless, the sheer volume of whistleblowing indicated in the previous section raises many issues for public sector management. One is that it is clearly not a rare activity—rather, it is probably better characterised as a regular feature of organisational life.

A natural question is whether this incidence of whistleblowing might have been unusually high (or low) during the study period. While this question can be properly answered only by continuing research, there is no particular reason to expect this, especially given the broad consistency of the outcome with similar international studies. In fact, studies in the United States and the United Kingdom indicate that the incidence of whistleblowing appears to be increasing over time (Dozier and Miceli 1985; Near et al. 2004; Vinten 1994). In our research, one indicator of the relative normality of the current incidence of whistleblowing was provided by the case-handler, manager and integrity case-handler surveys, which asked respondents whether they believed that the number of employees who had reported wrongdoing had changed in the previous five years. Table 2.9 sets out the results. Overall, while 48 per cent of case study agency case-handlers and managers indicated a belief that the number was 'about the same' as five years previously, 42 per cent believed that the number had increased and only slightly less than 10 per cent indicated that the number had decreased. The responses of integrity case-handlers followed a similar pattern.

A related issue is whether there is any reason to believe that this level of whistleblowing is likely to change, but this appears unlikely. A further indication of this is given by evidence that—contrary to a strong popular myth—many public employees are not deterred from reporting wrongdoing even if they anticipate, or have established from previous experience, that whistleblowing is not an easy process. In the earlier NSW study, 49 per cent of the stratified sample of 800 NSW public employees indicated a belief that they would still report corruption even if they knew they did not have the support of colleagues and 41 per cent would do it even if they knew their career would be adversely affected (Zipparo 1999a, 1999b). In the employee survey, 81 per cent of all those who had reported wrongdoing indicated that if they had their time over again, they would be either 'very likely' or 'extremely likely' to still report the activity (employee survey: Q34). As will be discussed in Chapter 5, even a majority of those whistleblowers who said they had been treated badly as a result said they would be at least 'somewhat likely' to still report if they had their time over again. These responses indicate that overall, the incidence of whistleblowing is unlikely to decline, other than perhaps in the event of a significant decline in perceived wrongdoing.

**Table 2.9 Change in number of employees believed to report (mean)**

| In the past five years, do you believe the number of employees who have reported wrongdoing in your organisation/to your agency has changed? | (a) Case-handlers (n = 288) | (b) Managers (n = 422) | (c) Integrity case-handlers (n = 70) |
|---|---|---|---|
| 1 = decreased a lot<br>2 = decreased somewhat<br>3 = about the same<br>4 = increased somewhat<br>5 = increased a lot | 3.53 | 3.29 | 3.47 |

**Sources:** Case-handler and manager surveys: Q15; integrity case-handler survey: Q10.

This level of whistleblowing has important implications since it makes clear that whistleblowing is not a process in which public sector managers can afford to simply be reactive. The survey data reveal, however, that the role of whistleblowing has already achieved widespread acceptance in basic ways in most agencies and for most case-handlers and managers, even if questions remain about how it might best be managed. Current levels of whistleblowing play an important role in an objective sense, as a contribution to the integrity-promoting efforts of organisations and the public sector generally. The assumption that whistleblowing has positive effects in bringing wrongdoing to light, which provides much of the reason for the existence of current whistleblowing legislation, is borne out in much of the attitudinal and opinion data collected in the surveys.

The first of three ways to assess the value of current whistleblowing is through the views of employees in general. According to the employee survey, far from being rejected as 'dobbing' or an act of peer or corporate disloyalty, the reporting of wrongdoing by staff appears to be highly valued by the bulk of public employees. While approval is highest among those who have reported, it is almost as high among those who have not observed wrongdoing or have observed it but have not reported it (Table 2.10). These results form part of a scale for measuring the different levels of 'whistleblowing propensity' in organisations, used further in later chapters.

**Table 2.10 Attitudes towards the reporting of wrongdoing (mean)**

| 1 = strongly disagree to 5 = strongly agree | (a) Did not observe wrongdoing (n = 2 188) | (b) Observed wrongdoing, but did not report the most serious (n = 3 123) | (c) Reported the most serious wrongdoing (n = 2 146) |
|---|---|---|---|
| I personally approve of employees reporting illegal activities within the organisation | 4.4 | 4.4 | 4.5 |
| I personally approve of employees reporting wasteful activities within the organisation | 3.9 | 3.8 | 4.0 |
| It is in the best interest of the organisation when an employee reports wrongdoing | 4.1 | 4.0 | 4.2 |
| Employees should be encouraged to report wrongdoing | 4.1 | 4.1 | 4.3 |

Source: Employee survey: Q15.

A second indicator of the value currently placed on whistleblowing, from the employee survey, is through the eyes of those who have reported wrongdoing. As already noted, a majority indicated they would do it again. Further, a majority (63 per cent of all those who reported wrongdoing and 56 per cent of public interest whistleblowers) also indicated that they knew their disclosure was investigated. The fact that a higher number did not know whether action was taken is cause for concern, for a number of reasons that become clear in Chapters 3 and 5. Of those who did know that there had been some investigation, however, a majority also indicated that the outcome of the investigation was positive. Sixty-five per cent of all reporters and 56 per cent of all whistleblowers whose issue was investigated (31 per cent of all whistleblowers in total) indicated that things became 'better' as a result of the investigation.

Given that wrongdoing inevitably occurs and is reported but is not able to be substantiated, this evidence from whistleblowers themselves is not consistent with any stereotype of a public sector in which internal disclosures about wrongdoing are always simply swept under the carpet. At a general level, even if only 31 per cent of all whistleblowing reports result in positive action, this compares favourably with substantiation or 'clear-up' rates for internal or external investigations on most available measures (see Brown et al. 2004). Of course, as with other rates contained in the data, this is only a broad average.

As will be seen in the next section, it masks great variability in key outcomes from the data, at the level of individual agencies.

A third way of assessing the value currently placed on whistleblowing is from an organisational perspective, including individuals in organisations with reason to know something about it. The agency survey asked organisations to estimate the total number of cases of alleged or suspected wrongdoing reported or detected in their agency for a recent period (2002–04) and the number of these cases that came to light due to reports by employees or organisation members. Only 76 of the 118 agencies that went on to complete the employee survey, covering about two-thirds of the total employee survey data set (5151 respondents), were able to supply most of this information. Further, the information recorded on central databases was often based on different categorisations. Where the categorisations in agency records aligned, however, there was at least some similarity with the results of the employee survey in terms of the relative incidence of different wrongdoing types.

Overall, as shown in Table 2.11, the results confirm the importance of internal reporting as an information source in the internal integrity investigation efforts of agencies. Most significantly, the agency survey revealed that in a like period to that covered by the employee survey, internal reports accounted for 67 per cent of all the wrongdoing cases recorded and dealt with by these agencies. While the misalignment of categories makes the subjects difficult to interpret, the responses indicate that in some major wrongdoing categories such as 'misconduct for material gain', more than 50 per cent of matters are already known within the management structure of the agency as having come to management attention because of the action of staff.

Further, final evidence of the organisational value of whistleblowing is found in the opinions of the case study agency case-handlers and managers, as well as integrity agency case-handlers. These surveys asked each group for their opinions on the content and significance of employee reporting of wrongdoing. Consistent with the above results, these groups responded in a way that confirmed that the internal reporting of wrongdoing served a good purpose, and was only infrequently baseless, trivial or unsubstantiated. Table 2.12 indicates that, while not all internal reports are entirely meritorious or accurate, case-handlers and managers generally regard the information provided via employee reporting as significant and valuable. In particular, they were not inclined to agree with the statements that most employee reports were 'wholly trivial' or that they were often vexatious or contained intentionally false information. In some circles, these are pervasive stereotypes about whistleblowing, but these data suggest that they should now be considered quite erroneous.

**Table 2.11 Wrongdoing detected and investigated by select agencies[a] over two years**

| Wrongdoing category | (a) Employee survey respondents indicating they reported this activity | (b) Total no. of cases reported or detected according to agencies (Q18) | (c) No. of cases reported by staff, etc., according to agencies (Q18) | (d) Proportion of cases detected, reported by staff (c/b) |
|---|---|---|---|---|
| | % (n = 1 493) | n | % (n) | % |
| Personnel or workplace grievances | 33.5 (472) | 258 | 7.4 (126) | 48.8 |
| Misconduct for material gain | 23.0 (324) | 921 | 28.7 (490) | 53.2 |
| Improper or unprofessional behaviour | 18.5 (236) | 1 688 | 38.2 (652) | 38.6 |
| Defective administration | 11.1 (157) | 1 667 | 15.0 (257) | 15.4 |
| Perverting justice or accountability | 8.5 (120) | 65 | 2.2 (37) | 56.9 |
| Waste or mismanagement of resources | 4.5 (63) | 126 | 4.4 (76) | 60.3 |
| Conflict of interest | 1.7 (24) | 280 | 4.2 (71) | 25.4 |
| Reprisals against whistleblowers | 0.9 (13) | 0 | 0 | 0 |
| Subtotal | 100 (1 409) | 5 005 | 100 (1 709) | 34.1 |
| Other | (51) | 5 044 | (5 026) | 99.6 |
| Wrongdoing type unknown | (33) | 0 | 0 | 0 |
| Total | (1493) | 10049 | (6735) | 67.0% |

[a] 76 agencies who answered agency survey Q18–23 and employee survey Q19, Q26.

Table 2.13 also sets out how case-handlers and managers responded to a direct question about the importance of employee reporting as a means of bringing wrongdoing to light, relative to other well-known methods of discovery. While several methods of discovery ranked as very or extremely important, 'reporting by employees' ranked overall as the single most important trigger for the uncovering of wrongdoing in the view of these respondents. Significantly, case study agency case-handlers and managers and integrity agency case-handlers ranked employee reporting as more important than routine controls, internal audits or external investigations. These judgments are all the more significant because they come from groups—especially in the case of case-handlers, including investigators—in a relatively objective position to assess the quality of information provided by whistleblowers. The results confirm that the unique position of employees within organisations gives them a strategic role as quality information sources. Together, these results confirm that, on the whole, whistleblowing is not only regular, but is recognised within organisations as highly important for uncovering organisational wrongdoing. Of course, they also increase the responsibility of agencies to manage the process of whistleblowing in a responsible fashion.

**Table 2.12 Value of information provided by employees (mean)**

| When employees/public employees report wrongdoing, what type of information do they provide? Please indicate your level of agreement with each of the following statements (1 = strongly disagree to 5 = strongly agree) | (a) Case-handlers (n = 292) | (b) Managers (n = 421) | (c) Integrity case-handlers (n = 76) |
|---|---|---|---|
| Most reports are partly trivial and partly significant | 3.19 | 3.09 | 3.33 |
| Most reports are wholly significant (all information merits investigation) | 3.17 | 3.38 | 2.70 |
| Reports often contain inaccurate or mistaken information | 3.16 | 3.20 | 3.33 |
| Reports are often vexatious (an abuse of process) | 2.48 | 2.53 | 2.36 |
| Reports often contain intentionally false information | 2.24 | 2.35 | 2.24 |
| Most employee reports are wholly trivial (no information merits investigation) | 2.12 | 2.09 | 2.12 |

**Sources:** Case-handler and manager surveys: Q27a–f; integrity case-handler survey: Q23 a–f.

**Table 2.13 Relative importance of employee reporting (mean)**

| How important do you believe each of the following is for bringing to light wrongdoing in or by your organisation/public sector organisations? (1 = not important to 4 = extremely important) | (a) Case-handlers (n = 285) | (b) Managers (n = 410) | (c) Integrity case-handlers (n = 70) |
|---|---|---|---|
| Reporting by employees | 3.42 | 3.30 | 3.51 |
| Management observation | 3.36 | 3.30 | 3.17 |
| Routine internal controls (eg., normal financial tracking, service monitoring) | 3.24 | 3.24 | 3.26 |
| Internal audits and reviews | 3.19 | 3.06 | 3.27 |
| Client, public or contractor complaints | 2.94 | 2.97 | 3.09 |
| External investigations | 2.66 | 2.59 | 2.94 |
| Accidental discovery | 2.45 | 2.37 | 2.36 |

**Sources:** Case-handler and manager surveys: Q14; integrity case-handler survey: Q9.

# High and low rates of reporting

The above evidence of the incidence and significance of employee reporting has yielded a more positive picture of the role of whistleblowing in modern Australian public sector management than previously described. While a higher than expected incidence of whistleblowing might be misread as an indicator of higher than expected wrongdoing, in fact, it can equally be regarded as an indicator of a healthy public sector environment, in which employees feel willing and able to speak up about perceived problems in their organisation. On this approach, higher rates of reporting are to be viewed primarily as positive. Conversely, where wrongdoing is being observed by employees but reported at a lower rate, this can be taken as one indicator of a less positive reporting climate.

Chapter 3 will examine the factors that appear most likely to give rise to whistleblowing by individual employees, as well as the primary disincentives to reporting indicated by the substantial number of employee survey respondents who elected not to blow the whistle. The remaining issue for the present analysis is the extent to which the average rate of reporting indicated earlier, in which perhaps 12 per cent of all public officials can be expected to blow the whistle in a two-year period, holds true for the many different agencies involved. If it doesn't, it is possible that the key factors that influence employees' preparedness to report wrongdoing are also to be found at the organisational level.

In fact, even if the overall incidence of whistleblowing might be interpreted as healthier than expected, it does vary considerably between organisations. In other words, different agencies are achieving very different levels of success in their efforts to encourage employees to report perceived wrongdoing. The data show this in two ways: first, in the opinions of the case-handlers and managers of the case study agencies; and second, through an agency-level comparison of reporting and inaction rates themselves.

Table 2.14 shows how the respondents to the case-handler and manager surveys rated their own agency's success in encouraging employees to report. They show little overall confidence that their agencies are more than 'somewhat' successful. Figure 2.3 breaks this result down into the responses of case-handlers and managers from each of the 12 case study agencies from which sufficient data were obtained (a minimum of 10 responses). The respondents from agencies A and B were much more optimistic about their agencies' success in encouraging reporting than those from agency L.

**Table 2.14 Perceived success of the organisation in encouraging reporting (mean)**

| How successful do you think your organisation is in encouraging employees/ public employees to voice concerns about perceived wrongdoing? | (a) Case-handlers (n = 297) | (b) Managers (n = 432) | (c) Case-handlers and managers combined (n = 729) | (d) Integrity case-handlers (n = 75) |
|---|---|---|---|---|
| 1 = not at all, 2 = not very, 3 = somewhat, 4 = very, 5 = extremely | 2.96 | 3.13 | 3.06 | 3.37 |

Sources: Case-handler and manager surveys: Q61; integrity case-handler survey: Q61.

**Figure 2.3 Perceived success of the organisation in encouraging reporting by case study agency (mean)**

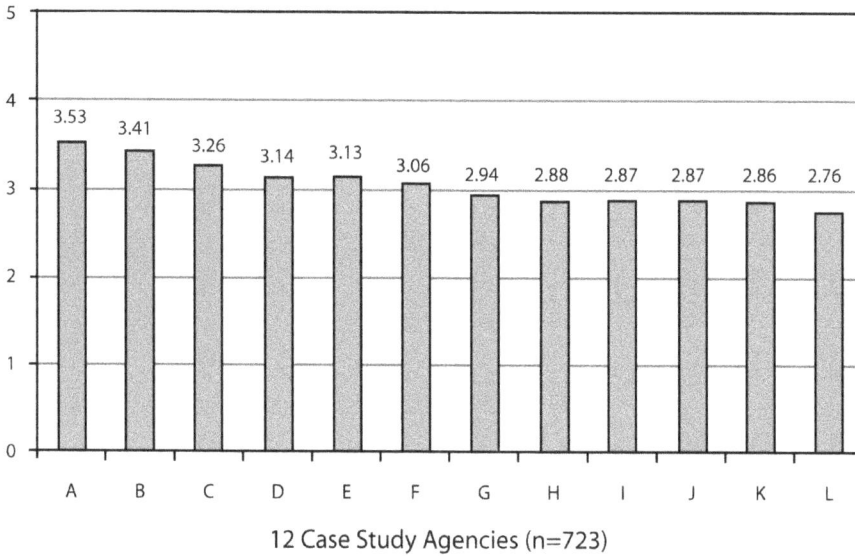

12 Case Study Agencies (n=723)

1 = not at all
2 = not very
3 = somewhat
4 = very
5 = extremely
Sources: Case-handler and manager surveys: Q61.

What do the data indicate about the reporting rate in different organisations? To answer this question, it was first necessary to establish a basis on which the incidence of reporting in different agencies could be validly compared. Comparison of raw numbers of reports or even different types of wrongdoing from the employee survey is insufficient, since the participating agencies have wildly varying sizes, functions and degrees of exposure to different risks of wrongdoing. A basic method of comparison is to examine agencies' individual 'reporting rates', or the proportion of respondents who see wrongdoing and then elect to report it. This is also a crude comparison, however, given that many employees might observe wrongdoing, but it might take only one to report it, in a healthy organisation, for management to be prompted to take appropriate action.

To allow for these differences, the basis for comparing agencies was refined in two ways. First, the comparison was confined to those instances of observed wrongdoing that employees considered either 'very' or 'extremely' serious on the five-point scale. This eliminated all those cases that on the respondents' own view might not have been serious enough to warrant reporting. Second, examination was made of the reasons given by respondents for not reporting this serious wrongdoing, which included whether someone else had already reported it and whether they took some other action by dealing with the matter themselves, formally or informally (employee survey: Q35a, b and c).

### Table 2.15 'Reporting' and 'inaction' rates by jurisdiction

| | | Cth | NSW | Qld | WA | Unknown | Total |
|---|---|---|---|---|---|---|---|
| | | (n = 2 307) | (n = 2 561) | (n = 1 729) | (n = 1 007) | (n = 59) | (n = 7 663) |
| | All respondents who observed wrongdoing | (1 676) | (1 826) | (1 242) | (686) | (43) | (5 473) |
| a | Respondents who regarded the wrongdoing as **very or extremely serious** | (968) | (1 048) | (735) | (368) | (28) | (3 147) |
| b | Staff in (a) who reported **(reporting rate)** | 50.5% | 54.5% | 54.8% | 49.7% | 39.3% | 52.7% |
| | | (489) | (571) | (403) | (183) | (11) | (1 657) |
| c | Staff in (a) who did not report, but dealt with it themselves (Q35a or b) or someone else reported it (Q35c) | 19.5% | 19.4% | 15.2% | 19.8% | 17.9% | 18.5% |
| | | (189) | (203) | (112) | (73) | (5) | (582) |
| d | Staff in (a) who did not report, did not deal with it themselves (Q35a, b) and did not indicate that anyone else reported it (Q35c) **(inaction rate)** | 29.8% | 25.9% | 29.7% | 29.9% | 2.9% | 28.6% |
| | | (288) | (271) | (218) | (110) | (12) | (899) |
| | Missing | 0.2% | 0.3% | 0.3% | 0.5% | -- | 0.3% |
| | | (2) | (3) | (2) | (2) | | (9) |
| | Total | 100% | 100% | 100% | 100% | 100% | 100% |
| | | (968) | (1 048) | (735) | (368) | (28) | (3 147) |

Source: Employee survey: Q19, Q20, Q22, Q26, Q35.

The key measure of the reporting climate, deduced from this, was not the reporting rate per se, but rather the 'inaction rate'—that is, the proportion of respondents who had observed very or extremely serious wrongdoing, but neither reported it nor gave any of the above reasons for not reporting it. Table 2.15 sets out the average national inaction rate across all agencies (28.6 per cent), as well as the rates for each jurisdiction. It shows the NSW and Queensland agencies to have, on average, slightly higher reporting rates than the Commonwealth and West Australian agencies, but that on the more accurate measure, only the NSW agencies had, on average, lower inaction rates, with the other three jurisdictions remarkably similar.

These similarities suggest that major differences in the reporting climate are not arising at the jurisdictional level, notwithstanding the substantial differences in the legislative regimes governing whistleblowing between the various sectors. The significance of this will be further analysed in Chapter 10. For the present purposes, what is clear is that the major differences are to be found at the agency level. Figure 2.4 sets out the reporting and inaction rates for the case study agencies shown in Figure 2.3. From left to right, the results shown are in order from the agency with the most positive result (the lowest inaction rate of 7.4 per cent) to the most negative (the highest inaction rate of 43.8 per cent).

**Figure 2.4 Select case study agency 'reporting' and 'inaction' rates (per cent)[a]**

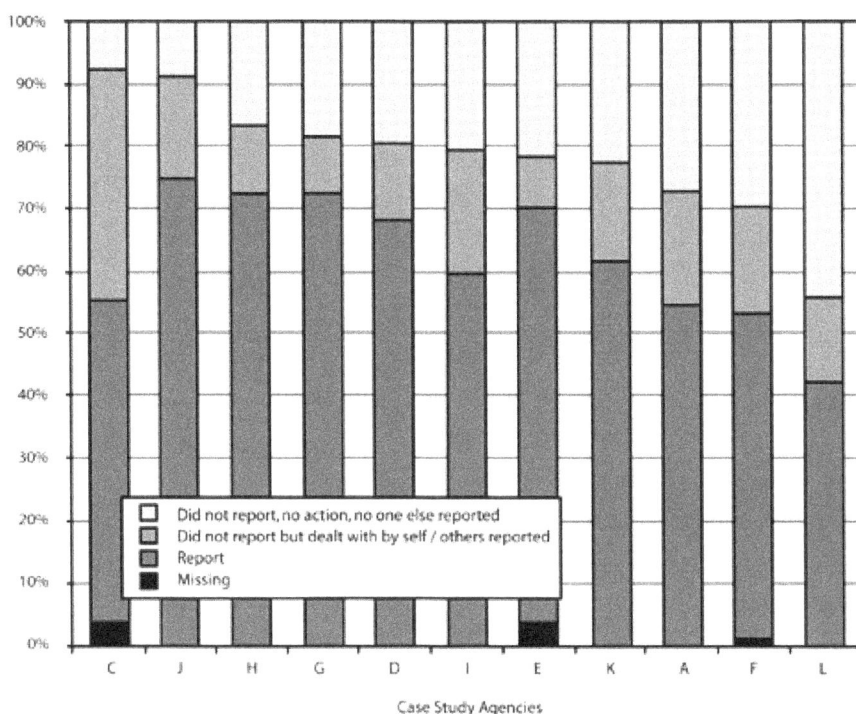

[a] Results provided for only 11 of the 12 agencies shown in Figure 2.3, because less than 10 employee survey respondents in agency B identified observed wrongdoing as 'very' or 'extremely' serious.
**Source:** Employee survey: Q20, Q22, Q26, Q35.

Interestingly, by comparing Figures 2.3 and 2.4, it is also possible to see which agencies' case-handlers and managers held, on average, the most accurate opinions about their agency's reporting climate. The respondents from agency L held the most accurate opinion, having the lowest opinion of their own reporting climate.

The variation in reporting climates was, however, even greater across the wider group of agencies that participated in the employee survey. Figure 2.5 shows the number of agencies whose inaction rates—the key measure—fall into each percentile band, again from low (positive) on the left to high (negative) on the right. Results are shown only for the 87 agencies in which at least 10 employee survey respondents identified observed wrongdoing as very or extremely serious. The range is considerably wider than that of the 11 case study agencies in the previous figure. While NSW government agencies have the lowest average inaction rate overall, they also have the widest range, including the agency with the highest inaction rate. All jurisdictions have at least one agency in which the inaction rate exceeds 55 per cent.

**Figure 2.5 Range of inaction rates by jurisdiction (national)**

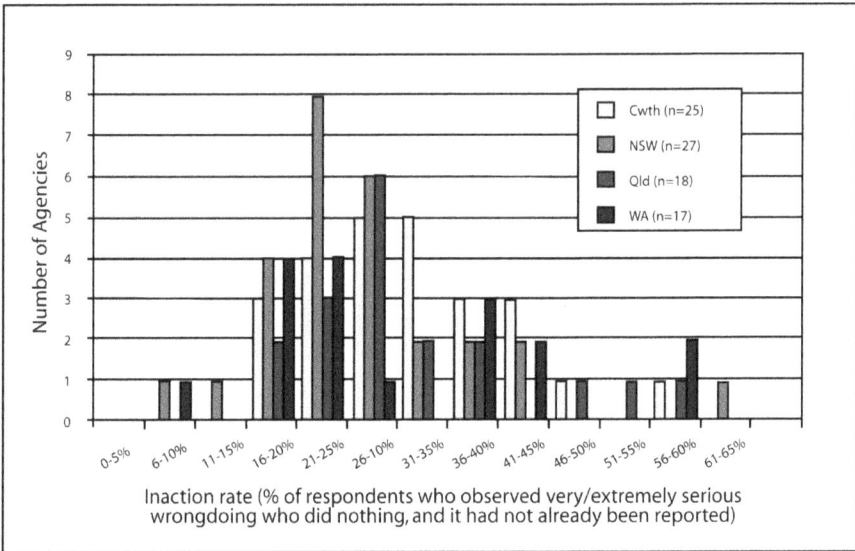

Source: Employee survey: Q20, Q22, Q26, Q35.

The reasons for this degree of variation in the reporting climate, and for such high inaction rates in some agencies irrespective of jurisdictions, will be explored in later chapters. Chapter 10 will examine the degree of correlation between these results and other key outcomes including employee trust in management, staff awareness of legislation, staff awareness of agency procedures and the real quality of these procedures. As will be seen, higher levels of reporting can and do appear to flow logically from a greater willingness by employees to speak up, based on a more positive culture in the organisation, encouraged by direct awareness raising. The reverse, however, also appears true: specific factors can be identified that correlate with reduced reporting rates and higher inaction rates. The identification of these begins in the next chapter.

It should be noted that the analyses in this section are not restricted to public interest whistleblowing, but include all categories of wrongdoing, including personnel and workplace grievances. Given the low number of cases of observed 'serious' wrongdoing in many agencies, these categories were retained so that the largest possible number of agencies could be compared. Since the reporting rates for personnel and workplace grievances appear to be generally lower than for public interest categories of wrongdoing,[1] and these grievances constitute a substantial amount of the wrongdoing in this analysis, an analysis restricted to public interest categories of wrongdoing would give a higher range of reporting rates and a lower range of inaction rates. For the purposes of this section, however, the inclusion of all wrongdoing types is considered to provide a no less—and possibly more—accurate view of variations in the overall reporting climate between agencies.

## Discussion and conclusions

This chapter has reviewed the basic incidence of whistleblowing in Australian public sector agencies revealed by the research, as well as new evidence about the recognised importance of whistleblowing. The results show a more positive picture than previously believed of a higher than expected level of employee reporting of wrongdoing in public sector agencies, with the value of whistleblowing widely recognised in agencies, notwithstanding its complexities.

The fact that a considerable amount of whistleblowing occurs and is organisationally recognised does not, however, necessarily mean that it is easy to manage, that associated intra-organisational conflicts and reprisals do not occur or that many of those who blow the whistle do not suffer as a result of the experience. Nor does it mean that whistleblowing in respect of different matters always carries the same level of risk, particularly when some types of perceived wrongdoing can by definition be easier to identify and remedy, while others can be more subjective or 'political' in nature. In short, the fact that whistleblowing is relied on heavily in Australian public sector integrity systems does not necessarily mean that it is being effectively encouraged and maximised as a process, or that all public sector agencies are fulfilling their responsibility to properly manage and protect the individuals involved. These are all important questions for later chapters.

Of most immediate concern is the fact that, while the overall incidence and recognition of whistleblowing might be higher than expected, there are clearly many individual public sector agencies in which a much lower proportion of serious wrongdoing observed by employees is reported, or otherwise acted on, than in others. Arriving at a better explanation of these differing reporting climates remains a major object of further study. Chapter 3 proceeds with a more complete analysis of why individual public officials do and don't report wrongdoing. Later chapters then analyse how officials report, the outcomes of reporting (including the experiences of reporters) and the nature of agencies' internal systems and procedures for managing those involved. All these issues have a bearing on the fundamental question of how reporting rates might be continually improved, and inaction rates reduced, whenever officials in public sector organisations perceive serious wrongdoing.

# ENDNOTES

[1] A paired-samples *t*-test showed that agency reporting and inaction rates differed significantly depending on whether the most serious wrongdoing observed was a 'personnel or workplace grievance' or a 'public interest' matter. In particular, reporting and action rates within agencies are lower for personnel and workplace grievances compared with public interest wrongdoing, while the inaction rates are higher:

| Outcome measure | Type of wrongdoing | Mean | Standard deviation | t value | Degrees of freedom |
|---|---|---|---|---|---|
| Reporting rate* | Public interest | 55.5 | 11.9 | | |
| | Personnel or workplace grievance | 49.0 | 10.9 | 2.79 | 43 |
| Action rate** | Public interest | 77.0 | 10.1 | | |
| | Personnel or workplace grievance | 64.6 | 12.2 | 5.61 | 43 |
| Inaction rate** | Public interest | 23.0 | 10.1 | | |
| | Personnel or workplace grievance | 35.4 | 12.2 | −5.61 | 43 |

* significant at p < 0.01
** significant at p < 0.0005

# 3. Who blows the whistle, who doesn't and why?

## Richard Wortley, Peter Cassematis and Marika Donkin

## Introduction

In the previous chapter, it was demonstrated that whistleblowing was more prevalent than was generally believed. Large numbers of employees, however, clearly observed wrongdoing within their organisation but neither spoke up nor took any other action in response. It was also shown that there were significant differences in reporting and inaction rates across organisations—that is, in the proportion of employees who, having perceived wrongdoing, spoke up about it, or, alternatively, who appeared to take no action. What explains these significant differences?

Later chapters will examine the relationship between different reporting and inaction rates in organisations and their approaches to whistleblowing, including the quality of their whistleblowing procedures. In this chapter, we drill further into the data from the employee survey to see what might explain differences in reporting rates at the level of the individual employee. Clearly, understanding the drivers of and impediments to reporting wrongdoing is crucial for the development of practices and programs to encourage those with evidence of wrongdoing to come forward—for example, by informing the development of new procedures or the content of workplace educational initiatives. This is especially so when organisational practices and the nature of the wrongdoing itself could be the primary determinants of whether or not an observer of wrongdoing will decide to report it.

There are two common explanations for why some individual employees choose to report wrongdoing they perceive, but others do not. The first is that some individuals are predisposed to blow the whistle, and hence any differences between reporters and non-reporters can be attributed to, and even predicted by, the personal characteristics of the individual observing the wrongdoing. According to some stereotypes, a reporter might be more likely to be diligent in their job or they might be predisposed to conflict. Such explanations might be attractive to some managers in organisations, for different reasons. If these characteristics could be identified, a manager seeking to encourage reporting might be able to staff the organisation only with those types of individuals. Conversely, a manager trying to pre-empt or manage some of the conflict that can be provoked by reporting could use such characteristics to try to anticipate in advance which staff members are more likely than others to report.

In fact, existing international research provides very limited support for this explanation. The first part of this chapter examines whether this is also true in the Australian public sector agencies in this study. Employee survey respondents who observed wrongdoing are divided into three groups (non-reporters, role reporters and non-role reporters) and are compared in terms of their individual characteristics, involving socio-demographic and attitudinal scales. The results confirm the international evidence that only very weak bases exist for trying to predict who is likely to blow the whistle using personal characteristics. It is more likely that, depending on the circumstances, almost any employee who perceives wrongdoing can be either induced or provoked to report it.

The second part of this chapter pursues this second explanation: that the individual human element is a less important influence on reporting behaviour than situational factors surrounding the perceived wrongdoing. It compares the same groups, focusing on characteristics of the wrongdoing they say they observed, including its perceived frequency, seriousness and the position in the organisation occupied by the perceived wrongdoers. The results show much more distinct trends in the circumstances in which the whistle is likely to be blown. They suggest that employees are more likely to report wrongdoing when it either threatens the core business of the organisation or when it is directed at them personally (or both), and when they perceive it to be serious and frequent. On the other hand, employees were less likely to report when more than one perceived wrongdoer was involved and when the wrongdoer(s) included people more senior than them in the organisation. These results suggest not only that the likelihood of reporting depends on the situation, but that the decision about whether or not to report is most often a rational act, reflecting normal assessments of risk in the context of the individual's organisational relationships.

Given the evidence in support of this second explanation, the reasons given by employees for reporting or not reporting become crucial; the third part of the chapter examines these. The reasons given for reporting confirm the earlier findings and also indicate that many employees will proceed to report wrongdoing if they believe the problem will be corrected, even if they have relatively low knowledge of or confidence in whether they will be supported and protected. The reasons for not reporting mirror this picture. Putting aside those who did not report because others already had, or because they took other action, the overwhelming reason given for not reporting was the belief that no action would follow. A lesser, but still very important reason for not reporting was the fear of reprisal—particularly of reprisal from the perceived wrongdoer, especially when the wrongdoer was more senior in the organisation than the employee concerned.

These results confirm the soundness of the basic objectives of whistleblowing legislation and procedures discussed in Chapter 1. The encouragement of the reporting appears to turn directly on employee confidence that the organisation will take effective action to stop or remedy the perceived wrongdoing. In many cases, the decision to report will also hinge on an employee's assessment of the associated risk, especially whether the organisation is capable of protecting them from adverse outcomes when more senior employees or management are involved. The same results show, however, that in many instances, current whistleblowing policies are struggling to deliver the levels of employee confidence necessary to satisfy these primary preconditions of reporting. Many of the solutions lie in the types of procedural and legislative reform discussed in later chapters.

In conclusion, this chapter also discusses the need for managers to abandon some of the stereotypical views of whistleblowers that receive little support from this analysis and focus on the encouragement and better management of reporting. The evidence suggests this might usefully be pursued by ensuring that management responses to whistleblowing reflect and embed a larger commitment to organisational justice. This concept recognises that the decision to report or not report is based most often on differing rational assessments about the outcome, considered in an organisational context (Colquitt et al. 2005). While the application of organisational justice to whistleblowing events and research has been suggested elsewhere (Trevino et al. 2006), it becomes clear from the present study that this concept can do much to inform better management responses to whistleblowing.

## Notes on the analyses

The results in this chapter are based primarily on the employee survey. As outlined in Chapters 1 and 2, respondents were asked to nominate the most serious type of wrongdoing for which they had direct evidence, with direct evidence defined as 'something that you personally observed, experienced or was formally reported to you'. Participants were then asked a number of questions about that wrongdoing and whether they reported it. The employee survey also contained questions about the employee's organisational experiences and perceptions.

In the previous chapter, and in later chapters, many of the analyses focus on public interest whistleblowing by excluding those respondents for whom the most serious type of wrongdoing falls into the category of 'personnel and workplace grievances'. In this chapter, however, it is useful to include all the wrongdoing types offered by the employee survey—for comparison and because of the conclusions this ultimately supports about the need for whistleblowing procedures to reflect a broader commitment to organisational justice. Key differences between the major wrongdoing categories are nevertheless shown for particular results.

For the current analyses, participants were divided into three main groups of employees who observed wrongdoing and: 1) did not report it (non-reporters: n = 3125); 2) reported it as part of their role as defined in Chapter 2 (role reporters: n = 619); and 3) reported it outside their role (non-role reporters: n = 1497). This group of non-role reporters corresponds most closely with the whistleblowing definition used elsewhere in this book, although for the reasons just given, in this chapter, it also includes employees who reported 'personnel and workplace grievances'.

The three groups were compared on a range of personal and situational variables, using MANOVA and Chi-square statistical procedures as appropriate. To facilitate readability, statistical results are not reported in detail and only findings for which there is a statistically significant difference ($p < 0.01$) are shown (indicated in tables with a tick: ✓).

## Employee characteristics

There are several reasons why an effort is often made to try to identify, or predict, whether particular types of employees are more likely than others to report wrongdoing. International research suggests, however, that demographic, personality and attitudinal variables are unreliable identifiers of prospective whistleblowers. For example, a literature review by Near and Miceli (1996) identified males as more likely to blow the whistle, but a recent meta-analysis found females were more likely to be whistleblowers (Mesmer-Magnus and Viswesvaran 2005). To present an attitudinal example, Near and Miceli (1996) reported that job satisfaction was unrelated to whistleblowing, but this finding was contradicted by Mesmer-Magnus and Viswesvaran (2005). Similarly, Brewer and Selden (1998) contradict Near and Miceli (1996) and Mesmer-Magnus and Viswesvaran (2005) in reporting that 'commitment' positively predicts whistleblowing.

The inconsistent results across different studies already constrain the validity of demographic and attitudinal variables as identifiers of whistleblowers. The present study also sought to establish whether this was the case in an Australian public sector context and, by so doing, to determine more clearly whether there was any value in any particular stereotypes of a whistleblower or, alternatively, whether other frames of reference were needed to explain when wrongdoing was or was not reported.

Data were collected on socio-demographic characteristics of employees and their responses on a number of scales and other survey items. Results for these data are presented separately.

## Socio-demographic variables

Results for demographic data are summarised in Tables 3.1 and 3.2. As shown in Table 3.1, age, tenure in the public sector and tenure in the current organisation significantly discriminated among the three groups. In discussing these and subsequent results, most attention is given to the comparison between non-role reporters and the other two groups, since non-role reporters are closest to the traditional notion of 'whistleblowers'. Accordingly, on average, those who reported outside their role:

- were older than non-reporters but younger than role reporters
- had longer tenure in the public sector than non-reporters but not as long as role reporters
- had shorter tenure in their current organisation than role reporters but did not significantly differ from non-reporters.

**Table 3.1 Reporting behaviour by characteristics of the employee (mean)**

| | Mean | | | Significance | | |
|---|---|---|---|---|---|---|
| | 1 | 2 | 3 | 1 v. 2 | 1 v. 3 | 2 v. 3 |
| Variable (years) | Non-reporter | Role reporter | Non-role reporter | | | |
| Age | 42.3 | 46 | 43.1 | ✓ | ✓ | ✓ |
| Tenure in public sector | 14.7 | 20.2 | 15.4 | ✓ | ✓ | ✓ |
| Tenure in organisation | 10.0 | 13.8 | 10.6 | ✓ | | ✓ |

Other demographic variables are shown in Table 3.2. Note that because of the nature of these data (categorical rather than continuous), it is not possible to conduct direct comparisons between each group, as was done for Table 3.1. The statistical analysis examines the overall significant difference in the variables shown, although, exercising caution, it is possible to make some inferences about where the difference lies among the various groups. For ease of interpretation, variables for which there were more than two categories (for example, level of education) were collapsed into two categories. There were overall significant differences for gender, role in the organisation, employment status, language and work-unit size. Employees who reported outside their role:

- were more likely than the other two groups to be female
- were markedly less likely than role reporters to be managers, but only slightly less likely to be managers than non-reporters
- were less likely than role reporters to have an audit role (or similar), but somewhat more likely to have an audit role than non-reporters
- earned less than role reporters, but did not differ from non-reporters
- were somewhat less likely to be permanent than role reporters but slightly more likely to be so than non-reporters
- were somewhat more likely than role reporters to speak a language other than English at home, but somewhat less likely than non-reporters to do so

- were more likely to be in smaller work units than role reporters, but were somewhat less likely to be in smaller units than non-reporters.

**Table 3.2 Reporting behaviour by characteristics of the employee (per cent)**

| Variable | Percentage | | |
|---|---|---|---|
| | Non- reporter | Role reporter | Non-role reporter |
| Gender: | | | |
| Male | 49.3 | 56.5 | 43.2 |
| Female | 50.7 | 43.5 | 56.8 |
| Role—management: | | | |
| Yes | 17.6 | 71.3 | 14.0 |
| No | 82.4 | 28.7 | 86.0 |
| Role—audit, etc.: | | | |
| Yes | 20.8 | 46.7 | 25.5 |
| No | 79.2 | 53.3 | 74.5 |
| Salary range: | | | |
| < $59 000 | 54.7 | 18.0 | 54.1 |
| ≥ $60 000 | 45.3 | 82.0 | 45.9 |
| Employment status: | | | |
| Non-permanent | 9.2 | 3.4 | 6.6 |
| Permanent | 90.8 | 96.6 | 93.4 |
| Language other than English spoken at home: | | | |
| Yes | 10.8 | 6.3 | 9.2 |
| No | 89.2 | 93.7 | 90.8 |
| Size of immediate work unit: | | | |
| < 20 | 66.0 | 51.5 | 62.8 |
| ≥ 20 | 34.0 | 48.5 | 37.2 |

It should be noted that a number of these variables are likely to be interrelated. Age, tenure in the public sector, tenure in the current organisation, role in the organisation, employment status and salary are all potentially related in varying degrees to respondents' seniority in the organisation. For example, managers are likely to be permanent employees, be older and earn more than others.

Our main interest is in identifying how employees who reported outside their role differed from the other two groups. There are major differences between non-role reporters and role reporters. In general, role reporters are more likely to have the cluster of characteristics associated with seniority. This is hardly surprising given that, by definition, many role reporters are in supervisory positions over other staff. Role reporters are also less likely to be female, which again probably reflects the lack of women in supervisory roles.

Of more interest is the comparison between non-role reporters and non-reporters; here, the differences are less extreme. In general, there is a tendency for non-role reporters to possess more seniority characteristics than non-reporters. Even though this seniority was not directly related to their reporting behaviour (inasmuch as it was not clear that they reported because of their role), it could be that seniority gave them greater confidence to report or more extensive knowledge of reporting procedures. The finding for gender is more interesting.

Women, if they have direct evidence of wrongdoing, are proportionately more likely to report outside their role than are men. At this stage, we can only speculate on the reasons. Perhaps women have a greater sense of duty or they could have higher reporting rates because they are less inclined to deal with the matter themselves.

Finally, it is worth noting variables for which there are no significant differences among groups. We found no evidence that reporting behaviour varied for Indigenous cultural background, union membership, level of education or work location (urban/rural).

## Attitude scales

The employee survey contained a number of standardised scales, as well as items written for this study. Scales are described in Table 3.3, beginning with measures of organisational citizenship behaviour (OCB) introduced in Chapter 1. All items in each scale run from '1 = strongly disagree' to '5 = strongly agree'. Alpha (α) levels describe the degree of internal consistency of each scale—that is, the extent to which each item in the scale contributes to the overall construct (they all measure the same thing). Possible values run from 0 to 1 and any score above 0.7 is considered satisfactory. On this basis, all scales with the exception of the 'personal industry' subscale can be considered to have good internal consistency, and 'personal industry' is sufficiently close to the criterion to proceed with its use in a research context.

**Table 3.3 Summary of measures used in the study**

| Measure | Description | Items | α |
|---|---|---|---|
| Organisational citizenship behaviour (Moorman and Blakely 1995) | | | |
| *Interpersonal helping* | Assisting others with work-related problems | 5 | 0.74 |
| *Individual initiative* | Being communicative and attempting to influence others in the workplace, and behaviour that could be seen as rocking the boat | 5 | 0.80 |
| *Personal industry* | Task-related behaviours that go beyond the standard required in terms of innovation, persistence, responsibility and being a good example to others | 4 | 0.67 |
| *Loyal boosterism* | Promoting, protecting and defending the organisation and remaining committed under adverse conditions | 5 | 0.83 |
| Whistleblowing propensity (Keenan 2000, 2002; Tavakoli et al. 2003) | | | |
| *Individual propensity to whistleblow* | Having favourable personal opinions towards whistleblowing | 5 | 0.83 |
| *Organisational propensity to whistleblow* | Possessing information on how to report whistleblowing | 5 | 0.84 |
| Trust in management (Robinson and Rousseau 1994) | Belief that management will treat employees fairly | 7 | 0.90 |
| Job satisfaction (Agho et al. 1992) | Enjoyment of role and working conditions | 6 | 0.86 |
| Opinion of legislation (new) | Belief in the effectiveness of existing whistleblower legislation | 6 | 0.76 |
| Management response (new) | Perceived level of openness to employee reports on the part of management | 13 | 0.94 |

Results of the analyses comparing the three employee groups with respect to these scales are shown in Table 3.4. There were significant differences on most scales (with the exception of 'personal industry'), although the pattern of significance between particular groups varied. It was found that, on average, employees who reported outside their role:

- had less trust in management than role reporters and non-reporters
- had less job satisfaction than role reporters and non-reporters
- had higher levels of 'interpersonal helping' than non-reporters but did not differ from role reporters
- had higher levels of 'individual initiative' than non-reporters but less than role reporters
- had lower levels of 'loyal boosterism' than role reporters but did not differ from non-reporters
- had higher 'individual propensity to whistleblow' than non-reporters but less than role reporters
- had lower 'organisational propensity to whistleblow' than role reporters, but the same as non-reporters
- had less favourable opinions of the legislation than role reporters and non-reporters
- had less favourable opinions of management response to whistleblowing than role reporters and non-reporters.

## Table 3.4 Reporting behaviour by attitudes of the employee (mean)

| | Mean | | | Significance | | |
|---|---|---|---|---|---|---|
| | 1 | 2 | 3 | 1 v. 2 | 1 v. 3 | 2 v. 3 |
| Variable | Non-reporter | Role reporter | Non-role reporter | | | |
| Trust in management team | 3.4 | 3.7 | 3.1 | ✓ | ✓ | ✓ |
| Job satisfaction | 3.5 | 3.7 | 3.3 | ✓ | ✓ | ✓ |
| Organisational citizenship behaviour | | | | | | |
| *Interpersonal helping* | 3.9 | 4.0 | 4.0 | ✓ | ✓ | |
| *Individual initiative* | 3.7 | 4.0 | 3.8 | ✓ | ✓ | ✓ |
| *Personal industry* | 3.8 | 3.9 | 3.9 | ✓ | | |
| *Loyal boosterism* | 3.5 | 3.8 | 3.5 | ✓ | | ✓ |
| Whistleblowing propensity | | | | | | |
| *Individual propensity to whistleblow* | 4.1 | 4.3 | 4.2 | ✓ | ✓ | ✓ |
| *Organisational propensity to whistleblow* | 3.4 | 3.9 | 3.4 | ✓ | | ✓ |
| Opinion of legislation | 3.2 | 3.4 | 3.1 | ✓ | ✓ | ✓ |
| Management response | 3.3 | 3.6 | 3.1 | ✓ | ✓ | ✓ |

Overall, the differences between non-role reporters and role reporters were greater than between non-role reporters and non-reporters. In either case, however, the differences between the groups were small. When sample sizes are large, such as in the present study, relatively minor differences can show up as being statistically significant. Caution needs to be exercised, therefore, when interpreting the results. For example, while non-role reporters were found to have significantly higher levels of 'interpersonal helping' than non-reporters, the difference was just 0.1 on a five-point scale (a 2 per cent variation). While there is therefore a statistical difference, from a practical point of view, not too much should be read into the finding.

With this caveat in mind, some tentative conclusions can be drawn. Looking first at the comparison between non-role reporters and role reporters, role reporters were more positive in their attitudes than non-role reporters on eight of the 10 scales (the exceptions being 'personal industry' and 'interpersonal helping'). As with the demographic data, these findings might be expected given the more senior position that role reporters typically hold.

For the non-role reporters versus non-reporters comparison, there are differences on seven scales (not 'personal industry', 'loyal boosterism' and 'organisational propensity to whistleblow') and, as noted, these differences are small. On the whole, employees who report outside their role see themselves as more dedicated corporate citizens than employees who do not report. This suggests that at least some of the motivation to report wrongdoing comes from a greater commitment to pro-social organisational behaviour and a belief that reporting is for the good of the organisation. As one might expect, these employees are also more positive towards whistleblowing. They are, however, slightly less positive towards their job, the whistleblowing legislation and the likely management response to whistleblowing and they are marginally less trusting in the management team than are non-reporters.

One problem with interpreting these results is that the directions of these effects are a matter of speculation. For example, it is not clear whether less trust in the management team encourages employees to report wrongdoing or whether the experience of reporting wrongdoing makes employees less trusting of the management team. The second of these possibilities seems the most likely, as further discussed in Chapters 4 and 5.

In addition, when interpreting the results, it needs to be borne in mind that, in absolute terms, none of the groups responded negatively on any scale. The lowest mean score was 3.1, which was just on the positive side of the scale midpoint ('neither agree nor disagree'). All other scores were positive. For example, therefore, when it was reported that non-role reporters had lower 'trust in management', this must be interpreted in relative terms.

## Summary

Leaving aside employees whose role includes reporting the wrongdoing, these findings indicate a number of personal differences between employees who have direct evidence of wrongdoing and who do not report it and those with direct evidence who do report. Non-role reporters are less senior and more likely to be female than non-reporters. They are also more likely to have somewhat more positive views with regard to their level of organisational citizenship and whistleblowing generally, but somewhat more negative views of management and the whistleblowing legislation. Together, these results give a picture of whistleblowers as possessing stronger personal motivations to report wrongdoing, but also as being more cynical about the process of reporting. Still, these differences are small and absolute scores are mostly positive.

There is little in the findings to support either of the main stereotypes that might justify attempts to develop a predictive model of whistleblowing, based on personal characteristics. While there is some evidence that reporters either begin or end the process with views consistent with higher organisational citizenship, overall there is little to differentiate them from the larger number of employees who elect not to report. For example, there was no significant difference between the reporters and non-reporters on the 'personal industry' scale—the main measure of perceived diligence. There is even less evidence to support a view of whistleblowers as predisposed to conflict—for example, because they are disgruntled and embittered employees, driven to report by perverse personal characteristics. This being the case, there are good reasons to believe that explanations for variations in reporting behaviour are more likely to lie outside the individual in other circumstances, such as the characteristics of the wrongdoing itself.

## Characteristics of the wrongdoing

This section examines variations in reporting behaviour as a function of the nature of the wrongdoing observed. As discussed at the outset, if the individual characteristics of reporters shed only limited light on who appears likely to report, other explanations are also needed. Internationally, characteristics of the wrongdoing and contextual variables have been shown to have a more consistent relationship with the decision to report wrongdoing. For example, Near et al. (2004) found that reporting rates differed by type of wrongdoing, with non-reporting most likely when employees believed nothing would be done to rectify the situation. Scenario-based research by Brennan and Kelly (2007) found that 96 per cent of participants would report the wrongdoing contained in a scenario rated as very serious, while only 70 per cent would report in a scenario rated as trivial. Similarly, Masser and Brown (1996) reported that whistleblowing was more likely to occur when the wrongdoing was seen to be serious, when there was a belief that there would be an improvement after the report and when the threat of retaliation was low. Brewer and Selden (1998) found that reports were made by employees who believed the wrongdoing constituted a threat to the public interest that they (as public servants) were supposed to protect.

Mesmer-Magnus and Viswesvaran (2005) reported that the seriousness of the offence positively predicted whistleblowing, but this accounted for only 3 per cent of the final decision. These researchers suggested that a number of contextual variables—including fear of reprisals, organisational climate and supervisor support—were incorporated into the decision to report or not. Further, they drew a distinction between those who stated an intention to make a report and those who really did report. For example, fear of reprisals was negatively correlated with the intention to make a report, but did not necessarily stop those who saw no other option than to make a report.

## Wrongdoing type

Table 3.5 shows the most serious type of wrongdoing nominated by respondents from the present study, categorised in terms of the same three groups used above: non-reporters, role reporters and non-role reporters. Results are shown in bold for each of the major categories of wrongdoing into which the survey responses are grouped for analytical purposes (see Chapter 2 and Appendix 1) and in italics for each of the individual wrongdoing types making up these categories. Because of the large number of wrongdoing categories, statistical analysis was not conducted on these data.

As can be seen, this comparison includes 'personnel and workplace grievances' in addition to public interest matters. For all three groups, the most common wrongdoing nominated was bullying of staff, particularly by non-role reporters, for whom this behaviour accounted for one in four of all responses. This suggests that when bullying is the most serious wrongdoing observed (or experienced) by employees, they are relatively likely to report it, compared with other forms of grievance such as favouritism in promotion. Across the whole category, however, there was little overall difference between non-reporters and non-role reporters as to the frequency of the relevant wrongdoing being a personnel or workplace grievance. Role reporters were somewhat less likely than the other groups to nominate personnel or workplace grievances, consistent with the fact these often have processes designed to be triggered by the aggrieved employee themselves. Consistent with their roles, role reporters were more likely than others to nominate the various recognised forms of employee misconduct (theft, sexual harassment, downloading pornography).

## Table 3.5 Most serious type of observed wrongdoing, by reporting behaviour

| Wrongdoing | Percentage | | |
|---|---|---|---|
| | Non-reporter | Role reporter | Non-role reporter |
| **Misconduct for material gain** | **24.3** | **32.3** | **17.1** |
| *Theft of money* | 2.6 | 7.6 | 2.7 |
| *Theft of property* | 3.2 | 8.1 | 2.8 |
| *Bribes* | 0.7 | 1.0 | 0.5 |
| *Using official position for services/favours* | 2.2 | 1.2 | 1.0 |
| *Giving unfair advantage to contractor, etc.* | 1.9 | 1.5 | 1.2 |
| *Improper use of facilities for private purposes* | 7.2 | 5.8 | 3.6 |
| *Rorting overtime/leave* | 5.6 | 5.6 | 4.5 |
| *Making false/inflated claims for reimbursement* | 1.0 | 1.7 | 0.8 |
| **Conflict of interest** | **1.3** | **1.9** | **1.4** |
| *Failing to declare financial interest* | 0.1 | 0.2 | 0.3 |
| *Intervening in a decision on behalf of a friend or relative* | 0.9 | 0.5 | 0.7 |
| *Improper involvement of a family business* | 0.3 | 1.2 | 0.4 |
| **Improper or unprofessional behaviour** | **12.3** | **25.6** | **11.6** |
| *Downloading pornography on a work computer* | 1.6 | 3.6 | 1.1 |
| *Being drunk/under the influence of illegal drugs at work* | 4.7 | 5.3 | 3.6 |
| *Sexual assault* | 0.2 | 1.7 | 0.4 |
| *Stalking (unwanted intrusion into personal life)* | 0.6 | 2.6 | 1.2 |
| *Sexual harassment* | 2.3 | 6.4 | 2.9 |
| *Racial discrimination against a member of the public* | 0.9 | 0.2 | 0.8 |
| *Misuse of confidential information* | 2.0 | 5.8 | 1.6 |
| **Defective administration** | **9.4** | **6.5** | **13.3** |
| *Incompetent or negligent decision making* | 6.9 | 2.6 | 8.1 |
| *Failure to correct serious mistakes* | 0.5 | 0.3 | 1.0 |
| *Endangering public health or safety* | 0.8 | 1.3 | 1.8 |
| *Producing or using unsafe products* | 0.1 | - | 0.2 |
| *Acting against organisational policy, regulations or laws* | 1.1 | 2.3 | 2.2 |
| **Waste or mismanagement of resources** | **6.5** | **3.1** | **4.6** |
| *Waste of work funds* | 3.4 | 0.5 | 1.0 |
| *Inadequate record keeping* | 2.6 | 2.1 | 3.3 |
| *Negligent purchases or leases* | 0.5 | 0.5 | 0.3 |
| **Perverting justice or accountability** | **7.3** | **6.4** | **9.1** |
| *Covering-up poor performance* | 6.5 | 4.5 | 7.4 |
| *Misleading or false reporting of agency activity* | 0.4 | 0.3 | 0.2 |
| *Covering-up corruption* | - | 0.2 | 0.5 |
| *Hindering an official investigation* | 0.1 | 0.3 | 0.2 |
| *Unlawfully altering or destroying official records* | 0.3 | 1.2 | 0.8 |
| **Personnel and workplace grievances** | **36.5** | **19.2** | **37.6** |
| *Racial discrimination against a staff member* | 1.8 | 1.3 | 1.6 |
| *Allowing dangerous or harmful working conditions* | 2.0 | 1.3 | 3.4 |
| *Unfair dismissal* | 1.5 | 0.5 | 0.5 |
| *Failure to follow correct staff-selection procedures* | 4.2 | 1.3 | 2.5 |
| *Favouritism in selection or promotion* | 11.6 | 0.3 | 5.6 |
| *Bullying of staff* | 15.4 | 14.5 | 24.0 |
| **Reprisals against whistleblowers** | **0.4** | **0.5** | **1.4** |
| Other | 1.9 | 4.3 | 4.0 |
| **Total (rounded)** | **100** | **100** | **100** |

In the 'public interest' categories, non-reporters and non-role reporters were somewhat more likely than role reporters to nominate wrongdoing affecting the business of the organisation or associated with the behaviour of management or failures of the organisation as a whole (such as incompetent decision making and covering-up poor performance). Non-role reporters were also somewhat more likely to nominate these types of wrongdoing—that is, to have blown the whistle on them—than the non-reporters, who were somewhat more likely to have observed, but not reported, various types of misconduct involving material gain.

## Seriousness, frequency and organisational context

Differences in reporting behaviour as a function of further characteristics of the nominated wrongdoing are summarised in Tables 3.6 and 3.7. Here, the differences become even more pronounced. The wrongdoing nominated by non-role reporters:

- was judged by them to be more serious than the wrongdoing nominated by non-reporters, but not as serious as that nominated by role reporters
- was judged to be more frequent than the wrongdoing nominated by both other groups
- was more likely to involve wrongdoing involving only one person than for non-reporters, but less likely than for role reporters
- was more likely to involve wrongdoing involving people below or at the respondent's position than for non-reporters, but less likely than for role reporters.

The wrongdoing nominated by non-role reporters was also more likely to involve wrongdoing that was directed at them, or for which they had direct evidence, than for non-reporters (role reporters by definition in most cases had the incident reported to them in their official capacity). As will be discussed below, however, much of this result relates to the retention of personnel and workplace grievances in this analysis.

**Table 3.6 Reporting behaviour by further characteristics of wrongdoing (mean)**

| Variable | Mean | | | Significance | | |
|---|---|---|---|---|---|---|
| | 1<br>Non-reporter | 2<br>Role reporter | 3<br>Non-role reporter | 1 v. 2 | 1 v. 3 | 2 v. 3 |
| Seriousness | 3.5 | 4.2 | 4.0 | ✓ | ✓ | ✓ |
| Frequency | 3.0 | 2.5 | 3.1 | ✓ | ✓ | ✓ |

**Table 3.7 Reporting behaviour by further characteristics of wrongdoing (per cent)**

| Variable | Percentage [a] | | |
|---|---|---|---|
| | 1 | 2 | 3 |
| | Non-reporter | Role reporter | Non-role reporter |
| How was it found out? | | | |
| *Directed at me* | 12.7 | 3.6 | 34.7 |
| *Invited to participate* | 3.0 | 0.8 | 4.9 |
| *Observed it* | 64.6 | 15.2 | 56.5 |
| *Direct evidence* | 9.6 | 10.5 | 25.5 |
| *Reported to me in my official capacity* | 8.1 | 80.5 | 10.0 |
| *Other* | 9.8 | 1.6 | 7.5 |
| How many involved? | | | |
| *Just one person* | 39.3 | 63.0 | 42.9 |
| *More than one person* | 60.7 | 37.0 | 57.1 |
| Position of wrongdoer: | | | |
| *Below/same as my level* | 40.8 | 86.1 | 44.6 |
| *Other* | 59.2 | 13.9 | 55.4 |

[a] Because multiple responses were permitted for this item, the column total exceeds 100 per cent. For this reason, statistical tests cannot be applied to this question.

In summary, wrongdoing that came to the attention of role reporters was relatively more serious, likely to have involved misconduct for material gain or improper behaviour and likely to have been carried out by one person below or at the level of the role reporter. This profile is consistent with someone in a supervisory role, who has observed or received reports from other employees about the misbehaviour of a subordinate.

Comparing the most serious wrongdoing observed by non-role reporters with that observed by non-reporters, it seems that perceived seriousness and frequency of the wrongdoing have a direct influence on the likelihood of a report being made. The likelihood of reporting also increases when an employee has direct evidence of the wrongdoing, in addition or as opposed to simply observing it. These results seem consistent with the types of wrongdoing in the non-grievance category that appear more likely to give rise to whistleblowing, tending to be either more serious by nature or more likely to directly affect organisational core business or perhaps are more clear-cut to prove. Together, these results suggest that in the majority of cases the decision to report is probably taken quite rationally.

On the other hand, when the wrongdoing involves multiple participants and participants at a higher organisational level than the observer, reporting is much less likely. This also tends to confirm the rational nature of most employees' decision about whether or not to report. In these circumstances, the wrongdoing is more likely to be systemic, to involve managers or to have been allowed to develop because of management laxity. The likelihood of anything being done is therefore also lower. Especially when superiors or managers are perceived as being directly responsible, it is reasonable to assume that reporting is also judged to be relatively risky and more likely to invite reprisal. The fact that these circumstances emerge as clear indicators of when employees are likely to report has important implications for the whistleblowing processes in place in the agencies surveyed.

## Degree of personal involvement

As noted above, in Table 3.7, it can also be seen that a major difference between non-role reporters and non-reporters is whether the wrongdoing is directed at the respondent. The likelihood of a report is also increased when the observer is the object of the wrongdoing. This is also not surprising, since the employee clearly has a greater personal stake in the issue in these circumstances.

How important is this factor, relative to others? If important, it could change the emerging picture of why and when employees are likely to report wrongdoing, because it could suggest a motive that is based on promoting one's self-interest. For example, the real determinant or 'tipping point' in the making of the report might not be the reporter's pro-social assessment of the impact of the wrongdoing on the organisation or the public, but simply the fact that they have become a direct victim of it. This could support a stereotype that irrespective of what public interest is 'objectively' involved, reporting is still likely only when an employee becomes disgruntled or personally aggrieved by conditions within the organisation.

To test this, comparisons were made to identify any systematic differences between the two groups of non-role reporters—those who indicated they learned of the wrongdoing because it was 'directed at me' (n = 526) and those who simply observed it or became aware of it in another way ('not directed at me', n = 1171).

Table 3.8 shows the primary explanation for the relative prevalence of 'directed at me' observers among the non-role reporting group. In more than 60 per cent of instances, the type of wrongdoing reported was a direct personnel or workplace grievance (mostly bullying). When the wrongdoing involved a range of other improper behaviour, such as sexual harassment or stalking, the fact that it was directed at the reporter was also understandably important. In no other category, however, did the fact that the wrongdoing was directed at the respondent take on any such importance; and, in most clear 'public interest' categories, such as misconduct for material gain and defective administration, it became relatively unimportant. In these categories, therefore, the earlier analysis stands.

**Table 3.8 Degree of involvement by type of most serious wrongdoing (per cent)**

| Variable | Percentage | | |
|---|---|---|---|
| | 1 Non-reporter | 2 Non-role reporter—not directed at me | 3 Non-role reporter—directed at me |
| Wrongdoing category: | | | |
| Material gain | 24.3 | 23.0 | 6.8 |
| Conflict of interest | 1.3 | 1.5 | 1.2 |
| Improper behaviour | 12.3 | 11.8 | 11.3 |
| Defective administration | 9.4 | 16.6 | 6.3 |
| Waste | 6.5 | 7.0 | 0.6 |
| Perversion of justice | 7.3 | 12.7 | 2.0 |
| Personnel and other grievances | 36.5 | 24.5 | 62.3 |
| Reprisals | 0.4 | 0.1 | 3.7 |
| Other | 2.0 | 2.8 | 5.8 |
| Total (rounded) | 100 | 100 | 100 |

Notwithstanding that the bulk of reporters were complaining about a personnel or workplace grievance, those non-role reporters at whom the wrongdoing was directed provided a general reminder that where the personal involvement was higher, there remained a higher likelihood of a report. There is also likely to be a higher degree of associated conflict within the relevant parts of the organisation and, whether before the report or as a result of it, a lower degree of trust in management's ability to respond properly to the situation. These results are apparent from the scales of differences in attitude shown in Table 3.9. While some of the differences might be slight, whatever the reasons, those who reported having the wrongdoing directed at them

- had lower trust in management than both other groups
- had lower job satisfaction than both other groups
- had lower levels of 'loyal boosterism' than 'not directed at me' reporters
- had higher levels of 'individual propensity to whistleblow' than non-reporters
- had lower levels of 'organisational propensity to whistleblow' than 'not directed at me' reporters
- had a poorer opinion of the legislation than both other groups
- had less faith in the management response to reporting than both other groups.

**Table 3.9 Degree of involvement by characteristics of the employee (mean)**

| Variable | Mean | | | Significance | | |
|---|---|---|---|---|---|---|
| | 1<br>Non-reporter | 2<br>Non-role<br>reporter—not<br>directed at me | 3<br>Non-role<br>reporter—directed<br>at me | 1 v. 2 | 1 v. 3 | 2 v. 3 |
| Trust in management team | 3.2 | 3.2 | 2.8 | | ✓ | ✓ |
| Job satisfaction | 3.4 | 3.4 | 3.2 | | ✓ | ✓ |
| Organisational citizenship behaviour | | | | | | |
| *Loyal boosterism* | 3.4 | 3.5 | 3.4 | ✓ | | ✓ |
| Whistleblowing propensity | | | | | | |
| *Individual propensity to whistleblow* | 4.0 | 4.2 | 4.2 | ✓ | ✓ | |
| *Organisational propensity to whistleblow* | 3.2 | 3.5 | 3.3 | ✓ | | ✓ |
| Opinion of legislation | 3.1 | 3.2 | 2.9 | | ✓ | ✓ |
| Management response | 3.2 | 3.2 | 2.8 | | ✓ | ✓ |

Tables 3.10 and 3.11 provide a useful further contrast between these groups. In addition to heightened conflict and risks that the employee has a sourer view of the organisation, the wrongdoing observed by 'directed at me' reporters

- is rated as more serious than the wrongdoing observed by both other groups
- is rated as more frequent than the wrongdoing observed by both other groups
- is more likely to involve multiple people than the wrongdoing observed by 'not directed at me' reporters
- is more likely to involve people above their level than the wrongdoing observed by both other groups.

In other words, irrespective of the presence of personnel and workplace grievances in this analysis, the fact the employee is directly involved does appear to influence the circumstances in which he or she is prepared to report. In particular, it likely contributes to the perceived seriousness of the matter to the employee, further increasing the likelihood of a report. Direct personal involvement will also likely offset the deterrents to reporting that are found when multiple people are perceived to be responsible and when they include more senior people. Employees who feel they are on the receiving end of wrongdoing are more likely to be prepared to report it, even when they normally might not, even though the risks of conflict or reprisal will objectively also appear to be higher. These results reinforce the need for an approach to the management of whistleblowing that shows a broader commitment to organisational justice, as discussed further below.

**Table 3.10 Degree of involvement by further characteristics of most serious wrongdoing (mean)**

| Variable | Mean | | | Significance | | |
|---|---|---|---|---|---|---|
| | 1<br>Non-reporter | 2<br>Non-role reporter—not directed at me | 3<br>Non-role reporter—directed at me | 1 v. 2 | 1 v. 3 | 2 v. 3 |
| Seriousness | 3.5 | 3.9 | 4.3 | ✓ | ✓ | ✓ |
| Frequency | 3.0 | 3.0 | 3.4 | | ✓ | ✓ |

**Table 3.11 Degree of involvement by further characteristics of most serious wrongdoing (per cent)**

| Variable | Percentage | | |
|---|---|---|---|
| | 1<br>Non-reporter | 2<br>Non-role reporter—not directed at me | 3<br>Non-role reporter—directed at me |
| How many involved? | | | |
| *Just one person* | 39.3 | 44.9 | 38.2 |
| *More than one person* | 60.7 | 55.1 | 61.8 |
| Position of wrongdoer: | | | |
| *Below/same as my level* | 40.8 | 50.6 | 30.0 |
| *Other* | 59.5 | 49.4 | 70.0 |

# Reasons for reporting or not reporting wrongdoing

Some of the reasons why an employee will report or not report can be inferred from the analyses conducted so far. Respondents were, however, also asked directly the reason for their decision. The results show a consistency with the evidence that reporting decisions are typically quite rational, reflecting the employees' desire for the problem to be rectified and their desire not to suffer as a result of bringing it to notice.

## Why employees report

Table 3.12 presents the reasons for reporting given by non-role and role reporters in response to the employee survey, ranked in order of importance given by the non-role reporters. For comparison, we have also included the reasons case-handlers and managers in the smaller number of case study agencies thought were important in their perception of decisions by employees to report wrongdoing (from a matching question in the case-handler and manager surveys). In both cases, the respondents were asked to rate these items on a four-point scale (1 = 'not at all important', 2 = 'somewhat important', 3 = 'very important', 4 = 'extremely important').

**Table 3.12 Reasons for reporting by actual and perceived reasons (mean)**

| Variable | Mean | | | |
|---|---|---|---|---|
| | Non-role reporters | Role-reporters | Case-handlers (perception) | Managers (perception) |
| I saw it as my ethical responsibility | 3.2 | 3.4 | 3.0 | 3.0 |
| The wrongdoing was serious enough | 3.1 | 3.2 | 3.2 | 3.2 |
| I believed my report would correct the problem | 3.1 | 3.2 | 3.3 | 3.2 |
| I had evidence to support my report | 3.0 | 3.1 | 2.9 | 2.8 |
| I knew who to report to | 2.9 | 3.1 | 2.8 | 2.8 |
| I trusted the person I should report to | 2.9 | 3.1 | 3.4 | 3.4 |
| I thought I would be supported by management | 2.8 | 3.0 | 3.2 | 3.2 |
| I thought I would be supported by co-workers | 2.7 | 2.5 | 3.0 | 3.0 |
| I believed I was under a legal responsibility | 2.5 | 3.1 | 2.6 | 2.5 |
| I believed I would have legal protection | 2.4 | 2.4 | 3.1 | 3.1 |

**Sources:** Employee survey: Q27; case-handler and manager surveys: Q25

Looking at the absolute value of scores, all except two scores are on or above the midpoint ('I believed I would have legal protection', as rated by role reporters and non-role reporters) and most are above 3, indicating that the reasons are judged to be at least 'very important'. It can be seen that there is a close parallel in the order of importance given by role reporters and non-role reporters, although non-role reporters generally rate all the reasons as somewhat less important. The consistent result is that once motivated by seriousness to report the wrongdoing, employees indicated they did so when they had confidence that action would result and knowledge of and/or confidence in the process they were meant to follow. Confidence that they were going to be supported or protected was either less often present or less of a consideration.

There is less similarity in the relative importance of reasons given by reporters and those given by case-handlers and mangers. An ethical responsibility to report was judged to be the most important reason by both groups of reporters, while trust in the receiver of the report was thought to be the most important reason by case-handlers and managers. Similarly, reporters gave less importance to legal protection than case-handlers and managers thought they would. Generally, reporters were more likely to rate reasons associated with a sense of duty and the nature of the wrongdoing, while case-handlers and managers thought that they would be more likely to rate guarantees of protection as the most important.

This provides some mixed results for agencies' approaches to whistleblowing. Reporters, it seems, are rather more pro-socially motivated than case-handlers and managers assume them to be. Their belief that a problem is serious and can and should be fixed often appears to rank more highly than their desire for self-protection. On one hand, this tends to confirm the pro-social value of whistleblowing and further explains its prevalence, as discussed in Chapter 2. On the other hand, it underscores the responsibility of agencies to provide safe and just processes for those who blow the whistle, given that many employees apparently do so notwithstanding the logical risks of intra-organisational conflict or reprisal.

## Why employees do not report

### Table 3.13 Reasons for not reporting by role (per cent)

| Variable | Percentage [a] | | |
|---|---|---|---|
| | Non-role | Role | Total |
| **Inadequate management response:** | | | |
| I didn't think anything would be done about it | 38.1 | - | 36.4 |
| I didn't trust the person I had to report to | 15.5 | - | 14.8 |
| I didn't think the organisation would protect me | 13.6 | - | 13.0 |
| I didn't think my identity would be kept secret | 13.5 | - | 12.8 |
| **Nature of the wrongdoing:** | | | |
| I didn't have enough evidence to report it | 21.4 | 9.2 | 20.8 |
| It wasn't important enough to report | 15.2 | 5.6 | 14.8 |
| **Resolved in some other way:** | | | |
| Someone else had already reported it | 18.6 | 51.8 | 20.1 |
| I dealt with the matter myself informally | 12.9 | 14.2 | 13.0 |
| I dealt with the matter formally as part of my role | 3.5 | 27.7 | 4.6 |
| **Fear of reprisal:** | | | |
| I was afraid the wrongdoer would take action against me | 18.7 | - | 17.8 |
| I was afraid my co-workers would take action against me | 8.4 | - | 8.0 |
| I was afraid the organisation would take action against me | 9.2 | - | 8.8 |
| **Other negative consequences:** | | | |
| It would have been too stressful to report it | 15.1 | - | 14.4 |
| I didn't want to get anyone into trouble | 11.3 | 0.7 | 10.8 |
| I was aware of others' bad experiences reporting wrongdoing | 7.8 | 0.7 | 7.5 |
| I had a previous bad personal experience reporting wrongdoing | 6.6 | 0.7 | 6.3 |
| Other people advised me not to report it | 4.0 | - | 3.8 |
| I didn't want to embarrass the organisation | 2.5 | - | 2.4 |
| I would not have the support of my family | 0.2 | - | 0.2 |
| **Unsure of process:** | | | |
| I didn't think it was my responsibility to report it | 10.9 | 2.1 | 10.5 |
| I didn't know my legal protection if I reported it | 7.9 | - | 7.5 |
| I didn't know who to report it to | 7 | 0.7 | 6.7 |

[a] multiple responses permitted

Table 3.13 shows the reasons selected by employees who had direct knowledge of wrongdoing but who did not report it. Non-reporters have been divided into two groups, those who: 1) did not have an official role-reporting position in the organisation (n = 2981); and 2) did have an official role-reporting position in the organisation (n = 144). For ease of analysis, we have grouped responses in terms of more general categories.

There are easily discernible differences between the two groups. In almost all cases, the reasons given by employees in reporting roles concerned the fact that the problem was resolved in another way or a lack of either sufficient seriousness or evidence. These responses were also popular with non-role observers, but relatively less so. If we accept their judgment about the wrongdoing, in these cases, the decision not to report is justifiable, and, in the case of role observers, they are not neglecting their responsibilities.

The reasons given for not reporting by employees who did not have an official role-reporting position (non-role observers) are more varied. They tend, however, to mirror all the evidence presented so far, producing an increasingly consistent picture of the circumstances that appear to give rise to reporting behaviour. The most common reasons for not reporting were to do with expected management reaction to a report. In particular, more than one-third of respondents believed that nothing would be done if they reported the wrongdoing. The other responses concerned a lack of faith in the ability of the organisation to properly handle the whistleblowing process. The frequency with which respondents indicated that they did not report because they did not have appropriate evidence is also significant. This could simply be an exculpatory reason. At the same time, it tends to confirm that the decision about whether or not to report is a rational one, in which issues of process and risk figure prominently.

In the middle lies another large cluster of responses showing the role that fear of reprisal has in deterring reporting. While fewer than 10 per cent of the respondents said they did not report because of fear of reprisal from management or co-workers, significantly more respondents (17.8 per cent) feared action from the wrongdoer. These categories are not, however, mutually exclusive. Taken together, 24.4 per cent of non-role observers gave fear of reprisal from any source as a reason for not reporting—making this the second largest reason overall. There is also a large degree of overlap between those who said they feared reprisal and those who did not think the organisation would protect them (from just such a reprisal).

Table 3.14 also confirms that when many of these respondents said they did not report the wrongdoing for fear of reprisal from the wrongdoer(s), they were referring to wrongdoer(s) who were higher than them in the management chain. Allowing that the respondents could make multiple responses, the table shows that, of the non-reporters who indicated fear of the wrongdoer to be a factor, 82 per cent were referring to cases in which this included their supervisor and/or higher-level managers. Of the non-reporters who indicated a fear of organisational reprisal, at least 91 per cent were referring to this same type of case. These results make it clear that fear of management reprisal is a major reason for non-reporting, particularly when management is also the perpetrator of the wrongdoing. The rational nature of this fear is reinforced by evidence in Chapters 5 and 6 about the extent to which those who do blow the whistle report being mistreated by management.

Some of the least common reasons for not reporting were often still significant. These included a range of possible indirect negative consequences of reporting, from the anticipation of stress to not wanting to embarrass the organisation. It is notable that one in 10 respondents did not want the wrongdoer to get into trouble. The least significant reasons were those to do with uncertainty about the reporting process. Most respondents, for example, did not seem uncertain about to whom they needed to report wrongdoing (or, if they were, it was not seen as a reason not to report).

**Table 3.14 Source of apprehended reprisal risk among non-reporters**

| Position of wrongdoer(s) in the organisation [a] | | Reason for not reporting | | |
|---|---|---|---|---|
| | | Afraid wrongdoer would take action against me | Afraid co-workers would take action against me | Afraid organisation would take action against me |
| | | % (n = 557) | % (n = 249) | % (n = 275) |
| Employee(s) below level | Only | 2 (9) | 5 (13) | 1 (4) |
| | Along with others | 4(25) | 11 (27) | 5 (15) |
| | Subtotal | 6 (34) | 16 (40) | 6 (19) |
| Employee(s) at level | Only | 15 (81) | 28 (69) | 7 (18) |
| | Along with others | 11 (59) | 19 (48) | 9 (26) |
| | Subtotal | 26 (140) | 47 (117) | 16 (44) |
| Immediate supervisor(s) | Only | 26 (140) | 20 (51) | 18 (49) |
| | Along with others | 15 (86) | 16 (41) | 17 (48) |
| | Subtotal | 41 (226) | 36 (92) | 35 (97) |
| High-level manager(s) | Only | 37 (205) | 19 (47) | 49 (135) |
| | Along with others | 14 (76) | 11 (28) | 18 (50) |
| | Subtotal | 51 (281) | 30 (75) | 67 (185) |
| Immediate supervisor(s) and/or high-level manager(s) | | 82(456) | 60(149) | 91(250) |

[a] Subtotals add to more than 100 per cent as multiple responses were permitted. Outside contractors or vendors have been excluded from this table.
**Source:** Employee survey: Q25, Q44.

**Table 3.15 What could be done to increase the likelihood of reporting (mean)**

| Variable | Mean |
|---|---|
| Training managers how to deal with reports of wrongdoing | 2.2 |
| Knowing that I would have support from my co-workers | 2.2 |
| My organisation having clear policies on the protection of whistleblowers | 2.1 |
| Training staff how to deal with reporting wrongdoing | 2.1 |
| My organisation having an active support system for whistleblowers | 2.1 |
| Being assured that I would be supported by management if my name was disclosed | 2.0 |
| My organisation having clear policies on reporting wrongdoing | 2.0 |
| Being assured my name would be kept secret | 1.9 |
| Having the opportunity to report without giving my name | 1.9 |

Finally, non-reporters were also asked if anything could have been done to increase the likelihood that they would have reported the wrongdoing (Table 3.15). Note that these items were rated on a four-point scale (1 = 'make no difference', 2 = 'somewhat increase likelihood', 3 = 'significantly increase likelihood', 4 = 'guarantee reporting'), so the notional midpoint was 2.5 (there was no real middle value on the scale). Ratings were within a very narrow band (1.9–2.2) and towards the lower end of the scale. For example, training managers was rated the most likely strategy to increase reporting, but only marginally so compared with other strategies, and, with a rating of 2.2, it was judged to do just slightly better than 'somewhat increase likelihood' of reporting. None of the strategies was therefore endorsed with any great enthusiasm, although all were seen to have some limited value.

## Discussion and conclusions

### Predicting reporting behaviour

The analyses reported in this chapter were conducted in order to test whether whistleblowers could be distinguished from non-whistleblowers on the basis of demographic characteristics, attitudinal measures and perceived characteristics of a wrongdoing. While some significant employee characteristics were identified, the majority of demographic variables did not distinguish between reporters, non-reporters or role reporters. Differences that did occur were most commonly between role reporters and non-role reporters. The demographic variables that offer the clearest distinction between role reporters and non-role reporters are age, gender, tenure in the public sector and organisation, playing a management role, employment status and the size of the immediate work unit. Compared with role-reporters, non-role reporters (many of whom would fit the description of whistleblowers) were more likely to be younger with less tenure in the organisation or public sector, female and in non-managerial roles. Non-role reporters were similar (in general) to non-reporters; however, they were slightly more likely to be older, female, managers and to have more tenure in the public sector.

These results are broadly consistent with previous research that has found that reporters are more likely to be female employees with higher seniority (Mesmer-Magnus and Viswesveran 2005). Seniority was also connected with reporting by Keenan (2002), who found upper-level managers to be more positive towards (and more likely to engage in) reporting than middle or lower-level mangers. Near and Miceli (1996) also connected seniority with reporting, although, in contrast with the present findings, they found males to be more likely to be whistleblowers than females. These results do not, however, provide a clear indication that demography alone will allow for reliable, accurate prediction of who will report. The effect sizes of the differences are small, especially when the large sample size is considered, which suggests that there are other relevant variables that contribute beyond demography (Miethe and Rothschild 1994). For example, MacNab and Worthley (2007) could not connect age with whistleblowing, nor did they find a direct predictive relationship between whistleblowing and tenure, managerial experience or age. What they did find was an indirect relationship between managerial experience and reporting through the person-centred variable 'self-efficacy'. Managers had higher self-efficacy and it was this variable that predicted the making of a report. In many cases, however, the relationship between managerial experience and reporting noted by other studies could simply capture those cases that in the present study have been identified as role-reporting, rather than non-role reporting, which aligns more closely with 'whistleblowing'.

Attitudinal variables also contribute to the decision to report or not, but the broad pattern across these variables does not support the idea that whistleblowers are malcontents who can be distinguished from non-whistleblowers by having a particular constellation of anti-organisational perceptions and attitudes. There were, however, a number of differences found between reporters and non-reporters. Non-role reporters had less trust in management, less job satisfaction, a lower opinion of legislation and less confidence that management would respond positively to whistleblowing than either non-reporters or role reporters. This could, however, have been based on their experience, as will be explored in later chapters. Non-role reporters also viewed themselves as organisational citizens of good standing, showing signs of being more helpful and exercising more initiative than non-reporters, while being just as loyal and industrious. Non-role reporters still also had a more favourable attitude towards whistleblowing, but no greater knowledge of reporting procedures than non-reporters.

Levels of trust and organisational citizenship are both markers of an individual's attachment to, and willingness to cooperate with, an organisation (De Cremer and Tyler 2007; Fassina et al. 2007). Research has found a positive association between trustworthiness and OCB and a negative association with counterproductive work behaviour (Colquitt et al. 2007). Therefore, if a lower level of trust was found together with lower levels of organisational citizenship among non-role reporters, it would suggest that these employees were more likely to make reports based on a willingness to cause or engage in conflict, with less regard for organisational or social consequences. In the present study, however, non-role reporters did not score any mean that fell below the 'neutral' level and the differences between groups were small, as were the effect sizes. The failure to find major distrust or lower levels of organisational citizenship among non-role reporters also suggests that whistleblowers in the current sample are neither markedly undesirable employees nor particularly antagonistic towards management or their organisation. Certainly, the idea of a whistleblower as a 'crackpot' (Miceli and Near 1996) or someone with a generally troublesome work attitude is not supported.

At the same time, there is also not necessarily support for opposite stereotypes of whistleblowers as always inherently altruistic and trusting. It is notable that neither non-role reporters nor non-reporters felt management to be particularly trustworthy. Both groups were effectively neutral in their confidence in management's handling of reports. Similarly, even though many employees showed a generally favourable attitude towards whistleblowing, it could not be claimed that this necessarily played a causal role in their decision to report wrongdoing, given the situational variables that emerged as important. Even though behaviour is generally expected to follow a favourable attitude, whistleblowing behaviour has been found to be an exception to the rule, with Ellis and Arieli (1999) and Mesmer-Magnus and Viswevaran (2005) having also found that a favourable attitude towards whistleblowing does not predict real whistleblowing behaviour. Based on the pattern of these results, we cannot conclude that individual attitudes will differentiate whistleblowers from other groups.

## Situation and context

In contrast with the above results, most of the analyses suggest that almost any employee can potentially come to fulfil the role of a whistleblower, depending on the circumstances. Among these, the perceived characteristics of the wrongdoing are clearly more influential than personal characteristics in the decision-making process. The evidence suggests that the first preconditions for most whistleblowing are perceptions by the employee that the wrongdoing involved is serious and frequent, followed closely by rational assessments about whether they have sufficient information or basis on which to make a report, and perhaps, above all, about whether any effective management action will flow as a result ('whether anyone will do anything about it'). This result is consistent with the connection between expected inaction and failure to report made previously by Masser and Brown (1996) and Near et al. (2004). This appears, then, to be followed, in most cases, by equally rational assessments of reprisal risk. When the wrongdoing involves more people (that is, appears to be more systemic) or people more senior than the observer, the likelihood of a report drops off considerably. This is confirmed by the evidence that for those who do not report, lack of confidence in management action and the fear of management reaction, in circumstances in which management is involved or perhaps complicit, represent the major disincentives to reporting. When employees do go ahead and report, it is usually because these risks are less present or because the perceived seriousness outweighs the risks and the employee is willing to take their chances.

The variable that best distinguishes between non-role reporters and non-reporters, across all the analyses, is whether the reporter is the direct target of the wrongdoing (Tables 3.7–3.11). This is, however, most commonly the case only for personnel and workplace grievances, and to a lesser extent other forms of improper interpersonal behaviour, rather than for categories of wrongdoing with greater 'public interest' content. In these situations, the earlier variables continue to tend to dictate whether a report will be made, including the degree of clarity and availability of evidence about the wrongdoing. Less clear-cut or 'subjective' forms of perceived wrongdoing, such as defective administration (for example, incompetent or negligent decision making), are more likely to be reported when the whistleblower has clear evidence that the organisation's core business or larger public interest are affected.

The presence of personnel and workplace grievances in the data set nevertheless poses the question: what motivates other non-role reporters (that is, public interest whistleblowers) to make a report when they are not the target of the wrongdoing, given that they do not differ from non-reporters on attitudes such as trust? The most likely explanation is again that most whistleblowing is pro-social not just in character, but in intent, irrespective of how much conflict might surround it. It also reinforces that in the absence of a personal motivating factor, such as experienced by those making a personal grievance, other strategies are needed in organisations to overcome the barriers to reporting. Unless the wrongdoing is very serious, such that the observer feels they really cannot ignore it, non-role reporting by those who are not also in a position of 'victim' is usually likely only when the reporter perceives they are in a personally safe situation. A vital question for later chapters becomes: how are more employees to be given greater confidence that it is safe to report, given the clearly rational basis of their concerns that the reporting of any wrongdoing that involves more people or more senior people is inherently risky?

## Organisational justice

From the evidence in this chapter, it appears that many organisations require a new frame of reference from which to approach the question of how to better manage whistleblowing. The encouragement of whistleblowing is motivated by public interest and organisational interest concerns. The question of whether it will really happen when it should—before wrongdoing becomes more serious, systemic or entrenched—depends, however, on how individual employees view the likely organisational responses. These anticipated responses include the organisation's response to the perceived/alleged wrongdoers and its response to the individual themselves, as a reporter or whistleblower.

At the outset, it was suggested that concepts of organisational justice could provide a better unifying framework for understanding not only when the whistle was or was not likely to be blown, but why this was the case and what could be done to influence this behaviour. The above results make it clear that organisational justice provides a better means of analysing the management actions needed to encourage whistleblowing, as a construct that unites offence and context.

Organisational justice can be considered along two dimensions: 'distributive justice' and 'procedural justice'. Distributive justice is considered to reflect the degree of equity in the allocation of an outcome based on judgments of what constitutes a fair return relative to inputs. While outcomes are generally thought of in terms of pay, promotion and privileges, they need not be limited to these. Procedural justice is defined in various ways, including trust in authority and intra-group respect (for example, De Cremer and Tyler 2007). Six common criteria of procedural fairness are: a) consistent application of rules; b) unbiased investigation; c) use of accurate information in decision making; d) corrective mechanism for mistakes; e) decisions that match prevailing ethical standards; and f) ensuring all relevant voices are heard (Colquitt et al. 2001). There is a common concern about the perceived fairness of methods used to arrive at an outcome across these different definitions (Ambrose and Arnaud 2005). More recently, 'interactional justice' has also been identified as a form of organisational justice, concerning the extent to which a person is valued by the organisation (Colquitt et al. 2001). Interactional justice refers to the level of dignity and respect that authorities or decision makers display in their treatment of employees (interpersonal justice) and to the provision of information about processes and explanations for decisions (informational justice).

The perceived justice climate was not measured directly in the present study. Justice perceptions, however, clearly align with a broad range of the variables relevant to whistleblowing, such as trust, OCB, organisational commitment, job satisfaction, outcome satisfaction, cooperation with organisational authorities and evaluation of organisational authorities (Colquitt et al. 2006; De Cremer and Tyler 2007; Fassina et al. 2007). Whatever its precise mix of motives, whistleblowing is often motivated by the desire of individuals to correct what is perceived to be a seriously incorrect situation, which itself is likely to often involve a concern for justice (Trevino et al. 2006). For example, Table 3.12

confirmed that 'having an ethical responsibility', 'seriousness' and a 'belief that making a report would correct the problem' were the most potent reasons for reporting.

At the same time, it is clear that the decision about whether to act is interwoven with an evaluation of the justice climate within the organisation. While it might be hoped that employees in a 'just' system will be less likely to need to blow the whistle, they should also feel more free to voice whatever concerns they do hold, as they should also feel that reporting will be managed in a way that maintains the ethical integrity of the organisation (Kray and Lind 2002; Trevino et al. 2006). Conversely, the belief that an organisation is unjust can be identified as having a wide range of negative organisational effects (Acquino et al. 2006; Bies and Tripp 2005). In the present study, a lack of faith in the organisation's capacity to provide justice can be seen when employees lack confidence that reported wrongdoing will be dealt with, or that their reporting role will be properly understood and respected. The organisation's view of whistleblowing (a correlation of intent to make a report) and evaluation of the justice climate are based on observations of how others are treated and on direct experience within the workplace (Kray and Lind 2002; Mesmer-Magnus and Viswesvaran 2005). The belief that the organisation will ignore a report of a wrongdoing perceived to be serious violates perceptions of procedural justice (Harlos 2001). It also violates perceptions of distributive justice in the sense that exerting the effort to make a report will not result in a fair hearing or any change.

Organisational justice is therefore a concept that is consistent with most of the data above, especially given that the major reasons cited for not reporting are expectations of organisational inaction and of reprisal. For example, the informational component of interactional justice helps explain why non-role reporters could not be separated from non-reporters on the basis of their knowledge of reporting procedures. It is reasonable to expect that those who made a report would be more familiar with the procedures. The absence of this difference, however, suggests that reporters are routinely kept outside the process that is triggered by their report. As indicated in Chapter 2, a large proportion of non-role reporters simply do not know if an investigation is ever carried out. For informational justice to be served, it needs to be clearly communicated that the report has been heard and acted on, with periodic updates on the progress of any investigation and the outcome (Bies 2005). These elements are reinforced by further evidence about the procedural satisfaction of whistleblowers presented in Chapter 5.

Similarly, many elements of procedural and interactional justice can provide managers with a ready guide for how to better encourage reporting, given that they must usually make their evaluations based on retrospective data (written reports, interviews and observation of the workplace). Interactional justice will be served by employees being made aware of the official complaints procedure. The analyses here also show that an organisation wishing to increase reports of wrongdoing can do so by ensuring procedures are just, by checking the accuracy of information, taking all reports seriously, referring all reports to an unbiased, well-respected arbiter, giving all involved the opportunity to provide input and the other features of good investigation reviewed in Chapter 8. Interpersonal justice demands that all interaction between investigators and those involved be polite, respectful and honest.

Organisational justice concerns become most salient when it comes to the role of perceived risk of reprisal from management. Those higher in an organisational hierarchy are clearly capable of influencing organisational culture and workplace climate through their ability to approve and enforce policies and through their behaviour (Appelbaum et al. 2005; Foote and Robinson 1999). Those higher in an organisation are also expected to exemplify ethical behaviour in order to set a professional example, if only to legitimise their roles. Those with less power, on the other hand, rely on organisational systems for protection, but clearly are likely to do so only when they believe the system is procedurally just (Acquino et al. 2006). If there is dissatisfaction with the way the organisation responds to a complaint, and especially if management itself is seen as responsible for or unable to protect a reporter from real harm, the perceived level of systemic procedural justice will have been violated.

Finally, procedural, interactional and distributive justice interact, as can be seen in later chapters. For example, receiving an unfavourable outcome (such as not having a complaint upheld) could lead to a perceived lack of distributive justice; this could, however, be offset if it is clear that, notwithstanding this, management will still respect and protect the role of the employee who made the complaint, demonstrating a high level of procedural and interactional justice (Ambrose and Arnaud 2005; Brockner and Wiesenfeld 2005; Brockner et al. 2007; Skarlicki and Folger 1997).

Overall, there is a clear potential benefit for organisations in ensuring that whistleblowing policies and procedures are embedded in, and reinforce, their other strategies for achieving organisational justice. The analyses here suggest that in the alternative, they can expect to continue to learn of many of the more systemic and complex types of wrongdoing only after they have already developed into serious threats to organisational integrity. Even if those involved are not always satisfied that the outcome is distributively just, it could be that other members of the organisation will have confidence that the outcome is fair if the organisation's whistleblowing practices and procedures are seen to be consistently fair across a number of separate events (Cropanzo et al. 2001). By managing reports in a just manner, there is good reason to believe that organisations can discourage malicious or retaliatory complaints and instead encourage the pro-social reporting of wrongdoing (Acquino et al. 2006).

## Summary

This chapter has confirmed the soundness of the basic objectives of whistleblowing legislation and procedures discussed in Chapter 1. The encouragement of reporting appears to turn directly on employee confidence that the organisation will take effective action to stop or remedy the perceived wrongdoing. In many cases, the decision to report will also hinge on an employee's natural assessment of the associated risk and especially whether the organisation is capable of protecting them from adverse outcomes if more senior employees or management itself are involved.

The same results show, however, that in a large proportion of instances, current whistleblowing policies are struggling to deliver the levels of employee confidence necessary to satisfy these primary preconditions of reporting. Many of the results suggest that the low reporting rates and high inaction rates in response to perceived wrongdoing described in Chapter 2 stem from the need for organisations to do more to gain the confidence of employees that reports or wrongdoing will be handled seriously and professionally.

Among those who are not currently inclined to report the wrongdoing they observe, the degree of ambivalence towards managerial responses or other strategies such as symbolic legislation (Table 3.15) confirms this is not necessarily an easy task. Many of the solutions lie in the types of procedural and legislative reforms discussed in later chapters. For its part, this chapter has demonstrated the need for managers to abandon some stereotypical views of whistleblowers and focus instead on the encouragement and better management of reporting, on the basis that, depending on the circumstances, almost any employee can be expected to speak up about wrongdoing. Similarly, depending on the circumstances, almost any employee might also remain silent. The focus of management needs to fall on these different circumstances, including whether the organisational environment is conducive to speaking up. In particular, the prospects for encouraging the early and more constructive forms of reporting may well depend on how effectively management responses to whistleblowing reflect a larger commitment to organisational justice.

# 4. How do officials report? Internal and external whistleblowing

Marika Donkin, Rodney Smith and A. J. Brown

## Introduction

How often do public officials blow the whistle on wrongdoing internally and how often do they do it externally? Having decided to report, what influences their decisions about to whom and how they should make their disclosure and who else they should go to if they need to take the matter further?

These questions are important for further understanding the nature and significance of current whistleblowing and identifying the types of organisational decisions that might influence the reporting behaviour of employees. As discussed in Chapter 2, organisations tend to respond more negatively to whistleblowing if they are equipped only to react to the relatively rare cases in which whistleblowing occurs publicly. The previous two chapters have shown that when internal and regulatory whistleblowing are considered, the reporting of public interest wrongdoing by officials is a frequent and relatively routine part of organisational life, with almost any official likely to do so depending on the wrongdoing they observe and the organisational context in which they find themselves.

Do these assessments hold for all types of whistleblowing—in particular, for those who blow the whistle externally as well as those whose reporting is only internal? What implications do current reporting patterns have for how organisations need to manage whistleblowing, especially given the evidence in Chapter 3 that trust in management's response to a report of wrongdoing is usually pivotal to whether public officials will blow the whistle at all?

The first part of this chapter gives an overview of the different reporting paths that whistleblowing currently follows in the organisations that participated in this research. In further contrast with a widely held stereotype, the bulk of whistleblowing recorded by the employee survey started (97 per cent) and ended (90 per cent) as an internal process. Only an extremely small proportion (less than 1 per cent) of whistleblowers went outside official channels to the media at any stage; and typically this was a last resort. While this is based on survey data that do not include former employees, the proportion is unlikely to increase significantly. A slightly larger proportion blew the whistle to external watchdog agencies, but again the overall proportion was small (less than 4 per cent at any stage). In the overwhelming majority of cases, officials confronted with wrongdoing blew the whistle internally in the first instance. Moreover, they did so mostly up the management chain (84 per cent) rather than through special internal units or processes (less than 10 per cent).

This result has many implications for how whistleblowing is managed and for procedural and legislative systems intended to encourage and govern public interest disclosures. It also demonstrates that reporting paths can be complex, with mixed internal and external dimensions, all of which are important for organisations to recognise in the way in which their reporting procedures are devised.

The second part of the chapter examines whether there are significant differences between those public officials who blow the whistle internally and those who do so externally, in terms of key measures of OCB, an organisationally functional form of pro-social behaviour introduced in Chapter 1. In Chapter 3, it was seen that those who reported wrongdoing did not differ significantly from other employees on any of the four relevant measures of OCB. This chapter continues that analysis by examining what differences—on measures such as initiative or loyalty—exist between those who blow the whistle internally and those who do so externally. On the whole, internal and external whistleblowers gave indications of high levels of OCB, further challenging the stereotype of an external whistleblower as a disgruntled, organisationally unhappy employee. This analysis provides strong confirmation of the usefulness of understanding whistleblowing as a form of pro-social behaviour, as outlined at the outset of the report. Officials who reported externally at any stage, however, indicated higher levels of initiative and lower levels of loyalty than purely internal whistleblowers. The reason for the second result is not known. Slightly lower loyalty could be a predictor of external reporting, or it could be a result of the conditions that lead an official to report externally. Either way, some lessons begin to emerge for the way that whistleblowing should be managed.

The third part of the chapter further analyses these results in light of the degree of trust in management held by respondents. As already shown in Chapter 3, there was no significant difference in job satisfaction for those who reported wrongdoing and those who did not report; but those who reported were marginally less trusting of the management team. Again, the reason for this is not known (for example, whether slightly lower trust is a predictor or a result of reporting). The question of trust becomes even more central to the question of how employees report. The analysis reveals higher trust in management among those who only ever reported internally, and lower trust among those who reported externally at some stage, including in many cases after having reported internally in the first instance.

The discussion examines the implications for organisational efforts to identify and rectify wrongdoing and to manage the individuals involved. While the pattern of internal reporting has many positive implications, these implications also have limits. Employees' trust in management is clearly a key factor influencing the options that employees see for reporting perceived wrongdoing—again, as shown in Chapter 3, this is a more important factor than the individual personalities of employees. This tends to confirm that when organisations can engender a higher level of trust, they should be able to encourage more employees to report internally rather than externally. The crucial importance of trust, in conjunction with the great likelihood that any reporting will occur internally, emphasises the importance of organisations' efforts to devise and implement quality internal disclosure procedures and increases their responsibility to manage reported wrongdoing effectively.

At the same time, the reporting patterns described here pose significant questions for current legislative and procedural arrangements. As will be seen in Chapters 7 and 10, employees frequently have a low awareness of the statutory provisions intended to encourage internal and regulatory disclosures. While it is encouraging that many officials have sufficient trust in their direct management chain to report wrongdoing, the fact that so few officials (less than 10 per cent of public interest whistleblowers) went outside the management chain to use specialist internal whistleblowing procedures suggests either a low awareness of, or low confidence in, those alternative internal avenues. If this is the case, the same is likely to be true of staff awareness and/or confidence in the availability of external regulatory avenues.

The overall picture is that despite recent legislative reforms, current whistleblowing systems rely very heavily indeed on the ability of ordinary managers to recognise and take appropriate action in response to public interest disclosures. Public sector employees who do not see this as a viable path, for reasons such as those set out in Chapter 3, are currently more likely to remain silent about perceived wrongdoing than they are to find an alternative whistleblowing avenue—even an authorised internal one. Moreover, when employees do report externally, this is usually after they have already reported internally. Given the reduced organisational loyalty and trust recorded by external whistleblowers, and further results on outcomes set out in Chapter 5, it is likely that a whistleblower's decision to use an external, authorised reporting path is often made after problems arise with the organisation's handling of the matter, rather than being identified by whistleblowers as a first option.

These results suggest the need for organisations to place greater effort on training and equipping their managers to handle disclosures appropriately and on educating employees about the availability of different reporting avenues. They also indicate the need for closer coordination between line and integrity agencies to ensure disclosures are managed in the most appropriate way as early as possible, including by direct reference to external agencies, rather than waiting for whistleblower dissatisfaction to become the trigger for further, external complaints.

## Reporting paths

Public sector employees who wish to report wrongdoing can do so via a large number of paths. The most basic choice they make is whether to confine their disclosure within their organisation or take it to individuals or bodies outside the agency; and, if they choose the latter, whether to confine the external report to regulatory authorities or make it more public. There is a range of possible recipients of reports within most organisations. These include generalist managers such as the reporter's supervisor, another senior manager and the CEO. Agencies also usually have one or more specialist officials or units to deal with reports, such as human resources units, equity and merit units, ethical standards units, audit or fraud investigation units, internal ombudsmen or other complaints units, counselling units and peer support programs. External recipients of wrongdoing reports potentially include government watchdog and investigation agencies, external anti-corruption hotlines, external counselling services, relevant trade unions, members of parliament and journalists.

Existing overseas studies show a number of factors impact on the decision to whistleblow externally as opposed to internally, including management support, awareness and communication about wrongdoing and the climate for retaliation (Dworkin and Baucus 1998; Miceli et al. 1991). Studies have also demonstrated that it is rarely a direct choice of 'either/or'—most external whistleblowers have tried first to report wrongdoing internally, but without success, and tend to view going outside the organisation as a 'last resort' (Rothschild and Miethe 1999). Research on these questions in Australia has been limited and has tended to suggest a different trend. For example, Zipparo (1999b) found that one-third of NSW public sector respondents expressed a preference for reporting corruption externally in the first instance, rather than to anyone within their own organisation.

Public debate about the management of whistleblowing has been dominated by the treatment of officials whose disclosures have appeared in the media (see Brown 2007; Chapter 11, this volume). This debate has given the impression that external whistleblowing is relatively frequent and that the management response to whistleblowers is likely to be negative, when in fact the frequency of external reporting and the full pattern of management responses to whistleblowers have been unknown.

In the present research, evidence about the reporting paths used by whistleblowers was gathered through the employee survey (conducted across 118 agencies) and the internal witness survey (conducted across 15 agencies). The results presented in this section are for those respondents defined in the preceding chapters as whistleblowers (that is, 'non-role' reporters who observed and reported 'public interest' matters, and not respondents who observed and/or reported only personnel and workplace grievances).

The employee survey and internal witness survey used slightly different methods for asking respondents to record the paths they took to report wrongdoing. The employee survey asked respondents to indicate the first category of person to whom they reported wrongdoing with the number '1', the second person (if any) with the number '2', and so on. The internal witness survey allowed respondents to circle as many categories of person as they liked to whom they had reported wrongdoing 'in the first instance', as well as to then circle all the categories of person to whom they had provided information in any subsequent reports. These differences mean that the data on the reporting paths of the two samples cannot be compared exactly. The employee survey represents reporting as a series of discrete steps (for example, the respondent first went to their manager, then to the union, then to the CEO, then to a government watchdog agency, and so on). In contrast, the internal witness survey represents reporting as two or more episodes of reporting, each possibly involving more or less simultaneous reporting to more than one category of person (for example, the respondent reported at more or less the same time to their manager and union and later reported to the CEO and a watchdog agency).

The results from both surveys confirm the variety of distinct reporting paths available to whistleblowers. In practice, the whistleblowers surveyed often did approach more than one type of person to report wrongdoing. The employee survey whistleblowers provided information to an average of 1.9 recipients. The internal witness survey whistleblowers approached an average of 4.3 recipients, suggesting that this group included a higher proportion of respondents with complex whistleblowing experiences than their counterparts in the employee survey. Both surveys show that public sector whistleblowing typically involves more than a single report to one individual.

The two surveys tell similar stories about reporting paths. Tables 4.1 and 4.2 set out the types of recipients of reports from employees, in order of the frequency of reporting to each type of recipient. In each table, the first column shows how often a type of recipient was the first person to whom a report was made, while the second column shows how often types of recipients were approached at any stage of whistleblowing. The tables show that the most common recipients of wrongdoing reports are generalist managers (supervisors, senior managers and CEOs) in the direct management chain of the organisation, rather than specialist internal bodies such as ethical standards units. Reports to external bodies occur only in a small minority of cases.

The first people who whistleblowers are likely to approach with their concerns are their supervisors. If whistleblowers follow up their initial report (Table 4.1) or simultaneously take their report to someone else (Table 4.2), their most likely course of action will be to approach a senior manager. Beyond these two groups of recipients, the targets of initial reports are spread mostly within organisations between CEOs, human resource, equity and merit and audit and fraud units, and externally between unions and government watchdog agencies. This pattern is clearer among respondents to the internal witness survey (Table 4.2) than among respondents to the employee survey (Table 4.1), perhaps because of the different ways in which the reporting path items were asked in the two surveys, because respondents from the internal witness survey tended to have more complex whistleblowing experiences, or both. The prominence of generalist managers, rather than specialist internal units, as initial recipients of whistleblower reports in both surveys could be partly because of the lack of availability of specialist units in some organisations.[1]

## Table 4.1 Recipients of reports from public interest whistleblowers, employee survey

| Recipient | Initial recipient (%)[a] | Overall recipient (%)[b] | Stage recipient contacted (average)[c] |
|---|---|---|---|
| Supervisor | 65.7 | 72.8 | 1.13 |
| Senior manager | 15.0 | 41.1 | 1.76 |
| Peer support officer | 3.5 | 8.5 | 2.13 |
| CEO | 3.4 | 13.1 | 2.27 |
| Human resources/equity and merit unit | 1.8 | 10.5 | 2.55 |
| Union | 1.8 | 8.3 | 2.71 |
| Internal audit/fraud unit | 1.1 | 4.3 | 2.64 |
| Internal ethical standards unit | 1.0 | 3.2 | 3.04 |
| Government watchdog agency | 0.8 | 3.5 | 3.69 |
| Internal ombudsman/ complaints unit | 0.5 | 2.4 | 3.40 |
| External hotline/ counselling service | 0.5 | 1.7 | 5.71 |
| Member of parliament | 0.4 | 1.1 | 5.56 |
| Internal hotline/ counselling service | 0.2 | 1.8 | 4.67 |
| Journalist | 0.1 | 0.7 | 9.17 |

[a] Respondents were asked to indicate the first person to whom they reported a case of wrongdoing, followed by the second person, if applicable, and so on. Percentages total less than 100 because an 'other' category has been omitted.
[b] Percentages in this column represent the percentage of whistleblowers who reported a case of wrongdoing to each type of recipient at any stage in the reporting process. The percentages in this column total more than 100 because respondents were able to indicate all the people to whom they reported wrongdoing and some reported to more than one.
[c] Figures indicate the average stage in the reporting process when particular types of report recipients were contacted by whistleblowers. Lower figures indicate contacts early in the process; higher figures indicate later contacts.
**Source:** Employee survey: Q28 (n = 835).

The broad patterns of reporting are presented in Figure 4.1 (employee survey) and Figure 4.2 (internal witness survey). The figures simplify the whistleblowing process by reducing the various recipients of reports into three categories: solely internal, solely external and mixed (internal and external). The figures also reduce reporting to two broad stages: the initial report (to one person in Figure 4.1 and to one or more people in Figure 4.2), and then all further reports.

**Table 4.2 Recipients of reports from public interest whistleblowers, internal witness survey (per cent)**

| Recipient | Initial recipient[a] | Overall recipient[b] |
|---|---|---|
| Supervisor | 37.5 | 40.3 |
| Senior manager | 36.8 | 45.1 |
| Human resources/equity and merit unit | 11.8 | 20.1 |
| CEO | 11.1 | 26.4 |
| Union | 10.4 | 20.1 |
| Internal audit/fraud unit | 10.4 | 22.2 |
| Government watchdog agency | 10.4 | 25.0 |
| Internal ethical standards unit | 5.6 | 16.7 |
| Internal ombudsman/complaints unit | 4.9 | 6.9 |
| Member of parliament | 4.2 | 13.2 |
| Internal hotline/counselling service | 2.8 | 6.3 |
| External hotline/counselling service | 2.8 | 4.2 |
| Peer support officer | 2.1 | 4.9 |
| Journalist | 1.4 | 6.3 |

[a] Percentages in this column total more than 100 because respondents were able to indicate all the people to whom they reported wrongdoing in their first stage of reporting and some reported to more than one person.
[b] Percentages in this column represent the percentage of whistleblowers who reported a case of wrongdoing to each type of recipient at any stage in the reporting process. The percentages in this column total more than 100 because respondents were able to indicate all the people to whom they reported wrongdoing and some reported to more than one.
**Source:** Internal witness survey: Q30 (n = 144).

**Figure 4.1 Reporting paths of public interest whistleblowers, employee survey (per cent)**

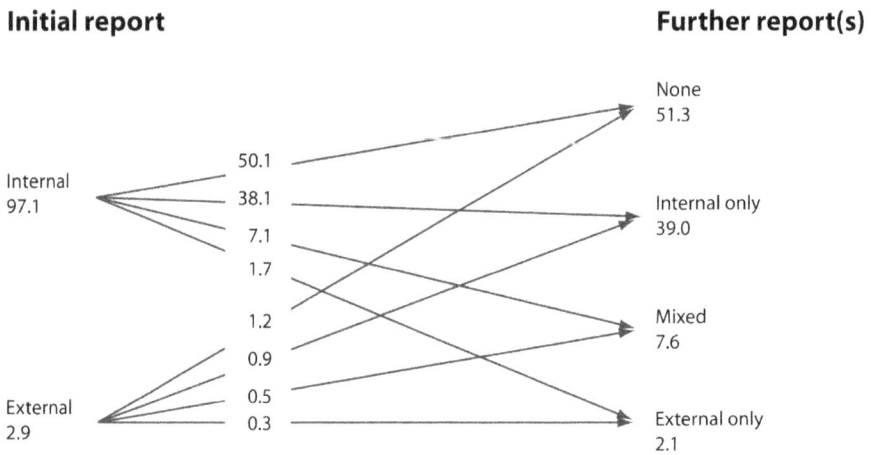

**Initial report**                                    **Further report(s)**

Internal 97.1

External 2.9

None 51.3

Internal only 39.0

Mixed 7.6

External only 2.1

50.1
38.1
7.1
1.7
1.2
0.9
0.5
0.3

**Notes:** 'Internal' includes reports to one of the following: supervisors, senior managers, CEOs, internal ethical standards units, internal audit or fraud units, internal ombudsmen or complaints units, human resource or equity and merit units, internal hotlines and counsellors and peer support officers. 'Internal only' includes reports made only to one or more recipients in the 'internal' category. 'External' includes reports to one of the following: external hotlines or counselling services, unions, government watchdog agencies, members of parliament or journalists. 'External only' includes reports made only to one or more recipients in the 'external' category. 'Mixed' includes reports made to 'internal' and 'external' recipients. **Source:** Employee survey: Q28 (n = 858).

In the first instance, almost all reporting (97 per cent in the employee survey and 80 per cent in the internal witness survey) is directed solely at internal recipients. Less than one-tenth of whistleblowers in either survey took their first report exclusively to someone outside their organisation. The reporting path taken by whistleblowers almost always begins within the organisation for which they work.

The second stage in Figures 4.1 and 4.2 concerns what happens next. Two-fifths to one-half of whistleblowers do not pursue their reporting beyond the initial stage. Their reports are resolved in one way or another, or else they let the matter drop. There is some movement towards involving external bodies and individuals in subsequent reporting. Nonetheless, external reporting remains a minority practice. Between one-half (internal witness survey) and four-fifths of whistleblowers who make subsequent reports keep them completely in-house. Only between 11.5 per cent (employee survey) and 37.7 per cent (internal witness survey) of whistleblowers ever take reports of wrongdoing outside their organisations at any time during their reporting.

**Figure 4.2 Reporting paths of public interest whistleblowers, internal witness survey (per cent)**

**Initial report**                                              **Further report(s)**

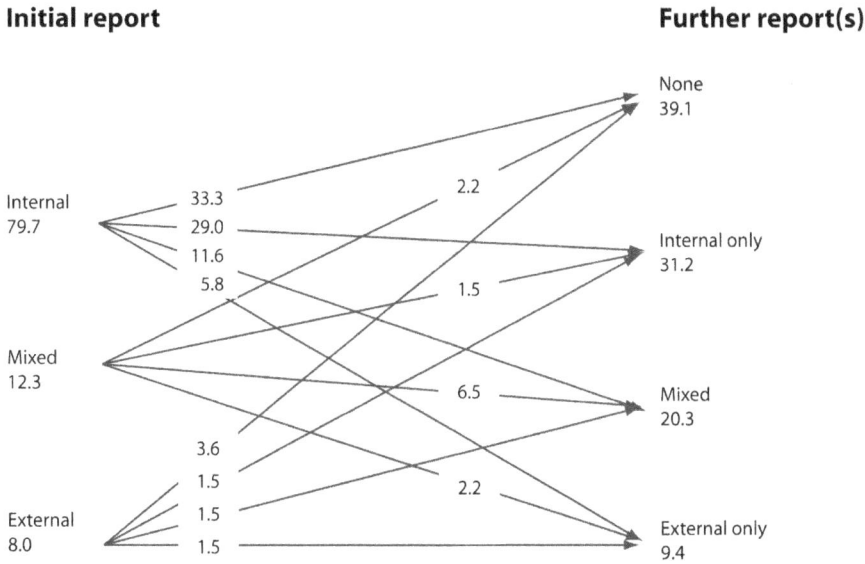

Initial report:
- Internal 79.7
- Mixed 12.3
- External 8.0

Path values: 33.3, 29.0, 11.6, 5.8, 2.2, 1.5, 3.6, 1.5, 1.5, 1.5, 6.5, 2.2

Further report(s):
- None 39.1
- Internal only 31.2
- Mixed 20.3
- External only 9.4

Source: Internal witness survey: Q30, Q38 (n = 138).

Even with the simplifications inherent in Figures 4.1 and 4.2, the broad patterns of reporting are complex. Also, when whistleblowers pursue their reporting beyond a first stage—and, as we see, only about half seem to do so—the recipients of their reports become more diverse, as they cast around for someone to deal with the wrongdoing they believe has occurred. As is shown in Tables 4.1 and 4.2, specialist units become more prominent, as do unions and government watchdog agencies (at least in Table 4.2). Even so, none of these bodies overtakes supervisors or managers in the volume of reports they receive. Even among the internal witness survey respondents, who showed stronger tendencies than their counterparts in the employee survey to spread their concerns widely, 30 per cent of whistleblower reports were dealt with exclusively by generalist managers.

What are the implications of these reporting patterns? At least four points can be made. First, public discussion of whistleblowing in Australia is almost certainly distorted by the relatively small number of cases that are eventually taken to journalists and members of parliament. Table 4.1 suggests that less than 2 per cent of whistleblower reports are ever received by journalists and parliamentarians, and they are almost never the first recipients. Within this total, less than 1 per cent of initial reports are made to the media. Indeed, the third column in Table 4.1 shows that, on average, parliamentarians are the fifth recipients of whistleblower reports and journalists are the ninth. As noted in

Chapters 1 and 2, the data captured by the employee survey do not provide a total picture of all whistleblowing, since the survey respondents did not include whistleblowers who had since left the organisation—a higher proportion of whom might be reasonably assumed to have pursued their grievance externally (and even been suspended or sacked as a result). Some indication of the extent to which this might change the overall picture is given by the more complex cases captured by Table 4.2, which are less representative of the public sector as a whole but in which the respondents are likely to have more diverse reporting paths (see also Figure 4.2). This evidence shows higher but still comparatively low rates of whistleblower contact with journalists and parliamentarians.

From this, it is clear that journalists and parliamentarians see only the tip of the whistleblowing iceberg, and are also more likely to encounter cases of whistleblowing that are already complicated, if not rancorous. While this more public whistleblowing may well be justified, on occasion, by the failure of organisations to address alleged wrongdoing in the first instance, the greater extent of internal whistleblowing does not automatically mean that wrongdoing is simply swept under the carpet (see Chapter 5).

Second, this confirms that in the majority of whistleblowing cases, public sector managers have the opportunity to deal with wrongdoing themselves. They get first opportunity to resolve the problem. It is almost always only after wrongdoing has been brought to management attention that whistleblowers look elsewhere for solutions. This suggests that effective public sector procedures for dealing with whistleblowing should be focused on anyone who has a supervisory role. The pattern appears so strong that procedures stipulating that only certain officers in the organisation can receive disclosures, perhaps removed from the immediate workplace of many employees, are unlikely to shake the frequency of this behaviour. In some instances, the solution could lie in training supervisors to act as effective 'post boxes' for the effective referral of disclosures to more appropriate locations in (or outside) the organisation. Strategies that rely only on designated people other than supervisors to receive disclosures are not, however, likely to prove effective for the management of reports, especially if they also reduce the extent to which supervisors feel able or willing to take responsibility for those concerns of which they become aware.

Third, the current heavy reliance on supervisors and line managers as the first points of disclosure could involve some risk that disclosures are first made to supervisors and line managers in circumstances in which they are not the best person to first receive the information. In some cases, the fact that a whistleblower elected to instead report first to a specialist internal unit, or to an external watchdog agency, could reflect a conscious decision by an employee that they were not prepared to trust line management with the disclosure. This could be due to the specific nature of the perceived wrongdoing or the people involved, including supervisors themselves. As shown in Chapter 3, however, and discussed further below, whistleblowers were not shown by the employee survey to be particularly untrusting of management on the whole. The strength of the reliance on supervisors and line managers therefore makes it likely that in at least some instances, staff could be blowing the whistle in an entirely trusting manner, without knowing or considering the full history (for example, when a problem has been going on for some time because a supervisor has previously failed to act). This likelihood also has implications for agencies' reporting procedures, including decisions about how the process is best managed once the whistle is blown.

Fourth, the motivations behind the strong tendency of whistleblowers to internally report to generalist managers need to be understood. Do whistleblowers report internally to generalist managers because they see this as the right thing to do, as part of being good organisational citizens? Does this reflect their first preference, or are they limited in their organisational choices? Given that many statutory regimes provide for multiple reporting avenues and given that most of the agencies surveyed have a range of internal reporting avenues including specialist units, what does the relatively low use of those avenues say about current whistleblowing policies? Finally, are those whistleblowers who go external necessarily less loyal or more disgruntled than those who remain internal? The remainder of this chapter takes up these questions.

## When do whistleblowers choose internal or external paths? Organisational citizenship behaviour

As seen in Figures 4.1 and 4.2, the majority of officials blow the whistle internally in the first instance; and, for the majority, the matter also remains internal throughout. Further questions arise from this pattern: what does it indicate about the character of whistleblowing? Do people prefer to blow the whistle internally because that is simply their instinctive reaction? Or is there evidence that they are blowing the whistle internally because of a sense of duty and loyalty to the organisation? Is the decision to go outside the organisation associated positively with any evidence of an increased tendency to disloyalty? What are the implications for management?

The analysis of who reported wrongdoing provided in Chapter 3 already provides a broad backdrop to these questions. On the whole, the employee survey provided little evidence consistent with a stereotype of whistleblowers as generally disgruntled or embittered employees. This was established by comparing the levels of OCB shown by respondents, between non-role reporters (whistleblowers), role reporters and those respondents who observed wrongdoing but who did not report it (non-reporters). Whistleblowers showed higher levels of 'interpersonal helping' and 'individual initiative' (sub-scales of OCB) behaviour than non-reporters, but did not differ from non-reporters on either the 'personal industry' or 'loyal boosterism' sub-scales used to measure levels of OCB.

OCB is a constellation of discretionary extra-role behaviours enacted by individual employees that benefit the organisation and its members (Graham 1989; Organ 1988:4; Penner et al. 2005). While many whistleblowers have their own motivations for reporting wrongdoing, the fact that they score either higher or the same as non-reporters on these behavioural scales, combined with the objectively beneficial effects of a good deal of this reporting, justifies the characterisation of whistleblowing as pro-social behaviour (Dozier and Miceli 1985; Miceli et al. 2001; Miceli and Near 2006; Chapter 1, this volume).

Whistleblowers' choices about whether to report internally or externally provide a further departure point for analysing the extent to which whistleblowing is best understood as pro-social, in an organisational context. This is because, while much internal whistleblowing might easily be imagined to be beneficial to the organisation, external whistleblowing immediately raises a range of broader challenges. Even though pro-social behaviour is by definition 'generally beneficial' to society, it can also at times be organisationally dysfunctional (Brief and Motowidlo 1986; Moorman and Blakely 1995). Nowhere is this better demonstrated than by the issue of external whistleblowing, which is generally recognised as good for society (at least when vindicated), but which can involve intense conflict between an organisation and its members and throw substantial parts of its management into turmoil, even if the organisation ends up better off.

By further examining levels of OCB among those who report internally versus those who report externally, we can therefore test whether the characterisation of whistleblowing as pro-social still holds at an organisational level, as well as a broader social level. For obvious reasons, pro-social behaviour and OCB have long been seen as related concepts (Brief and Motowidlo 1986; Podsakoff et al. 2000; Puffer 1987, cited in Williams and Anderson 1991). The match is, however, not necessarily perfect, because OCB is intended to describe behaviours that are inherently organisationally functional. In the present study, if whistleblowing is shown to also be organisationally functional through OCB, its character as pro-social will only be strengthened.

More specifically, two of the four OCB sub-scales used in the employee survey[2] provide measures of attitudes that are directly relevant to decisions to blow the whistle externally or internally. 'Individual initiative' provides a measure of willingness to communicate and attempt to influence others in the workplace, including behaviour that could be seen as 'rocking the boat' (Graham 1989:9; cf. Podsakoff et al. 2000). For example, one item asks respondents to indicate their agreement with the statement: 'For issues that may have serious consequences, I express opinions honestly, even when others disagree.' As noted above, whistleblowers generally showed higher levels of 'individual initiative' attitudes than non-reporters. 'Loyal boosterism' is also directly relevant, but for the reverse reason—since it is usually presumed to indicate a preference for keeping issues internal. These items are used to measure respondents' attitudes to promoting, protecting and defending the organisation under adverse conditions (Podsakoff et al. 2000)—for example: 'I defend the organisation when other employees criticise it.' As noted above, whistleblowers generally showed the same levels of 'loyal boosterism' as non-reporters. The question arises, however, whether this holds true for external whistleblowers compared with internal ones, given that going outside the management chain or outside the organisation is often viewed as disloyal—especially by anyone likely to be unexpectedly exposed or embarrassed as a result. Disloyalty could be associated with normal loyalty that has been compromised by selfish motives (Weinstein 1979) or simply having been sacrificed for the higher ethical principle of reporting the wrongdoing (Jubb 1999). In either case, many organisational responses reflect assessments about the degree of loyalty or disloyalty that should attach to someone who makes an external report.

In theory, the pro-sociality of whistleblowing and levels of organisational citizenship should be stronger for those who report internally compared with those who do so externally (Dozier and Miceli 1985). Internal whistleblowing is more likely to facilitate early detection of wrongdoing and create an opportunity for timely investigation and corrective action (Berry 2004). Even though the motivation (to help put a stop to wrongdoing) and process (notifying people who have the power to do something about it) might be the same, it is, however, reasonably apparent to the whistleblower that the repercussions for the organisation are likely to be more extreme if outside organisations are involved. Further, some types of external whistleblowing are more likely to be antisocial than pro-social, such as reporting to the media to gain an individual advantage without first raising concerns internally (Miceli et al. 2001; Miceli and Near 2006).

The reasoning outlined above suggests four hypotheses.[3]

H1. OCB should be more strongly positively related to a preference for initial internal whistleblowing, and less strongly related to a preference for initial external whistleblowing.

H2. OCB should be more strongly positively related to internal reporting as an initial real reporting path, and less strongly related to external reporting as initial real reporting path.

H3. OCB will also be more strongly positively related to real reporting that remains internal only, and less strongly related to any real reporting that includes external reporting (for example, including reports that were initially internal, but subsequently became external).

H4. As for Hypothesis 3, but comparing only 'non-role' reporters (that is, potential whistleblowers as explained in Chapter 2), since role reporters might be presumed to be more likely to remain internal and also to have higher levels of OCB.

## Hypothesis 1: OCB more strongly positively related to preference for initial internal whistleblowing than preference for initial external whistleblowing

This hypothesis involved examining the stated preferences of respondents to scale items about internal and external reporting in the employee survey, irrespective of whether they reported. Although this chapter is otherwise concerned with officials' real reporting behaviour, this hypothesis allows us to test the attitudes of all 7663 respondents to the survey. As outlined in Chapter 3, the employee survey (Q15) measured 'whistleblowing propensity' as well as real behaviour, including two items that asked respondents to indicate whether they would be 'most likely' to report wrongdoing internally to a supervisor, manager or similar 'in the first instance', or to make their first report externally, to a watchdog body, the media or similar 'in the first instance' (Q15f and 15g).[4] These items were adapted from those used by Zipparo (1999b).

The hypothesis was tested using a method described by Steiger (1980), which allows a comparison to be made of the correlations of the internal and external reporting variables with the four dimensions of OCB, including the 'individual initiative' and 'loyal boosterism' sub-scales noted as important above.

The hypothesis was supported by the analysis. It was found that all OCB dimensions were significantly more highly correlated with the expressed preference for internal rather than for external reporting. All dimensions were significantly positively related to internal reporting. They were also negatively related to external reporting, with 'interpersonal helping' and 'loyal boosterism' significant in this equation. Significance tests were conducted for all hypotheses and are available for all those that were supported, including this one.[5]

Table 4.3 sets out the correlations and whether they are positive or negative. Note that the 'trust' variable included in Tables 4.3 and 4.4 will be discussed in the next section.

This analysis is especially significant because it suggests that the tendency for public employees to report wrongdoing internally to management might not simply be a product of organisational constraints. For example, while that strong tendency might reflect respondents' lack of knowledge about or confidence in other reporting avenues, it is also consistent with an active preference to report internally—that is, to be able to disclose wrongdoing and have it addressed in ways that remain loyal and rock the boat the least.

This result is therefore also consistent with the fact that, while it could be necessary and desirable in some cases, external reporting is more likely to be damaging to an organisation and more difficult to manage for whistleblowers and organisations alike (Berry 2004). These difficulties flow from the simple fact that the repercussions for the organisation are likely to be more extreme if outside organisations are involved, before the organisation has an opportunity to respond (Dozier and Miceli 1985). It stands to reason that many employees would be broadly aware of this and would see internal reporting as more viable specifically because it could help to avoid negative publicity and allow problems to be dealt with internally. It might also seem that the welfare of the whistleblower could be managed better, as discussed in later chapters.

In fact, as many legislative and procedural arrangements make clear, internal reporting is not always the best way for wrongdoing to be addressed. In some circumstances, it would be better for the whistle to be blown first to an external regulatory agency. What this analysis shows, however, is that it is unwise to assume that other reporting avenues—even if their use should be promoted—will ever substitute entirely for internal reporting processes, as these are highly likely to remain the first port of call for large numbers of staff.

## Hypothesis 2: OCB more strongly positively related to internal reporting as real initial path than external reporting as real initial path

This hypothesis was tested by using a one-way ANOVA to examine the relationship between the OCB dimensions and the behaviour of all employee survey respondents who said they had reported wrongdoing. This analysis includes all types of real reporting—that is, it is not confined to whistleblowing.

As outlined earlier in the chapter, respondents were asked about their real reporting path, by indicating in what order they reported to different types of people internal and external to the organisation (Table 4.1). The main paths available were: 1) reporting internally initially and remaining internal (or reporting only once, which was an internal report); 2) reporting internally initially and then reporting externally; or 3) reporting externally initially and remaining external (or reporting only once, which was externally). Those who indicated that their first report was internal were divided into one group (Q28a–h, j) and compared with those who indicated that their first report was external (Q28i, k–n). Whether or not they made any subsequent reports, either internally or externally, was irrelevant to this analysis. For the reasons indicated earlier, there was an imbalance in the relative sizes of these groups of respondents. The number who reported internally initially was very large (n = 1935, 90 per cent of all reporters), while the number who reported externally initially was very small (n = 80, 3.7 per cent of all reporters). Since these variables are so highly skewed, interpretations of the findings can only be undertaken with caution.

# Table 4.3 Mean, standard deviations, reliability estimates, correlations (numeric variables) and F-values (categorical variables) for study variables

| | M (SD) | 1 | 2 | 3 | 4 | 5 | 6 | 7 | 8 | 9 | 10 |
|---|---|---|---|---|---|---|---|---|---|---|---|
| 1. Trust | 3.41 (0.83) | (0.90) | | | | | | | | | |
| 2. Interpersonal helping | 3.96 (0.47) | 0.07*** | (0.74) | | | | | | | | |
| 3. Individual initiative | 3.76 (0.54) | 0.06*** | 0.47*** | (0.80) | | | | | | | |
| 4. Personal industry | 3.84 (0.55) | 0.07*** | 0.40*** | 0.31*** | (0.67) | | | | | | |
| 5. Loyal boosterism | 3.55 (0.66) | 0.35*** | 0.34*** | 0.33*** | 0.32*** | (0.83) | | | | | |
| 6. Internal preference scale | 4.26 (0.71) | 0.22*** | 0.17*** | 0.21*** | 0.12*** | 0.22*** | n.a. | | | | |
| 7. External preference scale | 1.82 (0.87) | -0.13*** | -0.04*** | -0.02 | -0.001 | -0.07*** | -0.22*** | n.a. | | | |
| 8. Real whistleblowing behaviour (yes/no) | n.a. | 1.1 | 52.85*** | 150.58*** | 13.84*** | 37.15*** | 73.93*** | 1.09 | n.a. | | |
| 9. Internal v. external real initial reporting path | n.a. | 44.21*** | 0.06 | 0.09 | 1.09 | 1.17 | 26.91*** | 45.17*** | 1.72 | n.a. | |
| 10. Internal only v. some external | n.a. | 125.12*** | 7.85** | 6.64* | 0.29 | 15.02*** | 22.22*** | 49.43*** | 0.034 | n.a. | n.a. |

* significant at the 0.05 level
** significant at the 0.01 level
*** significant at the 0.001 level

**Notes:** Notes: The reliability estimates (coefficient alphas) are reported in the diagonal. For comparisons of scale variables, correlations were used and for categorical variables with scale variables, ANOVAs were used. Pearson correlations were two-tailed.

**Source:** Employee survey: Q1, Q2, Q15, Q26, Q28 (n = 7663).

In fact, the hypothesis was not supported. There were no significant differences between the mean scores on any of the OCB sub-scales for those whistleblowers who initially chose an internal reporting path and those who initially chose an external reporting path. Table 4.4 sets out the relevant mean. The importance of this finding is discussed below.

**Table 4.4 Comparison of OCB and trust in management (mean) by different reporting paths (all reporters)**

| Variables | Mean | | | | |
|---|---|---|---|---|---|
| | Interpersonal helping | Individual initiative | Personal industry | Loyal boosterism | Trust |
| Internal whistleblowing as initial reporting path | 4.02 | 3.90 | 3.86 | 3.59 | 3.30 |
| External whistleblowing as initial reporting path | 4.03 | 3.91 | 3.79 | 3.50 | 2.62 |
| Internal reporting only | 4.01 | 3.88 | 3.85 | 3.61 | 3.36 |
| Some external reporting | 4.09 | 3.96 | 3.87 | 3.45 | 2.76 |

Source: Employee survey: Q28 (n = 2015).

## Hypothesis 3: OCB will be more strongly related to real reporting that remains internal only and less strongly related to reporting that includes external reporting

This hypothesis compared those respondents in the employee survey who only ever reported internally (n = 1728, 81 per cent of all reporters) with those who reported externally at any point, including those who reported internally initially but subsequently reported externally (n = 324, 15 per cent of all reporters). Note that these percentages total less than 100 per cent due to missing data. Again, this analysis includes all types of real reporting and is not confined to whistleblowing. The hypothesis was tested using a one-way ANOVA. These mean figures are also shown in Table 4.4.

Significant differences appeared on three of the OCB sub-scales, going in different directions. Contrary to the hypothesis, those who reported externally at any point had higher scores than internal reporters for 'individual initiative' and, as expected, lower scores for 'loyal boosterism'. Accordingly, compared with those who only ever reported internally, those who reported externally at any point were more similar to the stereotype of being more prepared to rock the boat and having less loyalty, but not at the expense of their overall similarity in organisational citizenship. In particular, 'personal industry' for both groups remained the same and, contrary to what was hypothesised, those who reported externally at any point rated higher than the internal group for 'interpersonal helping' (see Endnote 5 for the significance tests).

## Hypothesis 4: For 'non-role' reporters, OCB might be more strongly related to real reporting that remains internal only and less strongly related to reporting that includes external reporting

This hypothesis was based on the previous one, but was restricted to comparison of the reporting behaviour of non-role reporters. In other words, the analysis was confined to potential whistleblowers who had reported wrongdoing outside their organisational role, but still included those who reported personnel or workplace grievances and was thus not confined to public interest whistleblowers. A total of 1157 non-role reporters only reported internally, compared with 256 non-role reporters who reported externally at some point.

Significantly, once again, a result contrary to the hypothesis was found. Despite narrowing the group towards the definition of whistleblowing used elsewhere in this book, the results did not change from Hypothesis 3. External reporters similarly scored higher for 'individual initiative' (mean includes external = 3.93; mean internal only = 3.82) and 'interpersonal helping' (mean includes external = 4.08; mean internal only = 4) and lower for 'loyal boosterism' (mean includes external = 3.33; mean internal only = 3.53), with no difference for 'personal industry' (mean = 3.85). See Endnote 5 for significance tests.

Taken together, these results give new insights into how whistleblowing should be viewed by organisations, based on the reporting paths preferred and chosen by employee survey respondents. The fact that higher levels of OCB correlated strongly with those who expressed a preference for reporting internally rather than externally in the first instance suggests that employees could recognise the desirability of internal reporting—for their own sake and that of their organisation. Consistent with some of the broad findings in Chapters 2 and 3, this result indicates that whistleblowing is not only accurately characterised as pro-social, it is seen as pro-social, at least if internal in the first instance.

While the preference for internal whistleblowing confirms its underlying pro-sociality, a different picture emerges in terms of the relationship between measures of OCB and real reporting behaviour. Here, the analyses were not confined to public interest whistleblowing, but the fact that all types of wrongdoing were included (including personnel and workplace grievances) makes the results even more significant. The internal and external initial reporting path groups demonstrated no differences in their OCB scores. This indicates that, contrary to the preference, even those who report externally in the first instance retain (on average) their positive view of their role and relationship with their organisation. The result must, however, be treated with caution given the small size of the latter group.

In response to Hypothesis 3, the comparison of two more balanced groups—those who only ever reported internally and those who reported externally at any point—suggests the picture is more complex. Some of the outcomes stand to reason. Employees who blew the whistle externally at some point were more likely to rate highly for 'individual initiative' (including 'rocking the boat'). They also tended to rate lower for 'loyal boosterism' (loyalty to and promoting the organisation), but here, as in Chapter 3, the direction of cause and effect is not clear. Given the strength of the preference for internal reporting shown above, it appears more likely that this drop in loyalty is owed to the respondents' perception of the response once the report is made internally rather than that those who report externally are necessarily always predisposed to be less loyal. This is consistent with the evidence that very few employees blow the whistle externally without first having blown it inside the organisation. Accordingly, the external reporters' higher scores for 'initiative' and lower scores for 'loyalty' could simply reflect their experience of having felt compelled to pursue the matter externally, against what would have been their normal preference, rather than the other way around.

Most importantly, the fact that external reporters also rated higher for 'interpersonal helping' and equivalently for 'personal industry' means that, overall, their characterisation as organisational citizens holds, as does the characterisation of reporting—even when external—as pro-social. In Hypothesis 4, these results also held when the analysis was narrowed from all reporters to simply non-role reporters. Even with personnel and workplace grievances still included, therefore, we have results consistent with those in Chapter 3. There is little evidence that those who report wrongdoing externally are any more likely to be disgruntled or organisationally unhappy employees than those who report internally, except perhaps as a result of what happens when they first make an internal report. Just as the nature of the perceived wrongdoing and organisational context appear to have more to do with who blows the whistle than individual attitudes, it appears to be factors other than the individual that explain how and to whom employees choose to make any report.

## Do whistleblowers' choices vary with trust in management?

Trust has been defined as 'one party's willingness to be vulnerable to another based on the confidence that the latter party is benevolent, reliable, competent, honest and open' (Tschannen-Moran and Hoy 2000:7). Chapter 3 showed that public employees who reported wrongdoing outside their role had, on average, somewhat lower trust in management and lower expectations of the management response to whistleblowing than those who observed wrongdoing but did not report it. On the one hand, this could indicate that some distrust is conducive to reporting. After all, trust is also consistent with deference to authority and a lack of critical review, while some wariness and suspicion is needed for resilient organisations (Kramer 1999).

On the other hand, the reasons given in Chapter 3 by those who did and did not report showed that levels of confidence in the management response were a crucial part of their decision about whether or not to report. This suggests that, on average, the employees who reported wrongdoing might have had higher trust in management when they reported and experienced a decline in trust as a result of their experience. As we will see in Chapter 5, even 'successful' whistleblowers commonly say that they felt less trust in their organisation as a result of the experience than they did before. In other words, the most logical explanation appears to be that—while still broadly trusting of the management team in their organisation—a majority of reporters do appear to become slightly less trusting as a result of reporting.

Another way to test this conclusion is through the evidence for reporting paths. This chapter has already shown that the bulk of reporting is internal and that for most staff, for better or worse, this appears to be the natural course of action. It has been hypothesised elsewhere that while the decision to take action in response to observed wrongdoing is dependent on the degree of trust placed in management by staff, this is especially true if the action is internal (Dozier and Miceli 1985; Ashforth and Anand 2003; Miceli and Near 2006). Internal reporting therefore should increase in line with trust, given existing evidence of the positive relationships between trust, pro-social behaviour and OCB (Podsakoff et al. 2000; Thau et al. 2004).

If distrust of management was a predictor of reporting, rather than a result of it, we might expect to see a relatively high level of external reporting. Although we already know that most reporting is instead internal, we can still further test the importance of trust by seeing whether internal reporting appears to increase or decrease in line with trust. Relatively little research has been done internationally on the relationship between trust and whistleblowing, although McLain and Keenan (1999) propose that there could be one. In particular, they believe that when there is conflict between an organisation's formal policies and informal structures and a culture of rationalising and accepting wrongdoing, organisational trust is weakened and faith in internal reporting is lowered. Confirming the relationship between trust and internal reporting will therefore also have implications for whether a good deal of wrongdoing is ever reported at all, given that the next option for most public employees in response to wrongdoing, if they do not report internally, is not the option of reporting externally but rather not reporting at all.

To better assess the relationship between trust and reporting, three further hypotheses were arrived at.

> H5. Trust will be positively related to internal whistleblowing preference in the first instance and negatively related to external whistleblowing preference in the first instance.

H6. Trust will be more strongly positively related to real reporting that remains internal only, and less strongly related to real reporting that includes external reporting.

H7. As for Hypothesis 6, but comparing only 'non-role' reporters (that is, potential whistleblowers such as those discussed earlier in the chapter), since role reporters might be presumed to be more likely to remain internal and also to have higher levels of trust in management.

## Hypothesis 5: Trust positively related to preference for initial internal whistleblowing and negatively related to preference for initial external whistleblowing

Trust in management was measured using Gabarro and Athos's (1976, cited in Robinson and Rousseau 1994) seven-item 'bases of trust' (employee survey: Q1). The items were reworded to read 'management team' to specify who respondents should consider when responding—for example: 'My management team (supervisor/line manager and above) is open and up front with me.' The Steiger (1980) method was again used to test the relationship between the trust results and the reporting preference discussed earlier as an element of whistleblowing propensity in relation to Hypothesis 1 (employee survey: Q15f and g).

The hypothesis was supported. Despite the fact that trust was slightly lower for reporters than non-reporters, it was significantly more highly correlated with the internal than the external reporting variable (Table 4.3). Trust was positively and significantly associated with internal reporting and negatively and significantly associated with external reporting (see Endnote 5 for significance tests).

## Hypothesis 6: Trust will be more strongly positively related to real reporting that remains internal only and less strongly related to real reporting that includes external reporting

This hypothesis was tested using a one-way ANOVA, again comparing the groups identified earlier in relation to Hypothesis 3: those who reported internally initially and never reported externally and those who reported externally at any stage. Again, this analysis includes all types of real reporting and is not confined to whistleblowing.

The hypothesis was supported. Trust was much higher for those who reported internally only than for those reporters who also used external reporting paths (or only external reporting paths), as shown by the mean figures in Table 4.4. Trust showed highly significant differences between the reporting paths (Table 4.5). This tends to confirm the association between having reported and a slightly lower overall level of trust, compared with employees who have not reported. The result is also consistent with a reduction in trust that has occurred as a result of the reporting process (having typically been internal first, then external) rather than as a predictor of the initial internal report. In any event, it tends to confirm the overall importance of high trust in management among the initial internal reporters, being also the bulk of people who ever report wrongdoing.

## Hypothesis 7: For 'non-role' reporters, trust might be more strongly related to real reporting that remains internal only and less strongly related to reporting that includes external reporting

This hypothesis was based on the previous one, but, like Hypothesis 4, it was restricted to comparison of the reporting behaviour of non-role reporters. Again, this brought the analysis closer to real whistleblowing, although all types of wrongdoing were still included. Notably, the results did not change, with internal reporters similarly scoring significantly higher on trust (mean = 3.21) than reporters who included external reporting (mean = 2.57). In comparison, role reporters who remained internal and those who included external reporting did not differ in their mean trust in management. Significance tests are reported in Endnote 5.

These results show that respondents who scored higher on the trust scale were more likely to follow the tendency towards internal reporting, as an expression of what they would expect to do hypothetically and as a description of their real behaviour in response to wrongdoing. Non-role reporters were much more likely to keep the information internal within the organisation, even if this meant continuing to report 'up the line', or to different groups or individuals they believed could do something about the issue. Others simply reported once, the most common report being to the supervisor. This supports the research of McLain and Keenan (1999), who find that trust encourages whistleblowing 'procedurally' through internal channels and distrust discourages whistleblowing or makes external reporting more likely. Rationalising of wrongdoing by management or a conflict between formal policies and informal culture can perpetrate mistrust, which impacts negatively on employee reporting of wrongdoing.

From Chapter 3, it will be recalled that there are many variables that seem to impact on the decision to blow the whistle internally, externally, or at all. In the above analyses, statistically significant demographic variables were held constant, but there were other possible variables of interest for which we did not control (see, for example, Near and Miceli 1996; Sims and Keenan 1998). Nonetheless, initiatives that build employees' trust in management should contribute positively to the preparedness of employees to report and to do so internally in a manner over which the organisation has greatest control. These findings have positive implications for organisations, some of which are discussed in the conclusions below.

# Discussion and conclusions

This chapter has shown that the majority of whistleblowing in the Australian public sector is internal to agencies, with public employees on the whole showing a tendency to report wrongdoing internally, predominantly to their supervisor or up the chain of management, at least before they make any further reports elsewhere, including outside the organisation. This contrasts sharply with stereotypes of whistleblowing based on cases that become prominent in the media, which are unlikely to be typical and instead to be cases that have involved many stages, many parties and many more complexities and conflicts than the bulk of whistleblowing matters. Chapters 5 and 6 will go on to analyse some of the differences in outcomes.

Nevertheless, this chapter has also shown that employees who blow the whistle externally—while statistically less frequent—no better fit the stereotype of the misfit, disgruntled or organisationally unhappy employee than the bulk of employees who report internally. Employees who expressed a hypothetical view that it was better to report wrongdoing internally than externally also indicated higher levels of OCB. In practice, however, there was little overall difference between those who only ever reported internally and those who reported externally at some stage. On some OCB sub-scales, there were understandable differences; overall, however, the OCB rating remained high even for external reporters, and particularly on those sub-scales that demonstrated the pro-social nature of reporting at the organisational level. OCB is positively related to whistleblowing propensity and real reporting behaviour, in some cases in different ways, but generally irrespective of whether an internal or external reporting path is taken.

All these analyses provide concrete evidence that it is accurate to conceive of whistleblowing as being generally pro-social in its nature. As a result, it becomes even clearer that agencies can ill afford procedures or a management culture in which employees who report wrongdoing are seen as destabilising or troublemakers. Instead, it is clear that whistleblowers, or those with a whistleblowing propensity, are predominantly conventional organisational citizens and 'not the disloyal, marginally socialized [people] they are frequently perceived to be' (Somers and Casal 1994:282). Even when public interest whistleblowing is triggered or accompanied by issues in which employees have strong personal interests, therefore, its character as pro-social behaviour should not be forgotten.

The final analyses have also confirmed the importance of public employees' level of trust in management—generally and in terms of anticipated response to wrongdoing if reported. Employees who report internally are likely to have high trust in management. Whether these trusting expectations are always met is less certain: the most logical explanation for the reporters' average slightly lower level of trust is that this flows from the way the cases are then handled. These results tend to confirm that were it not for substantial levels of trust in the organisational response, at least in terms of the wrongdoing being stopped or remedied, it is unlikely that current levels of internal reporting would occur.

Through measures that build employee trust, organisations can expect to maximise the amount of wrongdoing that is reported—internally—in a timely fashion, rather than being left to fester or eventually be reported only externally. The crucial importance of trust, in conjunction with the great likelihood that any reporting will occur internally, emphasises the importance of organisations' efforts to devise and implement quality internal disclosure procedures and increases their responsibility to manage reported wrongdoing effectively. The heavy current reliance on internal reporting therefore places considerable responsibility on agencies to respond well in their investigation and remediation of alleged wrongdoing and to ensure unnecessary adverse consequences do not befall those who report. Management is judged by its actions and by the outcomes of those actions. Accordingly, the trust on which effective internal reporting at least partly depends is itself dependent on whether management has a proven capacity to properly manage those involved.

While the pattern of internal reporting has many positive implications, these implications also have limits. This includes significant questions for current legislative and procedural arrangements.

As will be seen in Chapters 7 and 10, employees frequently have a low awareness of the statutory provisions intended to encourage internal and regulatory disclosures. While it is encouraging that many officials have sufficient trust in their direct management chain to report wrongdoing, the fact that so few officials (less than 10 per cent of public interest whistleblowers) go outside the management chain to use specialist internal whistleblowing procedures suggests the absence of, a low awareness of or low confidence in those alternative internal avenues. If this is the case, the same is likely to be true of staff awareness and/or confidence in the availability of external regulatory avenues.

Consequently, even if it is natural for public employees to have a preference to report wrongdoing internally and 'up the line' in the first instance, the fact that this is currently the overwhelming pattern poses two major challenges. First, it could help explain the significant amount of serious wrongdoing observed by employees about which no action is taken. Chapter 2 showed that 29 per cent of all employee survey respondents who observed very or extremely serious wrongdoing neither reported it nor indicated that anyone else had reported it, nor dealt with it in any other way. For almost one-fifth of the agencies for which that analysis could be performed, this inaction rate exceeded 40 per cent. The evidence in Chapter 3 and this chapter combines to suggest that if public officials are not prepared to report wrongdoing internally, the bulk will simply stay silent.

The overall picture is that despite recent legislative reforms, current whistleblowing systems rely very heavily indeed on the ability of ordinary managers to recognise and take appropriate action in response to public interest disclosures. Public sector employees who do not see this as viable are currently more likely to remain silent than they are to find an alternative whistleblowing avenue—even an authorised internal one. Moreover, when employees do report externally, this is usually after they have already reported internally. Given the lower organisational loyalty and trust recorded by external whistleblowers and further results on outcomes set out in Chapter 5, it is likely that the decision to use an external, authorised reporting path is often made after problems arise with the organisation's handling of the matter, rather than being identified as an option to start with.

These results increase the need for organisations to place greater effort on training and equipping their managers to handle disclosures appropriately, but also on educating employees about the availability of different reporting avenues. They also increase the need for closer coordination between line and integrity agencies to ensure disclosures are managed in the most appropriate way as early as possible, including by direct reference to external agencies. The alternative is to continue to assume that whistleblowers themselves will know how to make their disclosures to the most appropriate place and to wait for whistleblower dissatisfaction to become the trigger for further external scrutiny, potentially after it is already too late.

## ENDNOTES

[1] Another possibility is question bias, based on the response order for the relevant items in the questionnaires, since the first two responses are 'my supervisor' and 'another manager more senior than me'. The fact that respondents in both surveys used a wide range of responses when recording their overall reporting experiences (see the second columns in Tables 4.1 and 4.2), however, suggests that question bias was not a factor.

[2] Employee survey: Q2, based on Graham (1989) and Moorman and Blakely (1995). Respondents used a five-point Likert scale ranging from 1 ('strongly disagree') to 5 ('strongly agree'), in which a higher score indicated higher OCB. Although Moorman and Blakely (1995) used a seven-point scale, a five-point scale was used here to maintain consistency across the survey. Moorman and Blakely (1995) obtained the following alpha reliabilities: 0.61 ('personal industry'), 0.74 ('interpersonal helping'), 0.76 ('individual initiative') and 0.86 ('loyal boosterism').

[3] Demographic variables in the analyses: it was necessary to perform analyses to determine whether any of the demographic variables impacted significantly on the variables of interest. Those demographic variables that were associated significantly with any of the OCB dimensions—trust, the whistleblowing-propensity factors or internal reporting or external reporting variables (as tested by correlations and ANOVA)—were held constant in the analyses. To be conservative, significance was tested at an alpha level of 0.10. It was important to ensure that any effects found were the result of the hypothesised relationship being tested, rather than other confounding factors. The highest level of education, gender, age, tenure in the public sector, tenure in the organisation, role within the organisation, annual salary range, employment status, union membership, audit/fraud risk management/corruption prevention/investigation as part of job duties, size of immediate work section and work location were found to be associated with all or some of the variables of interest at an alpha

level of 0.10, and these were therefore held constant as required in the various analyses, dependent on which variables were entered in the model.

Statistical techniques: all surveys were used as there were no out-of-range responses or significant amounts of missing data. The small level of missing data did not adversely affect the analyses as it was accounted for by calculating the scales with a requirement of at least an 80 per cent response rate for each. The hypotheses were tested using the following statistical techniques: correlations and comparison of correlations, ANOVA at an alpha level of 0.05.

[4] Respondents used a five-point Likert scale ranging from 1 ('strongly disagree') to 5 ('strongly agree'), in which a higher score indicated a higher likelihood of reporting either internally or externally.

[5] Statistics for this and other analyses are as follows:

| Hypotheses | Statistics |
|---|---|
| 1 | Interpersonal helping: $t(7\ 376) = 11.91$, $p < 0.001$ Individual initiative: $t(7\ 376) = 12.41$, $p < 0.001$ Personal industry: $t(7\ 376) = 7.30$, $p < 0.001$ Loyal boosterism: $t(7\ 376) = 16.70$, $p < 0.001$ |
| 3 | Interpersonal helping: $F(12\ 046) = 7.85$, $p < 0.01$ Individual initiative: $F(12\ 045) = 6.64$, $p < 0.05$ Loyal boosterism: $F(12\ 029) = 15.02$, $p < 0.001$ |
| 4 | Interpersonal helping: $F(11\ 408) = 5.50$, $p < 0.05$ Individual initiative: $F(11\ 407) = 8.12$, $p < 0.01$ Loyal boosterism: $F(11\ 394) = 15.04$, $p < 0.001$ |
| 5 | $t(340) = 2.87$, $p < 0.01$ |
| 6 | $F(12\ 042) = 125.12$, $p < 0.01$ |
| 7 | $F(11\ 405) = 112.20$, $p < 0.001$ |

# 5. The good, the bad and the ugly: whistleblowing outcomes

Rodney Smith and A. J. Brown[1]

## Introduction

Public perceptions of the outcomes of whistleblowing are undoubtedly shaped by the mythic tales of triumph and failure presented in the news media and retold in popular films and books (see, for example, Dempster 1997). As previous chapters have already suggested, however, experiences of public sector whistleblowing are more diverse than popular stereotypes allow. This point holds for the outcomes that flow from whistleblowing.

The different outcomes of whistleblowing are interrelated in complex ways. Defining outcomes as good or bad will depend on which outcomes and whose perspectives are acknowledged. Consider the following statement from a respondent to the internal witness survey, whose report ultimately resulted in successful prosecution of wrongdoers:

> This incident has done nothing for my career in this organisation as I have tended to just stay in low-key positions and away from the stress of finding fraud again. Basically, I have withdrawn and taken on interests outside my work that involve me in more interesting projects and life experiences. Yet my experience could have been a lot worse, such as, conspiracy within the organisation or management not taking it seriously. It [was] the biggest fraud this organisation has experienced. Part of me is proud to have had the courage to report it, part of me doesn't want to know about it.

In this example, the outcome for the organisation was good, while the outcome for the whistleblower was mixed. The whistleblower's report was vindicated, the whistleblower was not harmed and management acted well. The whistleblower, however, felt ambivalent about the outcome and changed their behaviour and career goals in response to the experience and stresses of reporting.

This chapter will show that a greater understanding of the complex interrelationships between different types of outcomes is pivotal in understanding how whistleblowing might be better managed within organisations of the types studied here. The chapter explores good and bad outcomes of whistleblowing across five dimensions: 1) substantive outcomes, including organisational changes resulting from investigations into employee reports of wrongdoing; 2) the satisfaction of individual whistleblowers with the results of the investigation process; 3) the overall treatment of whistleblowers by others in the organisation; 4) deliberate mistreatment or reprisals; and 5) more general impacts on whistleblowers' lives and careers.

The results show that for the first of these dimensions, the results of whistleblowing are frequently positive. Most whistleblowers have their disclosure investigated and, in most cases in which investigation occurs, in the view of whistleblowers themselves this leads to at least some improved outcomes in the organisation. While the results vary depending on the type of wrongdoing reported, they are consistent with the evidence given in Chapter 2 about the value generally placed on whistleblowing in public sector organisations. They are also consistent with the findings in Chapter 3 that public employees are more likely to blow the whistle when they are confident that action can and will be taken in response.

The results for the second dimension—whistleblower satisfaction with results of the investigation process—indicate some reasons why the outcomes can readily become mixed. Whistleblowers are likely to be satisfied with the handling of their disclosure only if the investigation vindicates them and they are kept informed of the process. These data demonstrate the difficulty that organisations have in acknowledging the value of whistleblowing at a case-by-case level. This misunderstanding is often due to misaligned understandings between whistleblowers and responsible managers and case-handlers about the issues of greatest importance in the management of whistleblowing processes. In addition, the chances of improved outcomes increase only marginally with further investigations, which is currently the response sought by whistleblowers if an initial investigation appears unhelpful. These results reinforce those from Chapters 3 and 4, which are that unless the initial investigative and management responses to disclosures are well managed, a cycle of distrust and dissatisfaction can begin from which it is difficult to recover. These results point to ways in which organisations can help prevent and reduce the conflicts that can flow from whistleblowing.

The feasibility of managing the response to whistleblowing well is demonstrated by results on the third dimension: the overall treatment of whistleblowers. On average, most public interest whistleblowers (at least 70 per cent) are treated either well or the same by management and co-workers in their organisation. This crucial finding challenges assumptions that whistleblowers are always destined to suffer as a result of their experience and helps to confirm that it is possible for organisations and whistleblowers to emerge with broadly positive outcomes.

This result also holds three sobering lessons. First, contrary to a common assumption, when whistleblowers are treated badly, this mistreatment is much more likely to come from management than from colleagues or co-workers.

Second, achieving a good or neutral outcome depends greatly on the circumstances, including the type of wrongdoing and the organisational relationships involved, but also the management approach of the agency. In some organisations surveyed, the proportion of whistleblowers indicating bad treatment by management fell close to zero; in others, it rose to up to 46 per cent. Third, higher levels of perceived mistreatment have direct impacts on the reporting climate in organisations, a result consistent with the findings of Chapter 3. While the majority of whistleblowers say they would report again, the number decreases steadily among those who say they were treated badly. These findings raise important questions throughout the rest of the book.

This chapter provides further evidence of the nature of deliberate mistreatment or reprisals suffered by whistleblowers. When this occurs, it is most often intimidation, harassment, heavy scrutiny of work, ostracism, unsafe or humiliating work and other workplace-based negative behaviour. The findings here are based not simply on whistleblower experiences, but on the first data ever collected on this issue from case-handlers and managers. The evidence from case-handlers and managers also points to preventing mistreatment by management as typically a more crucial challenge than control of individual co-worker reprisals.

Finally, the chapter looks at a fifth dimension: the more general impacts of whistleblowing on whistleblowers' lives and careers. This analysis helps to explain the type of mixed outcome described at the start of the chapter. It indicates that even those whistleblowers who experience no active mistreatment and emerge broadly positive nevertheless often feel less trusting of the organisation as a result of the process and suffer the negative impacts of increased stress and anxiety, which can themselves lead to other preventable conflicts and problems. Maximum estimates of the proportion of public interest whistleblowers who currently suffer significant negative impacts, on this broader measure, range to more than 40 per cent. Exactly which circumstances are more likely to give rise to negative impacts, and the effectiveness of current strategies for addressing these, are topics for later chapters.

## A note on the data

The chapter draws on responses from the employee survey (conducted across 118 agencies) and the internal witness and case-handler and manager surveys (all conducted across the 15 case study agencies). Each of these surveys provides important data on the outcomes of whistleblowing.

Whistleblowers from the employee survey were drawn from a large, representative sample of public sector workers. The questions about whistleblowing experiences asked of this sample were not as detailed as those asked in the internal witness survey. The outcomes experienced by the two samples can be compared directly on only the third dimension addressed below: treatment by others in the workplace. The internal witness survey provides a richer set of responses on aspects of whistleblowing, but based on a much smaller and less representative sample, given that these respondents largely self-selected in reply to calls for volunteers made by their agencies or external integrity agencies. People whose whistleblowing experiences no longer loomed large in their lives were less likely to respond than those for whom whistleblowing was still a deeply felt part of their identity (see Goyder 1987). It is therefore not surprising that respondents to the internal witness survey generally had more negative experiences than whistleblowers who responded to the employee survey.

The data collected from the case-handler and manager surveys were different again. While potentially more representative and somewhat larger than the internal witness survey, the sample is similarly restricted to the case study agencies, unlike the larger sample pool of employee survey agencies. Respondents to the case-handler and manager surveys were also often asked for general judgments about whistleblower outcomes that they had observed, rather than providing precise information about particular cases. The three surveys therefore provide complementary but different evidence about the outcomes of whistleblowing.

The greater representativeness of the employee survey strongly suggests that whistleblowing outcomes are not as negative across the Australian public sector as they might appear to be from the internal witness survey or the case-handler and manager surveys. Despite the differences between surveys, however, the relationships between variables such as treatment by managers and willingness to report again are often the same. In important ways, the three surveys tell the same story about whistleblowing outcomes.

## Substantive outcomes, including organisational changes

As discussed in Chapter 2, one important way of assessing the significance of whistleblowing concerns the substantive outcomes of investigations triggered by whistleblower reports. The agency and case-handler and manager surveys documented the substantial role played by employee reporting in the internal investigations of agencies. Further, the employee survey indicated that two-thirds (63 per cent) of all those who reported wrongdoing, including more than half (56 per cent) of public interest whistleblowers, believed that their report was investigated.

The best information on general whistleblower judgments about the results of whistleblowing comes from the employee survey, which asked respondents: 'Overall, if the activity was investigated as a result of your report, what was the result?' Perceptions of the results of investigations were predictably mixed but, on balance, they were positive. Sixty-five per cent of all reporters whose issue was investigated, and 56 per cent of public interest whistleblowers, indicated that things became 'better' as a result of investigation of their reports. About one-third (31 per cent) of public interest whistleblowers responded that there was 'no change'. One-tenth (10 per cent) said that 'things' became 'worse'.

If we count 'no change' as a negative outcome—after all, whistleblowers who are concerned enough to report wrongdoing presumably want something positive done about it—the balance of good to bad outcomes of investigations is about three to two. On the other hand, if no change is counted on the positive side of the ledger—for a range of legitimate reasons, whistleblowers' reports of apparent wrongdoing might not have resulted in change—the balance of good to bad outcomes is nine to one. Either way, the overall balance revealed in the employee survey is encouraging and consistent with the value placed on whistleblowing by many organisations, as shown in Chapter 2.

Does this positive result apply equally to all forms of wrongdoing, or do agencies find it easier to deal with certain types of cases? If organisations are good at dealing with less serious matters, but fail when they encounter more serious issues of organisational integrity, the figures just cited might not reveal much. Table 5.1 shows the percentages and mean figures for each major category of wrongdoing (including personnel and workplace grievances), ranked in descending proportions of perceived positive outcomes. These results show that while the bulk of investigations yield positive outcomes for most categories, the proportions vary significantly depending on the type of wrongdoing alleged. Employee reports of 'waste and mismanagement of resources', 'improper behaviour' and 'misconduct for material gain' appear more likely to result in good outcomes than those relating to 'defective administration' and 'perversion of justice or accountability'.

This finding about the types of wrongdoing can be related to several others reported throughout this book. In the next section of this chapter, we show that achieving substantive outcomes is linked to whistleblower satisfaction—a result further reinforced in Chapter 6 examining risk factors for reprisals. Chapter 8 suggests that organisations are better at investigating certain types of disclosures than others. Taken together, these findings suggest that the better management of whistleblowing needs to include improvement in the handling of the specific types of wrongdoing that are currently more difficult to substantiate.

**Table 5.1 Overall outcome of investigations by type of wrongdoing reported (per cent and mean)**

| Wrongdoing category | What was the result of your report? | | | | | Total | Mean[a] |
| --- | --- | --- | --- | --- | --- | --- | --- |
| | Much worse | Little worse | No change | Little better | Much better | | (SD) |
| Waste or mismanagement of resources | 0 | 0 | 20 | 50 | 30 | 100 (56) | 4.11[b] (0.71) |
| Improper or unprofessional behaviour | 3 | 4 | 18 | 31 | 44 | 100 (249) | 4.07[b](1.04) |
| Misconduct for material gain | 2 | 1 | 27 | 35 | 35 | 100 (317) | 4.00[b] (0.923 |
| Conflict of interest | 5 | 0 | 35 | 15 | 45 | 100 (20) | 3.95[b] (1.15) |
| Defective administration | 1 | 4 | 28 | 41 | 26 | 100 (146) | 3.88[b] (0.87) |
| Personnel and workplace grievances[c] | 7 | 5 | 31 | 38 | 17 | 100 (423) | 3.56[b] (1.05) |
| Perverting justice or accountability | 6 | 6 | 35 | 39 | 16 | 100 (109) | 3.53[b] (1.01) |
| Reprisals against whistleblowers | 35 | 12 | 41 | 6 | 6 | 100 (17) | 2.35[b] (1.222) |
| Other | 9 | 5 | 28 | 33 | 26 | 100 (58) | 3.62[b] (1.18) |

[a] Mean values have been calculated on a five-point scale, in which 1 represents 'much worse' and 5 represents 'much better'.

[b] Statistically significant at the $p = 0.01$ level ($F = 13.616$; $df = 8$; $p = 0.0005$). *Post hoc* comparisons using the Tukey HSD test indicated that the 'reprisals' group differed significantly to all other groups of wrongdoing. The 'perverting justice' and 'personnel' groups differed from the 'misconduct', 'improper' and 'waste' groups, with the 'personnel' group also different to the 'defective administration' group.

[c] See Appendix 2 for wrongdoing examples categorised as lying in this and all other groups. 'Personnel and workplace grievances' included here for comparison, but not included in results for public interest reporting or whistleblowing shown in other analyses.

**Source:** Employee survey: Q20, Q33 (n = 1395).

The large number of respondents from a wide range of agencies in the employee survey means that these figures can be taken as a good picture of the outcome for whistleblowers whose reports are investigated. Nevertheless, the employee survey can give us only a broad snapshot of whistleblower perceptions of outcomes. The questionnaire item 'what was the result?' asked respondents to make a composite judgment about the outcome of investigations, a judgment that potentially combined the substantive findings of the investigation, any actions taken against wrongdoers, any changes to respondents' workplaces or their wider organisations and any repercussions for themselves at work and more generally.

The smaller internal witness survey contained a range of questions designed to tease out some of these more specific substantive outcomes for more detailed analysis. Table 5.2 presents these whistleblowers' perceptions of the substantive findings and resulting actions that followed one or more investigations of their reports. About one-sixth of the internal witness survey whistleblowers (17 per cent) were not sure of the outcomes of the initial investigation, in some cases because that investigation was still under way at the time the survey was conducted. One-fifth of the initial investigations (20 per cent) resulted in no wrongdoing being found. Wrongdoing was found in two-thirds of cases (63 per cent) but initial investigations that detected wrongdoing led to effective action in only one-fifth of all cases (19 per cent).

**Table 5.2 Perceptions of investigation findings and action among public interest non-role reporters (per cent)**

| Further investigation outcome (Q40) | Initial investigation outcome (Q32) | | | | | Total |
|---|---|---|---|---|---|---|
| | No wrongdoing, no action | Wrongdoing, no action | Wrongdoing, no effective action | Wrongdoing, effective action | Not sure | |
| No wrongdoing, no action | 7.2 | 0.7 | 0.7 | 1.4 | 1.4 | 11.5 |
| Wrongdoing, no action | -- | 3.6 | 1.4 | -- | 2.2 | 7.2 |
| Wrongdoing, no effective action | 0.7 | 3.6 | 10.8 | 4.3 | 0.7 | 17.3 |
| Wrongdoing, effective action | 3.6 | 1.4 | 2.9 | 1.4 | 0.7 | 12.9 |
| Not sure | 2.9 | 2.2 | 1.4 | 2.2 | 4.3 | 12.9 |
| No further investigation | 5.8 | 5.8 | 10.1 | 9.4 | 7.2 | 38.1 |
| Total | 20.1 | 17.3 | 27.3 | 18.7 | 16.5 | 100.0 |

Source: Internal witness survey: Q32, Q40 (n = 139).

The action taken in response to investigations of wrongdoing will vary from case to case. Some action will be individual, directed at wrongdoers, victims or whistleblowers. Other action will involve deeper, systematic changes to organisational structures, policies and procedures. Table 5.3 sets out the proportions of whistleblowers identifying these different types of change as having occurred in response to their reports of public interest wrongdoing.

According to whistleblowers in the internal witness survey, the most common organisational result of their reporting was no change—a result recorded by about half the respondents. About one-tenth of the respondents were not sure what changes had resulted from their reports of wrongdoing. These figures are consistent with the outcome figures recorded in Table 5.2. In perhaps the most extreme cases of ineffective action taken in the face of whistleblower reports, fully one-fifth of the respondents in Table 5.3 claimed that wrongdoers were rewarded with promotion or other means when reports were made against them.[2]

Where positive organisational change did result from whistleblowing, it occurred most commonly at an individual level. In one-fifth of cases, wrongdoers were subjected to sacking, discipline, punishment or other corrective action. Less commonly, particular decisions were changed, specific apologies made or compensation granted. In about one-tenth of cases, management or organisational changes were made in agencies. Sometimes, these management changes were more individual than systematic in nature, with individual managers sacked or reassigned.[3] In another one-tenth of cases, policies and procedures were altered. Overall, 22 per cent of the internal witness survey whistleblowers perceived at least one positive change and no negative changes to have occurred in their organisation after they reported wrongdoing. Another 10 per cent described a mixture of positive and negative changes, while 68 per cent identified no changes or solely negative changes.[4]

**Table 5.3 Changes in whistleblowers' organisations as a result of reporting, public interest non-role reporters (per cent)[a]**

| Individual changes | |
|---|---|
| Action taken against wrongdoers | 21.7 |
| Wrongdoers promoted or rewarded | 21.0 |
| Decisions reversed or changed | 5.6 |
| Compensation or apologies issued | 3.5 |
| **Systematic changes** | |
| Changed agency procedures/policies | 11.9 |
| Organisational or management change | 9.1 |
| **No change** | 51.0 |
| **Not sure** | 9.8 |

[a] Responses total more than 100 per cent because respondents could circle more than one response.
**Source:** Internal witness survey: Q45 (n = 139).

Overall, in more than three-quarters of the cases in which whistleblowers were aware of an outcome, their belief that wrongdoing had occurred was vindicated by the investigation. This is again a broadly encouraging finding, given that this is a higher proportion than revealed in the more representative employee survey. In most cases, however, the vindication of internal witness whistleblowers was not matched by what they would have considered to be effective action. Given that most initial investigations are internal, as shown in Chapter 4, these figures indicate that in the opinion of whistleblowers, public sector organisations are much better at finding wrongdoing from within their ranks than they are at effectively dealing with it.

Not surprisingly, whistleblowers were more likely to pursue further investigation of a matter when the first attempt did not result in wrongdoing being found or effective action being taken. The bottom two rows of Table 5.2 show that only one-quarter of whistleblowers who believed that the initial investigation had been completely fruitless let the matter drop, as opposed to one-third of those who at least had the satisfaction of having wrongdoing acknowledged. Interestingly, one-half of the internal witness survey whistleblowers whose initial report resulted in wrongdoing being shown and effective action taken still pursued the matter further. The reasons for this doggedness are unclear at present. They could concern the complexity of some matters (investigations get good results but cover only some of the issues at hand) or perhaps the unwillingness, or inability, of some whistleblowers to let matters rest.

Those whistleblowers who do pursue a further investigation do not usually achieve a better outcome. The most likely outcome of further investigation was the same result as before (represented by the 23 per cent of respondents who fell in the four bolded cells on the downward diagonal from the top left of Table 5.2). It is true that 12 per cent of the whistleblowers represented in the table perceived an improvement in outcome (those falling in the six cells directly to the left of the bolded diagonal). At the same time, however, a comparable 9 per cent (those falling in the six cells directly above the bolded diagonal) were left with a worse outcome than they gained from the first investigation. The most positive interpretation of these figures is that pursuing further investigations marginally improves the odds of gaining the best possible outcome 'somewhere along the line', from about one in five (19 per cent) to one in four (27 per cent). It also shows, however, that most whistleblowers who pursue further investigations are probably left disappointed. This calls for further analysis of the circumstances in which whistleblowers themselves are more likely to be satisfied with the outcomes of their actions.

## Whistleblower satisfaction

How satisfied are whistleblowers with the process that leads to the above results? This apparently simple question exposes a major dichotomy in assumptions about the objectives of processes for managing whistleblowing. On one hand, if investigations are conducted well, whether or not the whistleblower is satisfied with the results of the process might seem irrelevant. Like anyone else, the whistleblower should learn to accept the outcome. On the other hand, the reality of organisational life is not so simple. The above results suggest that whistleblower dissatisfaction can sometimes be a good indicator that an investigative or management response has not properly addressed the matter. Further, the relative satisfaction or degree of 'procedural justice' experienced by whistleblowers is likely to have a direct impact on the broader reporting climate in an organisation, by impacting on the perception of many other employees as to whether there is any value in reporting, which Chapters 3 and 4 showed to be a crucial issue.

The data from the internal witness survey show that a large proportion of whistleblowers are not prepared to accept the substantive outcomes of the investigation process with the dispassion of ideal Weberian civil servants.[5] Consistent with the fact that the internal witness survey whistleblowers were perhaps twice as likely as the employee survey whistleblowers to have experienced a substantive outcome they regarded as inadequate, a large majority expressed levels of personal satisfaction with the process that were very low. As Table 5.4 shows, three-fifths of these whistleblowers were not at all satisfied with the outcomes of investigations, a further one-fifth were not very satisfied and only one-fifth were at least somewhat satisfied. These negative dispositions hold for the initial investigation and any later investigations. As well as leading to changed outcomes in only about 10 per cent of cases, more investigations typically do not produce greater satisfaction for whistleblowers.

**Table 5.4 Satisfaction with outcomes of first and subsequent investigation/s, public interest non-role reporters (per cent)**

| How satisfied? | First investigation | Subsequent investigation(s) |
|---|---|---|
| Not at all | 61.5 | 62.4 |
| Not very | 19.2 | 20.0 |
| Somewhat to extremely[a] | 19.2 | 17.6 |
| Total | 100 (n = 52) | 100 (n = 85) |

[a] The categories collapsed to allow for analysis are 'somewhat', 'very' and 'extremely'.
**Source:** Internal witness survey: Q36, Q44 (n = 137).

Why are some whistleblowers satisfied with the investigation of their reports, while others are dissatisfied? One piece of this puzzle has to do with how well whistleblowers are kept informed of the outcome of investigation of their reports. When whistleblowers feel they are being kept in the dark, they are unlikely to jump to the conclusion that the outcome of their report is satisfactory, or remain confident that the disclosure has been valued by the organisation. As Table 5.5 indicates, the whistleblowers who are kept best informed about the outcomes of investigations are the most likely to think these outcomes are satisfactory. A strong relationship (Gamma = 0.69) exists between the two variables. Six-sevenths (86 per cent) of those who were not informed at all of outcomes were completely unsatisfied with those outcomes, compared with just one-third (34 per cent) of those who were at least 'somewhat' satisfied with the information they received.

**Table 5.5 Relationship between level of information about outcomes and satisfaction with outcomes (per cent)[a]**

| How satisfied? | How well informed of outcome? | | |
|---|---|---|---|
| | Not at all | Not very | Somewhat to extremely[b] |
| Not at all | 86.0 | 57.1 | 34.1 |
| Not very | 10.5 | 34.3 | 20.5 |
| Somewhat to extremely[b] | 3.5 | 8.6 | 45.5 |
| Total | 100 (n = 57) | 100 (n = 35) | 100 (n = 44) |

[a] Where respondents were involved in more than one reporting stage, only the final stage is considered here.
[b] Categories collapsed to allow for analysis are 'somewhat', 'very' and 'extremely'.
**Source:** Internal witness survey: Q35, Q36, Q43, Q44 (public interest non-role reporters; n = 136).

Despite this finding, openness and information should not be seen as panaceas for whistleblower dissatisfaction. While necessary, they are clearly not sufficient. Table 5.6 indicates that whistleblowers who learned that no wrongdoing was found or that no action was taken were just as likely to be completely unsatisfied as whistleblowers who were kept in the dark. Findings of wrongdoing accompanied by ineffective action were enough to reduce the total lack of satisfaction among whistleblowers to half; however, it took findings of wrongdoing accompanied by effective action to reduce the proportion of the totally dissatisfied to one-quarter and boost the proportion of satisfied whistleblowers to a bare majority.

**Table 5.6 Relationship between substantive outcome of, and satisfaction with, final investigation (per cent)[a]**

| Satisfaction with final investigation | Final investigation outcome | | | | |
|---|---|---|---|---|---|
| | Not sure | No wrongdoing, no action | Wrongdoing, no action | Wrongdoing, no effective action | Wrongdoing, effective action |
| Not at all | 81.0 | 76.9 | 79.2 | 48.6 | 25.0 |
| Not very | 19.0 | 7.7 | 12.5 | 35.1 | 20.8 |
| Somewhat to extremely | -- | 15.4 | 8.3 | 16.2 | 54.2 |
| Total | 100 (n = 21) | 100 (n = 26) | 100 (n = 24) | 100 (n = 37) | 100 (n = 24) |

[a] Where respondents were involved in more than one reporting stage, only the final stage is considered here.
**Source:** Internal witness survey: Q32, Q36, Q40, Q44 (n = 132).

These results are quite stark. Most whistleblowers in the internal witness survey are not dispassionate Weberian participants in the investigation process. The majority were not remotely satisfied unless the substantive outcome confirmed their belief that wrongdoing had occurred and involved action commensurate with that confirmation. Some whistleblowers clearly come to set a very high bar for their organisations and others involved in dealing with cases of wrongdoing. For a range of often quite legitimate reasons, organisations could fail to clear this bar.

Why do a very substantial proportion of whistleblowers come to have such a high degree of personal investment in obtaining a substantive result that vindicates them? It could be due to a range of factors, including personal ethical principles, individual doggedness, the fact that the wrongdoing also affects the whistleblower personally or personal conflict with others in the organisation (see Chapters 2 and 3). At least two other factors are, however, also suggested by later analysis. First, as Chapter 6 will show, a whistleblower whose disclosure is not formally substantiated faces a much greater risk of direct mistreatment or reprisals. Second, Chapter 9 outlines that whistleblowers currently experience a lack of organised support, with even 'well-treated' whistleblowers depending heavily on informal support networks such as peers. In conflict situations, these peers are themselves likely to look to the substantive outcome to validate their support ('See...he *was* right').

Whatever the mix of reasons, the study reveals that whistleblower dissatisfaction can be exacerbated by the fact that, frequently, those responsible for managing the process do not seem to appreciate the premium that whistleblowers place on substantive vindication. In the same case study agencies in which the internal witness survey was undertaken, the case-handler and manager surveys asked respondents to rate the importance of different outcomes for whistleblowers. Table 5.7 presents their perceptions of what constitutes the important outcomes for whistleblowers, as well as for themselves. Almost all case-handlers and managers (96 per cent) believed that fair treatment was 'very important' to whistleblowers, while the majority (86 per cent) thought an appropriate investigation was 'very important' to them. About two-thirds believed that appreciation of the whistleblower's role (66 per cent) and resolving organisational conflict (63 per cent) were 'very important' to whistleblowers. Strikingly, fewer than half the case-handlers and managers (45 per cent) believed that whistleblowers saw substantiation of their complaints as 'very important'.

**Table 5.7 Important outcomes when employees report wrongdoing (mean)[a]**

| Outcome | Outcomes respondent believes are important to **employees** who report wrongdoing | Outcomes respondents themselves believe are most important |
|---|---|---|
| That they are treated fairly | 2.96 | 2.95 |
| That an appropriate investigation is carried out[b] | 2.86 | 2.92 |
| That their role in providing information is appreciated | 2.63 | 2.65 |
| That organisational conflict is resolved | 2.60 | 2.58 |
| That the complaint is substantiated[b] | 2.38 | 2.06 |

[a] Mean values vary across a three-point scale from 1 ('not important') to 3 ('very important'), with a higher mean indicating outcomes considered to be more important.
[b] Difference statistically significant at the $p = 0.01$ level.
**Sources:** Case-handler and manager surveys: Q29, Q30 (n = 560).

Obviously, this assessment is quite inaccurate. As a group, case-handlers and managers do not appear to recognise the importance that substantiation of the complaint takes on for many whistleblowers. Instead, Table 5.7 indicates that the desired outcomes that case-handlers and managers attribute to whistleblowers closely match the outcomes that they themselves see as very important. This result strongly suggests that when case-handlers and managers confront whistleblowers, they see them as reflections of themselves—that is, public sector officials with a detached interest in working through processes (fair treatment, appropriate investigations) rather than as people with a deep commitment to achieving a particular substantive result. One strong risk in this misalignment of understandings is that, at least initially, whistleblowers could see case-handlers and managers as sympathetic figures who share their commitment to the 'truth' of the matter. Case-handlers and managers might not appreciate that their sympathetic response, being a commitment to process rather than outcome, is being misread. When the outcome is reached, and if whistleblower expectations are not met, the feasibility of achieving *ex post facto* whistleblower confidence in the process is remote. These results help to show that, quite early, a cycle of distrust and dissatisfaction could begin from which it is difficult for an organisation to recover.

What, if anything, can organisations do to improve whistleblower satisfaction with investigation outcomes? The first requirement is for highly competent investigations and management action in response to possible wrongdoing, especially given the evidence that the attitudes of whistleblowers are likely to be set in place by the initial organisational responses. Also important are strategies for ensuring that whistleblowers are kept adequately informed about the nature and process of investigations and are given accurate reinforcement about the value placed on their information. Organisations must also acknowledge the likely importance of the substantive outcome to whistleblowers, especially when reprisal risks are high and support networks are weak. This cannot reasonably mean, of course, that organisations will always give whistleblowers the result they want. Good investigation and due process will inevitably mean that some whistleblower reports are unsubstantiated. Organisations must therefore develop strategies to increase the extent to which the self-image and organisational survival of whistleblowers are assured by the respect and support that is given to their reporting, rather than leaving these things to rely, as is currently the de facto situation, on substantiation itself.

## Overall treatment of whistleblowers

So far, this chapter has focused on whistleblowers' perceptions and judgments of the impact of their reports and the nature and outcomes of the investigative process. Another set of outcomes concerns the impact of whistleblowing on whistleblowers themselves. As discussed in Chapter 1, a popular stereotype of whistleblowing, shared by some whistleblower support groups and academics, is that whistleblowers inevitably suffer harm as a result of their reports of wrongdoing. The culture of all organisations is sometimes painted as infected by an 'anti-dobber' mentality in which loyalty to the organisation and to colleagues is paramount and no whistleblower is able to find support (for example, de Maria 1999).

As a corollary to these stereotypes, and the reported pervasiveness of reprisals, pro-whistleblower advocacy has tended to focus on the importance of criminalising reprisals and seeking the prosecution of offenders. This policy response assumes that harm is caused predominantly by identifiable individuals acting to deliberately punish the whistleblower, who are therefore able to be held liable for discrete reprisal actions, such as physical assault, interference with property or direct threats and intimidation. This response reinforces the notion that the types of mistreatment against which organisations should primarily guard are the adverse reactions of affected peers, whether they are the alleged wrongdoers, the wrongdoers' friends or other co-workers with a negative view of anyone who would 'dob in their mates'. Since the types of adverse action most likely to be taken by managers are less easily identified as criminal, the focus on reprisals as criminal offences tends to suggest that management mistreatment of whistleblowers is at most a secondary issue.

Elements of these presumptions can be found among respondents to the case-handler and manager surveys. Asked how well employees who reported wrongdoing were treated by managers and by co-workers in the case study organisations, case-handlers and managers regarded co-workers as the more likely problem for whistleblowers. As shown in Table 5.8, on average, case-handlers responded that managers were likely to treat whistleblowers the same or slightly badly in their organisation, but that co-workers were likely to treat whistleblowers somewhat more badly again. Managers responded that their peers treated whistleblowers the same to quite well, but that, again, co-workers treated whistleblowers the same to quite badly. In short, case-handlers and managers were each more likely to blame co-workers than managers for bad treatment that occurred.

**Table 5.8 Perceived treatment of employees who report (mean)[a]**

| Source of treatment | Case-handlers (n = 224) | Managers (n = 304) | Total (n = 528) |
|---|---|---|---|
| How do you think employees who report wrongdoing are treated by **management**? | 3.2 | 2.8 | 3.0 |
| How do you think employees who report wrongdoing are treated by **co-workers**? | 3.4 | 3.3 | 3.3 |

[a] Mean values can vary across a five-point scale from 1 ('extremely well') to 5 ('extremely badly'), with a midpoint of 3 ('the same'). The lower the mean, the better is the perceived treatment.
Sources: Case-handler and manager surveys: Q31–6 (n = 528).

The results of the current study challenge the assumptions that all, or even most, whistleblowers suffer reprisals and that their bad treatment is most likely to come from co-workers. The best data on overall patterns of treatment of whistleblowers by co-workers and managers come from the employee survey. Table 5.9 sets out the mean responses for all respondents who had reported the most serious wrongdoing they observed, outside their organisational role, as explained in Chapters 2 and 3. The average reporter, including the average public interest whistleblower, felt that they were treated 'the same' or slightly better as a result of reporting—by management and by co-workers. The only mean response that crosses slightly into negative territory concerns management's treatment of employees who complain of personnel and workplace grievances.

**Table 5.9 Treatment of non-role reporters by management and co-workers (mean)[a]**

| Source of treatment | Personnel or workplace grievances (n = 541) | Public interest whistleblowers (n = 877) | All non-role reporters (n = 1 452) |
|---|---|---|---|
| How do you feel you were treated by **management** because you reported? | 3.1 | 2.8 | 2.9 |
| How do you feel you were treated by **your co-workers** because you reported? | 2.7 | 2.7 | 2.7 |

[a] Mean values vary across a five-point scale from 1 ('extremely well') to 5 ('extremely badly'), with a midpoint of 3 ('the same'). The lower the mean, the better is the perceived treatment.
Source: Employee survey: Q30, Q31.

For the most part, then, public interest whistleblowers did not report that they were treated badly. When reporters did see themselves as treated badly, they were more likely to point the finger at management than co-workers. Table 5.10 gives a more detailed breakdown of the treatment reported by the public interest whistleblowers in the employee survey. Almost two-fifths (39 per cent) were treated well by at least one group (managers and/or co-workers), with one-fifth (22 per cent) treated well by both groups. The most common experience of whistleblowers from the employee survey, reported by almost one-half of the respondents (46 per cent), was no change in treatment by either managers or co-workers. More than three-quarters of respondents (78 per cent) were treated the same or well by managers and co-workers as a result of reporting the wrongdoing. Less than one-quarter of respondents (22 per cent) indicated that they were treated badly by co-workers, managers, or both. Figure 5.1 sets out most of the same data in graphical form.

**Table 5.10 Treatment of public interest whistleblowers by managers and co-workers (per cent)[a]**

| Treated by co-workers | Treated by managers | | | Total |
|---|---|---|---|---|
| | Well | Same | Badly | |
| Well | 21.7 | 4.7 | 5.9 | 32.3 |
| Same | 6.2 | 45.7 | 7.0 | 58.8 |
| Badly | 0.9 | 2.7 | 5.2 | 8.9 |
| Total | 28.7 | 53.1 | 18.1 | 100.0 |

[a] The results for the employee survey whistleblowers in the 15 case study agencies were almost identical to those found across the total employee survey data set and presented in this table.
Source: Employee survey: Q30, Q31 (n = 877).

**Figure 5.1 Treatment by management and co-workers (per cent)**

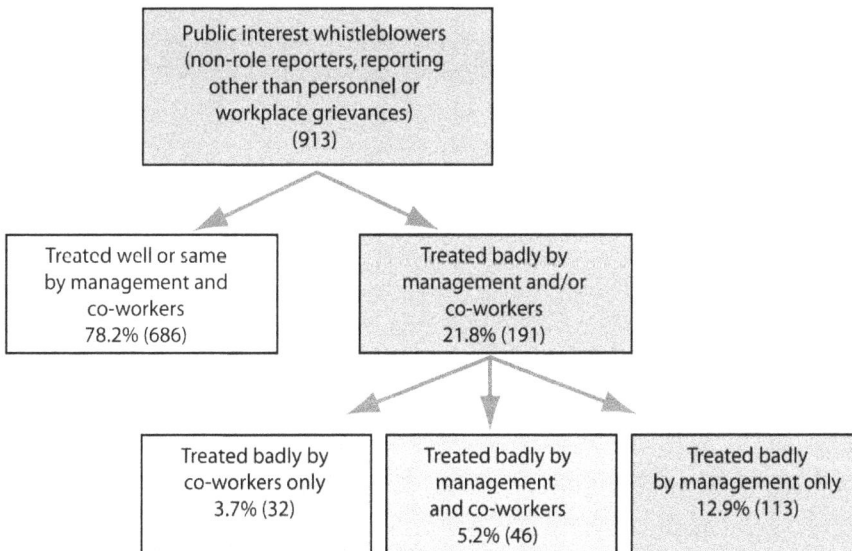

Source: Employee survey: Q30, Q31.

One limitation of the employee survey, noted in Chapter 2, was that all its respondents were still employees of the relevant organisation. Consequently, the survey did not capture any of those employees who had sufficiently bad whistleblowing experiences that they had left or had their position terminated by the organisation. It can reasonably be assumed that had these whistleblowers been included, the proportion reporting mistreatment would have been higher—but how much higher? A rough estimate can be made, based on one jurisdiction (Queensland) in which the total number of employees who separated from the public service in the two years covered by the survey equated to 6.4 per cent. If 24 per cent of these former public servants were public interest whistleblowers—twice the norm suggested by the survey—and 100 per cent of these, in turn, were treated badly as a result, the total proportion of all whistleblowers who were treated badly would rise from 22 per cent to about 30 per cent. Given that this estimate is excessively pessimistic, we can conclude that at least 70 per cent of whistleblowers do not feel they have been deliberately made to suffer for their experience.

As might be expected, the internal witness survey offers a somewhat bleaker picture of the treatment of whistleblowers (Table 5.11). Nonetheless, seven-tenths of the respondents reported that they were treated well or the same by co-workers after they blew the whistle, while two-fifths (40 per cent) were treated well or the same by managers. Without in any way discounting the difficulties they endured, it is worth noting that only one-quarter of whistleblowers in the internal witness survey (25 per cent) were treated badly by managers and co-workers. Given the generally worse experiences captured by this survey, it is notable that many of these whistleblowers still reported equal or good treatment. A major lesson of both surveys is that whistleblowers do not inevitably suffer ill treatment by fellow workers or managers and many whistleblowers are treated equally or well by members of their workplaces.

**Table 5.11 Treatment of public interest whistleblowers by managers and co-workers (per cent)**

| Treated by co-workers | Treated by managers | | | Total |
|---|---|---|---|---|
| | Well | Same | Badly | |
| Well | 8.6 | 6.5 | 17.3 | 32.3 |
| Same | 2.1 | 18.0 | 18.3 | 37.4 |
| Badly | 2.2 | 2.8 | 25.2 | 30.2 |
| Total | 12.9 | 27.3 | 59.8 | 100.0 |

Source: Internal witness survey: Q50, Q51 (n = 139).

These results confirm that it is possible for whistleblowers to emerge without suffering reprisals and that it is already feasible for organisations to successfully protect whistleblowers from deliberate adverse outcomes. They are, however, accompanied by three more sobering outcomes.

The first is the evidence that, contrary to the presumption outlined earlier, when bad treatment does occur, it is not most likely to come from co-workers. In response to the employee survey, only 4 per cent of whistleblowers indicated that they were treated badly by co-workers alone. Three times as many (13 per cent) claimed that they were treated badly by managers alone. Nine per cent were treated badly by co-workers, either alone or in conjunction with managers—half the number (18 per cent) who claimed to have been treated badly by management, either alone or in conjunction with co-workers. Mistreatment by management alone therefore produced more than half of the total bad treatment reported by whistleblowers. More than 80 per cent of the total cases of bad treatment involved management in some way.

In the internal witness survey, the most common source of poor treatment of whistleblowers was once again management rather than co-workers. The two-to-one ratio of bad treatment by managers and co-workers in the employee survey was repeated, where the relevant percentages were 60 per cent for managers and 30 per cent for co-workers. Reducing the incidence of bad treatment of whistleblowers by co-workers remains important. Nonetheless, these results show that policy attempts to control the risk of reprisals through criminalisation, as well as the common management expectation that the major risks of mistreatment lie among employees' peers rather than the management chain, are both misplaced. In Chapter 3, it became clear that there was a greatly reduced likelihood that an employee would report wrongdoing if they assessed it to be caused by their supervisor or other managers, with fear of reprisal emerging as an extra strong reason for not reporting in these circumstances. These results suggest that, in practice, it is indeed management reaction that poses the greatest potential problem for whistleblowers.

The second sobering result is that while it is positive that only 22 per cent of whistleblowers reported mistreatment, this is very much an average. Just as Chapter 2 showed the very variable reporting climates in different organisations, with some showing very low rates of employee inaction in response to wrongdoing but others very high rates, organisations differ widely in the proportion of whistleblowers who report being treated badly. Figure 5.2 provides an indication of this, for the 55 agencies across all four jurisdictions in the study in which at least 10 respondents had reported wrongdoing of some kind and also responded to the question about how they were treated by management

While three out of four jurisdictions had at least one agency for which this 'management mistreatment' rate was very low (less than 5 per cent, compared with the national mean of 18 per cent), all jurisdictions also had at least one agency for which the rate was double the national mean or greater (more than 36 per cent), with one agency ranging more than 46 per cent. Clearly, on this measure of outcomes, some agencies are managing whistleblowing quite well, but others are doing much less to successfully control the risks of perceived bad treatment.

**Figure 5.2 Proportion of reporters indicating bad treatment by management (per cent)**

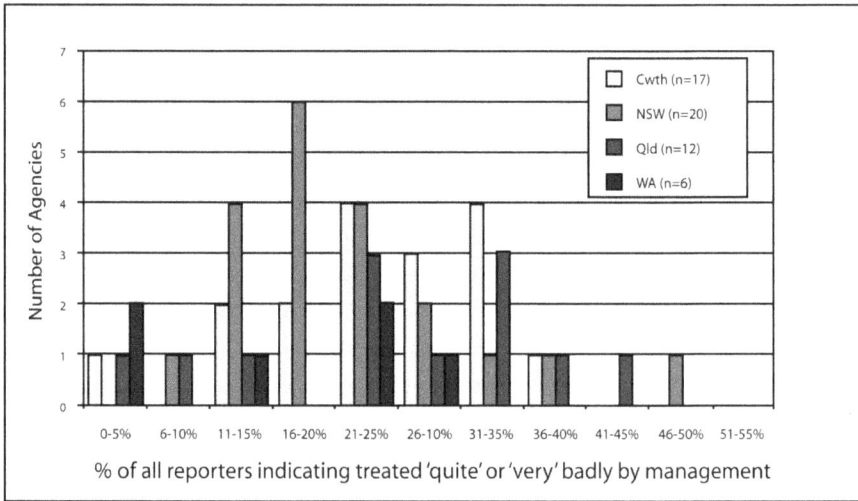

Source: Employee survey: Q30 (n = 55 agencies).

The third sobering result is that these issues of reported management mistreatment and the differing reporting climates in organisations are closely related. As set out in Table 5.12, the data from the employee survey and the internal witness survey show that the majority of all those who reported wrongdoing would do the same if they 'had [their] time over again'. This proportion, however, drops away markedly among those who indicate they were treated badly. More than one-third of the internal witness survey respondents (37 per cent) said they would be 'extremely likely' to report again, with another one-third either 'very likely' or 'somewhat likely' (30 per cent). Only one-third (33 per cent) would be 'not very' or 'not at all' likely to report again. A similar majority would be 'somewhat' (19 per cent), 'very' (20 per cent) or 'extremely' (25 per cent) likely to advise others in their organisations to blow the whistle if they encountered wrongdoing.[6] Only a minority of reporters (36 per cent) would be 'not at all' or 'not very' likely to advise others to follow the path they had taken.[7] The preparedness to report again is even higher on the part of employee survey respondents, where, in all, about 90 per cent of all reporters indicated they would report again. This suggests that the whistleblowers who responded to the internal witness survey are not necessarily substantially more dogged in their conviction that wrongdoing must be addressed, notwithstanding their generally worse experiences compared with respondents from the employee survey.

**Table 5.12 Likelihood of reporting again, by treatment (per cent)**

| Treated by managers and co-workers | Likelihood of reporting again | | | | | |
|---|---|---|---|---|---|---|
| | 'Not at all' or 'not very' | | 'Somewhat', 'very' or 'extremely' | | Total | |
| | ES[a] | IWS[b] | ES | IWS | ES | IWS |
| Well or same by both | 4.8 | 17.9 | 94.4 | 82.1 | 100.0 (n = 1 645) | 100.0 (n = 78) |
| Badly by co-workers only | 13.1 | 12.5 | 86.9 | 87.5 | 100.0 (n = 61) | 100.0 (n = 8) |
| Badly by management only | 26.4 | 26.0 | 73.6 | 74.0 | 100.0 (n = 258) | 100.0 (n = 73) |
| Badly by both | 41.0 | 65.3 | 59.0 | 34.7 | 100.0 (n = 100) | 100.0 (n = 49) |
| Total | 9.4 | 32.3 | 90.6 | 67.8 | 100.0 (n = 2 064) | 100.0 (n = 208) |

[a] ES = employee survey
[b] IWS = internal witness survey
**Sources:** Employee survey: Q30, Q31, Q34 (all reporters, n = 2064); internal witness survey: Q50, Q51, Q62 (all reporters, n = 208).

The table shows that, for both groups, bad treatment by managers and co-workers has a negative impact on preparedness to report again. In both samples, as bad treatment increases, preparedness to report again falls away. Given the strong correlation between whistleblowers' preparedness to report again and their advice to others, it is understandable that any level of perceived mistreatment will have repercussions for the broader expectations of employees throughout the organisation about the likely management response to reporting.

Finally, these more sobering lessons are all reinforced by the evidence from the case-handler and manager surveys, confirming that even if not as endemic as previously believed, poor treatment of whistleblowers is a definite problem. In the case study agencies, even 21 per cent of the manager respondents and as many as 41 per cent of the case-handler respondents thought that, overall, management treated whistleblowers either 'quite badly' or 'extremely badly' in their organisations. It is clear that there is no such thing as an objectively 'acceptable' level of mistreatment that should be tolerated in any organisation. The data confirm that the only safe course for organisations is one of continual improvement in efforts to reduce the proportion of cases resulting in perceived mistreatment, particularly by addressing deficiencies in the responses of management.

## Deliberate mistreatment and reprisals

The internal witness survey collected more detailed evidence about the nature of bad treatment and harm experienced by whistleblowers. In particular, in addition to asking about the overall good or bad treatment outlined in the previous section, the survey asked about deliberate bad treatment or harm in the workplace as a result of the respondent having reported or provided information about wrongdoing. Sixty-six per cent of respondents said that they did experience deliberate bad treatment or harm, a proportion that matches the proportion who had earlier responded that they had been treated badly by managers, co-workers or both (Table 5.11). Using the corresponding proportion of those treated badly by managers or co-workers in the employee survey, we can estimate that the overall proportion of whistleblowers who perceive themselves as having experienced a deliberate reprisal is likely to be about 20–25 per cent.

Respondents to the internal witness survey were asked to say what forms this deliberate harm or bad treatment took. The results are presented in Table 5.13. As even a cursory inspection shows, those whistleblowers who do endure reprisals are likely to encounter more than one type of deliberate bad treatment or harm. The average number of different types of reprisals recorded, among those suffering any at all, was 6.7. When reprisals occur, they are likely to take a range of forms. Some reprisals are also more common than others.

Table 5.13 also presents, alongside the reprisal experiences of whistleblowers themselves, the perceptions of reprisals among case-handlers and managers in the same agencies who indicated they had direct experience of cases involving action against whistleblowers. The two groups were asked different questions about reprisals. Whistleblowers were asked which reprisals they had experienced in their own particular cases of reporting wrongdoing, while case-handlers and managers were asked to reflect on all the cases of reprisals of which they had direct experience. Despite these different questions, with very few exceptions (unsafe and humiliating work, financial loss and essential resources withdrawn), the patterns of the most and the least common types of reported reprisals are remarkably consistent across both groups. This is believed to be the first time that data on this subject have been collected from case-handlers and managers, in addition to whistleblowers.

Key differences separate the most and least common types of reprisal. The most common types—threats, intimidation, harassment or torment, undermining of authority, heavier scrutiny of work, ostracism, questioning of motives, unsafe or humiliating work and being made to work with wrongdoers—centre on those that result in the whistleblower's position at work becoming more psychologically uncomfortable over time. If undertaken deliberately, these types of reprisals can all be achieved more or less surreptitiously and without formal change to the status of the whistleblower. Some of them are also highly subjective, in that while they could be very real in the mind of the whistleblower, the action could be relatively unconscious or unintended to cause harm on the part of co-workers or management. These contrast with the least common reprisals—loss of entitlements, sacking, suspension, demotion, forced probation and assault—which involve more drastic and tangible action against the whistleblower. Precisely because of this tangibility, they are riskier than the most common reprisals. For example, assault leaves physical evidence, while the other five all involve formal changes to the whistleblower's status that are more difficult to achieve and which leave a paper trail.

**Table 5.13 Types and frequency of bad treatment or harm after whistleblowing (per cent)[a]**

| Type of bad treatment and harm | Among all whistleblowers | Among whistleblowers experiencing any harm | Among case-handlers and managers[b] |
|---|---|---|---|
| Threats, intimidation, harassment or torment | 43.1 | 63.9 | 59.1 |
| Undermined authority | 29.9 | 44.3 | 38.2 |
| Heavily scrutinised work | 29.2 | 43.3 | 40.0 |
| Ostracism by colleagues | 28.5 | 42.3 | 56.9 |
| Questioning of motives for whistleblowing | 25.0 | 37.1 | 53.8 |
| Unsafe or humiliating work | 21.5 | 32.0 | 14.2 |
| Forced to work with wrongdoers | 20.8 | 30.9 | 25.8 |
| Financial loss | 18.1 | 26.8 | 9.8 |
| Essential resources withdrawn | 17.4 | 25.8 | 12.4 |
| Missed promotion | 16.7 | 24.7 | 22.7 |
| Poor performance report | 16.7 | 24.7 | 30.7 |
| Involuntary transfer | 16.7 | 24.7 | 29.3 |
| Reference denied or poor reference given | 16.0 | 23.7 | 16.0 |
| Training denied | 15.3 | 22.7 | 20.4 |
| Given little or no work | 15.3 | 22.7 | 20.4 |
| Overworked | 13.9 | 20.6 | 15.6 |
| Made to see psychiatrist or counsellor | 13.2 | 19.6 | 26.2 |
| Disciplinary action or prosecution | 13.2 | 19.6 | 15.1 |
| Forced to take leave | 11.8 | 17.5 | 20.4 |
| Harassment of friends, colleagues or family | 11.1 | 16.5 | 13.8 |
| Property destroyed, damaged or stolen | 11.1 | 16.5 | 11.6 |
| Lost entitlements | 7.6 | 11.3 | 8.4 |
| Sacked | 5.6 | 8.2 | 5.3 |
| Suspended | 4.9 | 7.2 | 8.0 |
| Demoted | 3.5 | 5.2 | 6.7 |
| Put on probation | 3.5 | 5.2 | 4.9 |
| Assault or physical harm | 1.4 | 2.1 | 6.2 |

[a] Percentages in each column total more than 100 because respondents could indicate as many categories of harm as applied to them. The response '[S]uffered a new or increased illness', recorded by 30.6 per cent of all whistleblowers and 48 per cent of case-handlers and managers who had direct experience of reprisals against whistleblowers, has been omitted from the table, since it does not refer directly to a type of action taken against whistleblowers.
[b] Column percentages are proportions of the total number of case-handlers and managers who reported direct experiences of whistleblowers alleging or experiencing reprisals. Each percentage refers to the proportion of such case-handlers and managers who believed that the relevant type of reprisal had occurred at least once in the cases with which they had direct experience.
**Sources:** Internal witness survey: Q53 (n = 141); case-handler and manager surveys: Q38 (n = 225).

These results show that when bad treatment does occur, or is perceived to occur, it is unlikely to involve a single decisive blow such as a sacking or demotion and is more likely to involve a series of smaller blows over time. Further, even though bad treatment is clearly real and all too common for the 20–25 per cent of whistleblowers who experience it, only in very rare cases is the nature of the reprisal such that it could meet the legal thresholds required to prove criminal liability on the part of any individual. Consequently, these data reveal even further questions about whether reliance on criminalisation, prosecution and the like is a well-founded strategy for addressing the bulk of reprisal risks or for trying to deal with most of the reprisals that do occur.

**Table 5.14 People 'mainly responsible' for deliberate bad treatment or harm (per cent)[a]**

| | |
|---|---|
| Senior managers | 74.2 |
| Supervisors | 52.6 |
| CEOs | 30.9 |
| Colleagues at same level | 24.7 |
| Colleagues below level | 20.6 |
| Officers from internal ethics unit | 16.5 |
| Officers from human resources unit | 16.5 |
| Unions or professional associations | 13.4 |
| Government watchdog bodies | 8.2 |
| Other internal specialist officers | 6.2 |
| Members of parliament | 4.1 |
| Internal support programs | 4.1 |
| Internal peer support people | 2.1 |
| Internal counselling or welfare services | 1.0 |
| External counselling or welfare services | 1.0 |
| Other community support groups | 1.0 |
| Whistleblower support groups | -- |
| Journalists | -- |
| Family members | -- |

[a] Percentages sum to more than 100 because respondents could indicate as many categories as applied to them.
**Source:** Internal witness survey: Q54 (public interest non-role reporters who experienced deliberate bad treatment or harm, n = 93).

Who takes reprisals against whistleblowers? Table 5.14 sets out the views of the respondents to the internal witness survey. Its basic theme is that reprisals almost always come from the workplace. Managers and co-workers occupy the first five places in Table 5.14 and, in one way or another, they are involved in all but 3 per cent of cases of reprisals. Again, contrary to popular belief, it is managers and not co-workers who are more likely to be responsible for reprisals. According to whistleblowers, two-thirds of cases (65 per cent) involved deliberate harm by one or more levels of management (immediate supervisors, other more senior managers and/or CEOs), with no involvement by co-workers (workers at or below the respondent's level). One-quarter of cases (25 per cent) involved managers and co-workers, while just one in 14 (7 per cent) involved co-workers and not managers. In about three-quarters of the cases of co-worker reprisals, managers were also involved. One interpretation of this finding is that co-workers need the covert or overt permission of managers before they will themselves engage in reprisals (see Strandmark and Hallberg 2007).

It is worth stressing again that the employee survey suggests that in the clear majority of cases, managers do not harm whistleblowers. At the same time, according to the internal witness survey, in the minority of cases in which whistleblowers do suffer reprisals, managers are very likely to be involved. As elsewhere in this book, our attention is drawn to the crucial role that managers play in the successful or unsuccessful handling of cases of whistleblowing.

This point is underscored in Table 5.15, which shows the relationship between the treatment of whistleblowers by managers and those whistleblowers' perceptions of the general change in organisations after their reports. The table shows that things are 10 to 17 times more likely to get worse in organisations when managers treat whistleblowers badly than when they treat them well or the same. Things can get better in an organisation when managers treat whistleblowers badly; however, things almost always will get better in an organisation when managers treat whistleblowers well. Once again, the actions and attitudes adopted by managers appear to play a pivotal role in the success or failure of whistleblowing.

**Table 5.15 Relationship between treatment by managers and overall judgment of result of investigation (per cent)**

| Overall result | Manager treatment after report | | |
|---|---|---|---|
| | Well | Same | Badly |
| Things better | 83.5 | 53.4 | 22.4 |
| No change | 14.2 | 42.5 | 37.8 |
| Things worse | 2.4 | 4.0 | 39.8 |
| Total | 100 (n = 212) | 100 (n = 247) | 100 (n = 98) |

Source: Employee survey: Q30, Q33 (n = 557).

## General impacts on whistleblowers

The final dimension of the outcomes of whistleblowing discussed in this chapter concerns more general impacts on whistleblowers' lives and careers, through changes in the way whistleblowers view themselves and their organisations. These changes were explored primarily through a series of semantic differential scale items in the internal witness survey. The scale items required respondents to rank their feelings as a result of their reporting experiences on five-point scales. The two ends of each scale represent negative and positive outcomes, with the most negative outcomes scoring '1' and the most positive outcomes scoring '5'.

Not surprisingly, given what we already know of the respondents to the internal witness survey, the changes they experienced as a result of their whistleblowing were generally negative. The average whistleblower felt decreased trust, disempowerment, betrayal, persecution, frustration, increased stress, anxiety, increased mood swings, withdrawal from others, decreased self-worth and decreased self-esteem. Table 5.16 shows these negative feelings organised according to the results of a factor analysis that suggested that the 11 feelings had three underlying factors. The first column (a) shows the results for all public interest whistleblowers. None of the individual items approaches the midpoint of the scale (3).

**Table 5.16 Respondents' feelings as a result of whistleblowing (mean)[a]**

| | | | (a) All public interest non-role reporters Mean (n = 144) | (b) Treated well/same by management and co-workers Mean (n = 47) |
|---|---|---|---|---|
| **Factor 1 'Feelings about others'** | | | | |
| Mean response for combined items a–e (1–5 scale):[b] | | | **1.78** | **2.60** |
| a. | Decreased... | Increased trust in organisation | 1.38 | 2.42 |
| b. | Powerlessness | Powerfulness | 1.95 | 2.58 |
| c. | Betrayal | Support | 1.81 | 2.62 |
| d. | Persecution | Affirmation | 2.03 | 2.96 |
| e. | Frustration | Satisfaction | 1.72 | 2.48 |
| **Factor 2 'Emotions about self'** | | | | |
| Mean response for combined items f–i (1–5 scale):[b] | | | **1.99** | **2.62** |
| f. | More stress | Less stress | 1.67 | 2.40 |
| g. | Anxiety | Confidence | 1.87 | 2.47 |
| h. | Increased... | Decreased mood swings | 2.23 | 2.62 |
| i. | Withdrawal from... | Connection with others | 2.18 | 3.00 |
| **Factor 3 'Individual worth'** | | | | |
| Mean response for combined items j–k (1–5 scale):[b] | | | **2.51** | **3.13** |
| j. | Decreased... | Increased self-worth | 2.57 | 3.21 |
| k. | Decreased... | Increased self-esteem | 2.44 | 3.04 |

[a] Items were ordered differently in the internal witness survey. They are presented here as suggested by a factor analysis that produced three distinct factors. All three scales are reliable (Cronbach's alpha 0.9 or better).
[b] Responses to the paired terms were indicated on a five-point scale, with the left-hand term in each pair scoring 1 and the right-hand term scoring 5.
**Source:** Internal witness survey (public interest non-role reporters, n = 144).

The first factor, 'feelings about others', comprises items that deal with whistleblowers' relationships. The scale based on these items produced the most negative mean score (1.78), indicating that the greatest damage to whistleblowers as a result of their experiences has to do with their relationships with others in their organisation. The second scale, based on a factor that deals with 'emotions about self', yields few more positive feelings. The third factor identified contains the two items—self-worth and self-esteem—for which whistleblowers scored most positively. This suggests that a core sense of individual worth is the most robust of all the feelings of whistleblowers. It could also suggest that while some elements of the experience might challenge that sense of worth, whistleblowing could also help to reinforce it. The opportunity exists for organisations to maximise this and potentially offset other more negative impacts, through strategies that acknowledge the whistleblower's role and the value of the disclosure, wherever honestly made, irrespective of any final substantive outcome.

In Table 5.16, the second column (b) also shows the results for all those public interest whistleblowers who indicated that they were treated either well or the same by management and co-workers. On the whole, the scores are more positive, as might be expected from whistleblowers who did not suffer bad treatment or harm. In particular, their sense of self-worth increased. It is important to note, however, that, overall, this was the only item against which well-treated whistleblowers recorded anything positive; and only in relation to two items on the first two scales ('affirmation' and 'connection') did the respondents reach the midpoint (3).

As the quotation from the whistleblower at the start of this chapter demonstrates, even whistleblowers who experience good treatment often end up with more negative feelings as a result of their experiences, including increased stress, frustration, anxiety and decreased trust in their organisation. To some extent, outcomes such as these can be considered unavoidable in the bulk of whistleblowing experiences, given that most whistleblowing either results from or has the potential to trigger some form of intra-organisational conflict. Moreover, it is easily forgotten that even before they make any disclosure, whistleblowers often might be suffering the stresses, frustrations and anxieties that go with being witness to the wrongdoing itself.

While at least some level of these impacts is almost impossible to separate from the whistleblowing experience, their prevalence across the spectrum of cases makes it all the more imperative that organisations have strategies for managing them. It is no surprise that whistleblowers left to manage such impacts are prime candidates for anxiety, distrust, dissatisfaction, conflict and real or perceived mistreatment by others. A de facto management policy of 'survival of the fittest' is unlikely to prove either effective or responsible.

To that end, it is useful to estimate what proportion of whistleblowing cases involves particular levels of these more general adverse impacts. These data were not collected in the employee survey. Nonetheless, we can make some estimates if we assume that the same levels of stress occurred among the sub-samples of whistleblowers in the internal witness survey and the employee survey who were treated well by their management and colleagues. Stress was chosen because it was the most commonly experienced adverse effect among respondents in the internal witness survey (Table 5.16). If we include any level of increased stress, the overall proportion of whistleblowers who currently suffer can be estimated to be about 62 per cent, or roughly three-fifths. If the estimate is limited to the most extreme level of stress (indicated by a score of '1' on scale item 'f' in Table 5.16), the overall proportion of whistleblowers suffering these extreme impacts is about 43 per cent—or about two-fifths. Taking an active approach to minimising and managing these less-direct impacts is one means of reducing the proportion of whistleblowers for whom the experience descends into larger conflicts and real or perceived reprisals. Where exactly the risks of these larger problems lie, and the mechanisms for addressing them, are topics for later chapters.

Finally, it is clear that the extent of negative impacts on whistleblowers is well known in the management structure of organisations. The case-handler and manager surveys asked these groups how often they believed employees who reported wrongdoing experienced 'emotional, social, physical or financial' problems as a result. While only 9 per cent of respondents indicated a belief that whistleblowers 'always' experienced problems, 44 per cent indicated a belief that whistleblowers 'often' experienced problems and a further 38 per cent believed that they 'sometimes' experienced problems. Less than 10 per cent of case-handlers and managers believe that whistleblowers rarely or never experience problems. These results are consistent with the evidence from the internal witness and employee surveys about the significant proportion of whistleblowers who suffer general negative impacts as a result of their experience, even when, on other dimensions, their whistleblowing can be considered successful.

## Discussion and conclusions

This chapter has provided a review of the various dimensions on which the outcomes of public interest whistleblowing can be measured. It has also provided new insights into the ways in which different types of outcomes interact. For example, substantive outcomes have a strong relationship with whistleblower satisfaction. Satisfaction could have a strong relationship with treatment by management; and treatment by management clearly has a strong relationship with the messages about the wisdom of reporting that whistleblowers are likely to transmit elsewhere through the organisation.

The findings of this chapter suggest a number of lessons for public sector whistleblowers and managers. First, when the outcome of whistleblowing is known, it is often likely to involve a finding that wrongdoing has occurred. Second, many such findings will not be accompanied by change within organisations, or at least the change seen as desirable by whistleblowers. Third, this contradiction is a deep source of potential frustration for many whistleblowers, given their frequently strong beliefs in the need for effective action commensurate with the truth of their allegations. Fourth, this frustration is likely to involve negative changes in whistleblowers' relationships with others in their organisations. Fifth, most whistleblowers nevertheless do not suffer direct reprisals or bad treatment at the hands of others, even if their overall experience is stressful, negative or causes problems in other ways. Sixth, those who do suffer reprisals suffer from actions that are difficult to prove, certainly to any criminal threshold. These are more likely to result from the actions of managers than from colleagues or co-workers.

The lessons for managers begin with the fact that they need to be recognised as very significant players in producing better or worse outcomes. As the first port of call for most whistleblowers (see also Chapter 4), they are in crucial positions to shape the outcomes of whistleblowing. Managers need to be aware that outcomes are more important than processes for most whistleblowers. The outcomes of an initial investigation of a wrongdoing report are also only rarely likely to be improved by later investigations. The treatment of whistleblowers by managers has important effects on whether or not whistleblowers view the outcome of their reporting of wrongdoing in positive or negative terms. While some organisations are clearly having success in preventing or containing whistleblower mistreatment, others are clearly struggling. Finally, any assumptions by managers that little can be done to protect whistleblowers or prevent workplace problems associated with reporting appear to be seriously misplaced and likely to only contribute to adverse results. All of these points suggest that public sector organisations need to pay careful attention to the training of managers and the development of more effective systems for the handling of wrongdoing reports.

## ENDNOTES

[1] The authors thank Lindy Annakin and Jane Olsen for assistance with analyses in this chapter.

[2] Intriguingly, in 3.5 per cent of cases, respondents reported that wrongdoers were both rewarded and punished. In these cases, some wrongdoers could have been protected and rewarded, while others were made scapegoats.

[3] A number of respondents made this point clear in additional written comments made on the questionnaires.

[4] These figures suggest a different pattern of experiences to those from the employee survey reported at the start of this chapter.

[5] Max Weber describes one of the three 'social consequences' of bureaucratic order as: 'The dominance of a spirit of formalistic impersonality: "Sine ira et studio", without hatred or passion, and hence without affection or enthusiasm. The dominant norms are concepts of straightforward duty without regard to personal considerations. Everyone is subject to formal equality of treatment; that is, everyone in the same empirical situation. This is the spirit in which the ideal official conducts his [or her] office.' (Weber 1978:225).

[6] Willingness to report again and likelihood of advising others to report are strongly associated (Gamma = 0.82).

[7] This might be termed the Trevor Haken response, after police whistleblower Haken's pithy reply when questioned about the advice he would give aspiring police whistleblowers: 'Tell them to f*** off' (see Padraic 2005:233).

# 6. Whistleblower mistreatment: identifying the risks

A. J. Brown and Jane Olsen

## Introduction

The previous chapter confirmed that even when the reporting of wrongdoing is vindicated, many public interest whistleblowers experience stress and difficulty. On average, it is a minority of whistleblowers who report bad treatment from management or co-workers (between 20 and 30 per cent), but this proportion is still sizeable, has direct impacts on the willingness of others to report and in some public agencies runs to a very much higher figure. Fairness, justice and the importance of fostering a positive reporting climate dictate that it is in everyone's interests—from whistleblowers to governments—to reduce this proportion to the lowest possible level. How is this goal best pursued?

Much of the answer lies in Part 2 of this book, which reviews the systems and procedures that public agencies currently have in place for the management of whistleblowing. Before leaving the data on the hundreds of individual whistleblowing incidents captured by this research, it is useful to mine this for a better understanding of which circumstances are most closely associated with higher levels of reprisal risk. Although mistreatment can arise in any type of whistleblowing case, clearly there are some types of cases in which the risks are generally higher. Identifying these not only helps complete the picture on the nature and impact of these types of whistleblowing outcomes, it is of practical importance in helping identify how agencies can better anticipate and manage reprisal risks.

Given the volume of whistleblowing that occurs and the fact that a large proportion can clearly be managed to a positive conclusion, it is logical that efforts to prevent and contain mistreatment should be focused on those cases involving the greatest risks. As will be seen in Chapter 9, there are currently few organised methods for assessing the risks that a reprisal will follow a particular act of whistleblowing. Moreover, it is already clear from Chapter 5 that some existing assumptions about likely sources of conflict and reprisal risk are misplaced. Effective appreciation of the risks, in individual cases, becomes important from a wide range of perspectives.

This chapter draws on the employee and internal witness surveys to identify those cases that might be considered at 'higher risk' of mistreatment and, in turn, the particular characteristics that contribute to the complexity of those cases. The core measure used is the third dimension studied in Chapter 5: whether respondents who reported wrongdoing said they felt themselves to have been treated well, the same or badly by management or by co-workers as a result of their whistleblowing.

The analysis is broken into three sections. First, the chapter continues an examination of the subjective elements of perceived mistreatment—in particular, the role of gaps between whistleblowers' expectations of what will happen and what actually happens. By analysing the relationships between whistleblowers' expectations about their treatment and the results, it is seen that employees often have expectations of positive treatment—no doubt reinforced by official efforts to encourage internal whistleblowing—that are not always met. It is also seen that this is not necessarily because the expectations are unrealistic. Whistleblowers are usually relatively accurate in self-assessing the reaction of co-workers to their disclosure, with their major problems arising in predicting the reaction of management. These results combine with those in the previous chapter to emphasise that whistleblowers are more likely to need support in navigating the management response to their disclosure, including the risk of management reprisals, than in anticipating and managing risks from co-workers. The implications of this are discussed further in the conclusion.

The second part of the chapter looks to the employee survey data to identify the 'risk factors' that point to circumstances in which it is more likely that a given disclosure will result in reported mistreatment. Logistic regression is used to compare public interest whistleblowers who do not report bad treatment (either from management or from co-workers) with those who do, across a range of variables. The result is a hierarchy of risk factors that agencies can use to identify those cases in which there is a higher likelihood of mistreatment. Where these factors combine, the proportion of whistleblowers who currently suffer mistreatment is very much higher than the average results indicated in Chapter 5. The key risk factors for whistleblower mistreatment by co-workers are identified, in order of significance, as:

1.  wrongdoing that is perceived as more serious
2.  lack of any positive outcome from investigation
3.  involvement of more than one person in the alleged wrongdoing
4.  situation of the whistleblower in a work group of less than 20 people.

The key risk factors for mistreatment by management are identified as:

1.  investigations that are not resolved internally and become external
2.  lack of any positive outcome from investigation
3.  wrongdoing directed at the whistleblower personally
4.  involvement of wrongdoers employed at a higher organisational level
5.  wrongdoing that is perceived as more serious and/or frequent.

The third part of this chapter reinforces this picture of reprisal risk factors, by undertaking two further comparisons. The analysis shows that a 'higher-risk' whistleblower could be considered to be one whose disclosure has not been substantiated and who has gone external to the organisation—yet, despite the odds, sometimes these report having been treated the same or well. What factors are associated with these cases, which do not turn out as badly as might be feared? Conversely, a 'lower-risk' whistleblower can be considered to be one who has been able to report internally and whose report is acted on with a positive substantive result. In theory, such whistleblowers should be easier for management to protect, however, some still report mistreatment, prompting the question: what crucial factors turn this potential success into a failure? These analyses confirm the salience of the factors listed above, providing new guidance on the processes that public agencies can use to better assess, reduce and manage the risks of whistleblower mistreatment.

## Expectations of treatment and support

Employees' experiences of reporting wrongdoing are shaped by objective and subjective elements: how they were really treated and how they feel they were treated. Outcomes also depend on the results relative to the expectations of employees about how they were likely to fare. As seen in Chapters 3 and 4, otherwise similar employees can arrive at very different assessments of how they will be treated, depending on the circumstances. This has direct implications for their differing decisions about whether to report and, if so, how to report. Their assessment of the risks also then shapes their interactions with authorities and colleagues and how they anticipate and manage their particular circumstances. Based on experience with public sector whistleblowers in Queensland, Anderson (1996) suggested that these different approaches to risk could place employees who observed wrongdoing in any one of a number of categories.

- **Risk avoiders**, who overestimate risks of reprisal, have low knowledge of or confidence in protection and are unlikely to come forward.
- **Risk managers**, who can realistically anticipate the risks and are more likely to come forward if they see a reasonable prospect of support.
- **Trusting** whistleblowers, who might anticipate a risk of reprisal but come forward expecting the risks to be lower than they perhaps are.
- **Naive** whistleblowers, who come forward unaware that there are risks of reprisal and who are therefore often at higher risk.
- **'Kamikaze'** whistleblowers, who come forward regardless of risk and therefore, depending on the circumstances, could be at very high risk.

Much of the employee survey data bear out this range of expectations. In Chapter 3, those who observed wrongdoing but took no action most often did so in circumstances in which there were obvious risks to be avoided, often for the explicit reason that that was the case. Table 6.1 extends this picture by comparing respondents' overall expectations about treatment and support, between all those who did not observe wrongdoing, those who observed but did not report and those who did report outside their role. The comparison confirms that those who did not report had lower than average expectations of support and higher than average expectations of mistreatment. Those who reported had slightly more negative attitudes again. This is another sign of the pattern that emerged from Chapters 3, 4 and 5—that even when they do not result in active mistreatment, the experiences of observing and reporting wrongdoing often result in a reduction in employees' trust and confidence in the organisation.

**Table 6.1 Comparison of expectations relating to risk of reprisals (mean)**

| 1 = strongly disagree<br>2 = disagree<br>3 = neither disagree/agree<br>4 = agree<br>5 = strongly agree | (a) Did not observe wrongdoing<br>(n = 2 114) | (b) Observed wrongdoing but did not report<br>(n = 3 245) | (b) Observed wrongdoing, reported outside role<br>(n = 1 470) | Total [a]<br>(n = 7 474) |
|---|---|---|---|---|
| **Management** is serious about protecting people who report wrongdoing | 3.45 | 3.04 | 2.93 | 3.17 |
| I am confident that my rights will be protected if I report wrongdoing and **am retaliated against** | 3.46 | 3.01 | 2.95 | 3.16 |
| I will suffer negative consequences from **management** for reporting wrongdoing | 2.53 | 2.91 | 3.01 | 2.78 |
| I will suffer negative consequences from **my fellow employees** for reporting wrongdoing | 2.75 | 3.10 | 3.13 | 2.97 |

[a] Includes role reporters and 30 reporters of whom it was unknown whether they could be classified as role or non-role reporters.
**Source:** Employee survey: Q18.

This pattern is also reinforced by Table 6.2, which shows the results for a range of attitudinal variables used in Chapters 3 and 4 for all public interest whistleblowers in the employee survey grouped according to their treatment. While the direction of any causality is again impossible to state, the most likely explanation for the significant differences is that the experience of reporting has impacted on personal attitudes to work, the organisation and others, more than the other way around. Equally important is the continuing lack of significant difference between the groups on many of these attitudinal variables (especially 'initiative' and 'industry') and the fact that even when differences occur, the results for whistleblowers who are treated badly remain at or above the mean. For example, on average, job satisfaction still does not fall into negative territory even for those treated badly by management. For those whistleblowers treated badly by management, the only organisational citizenship sub-scale on which this group scored lower was 'loyalty', which is again likely to be explained by their negative experience.

Just as Chapter 3 shows that personal attitudes cannot safely predict who will blow the whistle, these results confirm that they cannot be used to predict who will report that they suffered mistreatment. Overall, the data do not show that those whistleblowers who said they were mistreated were any more likely to be troublemakers, disgruntled employees or individuals predisposed to fall into conflict with management than those who were treated well or the same. While an existing history of poor performance, low job satisfaction and conflict with others would inevitably complicate any whistleblowing incident, there is no evidence that these are the typical features of the whistleblowers who report a bad experience.

**Table 6.2 Whistleblower treatment by whistleblower attitudes (mean)**

| Whistleblower attitudes<br>1 = very low to<br>5 = very high | (1a) Treated well/same by management<br>(n = 735) | (1b) Treated badly by management<br>(n = 160) | (2a) Treated well/same by co-workers<br>(n = 801) | (2b) Treated badly by co-workers<br>(n = 77) |
|---|---|---|---|---|
| Trust in management | 3.38**** | 2.44**** | 3.27**** | 2.58**** |
| Job satisfaction | 3.53**** | 3.01**** | 3.44* | 3.26* |
| Organisational citizenship behaviour | 3.84*** | 3.72*** | 3.81 | 3.86 |
| Helping co-workers | 4.01 | 4.07 | 4.00** | 4.15** |
| Initiative | 3.85 | 3.82 | 3.84 | 3.87 |
| Industry | 3.89 | 3.89 | 3.87 | 4.01 |
| Loyalty | 3.62**** | 3.14**** | 3.54 | 3.42 |

* difference statistically significant at $p < 0.05$
** difference statistically significant at $p < 0.01$
*** difference statistically significant at $p = 0.001$
**** difference statistically significant at $p < 0.0005$
**Source:** Employee survey: Q1, Q2.

The data in Tables 6.1 and 6.2 also reinforce the results from Chapters 3 and 4 that most whistleblowers enter into the process with a high degree of trust. Another feature of Table 6.1 is the extent to which all the expectations hover around the mean. This indicates that, while the bulk of respondents might not be harbouring strong fears about the organisational responses, they also do not appear to have a strong knowledge of or confidence in what those responses will be. It appears that a large proportion of public interest whistleblowers fall into the 'trusting whistleblower' category, with many also probably quite naive—for no fault of their own—about the processes involved.

Table 6.3 compares the same respondents according to the reasons they gave for reporting the wrongdoing, including some more specific indicators of their confidence that they would be supported or protected (bolded items). Whistleblowers who were mistreated placed a higher level of importance on all reasons than those who were not mistreated. On some variables, this could reflect the nature of the wrongdoing (for example, the fact that it was more serious), but the pattern could also suggest that individuals with negative experiences hold a stronger opinion about the importance of their act of whistleblowing, whether before or after they suffer mistreatment (or both). Most importantly, while expectations of support and protection remained only second-order reasons for reporting, they were stated as significantly more important for those who were then treated badly (especially by management) than for those treated the same or well. In other words, at least in retrospect, whistleblowers who were treated badly also appeared to have had higher original expectations about support and lower expectations that they would be left exposed to risks.

These results show that a higher degree of trust or naivety regarding the risk of a bad experience is probably a very good indicator that such a risk will be realised. In many respects, this stands to reason and comes as a reminder of the many subjective elements in any individual's assessment of the outcome. Lower expectations are by definition usually more easily met and outcomes are therefore regarded as relatively good; but if expectations are high, meeting them is more complex and an identical outcome could be seen as relatively bad. As seen in Chapter 5, small misunderstandings or failures in communication about the response to a disclosure can be enough to begin a breakdown in trust from which it is difficult to recover.

**Table 6.3 Whistleblower treatment by reasons for reporting (mean)**

| 1 = not at all important<br>2 = somewhat important<br>3 = very important<br>4 = extremely important | (1a) Treated well/same by management<br>(n = 647) | (1b) Treated badly by management<br>(n = 147) | (2a) Treated well/same by co-workers<br>(n = 721) | (2b) Treated badly by co-workers<br>(n = 73) |
|---|---|---|---|---|
| I saw it as my ethical responsibility to report it | 3.15**** | 3.41**** | 3.16*** | 3.48*** |
| The wrongdoing was serious enough | 2.97**** | 3.32**** | 3.00**** | 3.32**** |
| I had evidence to support my report | 2.91**** | 3.32**** | 2.95**** | 3.38**** |
| I believed that my report would help to correct the problem | 3.04* | 3.21* | 3.04** | 3.34** |
| **I thought that I would be supported by management** | 2.83* | 2.99* | 2.82*** | 3.19*** |
| I knew who I should report to | 2.85 | 2.97 | 2.83*** | 3.16*** |
| **I thought that I would be supported by my co-workers** | 2.58**** | 2.93**** | 2.64 | 2.78 |
| I believed I was under a legal responsibility to report it | 2.63* | 2.86* | 2.62**** | 3.09**** |
| **I believed I would have legal protection if I reported** | 2.36**** | 2.79**** | 2.41**** | 2.87**** |
| I trusted the person I should report to | 2.92* | 2.72* | 2.87 | 2.95 |

* difference statistically significant at p < 0.05
** difference statistically significant at p < 0.01
*** difference statistically significant at p = 0.001
**** difference statistically significant at p < 0.0005
Source: Employee survey: Q27.

The problem for agencies is that efforts to promote a higher consciousness of the risks among employees, before they report, will succeed only in converting potential whistleblowers into 'risk avoiders' who do not report at all. In other words, the encouragement of reporting relies on encouraging employees to be trusting, but this in itself will encourage higher expectations than might otherwise be held.

The only relief from this catch-22 situation is to ensure that there is an accurate assessment of the risks of mistreatment as soon as an employee makes a disclosure, in a manner that encourages whistleblowers and those responsible for them to proceed to manage these risks with a shared understanding. The importance of this risk-management approach has already been shown by the data in Chapter 5, which showed a mismatch between the outcomes of greatest apparent importance to whistleblowers and the assessments of most case-handlers and managers.

The need for such an approach is also underscored by the evidence of significant differences between the assessments reached by employees about the risk of mistreatment by their co-workers and the risk of mistreatment by managers. As seen in Chapter 5, until now, it has been widely believed that reprisals against whistleblowers are more likely to come from co-workers than from management. The results in Tables 6.1 and 6.3 confirm that this expectation is shared by many whistleblowers themselves. The analysis of outcomes in Chapter 5, however, reveal that co-workers per se are only infrequently the main sources of bad treatment or harm against those who do blow the whistle, with management more likely to be the main source of perceived mistreatment in practice. A contrasting result in Chapter 3 was that, in a majority of cases in which a fear of reprisal was given as a reason for not reporting, supervisors and managers were implicated in the wrongdoing.

These contrasting data suggest that while 'risk avoiders' who do not report are particularly conscious of the risk of mistreatment by management, the large body of more 'trusting' whistleblowers typically underestimates this risk. Results from the internal witness survey add to this picture. Table 6.4 sets out how all respondents to this survey answered further questions about their expectations of good and bad treatment. Unlike the employee survey respondents, this particular group said that they anticipated mistreatment by management as being more likely than mistreatment by co-workers. In other respects, however, their expectations appear relatively typical. Table 6.5 then shows the relationship between the level of support expected by internal witness respondents from management and co-workers respectively and their experience of how they were ultimately treated. There was a very strong inverse relationship between expecting support from co-workers and mistreatment by co-workers ($p < 0.001$), meaning that these expectations were usually right: if a reporter had low expectations of support from co-workers, they were more likely to report bad treatment from them.

The same was not true in relation to management. There was no identifiable relationship between the level of support expected by reporters from management and how they were treated. Clearly, on the whole, the reactions of management were more negative than reporters anticipated. The most crucial result, however, is that, notwithstanding the importance of the management reaction to their prospects, the same reporters were far less able to accurately predict the reaction of management.

### Table 6.4 Internal witness expectations of support, reprisals and protection (per cent and mean)

| | (1)<br>Not at all | (2)<br>Not very | (3)<br>Somewhat | (4)<br>Very | (5)<br>Extremely | Mean<br>(SD) |
|---|---|---|---|---|---|---|
| How supportive did you expect management to be?[a] | 14 (30) | 15 (32) | 16 (34) | 32 (67) | 24 (50) | **3.35**<br>(1.36) |
| How supportive did you expect immediate co-workers to be?[a] | 10 (22) | 14 (29) | 21 (44) | 35 (75) | 20 (43) | **3.41**<br>(1.24) |
| How likely did you think it was that managers would take action against you? | 21 (45) | 28 (60) | 22 (47) | 16 (33) | 13 (28) | **2.71**<br>(1.32) |
| How likely did you think it was that co-workers would take action against you? | 31 (65) | 31 (66) | 22 (46) | 11 (23) | 6 (13) | **2.31**<br>(1.19) |
| How likely did you think it was that you would be effectively protected? | 14 (30) | 26 (55) | 28 (60) | 21 (44) | 11 (24) | **2.89**<br>(1.21) |

[a] Correlation between expectation of management and co-worker support is statistically significant (Pearson $r = 0.404$; $p < 0.0005$).
**Source:** Internal witness survey: Q17, Q18, Q20, Q21, Q22 (n = 213).

### Table 6.5 Relationship between expectations of support and treatment

| Relationship between... | | Correlation |
|---|---|---|
| Expectation of management support<br>1 = not at all to 5 = extremely likely | Treatment by management[a]<br>1 = extremely well to 5 = extremely badly | Pearson $r = 0.040$<br>Not sig. at $p = 0.562$<br>(n = 211) |
| Expectation of co-worker support<br>1 = not at all to 5 = extremely likely | Treatment by co-workers[a]<br>1 = extremely well to 5 = extremely badly | Pearson $r = -0.375$<br>Sig. at $p < 0.0005$<br>(n = 208) |

[a] It was anticipated that these correlations would be negative because these outcome scales run from a good outcome scoring lowest to a poor outcome scoring highest.
**Source:** Internal witness survey: Q17, Q18, Q50, Q51.

In summary, while employees' judgments of risk appear rational, there are limits on the extent to which employees who report wrongdoing can be expected to self-assess and self-manage these risks in a comprehensive manner. The nature of the process dictates that many whistleblowers will be trusting or somewhat naive about the risks of mistreatment, because otherwise they will be more likely to follow a risk-avoidance path and simply not report. Most whistleblowers are nevertheless capable of accurately assessing the risks of mistreatment from their co-workers and are therefore better placed to manage these risks from the outset. The data suggest, however, that, just as many case-handlers and managers might not have an accurate assessment of the issues of most importance to whistleblowers, many whistleblowers might have difficulty anticipating when management is likely to react negatively to a report of wrongdoing, or otherwise fail to deliver the promised support.

There are many possible reasons why management reactions can be difficult to anticipate. Employees know from firsthand experience about the attitudes and personalities of their co-workers, but they might have little or no knowledge of the complex ways in which organisations must often handle investigations. They might report wrongdoing without realising that managers were involved or were already aware of the wrongdoing but had allowed it to continue. Even when employees have reason to believe that some managers will recognise that a problem needs to be fixed, they might not be aware of the extent to which others will see its exposure as potentially embarrassing.

These results emphasise the considerable extent to which the accurate, objective assessment of risk is a precondition for the effective management of many whistleblowing incidents. Unless an agreed understanding is reached about the sources and levels of risk from an early point in the reporting process, the prospects for successfully managing either the expectations or the real experiences of whistleblowers are immediately more doubtful. Risk assessment is crucial to closing the gaps in whistleblowers' understanding of how others might perceive their report and reducing the potential for conflict, including conflict with management about whether effective support was provided.

## Risk factors for mistreatment of whistleblowers

Clearly not all whistleblowing cases need to be managed equally intensively. Part of the utility of a risk-assessment approach is in helping identify which cases are more likely to warrant early intervention and active management. From the previous section, it can be seen that one indicator of high risk is subjective: the risk that expectations will not be met is naturally higher whenever a whistleblower has unrealistically low expectations about the chances of adverse reactions. At the same time, there could be other more objective indicators of risk.

In the United States, a number of studies have sought to identify the factors that predict retaliation against whistleblowers (Near and Miceli 1996; Miceli et al. 1999). Near and Miceli (1996) classified the predictors of retaliation into four categories.

1. **Personal characteristics of the whistleblower** and of the job situation that influence retaliation (for example, gender and other demographic variables; personality and other individual difference variables, such as OCB).
2. **Organisational variables** that are concerned with the context in which whistleblowing occurs and are relatively enduring characteristics of the

organisation or the reporter's work group (for example, size of organisation/work group, structure, ethical culture).

3.  **Characteristics of the wrongdoing** (for example, seriousness, systematic), which will affect the process by which reporting occurs and is responded to (for example, provision of support, external reporting).

4.  The **power and status of the wrongdoer**, which can influence whether the organisation protects or sanctions them (for example, seniority, tenure in the organisation).

The relative importance of each of these factors was considered in a sample of federally employed reporters (Miceli et al. 1999). Whistleblowers who suffered retaliation did not reliably differ from other whistleblowers in terms of most personal characteristics, such as age, gender, race, tenure in the organisation, pay, being a professional and so on. Whistleblowers with negative experiences, however, often felt that they had less support than others from managers and supervisors (notably, not from co-workers) and they were more likely to have used external channels to report the wrongdoing, rather than internal channels exclusively. The seriousness of the wrongdoing was also a fairly consistent predictor of retaliation.

Alternatively, an interview study of private sector employees indicated that no special method of disclosure or personal characteristics insulated whistleblowers from reprisals (Rothschild and Miethe 1999), while research in a large military base found that only gender predicted reprisals: women were more likely to suffer retaliation than men (Near et al. 2004). While these studies suggest a number of important factors to consider, they highlight the fact that predictors of poor treatment differ depending on the context in which the whistleblowing occurs. Which predictors of poor treatment appear to have currency in the context of the Australian public sector?

To examine the level of association between various risk factors and the poor treatment of whistleblowers, further analysis was conducted into the data provided by all public interest whistleblowers in the employee survey (n = 913). A logistic regression technique[1] was used to identify the relative importance of a range of variables in those cases that resulted in perceived mistreatment. By simultaneously controlling for a number of factors, logistic regression can identify the unique effect that each factor has on the variable(s) of interest—in this case, bad treatment by managers or co-workers. While the analysis cannot show causality, it shows where there is a strong association between a particular outcome and particular factors, helping identify not only the significant factors in isolation, but their relative significance in combination.

A large group of risk factors from the employee survey was selected for inclusion in the analysis based on previous studies and preliminary findings. This consisted of a variety of personal, organisational, wrongdoing and power characteristics.[2]

A first analysis established the extent to which each of these variables helped predict the likelihood of a respondent belonging to one of two groups: 1) those who said they were treated badly by co-workers; and 2) those who said they were treated the same or well by co-workers. The analysis was then repeated for the more complex problem of mistreatment by management, recognising that reprisals stemming from these two groups could have different explanatory factors.

## Mistreatment by co-workers

After adjusting for all variables in the model, the risk factors found to be significantly associated with poor treatment by co-workers are shown in Table 6.6. The column of particular note in this table is the 'odds ratio': this presents the probability of a public interest whistleblower experiencing poor treatment divided by the probability of them experiencing good or similar treatment. An odds ratio greater than 1 indicates higher odds of poor treatment.

The findings highlight four key risk factors associated with the poor treatment of whistleblowers by co-workers. The odds of being treated badly by co-workers were:

1. three and a half times greater when the wrongdoing was perceived to be more serious
2. more than three times greater if the report of wrongdoing did not have a positive outcome (that is, things did not become better as a result of investigation into the report)
3. more than two and a half times greater when more than one person was involved in the alleged wrongdoing
4. more than twice as great when the size of the whistleblower's work group was less than 20 people.

**Table 6.6 Risk factors for poor treatment of whistleblowers by co-workers[3]**

| Risk factors | Coefficient ($\beta$) | Standard error | Wald $\chi^2$ | P-value | Odds ratio | 95% CI |
|---|---|---|---|---|---|---|
| The wrongdoing was serious | 1.25 | 0.27 | 20.85 | < 0.0005 | **3.49** | 2.04–6.00 |
| No positive outcome from investigation | 1.17 | 0.36 | 10.78 | 0.001 | **3.23** | 1.60–6.50 |
| More than one person involved in wrongdoing | 1.02 | 0.35 | 8.52 | 0.004 | **2.77** | 1.40–5.47 |
| Size of immediate work group < 20 people | 0.75 | 0.37 | 4.16 | 0.041 | **2.12** | 1.03–4.37 |

Source: Employee survey: Q22, Q24, Q33, Q49 (n = 488).

This group of risk factors confirms much of what was already suspected regarding the 9 per cent of whistleblowers identified in Chapter 5 as reporting co-worker mistreatment. It is also consistent with the conclusions in the previous section, that the major factors associated with the risk of co-worker reprisal are readily apparent to most whistleblowers and are more likely to be accurately assessed by them.

In particular, it makes sense that reporters who observed wrongdoing involving more than one person had greater odds of poor treatment, given the power inequality between a group of wrongdoers and a sole reporter and the increased likelihood that the wrongdoing had become part of the workplace culture. Similarly, when the size of the reporter's immediate workgroup is smaller, there is greater opportunity for direct or indirect reprisals (given the likely higher level of workplace interaction with the wrongdoer[s]) and there is more likely to be an environment conducive to them. These are indicators of a classically stereotypical reprisal situation.

The top two factors nevertheless have more interesting implications. Chapter 5 discussed a range of explanations for why a positive substantive outcome, such as substantiation of the report, played such a pivotal role in shaping the overall outcome of the whistleblowing incident. One explanation was that whistleblowers whose reports did not lead to positive action could be inclined to regard that result as itself constituting bad treatment—that is, they were simply dissatisfied. Given the overall pattern of results in Chapter 5, however, and the personal attitudinal variables in the previous section, this explanation would appear to fit only a limited number of cases. Moreover, this procedural dissatisfaction is not likely to be directed at their co-workers, but rather at the management processes responsible for the investigation result, as discussed further below.

A more salient explanation, therefore, is that in a range of circumstances, unless there is formal substantiation or other positive action that vindicates their report, the whistleblower could be 'fair game' for direct or indirect reprisals. At present, it appears that many internal whistleblowers are left in the position of having to emerge either as a 'winner' or 'loser' from the experience, rather than being left with the possibility of a more neutral outcome. In these situations, achieving substantive vindication becomes a primary factor in avoiding mistreatment, which could explain the degree of dependence on a positive substantive result described in Chapter 5.

The salience of this factor is reinforced by the role of the seriousness of the wrongdoing. It was hypothesised that more serious wrongdoing, once exposed, might not necessarily lead to a greater risk of co-worker reprisal because others were also more likely to share the whistleblowers' view of the seriousness of the matter. Conversely, it was thought that more petty matters could lead to higher reprisal risk, because co-workers would be more likely to agree with the alleged wrongdoer that the matter should never have been reported. This analysis confirms, however, that the more serious the perceived wrongdoing, the higher is the likelihood of co-worker reprisal, presumably because of the more serious consequences for the wrongdoers. Clearly, this risk then becomes extreme when the allegation is also not substantiated.

Two further hypotheses were also not supported by this analysis. Logically, some types of alleged wrongdoing could be thought to be more likely to trigger reprisal risks, depending on the impact of the allegations on the perceived wrongdoer. In Chapter 5, it was also pointed out that certain types of wrongdoing were more likely to be substantiated than others. This analysis shows, however, that it is these other factors—seriousness and lack of substantiation—that are associated most closely with co-worker mistreatment, irrespective of what type of wrongdoing is involved. In other words, while some types of wrongdoing can be objectively considered more 'serious' and also more difficult to substantiate, it is not the wrongdoing type itself but these results that dictate whether mistreatment is likely to follow. Any kind of wrongdoing can therefore give rise to these risks, depending on the circumstances.

Contrary to expectations, the level of confidentiality maintained in respect of the whistleblowing incident also failed to emerge as a significant predictor of mistreatment. In total, 83 per cent of whistleblowers who said that they were treated well or the same by co-workers and by management said that either 'no-one' or just 'a few' people knew they had reported the wrongdoing—compared with 63 per cent of those who were treated badly by co-workers, management or both. The fact that confidentiality did not emerge as a clear protective factor confirms that while it could be important, in most circumstances, it is either simply unachievable or plays no protective role. For example, even if only a few people ever know the whistleblower's identity, this usually includes the people most directly concerned. This result has significant implications for the strategies that agencies use to try to control reprisal risk and, in particular, the need for agencies to be ready with other intervention strategies at the point that confidentiality ceases to be practical.

## Mistreatment by management

The second analysis examined the risk factors for mistreatment for those employee survey whistleblowers who indicated poor treatment from management (as distinct from co-workers). The results are set out in Table 6.7. The findings confirmed that, for the 18 per cent of whistleblowers who reported mistreatment by management, the factors associated with this result were more complex. Six key risk factors emerged, only two of which were common to mistreatment by co-workers. The odds of being treated badly by management were:

1. more than four and a half times greater in cases in which the investigation of wrongdoing did not remain internal to the organisation but progressed externally

2.  four times greater if the report of wrongdoing did not have a positive outcome (that is, things did not become better as a result of investigation into the report)
3.  three and a half times greater when reporters become aware of the wrongdoing because it was directed at them rather than via other avenues
4.  more than two and a half times greater when some or all of the wrongdoers were employed at a higher organisational level than the whistleblower
5&6. also increased when the wrongdoing was perceived by the reporter to be serious or frequent.

**Table 6.7 Risk factors for poor treatment of whistleblowers by management**

| Risk factors | Coefficient (β) | Standard error | Wald $\chi^2$ | P-value | Odds ratio | 95% CI |
|---|---|---|---|---|---|---|
| Investigation not kept internal | 1.54 | 0.35 | 19.52 | < 0.0005 | **4.65** | 2.35–9.20 |
| No positive outcome from investigation | 1.41 | 0.32 | 19.07 | < 0.0005 | **4.11** | 2.18–7.74 |
| Reporter became aware of wrongdoing because it was directed at them | 1.26 | 0.31 | 16.81 | < 0.0005 | **3.52** | 1.93–6.43 |
| The wrongdoer was at a higher level | 1.00 | 0.30 | 11.14 | 0.001 | **2.72** | 1.51–4.88 |
| The wrongdoing was serious | 0.59 | 0.21 | 8.14 | 0.004 | **1.80** | 1.20–2.70 |
| The wrongdoing was frequent | 0.40 | 0.16 | 6.34 | 0.012 | **1.48** | 1.09–2.02 |

Source: Employee survey: Q21, Q22, Q23, Q25, Q28, Q33 (n = 496).

The strongest common factor was the lack of any positive investigation result. This becomes an even stronger predictor of managerial mistreatment than of co-worker mistreatment. Its salience further confirms that, while some whistleblowers might be more likely than others to be dissatisfied by an unfavourable investigation result or push the matter in a way that generates more conflict, this is often likely to be the case because of the crucial protective value of achieving some form of vindication (fighting to emerge as a 'winner' rather than a 'loser'). The second common factor—the perceived seriousness of wrongdoing—was still present but not as important. This suggests that co-workers perhaps cannot be bothered reacting negatively in less serious matters, but that adverse management reactions can also flow in response to less serious matters, even though it is still more likely when the matters are serious.

The most dominant risk factor—the fact that managerial mistreatment is strongly associated with external reporting—combines with the issue of a substantive result to highlight again that any causality can run in either direction. Chapter 4 showed that most external whistleblowers had reported internally in the first instance. Therefore, it is likely that many whistleblowers are triggered to continue to pursue a disclosure externally because they experienced mistreatment within their organisation or because their claim could not be substantiated internally, or both. While it is more than possible that some whistleblowers experience mistreatment only after they disclose externally, in most cases, it can be presumed that external reporting follows the onset of reprisals or other conflict between the whistleblower and management, with external involvement then perhaps contributing to this real or perceived mistreatment in many cases.

This result nevertheless emphasises that in current circumstances—irrespective of the cause—by the time disclosures reach outside the organisation involved, crucial damage to the wellbeing of the whistleblower has often been done. This is further emphasised by the fact that this risk factor was not present for mistreatment by co-workers, but was the strongest of all factors associated with managerial mistreatment. These results further increase the obligations on agencies to manage their investigation and employee welfare processes actively and positively in the first instance. Failure to do so simply increases the likelihood of breakdowns in trust, external complaints and increasingly entrenched conflicts—all of which can have negative impacts on the organisation as well as any chance of a return to normality for the whistleblower.

The same results also support the conclusion that additional processes are needed to circumvent or reduce this risk of conflict, wherever internal processes are more likely to be tested by particular cases. Taken together, the remainder of the factors identify these classes of cases, in which the potential for internal processes to bring the matter to a successful conclusion is clearly more limited, at least without special measures or outside assistance. For example, it stands to reason that when a whistleblower reports a more serious or systemic matter, implicating managers, but an investigation does not or is not likely to resolve the matter in the whistleblower's 'favour', there is a very high risk that managerial action (or inaction) will occur that constitutes real or perceived mistreatment. This is clearly also compounded if the whistleblower feels that they are directly personally involved, with their capacity to independently self-manage the risks even further reduced, than if they are simply an observer or bystander.

Taken together, these factors emphasise why agencies need special processes for dealing with the welfare of the whistleblower and addressing the potential sources of conflict, outside the normal management chain. They also suggest the need for processes that monitor management responses to the whistleblower, before conflicts emerge or become too difficult to control. These issues, including the question of how earlier routine oversight by external integrity agencies might assist this process, are taken up in later chapters.

Again, it is salient that neither the wrongdoing type nor lack of confidentiality emerged as risk factors in this second analysis. Wrongdoing type could still remain indirectly relevant: not only are certain types of wrongdoing more likely to be substantiated than others, as shown in Chapter 5, certain types are more likely to come to the attention of whistleblowers as a result of having been directed at them personally, as shown in Chapter 3. It is, however, once again these other factors—lack of positive investigation outcome, personal involvement and, to a lesser extent, seriousness and frequency—that are most closely associated with management mistreatment, irrespective of what type of wrongdoing is involved. The absence of confidentiality as a protective factor is even less surprising than it is for co-worker mistreatment, given that, even if only a few people know, these are likely to be people in the management chain and are therefore well placed to undertake or be blamed for any reprisals.

The other very logical factor, confirming the realistic nature of these results, is that of the power differential between reporters and perceived wrongdoers. If more senior people are implicated, irrespective of their own level in the organisation, a whistleblower has double the chance of experiencing mistreatment from management, absent of any other factors. The lack of this factor in respect of co-worker mistreatment is perhaps unsurprising, but the difference tends to confirm that, overall, agencies have difficulty responding to upwards challenges to the integrity or competence of their own management. When other factors such as seriousness, frequency, personal involvement and difficulties in substantiation also combine, the risk of mistreatment is plainly extreme.

Taking both analyses together, it is clear that these very different listings of risk factors mean that the risks of mistreatment from each source need to be separated and independently assessed. The differences accord with the finding from Chapter 5 that only 5 per cent of whistleblowers experience negative treatment from both management and co-workers. The remaining 17 per cent of whistleblowers who recorded mistreatment perceived it as coming from either one or the other. The fact that the single largest group—13 per cent of all whistleblowers—perceived the mistreatment as coming from management alone, and that the risk factors for this group were more numerous, more complex and in some instances stronger in terms of significance, confirms that this is a major area for further inquiry and investment.

## Against-the-odds outcomes

Chapter 5 stressed the crucial role of managers in shaping whistleblowing outcomes through their important influences on whether or not public sector employees would ultimately view reporting in a positive or negative light. The previous section found two key risk factors associated with managerial responses that come to be perceived as mistreatment, increasing the likelihood by a magnitude of four that a whistleblower will perceive their treatment this way: first, if for whatever reason the reporting path has gone external, and second, if the event has failed to result in a positive substantive outcome. This second risk factor was also prominent among those associated with co-worker mistreatment, where its presence made the odds of poor treatment more than three times greater.

The final analyses in this section use these high-risk indicators to identify any factors associated with employee survey cases at the extreme ends of the risk spectrum. First, an analysis can be undertaken to examine the cases of 'higher-risk' respondents for whom both these high risk factors were present, but who, against the odds, did not record mistreatment by co-workers and/or management. By comparing these 'higher-risk, good-outcome' respondents with higher-risk respondents who recorded the more predictable bad outcomes, it is possible to identify any reasons why even in difficult cases some reporters manage to emerge relatively unscathed.

Second, the reverse analysis can be undertaken to examine 'lower-risk' respondents who reported wrongdoing, for whom neither of the high risk factors were present and whose cases should therefore have been much easier for agencies to manage to a positive conclusion, yet who nevertheless still recorded mistreatment. By comparing these 'lower-risk, bad-outcome' respondents with lower-risk respondents who did not record bad outcomes, it is possible to identify some reasons why even more straightforward cases still result in problems. Both analyses provide insights into how whistleblowing cases might be better managed.

Because the groups in each case are relatively small, these analyses are not limited to public interest whistleblowers; rather, they take in all non-role reporters, including those who reported personnel and workplace grievances. The extent to which this can influence the outcome is discussed. As the statistical tests for this section could not be repeated using logistic regression, alternative significance tests were used.

## Positive treatment of higher-risk reporters

When employees who report wrongdoing are at higher risk of mistreatment but, against the odds, do not record it, are there distinctive factors that explain these better-than-expected outcomes? Such cases are clearly valuable for their potential insights into how whistleblowers might be more effectively protected in a wide range of high-risk situations. In these cases, the report did not result in any substantive improvement in relation to the alleged wrongdoing, despite the reporter having pursued the matter outside the organisation, yet the reporter recorded being treated well or the same by co-workers and management as a result of the process.

Table 6.8 sets out the features of this group, comparing first those who recorded good and bad treatment by management, and secondly those who recorded good and bad treatment by co-workers. The group is small (n = 105), making up less than 7 per cent of all reporters. Nevertheless, these respondents were spread widely across the employee survey agencies, suggesting this less common combination of outcomes could potentially arise in any agency. Despite the fact that the analysis now includes all reporters, including those whose reports concerned personnel or workplace grievances, all the risk factors identified in the previous section hold, but now in reverse. For those treated well, it remained the case that the wrongdoing was perceived as less serious, occurred less frequently, was less likely to have been directed at the reporter personally, was less likely to have involved multiple wrongdoers or wrongdoers more senior than the reporter and involved an immediate work unit of 20 or more people.

Only one new factor emerged as providing additional 'protection' for reporters, further reducing the likelihood of mistreatment by co-workers, notwithstanding the otherwise high risks of this occurring. This factor was the reporter's age, with reporters who escaped mistreatment by co-workers being significantly older (mean of 46 years) than those who recorded mistreatment (mean of 40 years). This result suggests that, again, power differentials are in play, with older employees better able to ride out the storm even when the risks of mistreatment are otherwise high. In all other respects, however, no magic answer emerged from this analysis. This result confirms that, if agencies are to minimise the risks of whistleblower mistreatment, this can reliably be pursued only through policies and processes that offset the many situational and outcome variables that currently contribute to poor outcomes and by actively intervening in the normal operations of the organisation, rather than letting 'natural' organisational processes take hold.

**Table 6.8 Significant factors for treatment of higher-risk reporters (mean, per cent)**

| Risk factor | Means and frequencies | | | |
|---|---|---|---|---|
| | (1a) Treated well/same by management (n = 33) | (1b) Treated badly by management (n = 71) | (2a) Treated well/same by co-workers (n = 81) | (2b) Treated badly by co-workers (n = 24) |
| **The wrongdoing was frequent** | | | | |
| 1 = just this once | 3.24** | 3.82** | 3.52* | 4.04* |
| 5 = all the time | | | | |
| **The age of the wrongdoer** (years) | n.s. | n.s. | **46.21*** | **40.23*** |
| **How became aware of wrongdoing?** | | | | |
| Directed at me (n = 60) | 15% (9)*** | 85% (51)*** | n.s. | n.s. |
| Not directed at me (n = 44) | 55% (24)*** | 45% (20)*** | n.s. | n.s. |
| **How many people involved?** | | | | |
| One (n = 19) | n.s. | n.s. | 95% (18)* | 5% (1)* |
| A few/large number/ widespread (n = 85) | n.s. | n.s. | 73% (62)* | 27% (23)* |
| **Position of wrongdoer** | | | | |
| Below or at same level (n = 23) | 57% (13)** | 44% (10)** | n.s. | n.s. |
| Higher level (n = 81) | 25% (20)** | 75% (61)** | n.s. | n.s. |
| **Size of immediate work group** | | | | |
| Less than 20 (n = 57) | 21% (12)* | 79% (45)* | n.s. | n.s. |
| 20 or more (n = 46) | 43% (20)* | 57% (26)* | n.s. | n.s. |

n.s. = not significant
* difference statistically significant at $p < 0.05$
** difference statistically significant at $p < 0.01$
*** difference statistically significant at $p < 0.0005$
Source: Employee survey: Q21, Q23, Q24, Q25, Q39, Q49.

## Negative treatment of low-risk reporters

When employees who report wrongdoing are at lower risk of mistreatment but nevertheless still record it, are there distinctive factors that continue to explain these worst of all outcomes? Such cases might be considered a classic 'reprisal scenario', in which the reporter loyally kept the matter internal to the organisation and regarded their report as having been vindicated, but they were still made to suffer. In this case, the perception of mistreatment cannot be attributed simply to whistleblower dissatisfaction with the outcome, because there is less basis for conflict about the truth of the matter or frustration over inaction. What factors are associated with these outcomes?

Table 6.9 sets out the features of this group, comparing first those who recorded good and bad treatment by management and, second, those who recorded good and bad treatment by co-workers. Despite the fact that the analysis now includes all reporters, all the risk factors identified in the previous section still hold. For those treated poorly, it remained the case that the wrongdoing was perceived as more serious, occurred more frequently, was more likely to have been directed at the reporter personally and involved wrongdoers more senior than the reporter, with more than one wrongdoer involved.

**Table 6.9 Significant factors for treatment of lower-risk reporters (mean, per cent)**

| Factor | Mean and frequencies | | | |
|---|---|---|---|---|
| | (1a) Treated well/same by management (n = 390) | (1b) Treated badly by management (n = 20) | (2a) Treated well/same by co-workers (n = 390) | (2b) Treated badly by co-workers (n = 20) |
| **The wrongdoing was serious** 1 = not at all, 5 = extremely | 3.89** | 4.45** | 3.88**** | 4.63**** |
| **The wrongdoing was frequent** 1 = just this once, 5 = all the time | 2.64** | 3.30** | n.s. | n.s. |
| **How became aware of wrongdoing?** | | | | |
| Directed at me (n = 104) | 89% (92)**** | 12% (12)**** | n.s. | n.s. |
| Not directed at me (n = 306) | 97% (298)**** | 3% (8)**** | n.s. | n.s. |
| **How many people involved?** | | | | |
| One (n = 215) | n.s. | n.s. | 98% (211)** | 2% (4)** |
| A few/large number/ widespread (n = 183) | n.s. | n.s. | 92% (168)** | 8% (15)** |
| **Position of wrongdoer** | | | | |
| Below or at same level (n = 253) | 98% (248)**** | 2% (5)**** | 98% (244)*** | 2% (5)*** |
| Higher level (n = 149) | 90% (134)**** | 10% (15)**** | 90% (132)*** | 10% (14)*** |
| **Number of reporting stages** | | | | |
| Only 1 (n = 236) | 98% (231)** | 2% (5)** | 97% (222)* | 3% (6)* |
| More than 1 (n = 174) | 91% (159)** | 9% (15)** | 93% (161)* | 8% (13)* |
| **Investigation into report** | | | | |
| Yes (n = 385) | 96% (369)** | 4% (16)** | n.s. | n.s. |
| No/don't know (n = 21) | 81% (17)** | 19% (4)** | n.s. | n.s. |
| **Employment status** | | | | |
| Full-time (n = 358) | 96% (344)* | 4% (14)* | n.s. | n.s. |
| Part-time/contractor/ casual (n = 52) | 89% (46)* | 12% (6)* | n.s. | n.s. |

n.s. = not significant
* difference statistically significant at p < 0.05
** difference statistically significant at p < 0.01
*** difference statistically significant at p = 0.001
**** difference statistically significant at p < 0.0005
**Source:** Employee survey: Q21–5, Q28, Q33, Q46.

Three previously unidentified factors also appear to be significant in the poor outcomes of these lower-risk reporters. As none of these appears unique to personnel or workplace grievances, they can also be used to interpret the results for public interest wrongdoing.

First, even though all reporting remained internal for these groups, reporters were more likely to record mistreatment by management and co-workers if their report went through a larger number of internal stages before leading to positive action. When the number of internal reporting stages was restricted to one, reporters were much less likely to indicate poor treatment. This supports Miceli and Near's (1988) finding that allegations of wrongdoing that were resolved after the first report were less likely to be associated with reprisals, but that whistleblowers who were required to make their allegations in successive reports (usually to higher levels of authority) were more likely to experience retaliation. These findings further reinforce the importance of a competent initial response to a disclosure, preventing the need for a second or further report, if the chances of protecting even lower-risk whistleblowers are to be maximised. Given the evidence in Chapter 4 that most employees' first reaction is to report wrongdoing to their supervisor or another manager, irrespective of whether this is always wise, the importance of the first investigative response also reinforces the need for agencies to increase efforts for ensuring that disclosures reach the right place.

Second, the likelihood of lower-risk reporters recording management mistreatment was increased when—even though the problem was addressed—this was either without a formal investigation or without any of which the reporter was aware. When the reporter was confident that an investigation was held or, in other words, that it was their disclosure that led to the matter being addressed, close to only one in 20 from this group recorded managerial mistreatment. The mistreatment rate increased, however, to one in five of the group if the disclosure was either not investigated or the response was unknown. Given that the entire group believed that overall things became better in the organisation, it is likely that there was an investigation or other action, but clearly these reporters were not kept informed of its progress or outcome.

This result is consistent with the evidence in Chapter 5 that a failure to keep whistleblowers informed of the organisational response can contribute directly to stress and other negative outcomes. It is also likely to be an indicator of an environment conducive to direct reprisals, given that the whistleblower has not been armed with the information necessary to claim vindication and, indeed, management might have addressed the problem without any recognition or support of the whistleblower whatsoever. This result can therefore indicate a situation in which the whistleblower is correct but is either 'left in limbo' or 'hung out to dry'.

The third additional factor is the employment basis of the reporter. Lower-risk reporters who were nevertheless still treated badly by management were more than three times more likely to be employed on a part-time, casual or contract basis. Even when the level of conflict surrounding a report is otherwise low, the reporter's relative position in the organisational structure continues to be a major risk factor for reprisal. This result is consistent with other more general findings, here and elsewhere (Miceli et al. 1999), that the power of a whistleblower relative to that of wrongdoers is a direct determinant of the likelihood of negative treatment. When considering which cases deserve additional support and protection, it is imperative that agencies focus on low-status employees even when the risks otherwise appear low.

This section has highlighted that, for those whistleblowers with extreme levels of risk (either high or low), a number of additional risk factors come into play. If an investigation into a disclosure is kept internal to the organisation and things become better as a result, this ordinarily suggests a good outcome for the whistleblower; this group can therefore be considered 'low-risk' reporters. These analyses show, however, that, even if an investigation is conducted internally and is resolved, it is important that this occurs as early as possible (so that the whistleblower does not have to report more than once, if at all possible) and for the whistleblower's role to be recognised through advice and information. For high-risk whistleblowers (those with an unsuccessful outcome, in which the investigation was external to the organisation at some point), the results reinforce that the key to obtaining reasonable outcomes lies in assessing and compensating for the power differentials between reporters and suspected wrongdoers.

## Discussion and conclusions

This chapter has emphasised that the risk of bad treatment after a report of wrongdoing does not fall evenly across all whistleblowers in all circumstances. What is it about the successful cases that makes them easier to manage? Conversely, which are the more difficult cases for whistleblowers and agencies to manage and what might be done to reduce the number of them that turn into damaging conflicts?

The first part of this chapter showed that the opportunity for effective intervention in potentially difficult cases begins with the risks inherent in the original disclosure, and in particular a more accurate understanding of the expectations held by whistleblowers at the point of disclosure. If they are to encourage internal disclosures, public sector organisations have no choice but to promise high levels of fairness, support and employee protection in response to reports of wrongdoing. Given this, organisations must expect many employees to make their reports with trusting or even naive expectations and be ready to extend management protection accordingly.

Evidence from Chapter 5 and above reinforces the responsibility that lies with agencies to take an active management approach because, even when they capable of assessing the risks of reprisal from familiar sources such as co-workers, many employees are not equipped or positioned to accurately assess the factors that can cause managers to take a negative stance. The dilemma becomes how to honour the commitment to employee protection that accompanies a commitment to integrity and transparency, even in more complex cases in which management itself is implicated in wrongdoing, or is incapable of substantiating the matter.

The second and third parts of the chapter used data from the employee survey to more closely identify the risk factors associated with the mistreatment of whistleblowers and other reporters, pointing directly to the features of these more complex cases, which demand attention. These comparisons across samples have shown that it is possible to identify a range of whistleblowing events as involving a higher risk of reported reprisals. Whistleblowers are more likely to suffer negative outcomes when the investigation of the wrongdoing is not kept internal to the organisation and does not result in an overall positive outcome. The risks of reprisal also increase if the reporter is in a vulnerable position, particularly relative to the suspected wrongdoer(s). Other basic, perhaps obvious factors, such as the seriousness and incidence of the wrongdoing, also play a role in increasing the likelihood of mistreatment.

Overall, the mistreatment reported by respondents inevitably includes many subjective elements, including a proportion of cases in which the perception of mistreatment is simply an expression of dissatisfaction with the outcome, or in which no reasonable management action could have succeeded in preventing reprisals or containing conflict. While this proportion is impossible to quantify, the results in this and the previous chapter suggest it is small. Especially when considered in light of the evidence from the case-handler and manager surveys in Chapter 5, and compared in this chapter with the different sources of perceived mistreatment, the risk factors associated with mistreatment emerge as logical products of the different situations in which almost any employee might find themselves in any organisation.

Importantly, these factors also tend to mirror many of the features present in cases in which wrongdoing is observed but not reported, identified in Chapter 3. This reinforces that when employees choose not to report because of anticipated risks of mistreatment, as discussed in Chapter 3, their assessment is probably quite reasonable. These results make it clear that if agencies are genuine about encouraging internal and regulatory reporting, they must have credible strategies for directly addressing and offsetting the risks of reprisal in these cases, and they must make these strategies readily visible and accessible to their employees.

Fortunately, the risk factors for mistreatment identified in this chapter all reflect circumstances that, while difficult to address, can indeed be targeted by special programs within agencies, by early intervention strategies and by measures to expedite external oversight of how more complex cases are being handled. The results provide insights not only into the different ways that whistleblowers themselves assess risk, but where the focus of prevention efforts can usefully lie. The analyses reinforce several needs: for whistleblowers to be actively engaged, early, in the process of assessing the risks of mistreatment or conflict surrounding their own report; for greater certainty and clarity about how the management response will unfold; for continuing communication about the response; and for continuing efforts to ensure that the whistleblower is receiving organisational support appropriate to the individual case. Finally, when mistreatment is not successfully prevented or contained and organisations wish their efforts to have credibility in the eyes of employees, viable mechanisms must exist for restitution or compensation.

This chapter demonstrates that, whatever the mix of strategies adopted by organisations, the process begins with an obligation to systematically 'size up' and address the risks of negative outcomes at an early stage, before stresses emerge and the trust of participants begins to unravel. With a better understanding of these risks, it is possible to identify the types of cases that should be targeted by whistleblower support programs. It is also likely that efforts to address them, through higher levels of intervention, can reduce the proportion of cases that result in reportedly bad outcomes. The types of reforms needed to realise this potential become the subject of the second part of this book.

# ENDNOTES

[1] Methodology of logistic regression analysis in this chapter:

- Forward stepwise selection was performed in SPSS to identify which of the independent variables (risk factors) considered were significantly associated with the outcome variable. SPSS included the variable in the model if it was significant at the 7.5 per cent level ($p < 0.075$). (As explained below, the final model used a more stringent significance level of 5 per cent [$p < 0.05$], but a more generous criterion was used at this initial stage of model selection to avoid excluding variables of borderline significance.) The level of the exclusion criteria was 10 per cent ($p > 0.1$).
- A variable was included in the final model if it was significant at the 5 per cent level ($p < 0.05$). Once the likely variables to be included in the model had been determined, the final model was then rerun. Respondents who did not answer all of the questions of interest were excluded from the analysis.
- For each outcome there is an infinite number of models that could be examined and no one model should be considered as the 'correct' model. In practice, the aim is to produce a sensible, simple model. It is possible that a different selection of risk factors or an alternative method of model selection might lead to different results.

[2] The risk factors initially considered in the logistic regression analysis were:

- the reporter's gender (employee survey: Q38), age (Q39), tenure with organisation (Q42), managerial status (Q44), salary (Q45), employment status (Q46)
- the type of wrongdoing (Q20), its perceived seriousness (Q22; scale from 1 = not at all to 5 = extremely) and its perceived frequency (Q23; scale from 1 = just this once to 5 = all the time)
- whether the reporting path was internal or external (Q28) and the number of stages it took (Q28)
- whether the report was kept confidential (Q29), whether the activity was investigated (Q32) and the overall outcome of reporting (Q33)
- the size of the immediate workgroup (Q49) and whether the work location was metropolitan or regional (Q50)
- whether the employee became aware of the wrongdoing because it was directed at them (Q21), whether one or more than one person was involved in the wrongdoing (Q24) and whether the position of the wrongdoer was at a higher level than the reporter (Q25).

[3] Technical notes to Tables 6.6 and 6.7:

- Odds ratios indicate the strength of associations. The 'odds' of an outcome occurring is the ratio of the probability of its occurring to the probability of its not occurring. Odds ratios greater than 1 indicate that, as the predictor increases, the odds of the outcome occurring increase. Conversely, a value less than 1 indicates that, as the predictor increases, the odds of the outcome occurring decrease. The larger the size of the odds ratio, the greater is the magnitude of the association between a risk factor and an outcome.
- 'p' values indicate the statistical significance of the results by providing a measure of whether a risk factor is significantly associated with the outcome variable. A small p-value implies that it is.
- The confidence interval indicates the amount of variability and therefore the precision of the findings and the confidence that can be placed in the odds-ratio estimate. These can be interpreted as meaning that there is a 95 per cent chance that the given interval will contain the 'true' odds ratio. For example, a confidence interval of 1.3–1.8 indicates a much smaller degree of variability than one of 1.2–7.6 and is much more informative about the true magnitude of the odds ratio.

# Part 2

## *Managing whistleblowing: organisational systems and responses*

# 7. Support for whistleblowing among managers: exploring job satisfaction and awareness of obligations

Paul Mazerolle and A. J. Brown[1]

## Introduction

In the remaining chapters of this book, attention turns from whistleblowers and their treatment to the organisational cultures and systems within which whistleblowing occurs and the different elements of how individual organisations currently respond. In understanding organisational responses and some of the possible explanations for the results in Part 1, no issues are more important than those of the roles, knowledge, awareness and attitude of managers.

Among the contradictions in current research on whistleblowing is the dual role that managers often play. On one hand, managers can foster unhealthy work environments that lead to employee complaints, low staff morale and high employee turnover. In an environment in which abusive supervision practices are prevalent, reports of wrongdoing can be expected, especially among employees with moderate levels of organisational commitment (Somers and Casal 1994). In contrast, some managers, for a range of reasons, foster productive and professional work environments that engender more positive experiences among employees. In this context, managers can be expected not only to promote and foster a positive reporting climate, but demonstrate the commitment and capacity to provide more professional and effective responses to whistleblowing. The confidence that effective managers provide to their staff could therefore promote greater employee communication intended to resolve concerns informally or strong assurances that effective responses will be available in the event that formal reports are made.

This duality of roles is well demonstrated in some of the previous chapters. For example, in Chapter 4, we saw that most employees who were prepared to come forward with concerns about wrongdoing were inclined to trust their managers with that information. This predisposition to trust managers is clearly in the organisation's interests. In Chapter 5, however, which focused on outcomes largely from the perspectives of whistleblowers, we saw that managers were likely to be regarded as the source of most bad treatment or harm that whistleblowers experienced. In some cases, the perception that management has failed or deliberately mistreated the whistleblower is unavoidable. Chapter 6 reinforces that especially when managers are implicated in the allegation of wrongdoing, the risks of reported whistleblower mistreatment can become very high.

From all of this evidence, there are good reasons to expect that the competence, attitudes and qualities of managers make a material difference in their commitment to the practice of whistleblowing, as well as their support for procedures for handling it. In short, the role of managers within organisational settings is crucial in relation to whether whistleblowing occurs, whether whistleblowing reporting procedures and attitudes to reporting wrongdoing are endorsed or promoted and whether such incidents are managed in a professional and competent manner (Masser and Brown 1996; Vandekerckhove 2006).[2] While it is often acknowledged that the role of management is crucial in the handling and support of whistleblowing, important questions remain regarding the interaction between organisational experiences and workplace attitudes in determining a manager's level of support for whistleblowing. There has been a limited set of studies linking various organisational characteristics such as workplace culture to whistleblowing (cf. Zhuang et al. 2005), but much of this research has not focused especially on the role of managers. The relationship, therefore, between the workplace attitudes of managers and their attitudes towards whistleblowing is poorly understood.

In this chapter, we examine the relationships between organisational and personal factors and levels of managerial support for whistleblowing. More specifically, we examine whether managers with positive attitudes towards their organisation—as indicated by their job satisfaction, trust in management and organisational citizenship—disproportionately support whistleblowing when compared with other managers and non-managers. The results show job satisfaction to be a salient facilitating factor in managers' support for whistleblowing 'in principle', as well as their reported knowledge of reporting procedures. The findings therefore illustrate how experiences at work, in terms of whether one is satisfied or not, can lead to various tangible benefits across organisations.

We then explore the extent to which managers appear conscious of their specific obligations in respect of the management of whistleblowers, as a continuation of the broader inquiry into how effectively these positive outlooks translate into practice.[3] These results show that managers are far less certain about rights and obligations relevant to their own role in respect of real whistleblowing incidents. There are also strong signs that managers themselves recognise the need to close the gaps between broad principle and practical realities. While it is clear that managers have a unique role to play in encouraging whistleblowing, the results suggest that a concerted effort is needed if the potential contribution of good management cultures and styles to the productive management of whistleblowing is to be maximised. The major question becomes, how can agency systems and procedures build on the general support for whistleblowing that has been found among individual managers? By investing in the job satisfaction of managers as well as by promoting greater awareness among managers of their whistleblowing reporting obligations and procedures, organisations can do a great deal to reduce the risks of some of the outcomes described in earlier chapters and increase the prospects of the whistleblowing process being handled well.

## Research focus and method

Support for whistleblowing generally, as well as knowledge of and support for specific procedures involved in managing whistleblowing, are arguably a reflection of a more professionalised management culture within an organisational setting. In these circumstances, a much lower prevalence of abusive management practices could be expected (Zellars et al. 2002). Our specific concerns in the current chapter involve exploring relationships between managers and non-managers across public sector organisations on various organisational climate indicators, as well as their attitudes and commitment towards whistleblowing generally and knowledge of procedures for reporting whistleblowing.

Our first set of research expectations is that, all else being equal, managers when compared with non-managers should demonstrate significantly more trust in management, job satisfaction, organisational commitment and loyalty (for example, overall stronger organisational citizenship) and will exhibit greater support of whistleblowing. Further interest concerns how employee levels of job satisfaction relate to commitment to and support for whistleblowing. Does job satisfaction impact on levels of support for whistleblowing? Are such relationships magnified for managers? It could be expected that among dissatisfied employees, lower levels of support for whistleblowing would be observed, given that whistleblowing could itself gauge beliefs about procedural justice, fairness, organisational loyalty and commitment. In contrast, levels of support for whistleblowing as well as knowledge of the procedures for reporting it could be much greater among managers and employees generally who are satisfied with their work. In these circumstances, job satisfaction could link directly to trust, organisational citizenship and loyalty, which could foster a greater sense of awareness of the role of whistleblowing as well as the importance of effectively managing such events. It is therefore reasonable to expect that support for whistleblowing among managers and non-managers alike could be accentuated for employees with higher levels of job satisfaction.

Our second set of expectations is that managers will also demonstrate greater knowledge of the procedures triggered by the reporting of wrongdoing, including their own obligations in respect of it. Does job satisfaction impact on knowledge of procedures for reporting whistleblowing? Do managers have greater understanding of specific legal provisions in relation to whistleblowing? Our approach will explore whether managers differ from non-managers in this key aspect of whistleblowing management.

It is recognised that, all else being equal, managers as a group could be reasonably expected to have higher levels of trust and commitment to their organisations (especially in their own management—that is, themselves) as well as greater awareness of the importance of whistleblowing and the related procedures for handling internal disclosures. Part of the value of the current research is in attempting to gauge this empirically across a large sample of public sector employees in Australia. Absent any strong empirical base, beliefs and expectations about whether managers hold greater levels of organisational trust, job satisfaction and citizenship as well as support for whistleblowing when compared with non-managers are based simply on hunches and anecdotal information. Our aim is to examine and test such relationships (even ones that appear obvious) with hard data to provide more empirical evidence and therefore facilitate a broader, more in-depth body of knowledge in this area.

The first expectations are explored by examining whether managers differ from non-managers on a range of key organisational climate measures, drawn from the employee survey. Of the 7663 respondents to the survey, 1620 (21 per cent) identified as managers. Additionally, differences across employees with varying levels of job satisfaction are directly assessed. In this way, it can be explored whether there are consistent relationships linking job satisfaction to whistleblowing knowledge and attitudes. We also examine whether support for whistleblowing is a direct function of organisational role, such as being a manager. Finally, the direct predictive relationships between managerial status and support for whistleblowing are examined to assess whether managers have an increased probability of supporting whistleblowing net of various organisational dimensions including job satisfaction.

Measures used are similar to those employed in Chapter 3, including OCB (Graham 1989), trust in management (Robinson and Rousseau 1994), job satisfaction (Agho et al. 1992) and whistleblowing propensity (Keenan 2000, 2002; Tavakoli et al. 2003).[4] The analysis proceeds in stages. First, mean-level comparisons between managers and non-managers on a range of organisational measures are presented. Statistical comparisons are employed using t-tests. Second, comparisons of measures of organisational characteristics for respondents differentiated on their levels of job satisfaction (for example, low, medium-low, medium-high, high) are presented using ANOVA procedures. These groups are constructed by creating quartiles across the distribution of the job-satisfaction variable. In the final stage of the analysis, the results are presented from an ordinary least squares (OLS) regression model to predict levels of support for whistleblowing net of other influences.

The second set of expectations is explored using those items relating to knowledge of reporting procedures from the whistleblowing-propensity scale. We also examine whether knowledge of reporting procedures is a direct function of organisational role, such as being a manager. This analysis is, however, extended by examining descriptive statistics regarding the level of knowledge indicated by managers and non-managers about relevant legislation. Given the special role played by legislation in setting general standards for the management of whistleblowing, and in particular setting frameworks for managers' obligation as managers, this provides a window into perceived needs as well as current strengths.

## Managers, job satisfaction and support for whistleblowing

The first series of comparisons involves directly comparing managers with non-managers on a series of organisationally relevant measures. The comparisons are reported in Table 7.1. The findings demonstrate a fairly consistent picture. The broad trend across the reported attitudinal variables suggests the manager sample has a more positive view of the organisation than non-managers. Managers, as a group, across the sample demonstrate significantly higher mean levels of trust in management, higher job satisfaction and higher levels of OCB. In particular, managers see themselves as more helpful to their fellow employees and as showing greater initiative than non-managers. The only OCB in which managers did not report higher levels than non-managers was the 'industry' factor, with managers and non-managers reporting the same levels. Furthermore, managers as a group demonstrated greater levels of support for whistleblowing, measured in terms of having a favourable personal attitude to whistleblowing. Perhaps not surprisingly, comparisons also show that managers as a group held significantly longer terms of employment with their current employer when compared with non-managers.

## Does job satisfaction relate to whistleblowing support?

Table 7.2 reports the relationship between levels of job satisfaction and various organisationally relevant variables including whistleblowing support. Inspection of the results also reveals a consistent finding. Levels of employee job satisfaction appear directly related to salient organisational variables including trust in management, organisational citizenship and support for and knowledge of whistleblowing procedures. Employees with high levels of satisfaction, as indicated by the respondents in the upper quartiles of the scale distribution, score significantly higher than other respondents.

**Table 7.1 Comparing managers with non-managers for various organisational dimensions**

|  | Managers (n = 1 612) | Non-managers (n = 5 912) | t-value |
|---|---|---|---|
| Trust in management | 3.59 | 3.34 | 10.57* |
| Job satisfaction | 3.61 | 3.43 | 8.62* |
| Organisational: |  |  |  |
| *Citizenship* | 3.90 | 3.74 | 14.28* |
| *Helping* | 4.02 | 3.94 | 5.89* |
| *Initiative* | 4.02 | 3.69 | 22.37* |
| *Industry* | 3.84 | 3.84 | 0.35 |
| *Loyalty* | 3.72 | 3.49 | 11.96* |
| Whistleblowing propensity: |  |  |  |
| *Attitudes to whistleblowing* | 4.26 | 4.07 | 12.57* |
| *Knowledge of procedures* | 3.66 | 3.34 | 14.46* |
| Length of time with organisation | 13.60 | 9.56 | 15.24* |

* $p < 0.01$ two-tailed

**Table 7.2 Relationships between job satisfaction and organisational characteristics**

|  | 1st quartile: low | 2nd quartile: low–medium | 3rd quartile: medium–high | 4th quartile: high | *F* value |
|---|---|---|---|---|---|
| Trust in management | 3.02 | 3.51 | 3.77 | 4.01 | 111.10* |
| Organisational: |  |  |  |  |  |
| *Citizenship* | 3.69 | 3.82 | 3.91 | 4.18 | 133.25* |
| *Helping* | 3.89 | 3.94 | 4.00 | 4.25 | 48.01* |
| *Initiative* | 3.88 | 3.94 | 4.02 | 4.24 | 54.62* |
| *Industry* | 3.70 | 3.77 | 3.80 | 4.12 | 46.97* |
| *Loyalty* | 3.28 | 3.63 | 3.83 | 4.11 | 122.41* |
| Whistleblowing propensity: |  |  |  |  |  |
| *Attitudes to whistleblowing* | 4.19 | 4.22 | 4.22 | 4.44 | 21.79* |
| *Knowledge of procedures* | 3.34 | 3.53 | 3.78 | 3.98 | 51.10* |

* $p < 0.01$ two-tailed

The consistent pattern of results suggests that employee satisfaction could be an important ingredient for organisational harmony and performance. The comparisons suggest that satisfied employees provide additional benefits to organisations including trust, loyalty and, importantly for present purposes, support for whistleblowing. At this stage, however, we cannot rule out the possibility that additional factors influence job satisfaction as well as some of the organisational factors, including support for whistleblowing.

# Comparing support for whistleblowing across levels of job satisfaction for managers and non-managers

The next phase of the results considers whether support for whistleblowing among managers and non-managers is in part conditional on levels of job satisfaction. Given the prior results linking managerial roles and job satisfaction levels with support for whistleblowing, it raises the possibility that being highly satisfied at work, as opposed to being a manager, facilitates support for whistleblowing. Results reported in Figure 7.1 bear directly on this issue.

## Figures 7.1a–d Support for whistleblowing among managers and non-managers by varying levels of job satisfaction

Figure 7.1a. Support for Whistleblowing Among Managers and Non-Managers by Low Job Satisfaction (0-25$^{th}$ Percentile)

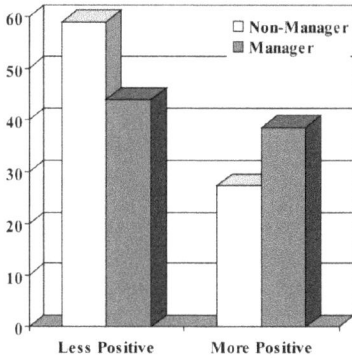

Figure 7.1b. Support for Whistleblowing Among Managers and Non-Managers by Low- Med Job Satisfaction (26-50$^{th}$ Percentile)

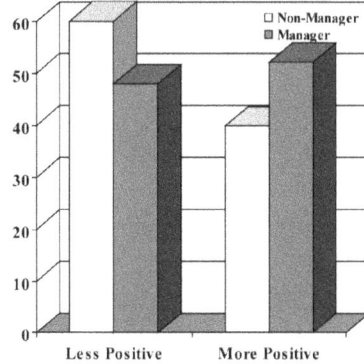

Figure 7.1c. Support For Whistleblowing Among Managers and Non-Managers by Med-High Job Satisfaction (51-75$^{th}$ Percentile)

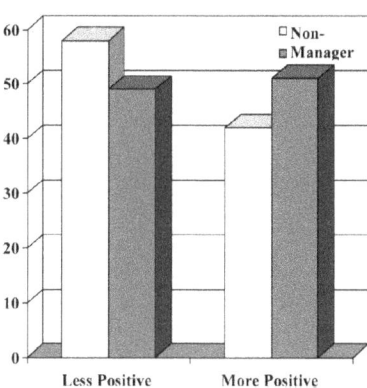

Figure 7.1d. Support For Whistleblowing Among Managers and Non-Managers by High Job Satisfaction (76-100$^{th}$ percentile)

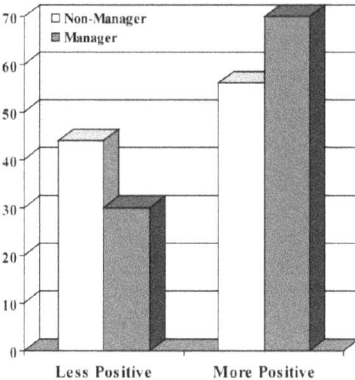

Results in Figures 7.1a–d show comparisons between managers and non-managers, across various levels of job satisfaction, on their specific levels of support for whistleblowing. For this comparison, the responses for the whistleblower support measure were differentiated at the fiftieth percentile to assess lesser or greater levels of support for whistleblowing. The picture emerging from the comparisons is clear: support for whistleblowing among managers and non-managers alike appears conditional on levels of job satisfaction. The findings reported in Figures 7.1a, 7.1b and 7.1c show that support for whistleblowing among managers is generally mixed between less and more support for respondents at the low or low–medium levels of job satisfaction. At higher levels of job satisfaction, however, a clear picture emerges, in which support for whistleblowing increases considerably. For example, at the seventy-sixth to the one-hundredth percentiles—indicating the highest level of job satisfaction—70 per cent of managers supported whistleblowing compared with 30 per cent who were less positive. At lesser levels of job satisfaction, no marked differences were observed. In sum, support for whistleblowing among managers and non-managers appears accentuated at higher levels of job satisfaction and the relationship appears stronger for managers.

## Predictors of support for whistleblowing

The next stage of the analysis examines a series of predictors of whistleblowing support. It is especially important to examine the predictive relationships to whistleblowing support in a multivariate context, given the range of possible influences that could affect such an outcome. Previous analysis suggested that managerial status was salient for whistleblower support, especially at higher levels of job satisfaction. In the next analysis, we explore whether these relationships remain while considering other actors, including demographic characteristics such as age and gender.

Because the outcome measure in this analysis—attitudes towards whistleblowing—comprises a continuous range of numbers, an OLS regression is appropriate. The results of an OLS regression allow researchers to gauge the amount of change in the outcome variable that results for every one-unit increase in the relevant predictor variable. The multiple-regression model results consider the precise relationships between individual independent variables, net of the effects of other influences. The results are reported in Table 7.3.

**Table 7.3 Predictors of support for whistleblowing**

|  | B | Std error | t value |
|---|---|---|---|
| Trust in management | 0.044 | 0.008 | 5.68* |
| Job satisfaction | −0.044 | 0.009 | 4.82* |
| Organisational citizenship | 0.413 | 0.016 | 25.12* |
| Managerial status (1 = manager) | 0.107 | 0.015 | 6.98* |
| Age | 0.002 | 0.001 | 3.12* |
| Gender (1 = female) | 0.018 | 0.012 | 1.45 |
| Tenure with organisation | −0.0006 | 0.001 | 0.82 |
| Education | 0.031 | 0.006 | 5.16* |
| Constant | 2.35 | 0.065 | 35.87* |
| Adjusted $R^2$ | 0.115 |  |  |
| N | 7 337 |  |  |

* $p < 0.01$ two-tailed

Results from multiple-regression statistical models predicting support for whistleblowing reveal a range of statistically significant relationships. Table 7.3 reveals that having greater levels of trust in management, job satisfaction and organisational citizenship significantly increases the probability of support for whistleblowing. At the same time, older and more educated workers supported whistleblowing. Of significance was that being a manager increased the probability of supporting whistleblowing, net of other influences.

## Managers, job satisfaction and knowledge of whistleblowing procedures

In assessing knowledge about whistleblowing policies in the workplace, a similar picture emerges. The relationships are reported and demonstrated in Figures 7.2a–d. The series of comparisons reveal that confidence in the ability to navigate whistleblowing policies is clearly stronger for managers who are more satisfied at work. For managers at low to low–medium levels of satisfaction, their professed familiarity with whistleblowing policies is equivocal. At higher levels of job satisfaction, reported knowledge of whistleblowing policies was much greater among managers—approaching 80 per cent. These results suggest there is a potential organisational benefit in having highly satisfied managers. Specifically, managers who are especially satisfied at work (on average) will not only have a more favourable personal attitude towards whistleblowing, they could be more able to put this attitude into practice through greater knowledge of relevant procedures.

## Predictors of knowledge of whistleblowing reporting procedures

Findings reported in Table 7.4 reveal even more consistent predictors of knowledge of whistleblowing reporting procedures. The relationships reveal that job satisfaction, trust in management, organisational citizenship and being a manager are all predictive of knowledge of whistleblowing reporting procedures. Significant relationships were also observed for various demographic factors, with older workers, males, more educated staff and employees with lengthier tenure proving more knowledgeable about whistleblowing policies and practices. While these findings are not unexpected, it is important to assess empirically whether managers understand and support whistleblowing practices to a greater extent than non-managers, net of other salient organisational factors.

## Figures 7.2a–d Knowledge of whistleblowing procedures among managers and non-managers by varying levels of job satisfaction

*Figure 7.2a. Knowledge of Whistleblowing Policies Among Managers and Non-Managers by Low Job Satisfaction (0-25$^{th}$ Percentile)*

*Figure 7.2b. Knowledge of Whistleblowing Policies Among Managers and Non-Managers by Med-Low Job Satisfaction (26-50$^{th}$ Percentile)*

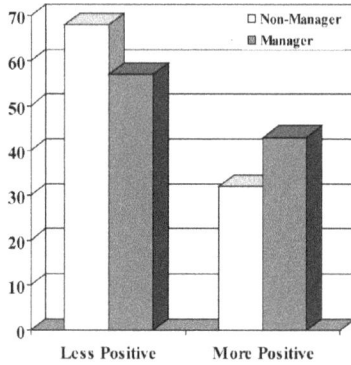

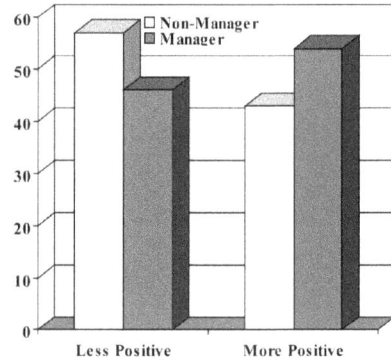

*Figure 7.2c. Knowledge of Whistleblowing Policies Among Managers and Non-Managers by Med-High Job Satisfaction (51-75$^{th}$ Percentile)*

*Figure 7.2d. Knowledge of Whistleblowing Policies Among Managers and Non-Managers by-High Job Satisfaction (76-100$^{th}$ Percentile)*

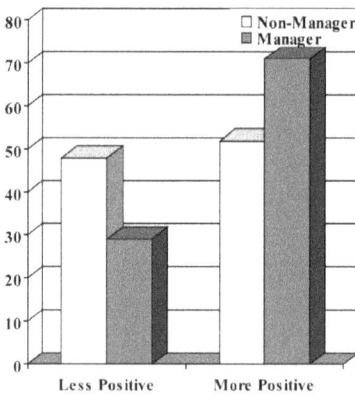

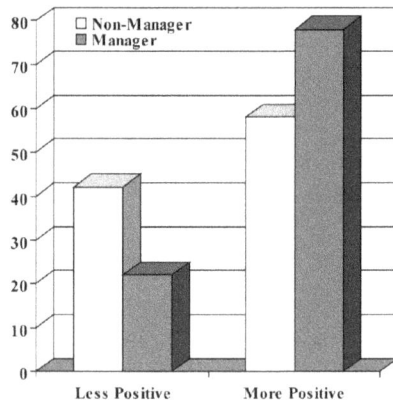

**Table 7.4 Predictors of knowledge of whistleblower reporting procedures**

|  | *B* | Std error | *t* value |
|---|---|---|---|
| Trust in management | 0.208 | 0.011 | 19.42* |
| Job satisfaction | 0.056 | 0.013 | 4.41* |
| Organisational citizenship | 0.376 | 0.023 | 16.53* |
| Managerial status (1 = manager) | 0.145 | 0.021 | 6.87* |
| Age | 0.004 | 0.001 | 4.23* |
| Gender (1 = female) | −0.117 | 0.017 | 6.83* |
| Tenure with organisation | 0.005 | 0.001 | 4.44* |
| Education | −0.028 | 0.008 | 3.36* |
| Constant | 0.996 | 0.091 | 10.99* |
| Adjusted $R^2$ | 0.17 |  |  |
| N | 7 338 |  |  |

* $p < 0.01$ one-tailed

# Managers and knowledge of whistleblowing legislation

In the final analysis, it is important to relate the above findings back to the systems and procedures in the agencies under study and the proven duality in managers' roles. Given the marked tendency of employees to blow the whistle internally, shown in Chapter 4, the results above help explain why a lower than expected proportion of whistleblowers report bad treatment, shown in Chapter 5. Nevertheless, 18 per cent of all public interest whistleblowers did report that management treated them badly, with the proportion rising much higher in many agencies. A major goal of this research is to identify how that proportion of whistleblowers might be reduced.

While the above analysis indicates that job satisfaction of managers is an important variable, other factors influencing outcomes are likely to include the nature or extent of managers' knowledge of the relevant procedures and whether the content of the procedures themselves is appropriate. This last issue will be taken up in the following chapters. While managers might indicate a general confidence in and familiarity with whistleblowing procedures, the questions become how comprehensive is that knowledge and how well equipped are they to operationalise this generally favourable recognition of whistleblowing in their day-to-day roles? These questions are reinforced by the fact that the indicators of procedural knowledge reported above are the same as those used to gauge knowledge by all staff (that is, the scale-measured agreement with statements such as 'I have enough information about where to report wrongdoing, if such activities came to my attention' and 'I know what support my organisation provides for employees who report alleged wrongdoing'). The variables gauge respondents' confidence in the procedural aspects of blowing the whistle more than procedures relevant to managers' role as managers in this process.

To answer these questions, comparisons were also conducted to examine whether managers and non-managers answered questions relating to their knowledge of relevant legislation differently. Previous studies have recorded relatively low levels of awareness of relevant legislation among public employees (for example, Zipparo 1999a, 1999b), but the present study was not necessarily looking for either confirmation or change in that overall result—the need for most employees to know the specifics of legislation might be low, especially if the extent to which legislative principles are implemented by agency procedures is high. There is, however, reason to expect that managers should have a higher awareness of any relevant legislation. This is especially the case for the management of whistleblowing, where legislative reform has been a principal driver of new procedures and is directly intended to increase the overall responsiveness of management to whistleblowing. While the extent and quality of current legislation is further discussed in Chapters 10 and 11, the fact is that for most of the agencies studied, the management of whistleblowing has been the subject of relatively recent and topical legislative reform.

Table 7.5 displays the responses to the question asking whether respondents believe they are covered by legislation setting out their 'rights and responsibilities associated with reporting alleged wrongdoing' involving their organisation. The differences by jurisdiction highlight the many factors influencing awareness of legislation, including whether such legislation does in fact exist, whether the respondents' specific agency is covered and what efforts have been made to promote awareness of the legislation.

The responses confirm a high level of uncertainty about whether employees are covered by legislation, with 54 per cent of respondents indicating they did not know. As already noted, however, this is not necessarily surprising. The question is whether managers share this uncertainty in equal measure.

### Table 7.5 Awareness of legislation relating to whistleblowing

| Are your rights and responsibilities covered by legislation? | Cth (n = 2 307) | NSW (n = 2 561) | Qld (n = 1 729) | WA (n = 1 007) | National (n = 7 604) |
|---|---|---|---|---|---|
| Yes | 42.4% (935) | 46.7% (1 144) | 47.6% (788) | 33.3% (320) | 43.8% (3 187) |
| No | 2.1% (46) | 1.7% (41) | 1.1% (18) | 2.2% (21) | 1.7% (126) |
| Don't know | 55.5% (1 224) | 51.7% (1 267) | 51.3% (848) | 64.5% (620) | 54.4% (3 959) |
| Subtotal | 100% (2 205) | 100% (2 452) | 100% (1 654) | 100% (961) | 100% (7 272) |
| Missing | 102 | 109 | 75 | 46 | 332 |

The results displayed in Table 7.6 reveal that managers do not share the same level of uncertainty as non-managers about whether they are covered by legislation. As the findings in Table 7.6 reveal, managers, as a group, are significantly less likely to indicate a lack of knowledge. Furthermore, and consistent with earlier results, managers also reported significantly greater confidence in the legislation they believed covered them, as shown in Table 7.7.

**Table 7.6 Manager and non-manager awareness of legislation**

| Are your rights and responsibilities covered by legislation? | Managers (n = 1 620) | Non-managers (n = 5 966) |
|---|---|---|
| Yes | 58.1% (901) | 40.0% (2 287) |
| No | 1.5% (240) | 1.8% (104) |
| Don't know | 40.3% (625) | 58.2% (3 324) |
| Subtotal | 100% (1 550) | 100% (5 715) |
| Missing | 70 | 251 |

**Note:** Significant at p = 0.01 using Chi-square test.

**Table 7.7 Manager and non-manager confidence in legislation**

| 1 = strongly disagree 5 = strongly agree | Managers (n = 1 012) | Non-managers (n = 2 735) |
|---|---|---|
| The existence of the legislation makes it easier for me to consider reporting corruption. | 3.71 | 3.58 |
| I am confident that the legislation has the power to protect me from any negative consequences if I were to report corruption. | 3.11 | 3.04NS |
| I believe that the legislation is ineffective. | 2.69 | 2.80 |
| The legislation is in need of major change to improve employee reporting of wrongdoing | 2.85 | 2.99 |

**Note:** All significant at p = 0.01 using Chi-square test (except where indicated by 'NS').

While these results are positive for managers and at a broad level continue to reinforce the results of the earlier analyses, there are nevertheless also signs that managers' knowledge of their specific obligations as managers in the whistleblowing process could be much stronger. In Table 7.6, the proportion of managers who did not know whether their rights and responsibilities were covered by legislation was still high (40 per cent). Apart from indicating a lack of awareness of specific obligations on them as managers, these results also show a substantial proportion of managers do not know whether their own staff are covered by relevant legislation.

There is also evidence that many managers themselves recognise their lack of knowledge when it comes to specific obligations. Among those respondents who did believe they were covered by legislation, there was still a significant desire for more information and training about the legislation. This is confirmed by Table 7.8, which shows that the perceived need for more information and training is particularly acute among managers, at whatever level of the organisation. Managers were significantly more likely than non-managers to indicate that they required greater information and training, notwithstanding that many managers were already confident that they were probably covered by the legislation. The higher perceived need for further information and training on the part of managers could in part reflect their role within the organisation, as well as their higher levels of organisational investment as indicated by their greater levels of citizenship (that is, loyalty, helping, and so on), trust in management and job satisfaction, which were demonstrated in earlier analysis reported in Table 7.1. It is, however, also probably an indicator that notwithstanding the generally positive attitude towards whistleblowing described earlier, the impacts of specific policies and procedures on the working lives of managers are not strong.

**Table 7.8 Need for more legislative information and training by managerial status**

| I require more information and training about the legislation. | Managers (n = 1 034) | Non-managers (n = 2 836) | Total (n = 3 900) |
|---|---|---|---|
| 1 = strongly disagree | 3.39* | 3.26* | 3.36 |
| 5 = strongly agree | (SD = 0.96) | (SD = 0.93) | |

* significant at $p = 0.01$ (two-tailed test)

## Discussion and conclusions

This chapter examined the unique role of managers in relation to their support for whistleblowing as well as whether that support was conditional on their levels of job satisfaction. The results reveal a relatively consistent set of findings in relation to comparisons between managers and non-managers. Managers tend to have a much greater stake in their workplaces. They reveal higher levels of organisational affiliation in terms of organisational citizenship, trust in management and job satisfaction. At the same time, they appear to have a stronger recognition of the value of whistleblowing in the workplace.

An additional part of the analysis involved assessing independently whether job satisfaction was related to whistleblower support. The results show that respondents with the highest level of job satisfaction tend to also have the highest degree of support for whistleblowing, as well as the highest scores for other organisational variables. Given the salience of job satisfaction, comparisons were conducted to assess whether managerial support for whistleblowing was a function of levels of job satisfaction. The results reveal that job satisfaction was a salient facilitating factor of support for whistleblowing, as well as reported knowledge of reporting procedures. The findings therefore illustrate how experiences at work, in terms of whether one is satisfied or not, can lead to various tangible benefits across organisations. One of the hidden benefits for satisfied employees, regardless of their managerial status, is that they demonstrate much greater awareness of and competency towards whistleblowing.

This observation was largely reinforced in the multivariate analyses that revealed that being a manager increased the probability of support for whistleblowing net of various demographic and organisational influences. In short, over and above the role of organisational climate influences, it is clear that managers have a unique role to play in encouraging whistleblowing, even if this role is also often complex.

These results illuminate a suite of implications for managing whistleblowing in public sector organisations. The findings illustrate that managers are very well placed to materially affect their work environments. As mentioned at the beginning of this chapter, managers are crucial for providing a professional and productive work setting. Unfortunately, however, there are numerous examples whereby managerial competence is stretched and workplace experiences begin to unravel. In such settings, employee morale and concerns about fair work and decision making might no longer take priority (Byrne 2005). The results suggest that a concerted effort is needed if the potential contribution of good management cultures and styles to the productive management of whistleblowing is to be maximised.

Underscoring the potential for maximising the generally positive culture of management in the agencies studied is the evidence in the final part of the chapter that managers are far less certain about rights and obligations relevant to their own role in respect of real whistleblowing incidents. There are strong signs that managers themselves recognise the need to close the gaps between broad principle and practical realities. How this might be done becomes a question of agency systems and procedures, building on the general support for whistleblowing that has been found among individual managers. The environment exists for the development of better systems and procedures. This fact reinforces the imperatives that can now be more clearly identified for doing so, based on the current standard of systems and procedures described in subsequent chapters.

The current research is not without limitations. In addition to some of the methodological constraints outlined in Chapter 1, the findings presented illustrate the need to conduct further, more fine-grained analyses. The findings suggest that many of the relationships between managers and whistleblower support and commitment are complex and various organisational context variables (for example, citizenship, loyalty, and so on) need to be further explored to assess the interactive or multiplicative influences. Additionally, the specific attributes of managers need to be further considered. Managers are clearly not a 'one-size-fits-all' category. Further analysis will need to explore a range of competencies as well as the possible relationship to gender and age to more fully consider the full range of influences that affect managers in their responses to and handling of whistleblowing. At the same time, a host of organisational context variables needs consideration. For example, there is reason to believe that organisational size can be a salient influence on job satisfaction and whistleblower support. Further analysis is needed to explore these issues in greater detail in a concerted attempt to understand the unique role of managers in handling whistleblowing in public sector organisations.

In summary, the findings from this research point to more effective strategies for promoting the importance of whistleblowing as well as the knowledge required to advance whistleblowing management practice. Strategies to promote an effective organisational climate appear salient to the extent that they facilitate job satisfaction among employees. Uncovering the key ingredients for facilitating job satisfaction for managers and non-managers alike provides the added benefits of there being more direct impact on the overall organisational health across public sector agencies. These results strengthen the evidence that whistleblowing is often recognised as necessary and even healthy in organisations and confirms the potential for building stronger systems for ensuring that the incidence of unfair treatment of whistleblowers is minimised. Perhaps most importantly, these results suggest that by investing in the job satisfaction of managers, as well as by promoting greater awareness among managers of their whistleblowing reporting obligations and procedures, organisations can do a great deal to reduce the risks of some of the outcomes described in earlier chapters, and increase the prospects of the whistleblowing process being handled well.

## ENDNOTES

[1] The authors thank Dr Peter Cassematis for research support on aspects of this chapter.

[2] We accept that managers operate across varying levels within organisations and that junior as opposed to more senior managers can shape their organisational settings in relation to whistleblowing (and other issues) in varying ways. It is the intention of the research team to further explore whether and to what extent support for whistleblowing as well as other organisational factors varies across levels of managers.

[3] Of course, if individual managers are the targets of a whistleblowing event (that is, the perceived wrongdoers), their personal support for that act of whistleblowing will likely be low. This issue can be explored in further research as part of this larger project.

[4] The measure for OCB (Graham 1989) comprises the sub-components of helping (five items; alpha = 0.74), initiative (five items; alpha = 0.80), industry (four items; alpha = 0.67) and loyalty (five items; alpha = 0.83). Trust in management (Robinson and Rousseau 1994) is assessed by a seven-item scale that gauges the extent to which respondents believe that managers will treat employees fairly (alpha = 0.90). Job satisfaction (Agho et al. 1992) is gauged with a six-item scale to assess employee job satisfaction and enjoyment with their employment role and working conditions (alpha = 0.86). Whistleblowing propensity is assessed using a scale developed by Keenan (2000), which has two discrete components: attitudes towards whistleblowing (five items; alpha = 0.84) and knowledge of reporting procedures (five items; alpha = 0.84).

# 8. Investigations: improving practice and building capacity

Margaret Mitchell[1]

## Introduction

Whistleblowing provokes many responses from individuals in organisations and from organisations as a whole. All the evidence on whistleblowing in the Australian public sector, reviewed so far, shows two main responses to be of overwhelming importance in shaping the outcomes from any public interest whistleblowing incident:

- how well employee reports of wrongdoing are investigated and (where necessary) acted on
- how well employees who disclose wrongdoing are managed, supported and (where necessary) protected, during and after the investigation process.

This chapter and the next address, in turn, each of these crucial issues.

Proper investigation of workplace complaints and concerns is a cornerstone of the practical implementation of whistleblowing legislation, resulting in reports being dealt with appropriately and the facts of the situation discovered. As seen in Chapters 2 and 5, many whistleblowing cases are successfully investigated by the agencies involved. The results from the employee survey indicated that more than half (56 per cent) of public interest whistleblowers believed that their report was investigated and, of these, the same proportion believed the investigation result led to a positive change in their organisation. Given that not every report about wrongdoing is correct, and that even if correct, many reports might not be capable of substantiation for evidentiary or other reasons, these results are seen as broadly positive.

The previous chapters, however, also provided evidence that some investigations do fail or fail to occur when they should. A worrying indicator was the substantial proportion of whistleblowers who simply did not know whether any investigative action was taken. Frequently, the organisation's failure to inform its employees of the resulting action could be a sign that no effective investigation has occurred—and, even if this is not the case, it is likely to contribute to that impression within the organisation. In Chapter 3, the general confidence of employees that a disclosure will be competently investigated and acted on emerged as pivotal to whether or not they would bother reporting their concerns. It is also reasonable to assume that widely held confidence in the thoroughness, fairness and professionalism of investigative responses will help dissuade employees from trying to use whistleblowing processes for other purposes.

From these results, the conduct and management of internal investigations represent major, continuing challenges for public sector agencies. This chapter focuses on evidence gathered about three main aspects of investigating wrongdoing: who conducts the investigations, their level of training and how the investigatory capacity of agencies might appear to impact on current outcomes from whistleblowing. Fundamentally, investigations are fact-finding processes that involve gathering information, interviewing relevant people and preparing a report for action (Ferraro and Spain 2006). Sennewald (1991:3) describes an investigation as 'the examination, study, searching, tracking and gathering of factual information that answers questions or solves problems [and] a comprehensive activity involving information collection, the application of logic, and the exercise of sound reasoning'. Investigation needs arise within agencies for a range of purposes, not restricted to whistleblowing reports. As indicated in Chapter 2, a range of triggers exists by which information about internal wrongdoing comes to light. Whistleblowing is simply one of the most important, in which the interactions between investigators, management, informants and the attitudes of other employees to reporting become very complex.

When a report of wrongdoing is made in an organisation, it has the potential to trigger a number of investigations. The first of these is the primary investigation. In some circumstances, as seen in Chapters 4 and 5, the primary investigation might not resolve matters or there could be further complaints, causing the issue to be reviewed. This review, if undertaken, can result in a further internal investigation or an investigation from an external integrity agency. Further, as seen in Chapters 5 and 6, if the complainant suffers a reprisal there could be an independent investigation into that reprisal, as distinct from the original wrongdoing. For simplicity, this chapter looks on all these investigations as a whole, on the assumption that the basic skills, expertise and experience required are often very similar.

The first part of the chapter examines who conducts investigations on behalf of the agencies studied, confirming that a wide variety of internal organisational units and individuals and external resources are used. As we have seen, almost all disclosures are made internally and the responsibility for investigating reports of alleged wrongdoing rests primarily within the organisation, even if decisions are made to involve outside parties.

The results show that the complex matter of conducting investigations cannot be taken lightly nor can the skills required be taken for granted. Those responsible for carrying out internal investigations should be experienced and qualified investigators aware of the sensitivities of investigating workplace reports of wrongdoing. Less-qualified and less-experienced staff members need active and continuing external guidance, training, support and management. Furthermore, agencies need to ensure that private companies and other external resources that they use are appropriately qualified to conduct investigations and that the other responsibilities that internal investigators often undertake do not fall through the cracks.

The need for appropriate expertise is underscored by evidence that not all management roles can be considered to be routinely compatible with investigation roles and that this impacts on the perceived quality of investigations. The data also point to the need for careful consideration of the way in which institutional responsibilities for investigations are configured. This includes the responsibility for managers who receive disclosures to automatically consult with specialists in their organisation, where available, and the need for more effective relationships between agencies and integrity agencies to help ensure that, wherever possible, the primary investigation of a disclosure is properly undertaken.

The second part of this chapter describes the training in investigation that is provided and/or required by the agencies, indicating considerable variation in what is required. The results give cause for concern in revealing a clear shortage of training in how to deal with disclosures and awareness on the part of many case-handlers and managers that they feel under-equipped to deal with whistleblowing. The degree to which current levels of training confer a sense of being able to deal with complex whistleblower reports is also examined. Not surprisingly, having professional training in investigation leads to more confidence, while informal training—which is found to be the most frequent form of training provided or required—leads case-handlers and managers to feel little more confident than the very substantial number with no training at all.

The analysis also identifies a number of relationships between the level of available training and other outcomes, in a manner that underlines the complexity of the issues. In terms of creating a working culture in which staff members feel comfortable about reporting, it appears that those with professional training are somewhat less negative and judgmental about whistleblowing. The knowledge and understanding of the issues that could be conferred by professional training appear to be associated with less harsh or stereotypical views about the usefulness of whistleblowing and the feasibility of managing whistleblowing incidents to a positive outcome.

Finally, the third section of the chapter examines whether the 'investigatory capacity' of agencies impacts on current outcomes from whistleblowing. The analysis examines differences, on a number of outcome measures, across 12 of the project's case study agencies using a proxy measure of 'investigatory capacity'. This examination indicates that investigatory capacity is indeed related to the likelihood of wrongdoing being reported in a given agency. This result reinforces the importance of the institutional and training issues raised in the first parts of the chapter, demonstrating that those agencies that do not take steps to ensure their investigatory capacity is high are less likely to find their employees will be prepared to help bring known wrongdoing to light. These findings therefore reinforce the crucial importance of good investigation practice and capacity to the process of realising the benefits of whistleblowing.

## Who conducts investigations?

Workplace complaints are investigated using internal and/or external resources. Table 8.1 details who, within each organisation, conducts the investigations, based on data supplied by the agencies in response to the agency survey. Decisions by each agency about who should investigate naturally depend in part on the size of the agency and the range of resources at its disposal. Given the results in Chapter 4, it is not surprising that by far the majority of investigations are conducted internally—a fact that underlines the need for good internal processes and practices and well-trained professional staff, especially given the inherent risk of internal organisational conflict that goes with any whistleblowing report. External investigators are discussed later in the chapter.

**Table 8.1 Who investigates reports of wrongdoing? (per cent)**

| Category | Percentage of agencies who use [a] |
|---|---|
| Senior manager(s) (eg., group/division heads) | 59.2 (180) |
| CEO or equivalent | 56.6 (172) |
| Human resources/equity and merit unit | 50.7 (154) |
| Internal audit/fraud investigation unit | 44.1 (134) |
| External government agencies (eg., police, ombudsman) | 33.9 (103) |
| Staff grievance/appeals units | 31.6 (96) |
| External audit/accounting firms | 27.6 (84) |
| Other specialist investigators | 25.9 (79) |
| Middle or junior managers (eg., branch/section heads) | 23.0 (70) |
| Administrative review/legal units | 20.4 (62) |
| Internal ethical standards/investigation units | 20.1 (61) |
| Internal ombudsman/complaints | 7.9 (24) |
| Quality-assurance units | 5.6 (17) |
| External retired managers | 5.6 (17) |
| Other | 25.7 (78) |

[a] Total exceeds 100 per cent as agencies were asked to indicate all those used.
**Source:** Agency survey: Q16 (n = 304).

## Internal investigators

About half of all agencies responded that senior managers, the CEO, human resource units and internal fraud and audit units had responsibility for conducting investigations. The term 'investigate' might also be interpreted to mean the person who has overall management of the investigation and/or responsibility to ensure that it is conducted appropriately rather than the person who conducts interviews, collects evidence and writes the report.

Given the range of investigatory resources used, case-handlers and managers in the 15 case study agencies were asked who they thought was most appropriate to conduct investigations, as shown in Table 8.2. A high mean score is 'usually appropriate' and a lower mean score is 'rarely appropriate'. Specialist units such as internal audit, fraud-investigation and ethics units were considered the most appropriate, followed by a manager from 'another area' and human resource units. Not surprisingly, journalists and 'parliament' were only rarely considered to be appropriate. An overall significant difference was found ($F(8, 6404) = 403.88$, $p \geq 0$) between these ratings.

**Table 8.2 Who case-handlers and managers think is most appropriate to conduct the investigation into employee reports of internal wrongdoing?[a]**

| Unit or individual (mean and std deviation of rating) | Usually appropriate | Sometimes appropriate | Rarely appropriate |
|---|---|---|---|
| Internal audit, fraud, investigation or ethics unit (2.42, 0.61) | 49.0% (353) | 44.7% (322) | 6.4% (64) |
| Manager from another area (2.14, 0.65) | 29.0% (207) | 55.8% (398) | 15.1% (108) |
| Human resources/equity and merit unit (2.10, 0.65) | 26.9% (192) | 56.5% (403) | 16.5% (118) |
| Supervisor of the area reported on (1.87, 0.70) | 18.7% (133) | 49.6% (353) | 31.6% (225) |
| External government watchdog agency (1.86, 0.65) | 15.0% (107) | 55.9% (400) | 29.1% (208) |
| Supervisor of employee who reports (1.83, 0.67) | 15.6% (111) | 52.2% (372) | 32.3% (230) |
| CEO or equivalent (1.62, 0.69) | 11.9% (85) | 38.4% (274) | 49.6% (354) |
| Parliament (1.14, 0.37) | 0.8% (6) | 12.6% (89) | 86.6% (613) |
| Journalist/media (1.04, 0.22) | 0.3% (2) | 4.0% (28) | 95.8% (676) |
| Other (2.20, 0.80) | 43.3% (13) | 33.3% (10) | 23.3% (7) |

[a] 'Valid' percentages are used—that is, the percentage of those who responded to each item rather than the total sample.
Sources: Case-handler and manager surveys: Q28 (n = 828, missing data in each cell).

To ascertain what underpinned these judgments, further analysis found that objectivity or 'social distance' was an important consideration reflected in respondents choosing organisational units or individuals whose role and responsibilities implicitly required objectivity—such as internal fraud investigation or human resource units. These units might also be expected to have the requisite training and knowledge to conduct investigations, although, as will be seen, that assumption is also questionable. The idea of distance is also reflected in respondents choosing 'a manager from another area'.

Appropriateness to investigate is not necessarily a static judgment, but it is likely to depend on such issues as the need for specialised knowledge in particular cases or on the increasing complexity of cases as they proceed. In other words, 'it depends' on the individual circumstances. This accounts for the frequency with which 'sometimes appropriate' was endorsed. This is of particular note in the frequency with which it was seen as 'sometimes' appropriate for an investigation to be conducted by the 'supervisor of the area reported on' (49 per cent, 353), an 'external government watchdog agency' (56 per cent, 400), the 'human resources/equity and merit unit' (56 per cent, 403) or even the 'supervisor of the employee who reports' (52.2 per cent, 372). These results do not mean that the decision about who should investigate is arbitrary; rather, they suggest that criteria such as distance from the reporter (to ensure objectivity) and the investigator's role and responsibility (to ensure they have appropriate knowledge, qualifications or seniority) are primary considerations.

Comparison of Tables 8.1 and 8.2 also begins to point, however, to ways in which the choice of who is best to investigate can be constrained. In Table 8.2, the 'CEO or equivalent' did not rate highly in terms of frequency of appropriateness, in the view of case study agency case-handlers and managers. These were mostly large agencies with a wide range of resources. Possible reasons for this view include not just the availability of these other resources, but the fact that many CEOs are simply too busy to conduct detailed investigations and the desirability of separating investigation findings from decisions about management action. Once the CEO has investigated and reached a view, they might be less well placed to act dispassionately in instituting any action, without at least some appearance of partiality or prejudgment. If the CEO has done the primary investigation, there are also no options left for review of the outcome without heightened risk of conflict between the organisation and the whistleblower. The situation can also be little different if other senior managers, close to the CEO, are used, unless they and the CEO have a robust relationship and well-developed understanding of these sensitive differences.

Table 8.1, however, shows that, in general, public sector organisations do rely heavily on using their CEOs to investigate matters. This could reflect the circumstances that exist in smaller agencies, where other resources are less available, especially when combined with a CEO who takes whistleblowing seriously and is therefore prepared to give high priority to a matter. Nevertheless, these data do point to the likelihood that lack of resources and/or lack of a senior management's grasp of the need for a professional, differentiated approach could be impacting on the ability of many agencies to meet the highest possible investigation standards. As managers might have the responsibility to implement any changes as a consequence of an investigation, prima facie these are competing or even conflicting roles for investigators. The extensive overlap of roles indicates an area that agencies might have to review.

The evidence provided by respondents to the internal witness survey in the case study agencies further complicates this picture. Table 8.3 shows the level of satisfaction of those who reported wrongdoing, with the progress and the outcome of the investigation, according to who conducted the primary investigation.

**Table 8.3 Satisfaction with the performance of the person who first dealt with the report**

| Who dealt with the matter? (n) | How satisfied with progress? | How satisfied with outcome? |
|---|---|---|
| | 1 = not at all satisfied | |
| | 5 = extremely satisfied | |
| | Mean (SD) | Mean (SD) |
| Ethical standards unit (14) | 2.64 (2.10) | 2.36 (2.17) |
| CEO (or equivalent) (27) | 2.04 (1.34) | 2.15 (1.90) |
| Internal witness's supervisor (43) | 1.95 (1.23) | 1.77 (1.17) |
| Human resources/equity and merit unit (13) | 1.92 (1.19) | 1.77 (1.30) |
| Internal audit/fraud investigation unit (13) | 1.92 (1.19) | 1.62 (1.04) |
| Internal ombudsman/complaints unit (7) | 1.86 (1.21) | 1.86 (1.46) |
| Manager senior to the internal witness (62) | 1.85 (1.38) | 1.74 (1.61) |
| External government watchdog/investigation agency (9) | 1.67 (1.22) | 1.56 (1.33) |
| Union/professional association (6) | 1.50 (1.22) | 1.50 (1.22) |
| Other (5) | 1.73 (1.27) | 1.54 (0.69) |

Note: Internal hotline/counselling service (3), member of parliament (2), external hotline or counselling service (0) and journalist (0) were either not nominated by any respondents or were nominated but not rated. An anomalous high rating for 'peer support officer' was excluded as these were very unlikely to have conducted the investigation.
Source: Internal witness survey: Q31, Q34, Q36 (n = 206, data missing).

A high mean score reflects high levels of satisfaction and a lower score reflects the opposite. Given that a score of 3 on both these items was needed to indicate the respondent was even 'somewhat satisfied' with progress or the outcome, the fact that all the mean values fell below this score indicated that, generally, there was a low level of satisfaction with the people who first dealt with the reports. As discussed in Chapter 5, however, this is likely to reflect the fact that internal witness survey respondents were generally less satisfied than respondents from a more random sample.

Satisfaction with the two aspects of the investigation (progress and outcome) closely paralleled each other, as one would expect, since the latter was likely to colour perceptions of the former. No significant difference in satisfaction was found according to who investigated the report (F $(12,165=) = 0.57$, $p > 0.85$). This again indicates that, depending on the situation, a wide variety of potential investigators could be appropriate for the task; or, conversely, whoever investigates faces a similar level of challenges. In either case, this lack of difference points to the need for adequate investigation expertise and knowledge to be available to a wide range of actors. One standardised approach, in terms of who conducts the investigation, is not necessarily required—but the diversity of actors increases the challenge of ensuring that consistently high standards of investigatory practice are achieved across individual organisations and across the public sector as a whole, regardless of who does the work.

Alongside this general finding, the differences in mean ratings in Table 8.3 provide food for thought. Internal witnesses appeared most satisfied with investigations conducted by an ethical standards unit. This could be explained by the professionalism that one would expect to be shown by an ethical standards unit, also indicating that the report is being taken seriously. It is more difficult to explain the lower level of satisfaction with investigations conducted by other specialist units (internal audit and investigation units or human resource units). Different perspectives are coloured in many instances, no doubt, by personal experiences, logistical considerations within agencies and the nature of the report. There could, however, also be some variation across different agencies in who works in these apparently similar organisational units, their specific scope and their governance arrangements. These results could indicate that the newer terminology of 'ethical standards' is indicating a more flexible or reflexive approach, better capable of getting to the bottom of whistleblowers' concerns than older, more functional units. Despite the fact that these are also specialist units, internal witnesses could perceive that their investigation is simply one of many issues being dealt with by these areas.

It remains salient, nevertheless, that internal witnesses, case-handlers and managers all agree that investigations are most often well handled if undertaken by at least some kind of specialist unit, whatever its precise title. This coincidence of view is especially significant given the evidence in Table 8.1 that such units are not necessarily the most present or relied on resource and the evidence from Chapter 4 indicating these units are only infrequently the first people to whom disclosures are made. Instead, the bulk of initial reports are made to first and second-level managers. It will be recalled from the previous chapter that although managers are generally supportive of whistleblowing, they often suffer from an acknowledged lack of awareness of the specific obligations that should govern their response. Together, these data indicate the need for procedures that require all managers to at least notify the relevant specialist units in their organisations when a disclosure is made, at the earliest available opportunity, with a view to referring or sharing the crucial initial decisions about investigation. Assumptions by frontline managers that they can or should investigate the matter alone, or seek to avoid the involvement of others unless problems arise, are only occasionally likely to be safe.

A similar query arises in relation to the very low satisfaction expressed in respect of external watchdog or investigation agencies (that is, integrity agencies). Clearly, these agencies do not currently enjoy much confidence from internal witnesses, and Table 8.2 indicate that they also do not enjoy strong confidence from agency case-handlers and managers. In cases (n = 112) in which case-handlers and managers had experienced the involvement of external agencies in dealing with alleged reprisals against whistleblowers, 40 per cent felt the external agencies had not handled the matter well, with another 40 per cent feeling the external agencies had handled the matter only 'somewhat' well. Only 20 per cent felt external agencies had handled it very or extremely well. Whereas some distance from the incident appears to favour quality investigations, it also appears that too much distance from the issues involved poses a difficult problem, which is usually the case for integrity agencies in terms of direct familiarity and the timeliness of involvement.

A more discordant result from the data is the relatively high satisfaction that internal witnesses had with investigations conducted by the CEO. The high levels of satisfaction with the CEO dealing with the report—which contrast with the views of case-handlers and other managers as to appropriateness—might similarly be explained by the internal witness seeing this as an indication of how important the organisation feels his or her concern to be. It also likely that notwithstanding the risks discussed above, in which a CEO becomes involved early and decisively in a whistleblower's favour, this can short-circuit a variety of potential real and perceived reprisals. The same can be true if the matter is dealt with directly in the first instance by the employee's supervisor. Nevertheless, the risks remain that if the result is not immediately favourable, the consequences for a well-meaning whistleblower can also be dire. One question becomes whether the potential advantages of decisive management intervention can be achieved by other means—for example, in the manner in which support is provided to whistleblowers, without needing to rely so heavily on CEOs or immediate supervisors to conduct the investigation themselves.

On a similar note, the perceived adequacy of internal investigations can be influenced by the fact that those responsible for investigation also have other roles—including a responsibility to provide support to those involved. As reviewed in more detail in Chapter 9, only 162 (54 per cent) of the 304 agencies that responded to the agency survey indicated they had procedures for identifying internal witnesses who needed 'active management support' during or after an investigation. When they did have procedures, the qualitative detail confirmed that it often fell to investigators to initiate or provide this support. For example, one agency commented: '[The] investigator would explain the process, [and] invite [the] internal witness to have a support person present at meetings/interviews.' Another stated that 'people needing support are also identified in the investigation process', while another stated that the people involved could seek 'support from the investigating officer'; another stated that assessing the need for support was 'part of [the] normal investigation'.

While these responses indicate that agencies understand the stress associated with participating in an investigation as an internal witness or interviewee, it also demonstrates the central role investigators play in the overall management of the people involved. In other words, not only do certain individuals in agencies—often managers—receive reports and conduct the investigation, they often have the responsibility to assess whether an internal or a witness requires support, and to provide it. Moreover, the data suggest that often they are the only people expected to ensure this occurs. The issue of support provided to internal witnesses is dealt with more fully in Chapter 9, but these results indicate that, like CEOs and other senior managers, many other types of investigators also have potentially conflicting roles. Keeping an internal witness happy and investigating their disclosure in a professional and impartial manner are not always compatible objectives. These data therefore reinforce the general issue of how investigation capacities can be institutionally configured so as to reduce or remove the effects of possible conflicts, as well as the need for basic training, to be discussed below.

## External investigators

As shown in Table 8.1, additional information was provided by more than 100 agencies in the agency survey about the use of external investigators. Almost one-third of agencies described using external contractors or consultants with human resource, legal or other investigative backgrounds, while about another 10 per cent used external government agencies such as police, ombudsmen or state corruption commissions. Of particular interest was the relatively frequent practice of drawing on an established panel of contract investigators.

Decisions regarding who conducts an investigation on behalf of the agency depend on criteria of complexity, sensitivity and whether the investigation requires specialist knowledge held outside the agency. Agencies explained that the nature of the alleged wrongdoing often dictated who conducted the investigation. For example, one agency mentioned specific 'contract investigators for discrimination, harassment and major policy breaches' and another a 'security firm to investigate a breach of a computer system', while a third used a company to investigate Workcover claims. In a further example, a respondent from one large department used specialist investigators who would be called on if this were ever necessary to deal with matters of child abuse. In other cases, 'consultants recommended by an integrity agency and/or recognised as qualified investigators' were used. The police and law firms were also mentioned for serious or criminal matters; former police officers appeared to be used because of their solid background in criminal investigation.

This frequent use of external investigators highlights a different range of issues. As can be seen, professional skills and capacity are less likely to be an issue, because, especially where contracted, the purpose of contracting the firm is to access these skills. Similarly, the use of external investigators is likely to achieve the desired qualities of distance and objectivity and to escape conflict between investigation and other organisational roles, such as management action and employee support. External contractors are also available to smaller agencies that could otherwise struggle to meet investigation needs in-house.

The involvement of an external investigator, however, relies on internal management action to identify the disclosure and initiate the investigation. When employee reports of wrongdoing raise issues that are potentially sensitive or embarrassing to the organisation, there is an inevitably increased risk that external resources will not be accessed, even if they might be in other circumstances. Further, if in many agencies it falls to investigators to become involved in internal witness support, this role is less likely to be fulfilled by external investigators engaged simply to complete the investigation task. Consequently, in some organisations, the use of external investigators could indicate that no-one is providing this support. These risks can increase the need for external integrity agencies to take a more active role in ensuring that some organisations are providing adequate support, as well as the relevance of other findings in Chapter 9.

## Training and qualifications of investigators

Training in investigation can be obtained through prior professional training—for example, as a detective in police work, forensic accounting training among finance professionals, grievance resolution training among human resource professionals and applied legal experience. Training can also occur through professional investigative qualifications (graduate certificates) offered by tertiary institutions such as Charles Sturt University, the University of Western Sydney and the TAFE level 'Certificate IV' in fraud investigation. Short courses, training sessions and awareness raising in administrative investigation are also available through some integrity agencies. All of these training options, and more, were mentioned in responses to the agency survey. These data make it clear that a wide variety of training and education resources are available to public sector organisations and their staff.

The important questions relate to how many agencies avail themselves of this training and how many case-handlers and managers dealing with whistleblowing issues have the benefit of it. Table 8.4 shows how organisations responded to the agency survey question 'What training does your agency provide or require for staff who investigate reports of wrongdoing?'. Among the options given, 'professional training' was defined as 'training accredited as contributing towards a qualification on criminal or administrative investigations, or formal training courses provided or funded by the agency'.

These results give real cause for concern. They are not clear-cut, as some agencies indicated a mixture of options, including professional training for some staff, only informal or 'on-the-job' training for others and 'no particular training' for others. Only one-quarter of agencies, however, provided or required professional training for any of their staff. Since professional training was specifically defined in terms of an accredited qualification, the range of training modalities included in 'informal/on-the-job training' could be very wide, including one-day seminars or information sessions, as well as learning from colleagues or literally 'learning as you go'. On the positive side, respondent agencies could also have included the high-quality training provided by integrity agencies under this 'informal training'. If so, these staff could still have good foundational information. Nevertheless, the fact that such a low proportion of agencies indicated that they had any investigation staff who were professionally qualified, and that the single largest group of agencies indicated they neither provided nor required any training whatsoever, is great cause for concern.

In order to achieve a more detailed picture, case-handlers and managers in the case study agencies were also asked for information on their level of training. 'Professional training' was here defined as 'accredited training as contributing towards a university or TAFE qualification, or formal training courses provided or funded by the agency'. A distinction was also made between professional training 'prior to taking up my current role' and 'once I took up my current role'. Table 8.5 shows the proportion of respondents who had received each of the eight possible combinations of types and sources of training.

## Table 8.4 Training provided or required by your agency for staff who investigate reports of wrongdoing (agencies)

| Level of training | % (n) |
| --- | --- |
| No particular training | 39.4 (117) |
| Informal/on-the-job training | 35.0 (104) |
| Professional training | 9.8 (29) |
| Mixture of professional and other training (including none) | 15.8 (47) |

Source: Agency survey: Q17 (n = 297).

## Table 8.5 Types of training for managers and case-handlers

| | No particular training | Informal/ on-the-job training | Professional training before taking up current role | Professional training at agency after taking up current role | % (n) |
| --- | --- | --- | --- | --- | --- |
| 1 | Yes | | | | 24.4 (188) |
| 2 | | Yes | | | 42.8 (330) |
| 3 | | | Yes | | 10.9 (84) |
| 4 | | | | Yes | 11.0 (85) |
| 5 | | Yes | Yes | | 2.6 (20) |
| 6 | | | Yes | Yes | 3.9 (30) |
| 7 | | Yes | | Yes | 2.1 (16) |
| 8 | | Yes | Yes | Yes | 2.3 (18) |
| | | | | | 100 (771) |
| | 24.4% (188) | 49.8% (384) | 19.7% (152) | 19.3% (149) | |

Sources: Case-handler and manager surveys: Q22 (n = 828, missing data n = 57).

In general, as will be seen through the next two chapters, these case study agencies had more developed systems and procedures for dealing with whistleblowing than other agencies. Nevertheless, even in these agencies, these results give continuing cause for concern. Indeed a large number of case-handlers and managers (24 per cent) had no particular training at all. Agencies relied heavily on informal training, which was the only source of training for 43 per cent of respondents. Thirty-three per cent of respondents had experienced professional training: 14 per cent before taking up their role, 13 per cent after taking up their role and 6 per cent both before and after taking up their role.

Given that case-handlers and managers responded to this survey, it was possible that any shortage of training was concentrated among certain types of respondents—for example, managers—and that those with more training were also those called on more regularly to deal with whistleblowing cases, such as the staff of internal investigation units. If so, then any shortage might not have such dire implications. Accordingly, Table 8.6 examines the level of training of those respondents employed in the internal investigation units most frequently used to deal with employee reports. The question 'Do you work, or have you worked, in any of the following [internal/investigation] units or roles?' was analysed with reference to the level of training, including only those currently employed in these two types of nominated units. Percentages of the different levels of training are calculated according to the total number of respondents working in such units.

**Table 8.6 Level of training of staff in internal investigation units**

| Level of training | Unit | |
| --- | --- | --- |
| | Internal audit/fraud/ investigation/ethics (n = 81) | Human resources/equity/merit (n = 72) |
| No particular training | 24.3% (20) | 18.0% (13) |
| Informal/on-the-job training | 33.3% (27) | 48.6% (35) |
| Professional training before taking up current role | 14.8% (12) | 6.9% (5) |
| Professional training at agency after taking up current role | 11.1% (9) | 8.3% (6) |
| Professional (before or after) plus informal training | 16.0% (13) | 18.0% (13) |
| | 100% (81) | 100% (72) |

Sources: Case-handler and manager surveys: Q2 and Q22.

Unfortunately, the results in Table 8.6 tend to worsen rather than improve the picture. These data are comparable with the overall results for all case-handlers and managers and reveal a surprisingly low level of training among staff in internal investigation units. Human resource units were more likely to rely on informal training than internal audit, fraud, investigation or ethics units; and, most surprisingly, these units were more likely than human resource units to comprise staff without any specific training at all. That a high percentage of internal investigation unit staff are not professionally trained, based on these data, is a concern, given that they are the most likely to be given the job of dealing with whistleblowing incidents, and with more complex or sensitive incidents.

Overall, it becomes hard to avoid the conclusion that even in the case study agencies, internal investigations and complaint handling are not seen as complex professional skills requiring appropriate training. The results suggest that a thorough audit is needed of investigatory expertise, training and experience, with the aim of understanding the skills and qualifications of investigators in this important area of administrative investigation. This audit should directly inform the training requirements of administrative investigators—including managers who are assigned this task on an ad hoc basis, but, as a priority, those with more full-time responsibility for investigations and case-handling.

What are the current impacts of this lower than expected level of training? The next section will examine whether there is a direct relationship between investigatory capacity and desirable outcomes from whistleblowing, including employee confidence in the ability of organisations to respond effectively to reports. Before moving to this analysis, it is possible to examine whether any relationship exists between current training levels and the experiences and perceptions of case-handlers and managers themselves.

In order to compare levels of training with other measures, respondents to the case-handler and manager surveys who circled only one source of training or a combination of informal and professional training (either before or while performing the role) were used to generate five levels of training—namely: no training; informal training; professional training before beginning role; professional training after beginning role; and a combination of informal and professional training (levels of training from '0' to '4'). Those who circled that they currently or had previously worked in relevant organisational units were excluded from the analysis to ensure that any significant differences in attitudes or knowledge were less likely to have been influenced by other organisational experience and more likely to result from their distinct levels of training. In practice, this meant that the respondents being compared involved fewer full-time case-handlers and more managers.

First, these respondents were asked how well they felt their training prepared them for dealing with cases of employee reports of wrongdoing, on a scale of 1 (not at all well) to 5 (extremely well). As shown in Table 8.7, a significant difference between training regimes was found (F (4651) = 188.16, p = 0.000, $\eta2 = 0.54$). Those with professional training before taking up their role felt most prepared, as did those who had professional training before and since starting their role. It is likely that this group comprised several former police officers since this is the group most likely to have had previous training in investigation. Those with no training, not surprisingly, felt the least prepared.

**Table 8.7 Level of training by quality of training ('How well did your training prepare you for dealing with these cases?')**

| Level of training | Quality (mean) | Std error | 0 | 1 | 2 | 3 | 4 |
|---|---|---|---|---|---|---|---|
| None (0) | 1.51 | 0.06 | | ** | ** | ** | ** |
| Informal (1) | 2.92 | 0.04 | ** | | ** | ** | ** |
| Professional before (2) | 3.60 | 0.07 | ** | ** | | | |
| Professional during (3) | 3.50 | 0.08 | ** | ** | | | |
| Informal and professional combined (4) | 3.46 | 0.07 | ** | ** | | | |

* p = < 0.05
** p = < 0.01
Source: Case-handler and manager survey: Q22, Q23.

These results confirm that the level of training is not merely an abstract or academic issue. It appears to matter in terms of how well case-handlers and managers themselves feel they are equipped to deal with whistleblowing cases. This resonates with the findings from the previous chapter that even when managers are broadly positive in their outlook towards whistleblowing, they are also often conscious of their low awareness of specific obligations when really confronted with it.

The level of training can also influence the attitudes that case-handlers and managers have towards whistleblowers and their reports, as well as their understanding of the risks and options for managing whistleblowing. Table 8.8 shows that, when asked to agree or disagree with the statement 'Most employee reports are wholly trivial (no information merits investigation)', those without training were significantly more likely to agree than those who had professional training before taking up their role, with or without additional training on the job (F (4688) = 4.22, p = 0, $\eta2$ = 0.02). This result indicates that those without the insights and knowledge conferred by prior professional training and experience could be more inclined towards more harsh, stereotypical views of whistleblowers. If so, the high proportion of under-trained investigators is likely to impact on the manner in which investigations are conducted and the ability of investigators to help manage the individuals involved to a positive conclusion. In addition to skills acquisition, training can be useful in that it can increase recognition of the value and legitimacy of whistleblowing for the improvement of the organisation.

**Table 8.8 Level of training by agreement with statement: 'Most employee reports are wholly trivial (no information merits investigation)'**

| Level of training | Agreement with statement (mean) | Std error | 0 | 1 | 2 | 3 | 4 |
|---|---|---|---|---|---|---|---|
| None (0) | 2.29 | 0.06 | | | * | | * |
| Informal (1) | 2.12 | 0.04 | | | | | |
| Professional before (2) | 1.96 | 0.09 | * | | | | |
| Professional during (3) | 2.00 | 0.09 | | | | | |
| Informal and professional (4) | 1.95 | 0.08 | * | | | | |

* p =< 0.05
Sources: Case-handler and manager surveys: Q27a.

A similar result was found when examining case-handlers and managers' perceptions of how those who report wrongdoing are treated by management. As shown in Table 8.9, respondents were asked how well they thought employees who reported wrongdoing were treated by management in their organisation. On a scale from 1 to 5, 1 indicated 'extremely well' and 5 indicated 'extremely badly'. A statistically significant difference in the belief about management treatment was found according to the level of training (F (4697) = 5642.88, p = 0.000, $\eta2 = 0.03$). Those without training were more inclined to believe that management treated whistleblowers poorly than those with professional training, again suggesting that those without the insights and knowledge of training had a more stereotypical, negative view of the whistleblowing process. Perhaps because they also then become exposed to more cases, those with more training appear to have a slightly more accurate assessment of the overall results suggested in Chapter 5 and a more positive outlook of, or confidence in, the ability of organisations to manage whistleblowing well.

**Table 8.9 Relationship of level of training with perceptions of how employees who report wrongdoing are treated by management**

| Level of training | Perception of treatment (mean) | Std error | 0 | 1 | 2 | 3 | 4 |
|---|---|---|---|---|---|---|---|
| None (0) | 3.19 | 0.07 | | | * | * | * * |
| Informal (1) | 2.96 | 0.05 | | | | | |
| Professional before (2) | 2.80 | 0.10 | * | | | | |
| Professional during (3) | 2.80 | 0.10 | * | | | | |
| Informal and professional (4) | 2.74 | 0.10 | * * | | | | |

* p =< 0.05
** p =< 0.01
Sources: Case-handler and manager surveys: Q32.

These analyses suggest that a lack of training in investigation is related to small, but statistically significant differences in attitudes to whistleblowers and the management of reports. Those with no specific professional training feel less well prepared to investigate cases and are slightly more inclined to see reports as trivial compared with those with professional training. A general conclusion is that professional training for those dealing with and investigating reports will contribute to higher skills and more constructive attitudes towards reporters and the agency's management of whistleblowers.

## Comparing investigation practices across agencies

The preceding sections suggest that investigation capacity is lower than desirable in many agencies and confirms that issues of capacity are important. Is there also clear evidence that these issues make a difference in terms of other outcomes—for example, that when investigation capacity is higher, this is contributing to more favourable reporting climates?

To answer this, comparisons of a number of agencies were carried out based on their differing levels of 'investigatory capacity'. A proxy measure of investigatory capacity was generated from a composite of several different measures from the employee survey and the case-handler and manager surveys. Only the 12 case study agencies for which there was sufficient data from these surveys could be included. The data used to form this composite measure were: the percentage of agency employees from the employee survey who reported that their complaint was investigated; the extent to which respondents to the case-handler and manager surveys in the agency felt their level of training prepared them for dealing with whistleblowing reports; and the agencies' mean scores on an 'overall perception' scale developed for this analysis, using the results from three further questions from the case-handler and manager surveys ('Overall, how committed do you think your organisation is to dealing respectfully and properly with employees who report wrongdoing?' [Q59]; 'How successful do you think your organisation is in encouraging employees to voice concerns about perceived wrongdoing?' [Q61]; and 'Based on your experience, how likely would you be to advise employees to report or provide information about wrongdoing in your organisation?' [Q62]).

The proportion of investigated complaints (as a percentage of agency participants) was weighted most heavily in the ranking, based on the assumption that a lower proportion of investigated reports signified either less ability or willingness to investigate. The next heaviest weighting was given to the mean score on the 'overall perception' scale and the perceived quality of training was considered last.

The resulting composite proximal measure can be thought of as a guide only. It divides the 12 agencies into two groups, reflecting the relative quality of investigative capacity rather than a definitive measure. The two groups comprise those agencies with 'average' and 'slightly better than average' investigatory capacities, rather than agencies that are clearly 'bad' or 'good'.

These two groups were then compared, via Chi-square, on a number of outcome measures:

- those agencies' inaction rates in response to serious observed wrongdoing
- the proportion of respondents who did not report, who gave a belief that 'nothing would be done' as a reason (employee survey: Q35k)
- the reporting rate in response to observed wrongdoing (employee survey: Q26)
- the proportion of reporters who said that they would report again (employee survey: Q34).

Given the nature of the measure, large differences were not anticipated. Further, it was not necessarily to be expected that employees would directly consider issues such as the likely nature and quality of the investigation when calculating whether to report. When all employee survey respondents were asked whether they believed that 'management carefully investigates employee concerns about wrongdoing', a substantial proportion (42 per cent) neither agreed nor disagreed, suggesting simply that they probably did not know what investigation responses usually followed employee reports in their organisation. Slightly less than 40 per cent of respondents agreed and approximately 20 per cent disagreed or strongly disagreed. A similar limitation is suggested if the above measure of the case study agencies' investigatory capacity is used to compare the strength of particular reasons why employees said they reported. An important reason was the confidence of reporters that their 'report would help to correct the problem' (employee survey: Q27e). There was, however, no significant difference in the level of importance given to this reason by reporters in those agencies with only 'average' investigatory capacity (mean = 3.09) when compared with reporters in agencies with 'slightly better than average' capacity (mean = 3.07; $F(1633) = 0.08$, $p = 0.78$). This suggests that employees' beliefs about whether or not organisational improvement is likely to follow from their report, as a motivating factor, are formed independently of any evaluation they might make about the likely quality of investigations—assuming they are in a position to judge.

These limitations could explain the results from the first and second comparisons listed above, which showed no significant difference between the agencies. The inaction rates of the two groups of agencies were calculated in the manner outlined in Chapter 2, by identifying the proportion of employee survey respondents who observed 'very' or 'extremely' serious wrongdoing but did not report it and did not deal with it themselves, without anyone else having reported it. This comparison did not identify a statistically significant difference ($\chi2(1) = 0.82$, $p = 0.37$). Similarly, there was no significant difference between the two groups of agencies in terms of the proportion of respondents who declined to report the reason why they believed nothing would be done ($\chi2(1) = 1.7$, $p = 0.20$).

While this could initially suggest that differences in investigatory capacity had no observable impact on reporting behaviour, the two remaining comparisons did show a positive result. In agencies with a 'slightly better than average' investigatory capacity, a higher proportion of employees who observed wrongdoing went on to report the most serious instance (49.9 per cent) than in agencies with an 'average' capacity (44.1 per cent). This was a statistically significant difference ($\chi2$ (1) = 4.55, p = 0.03, $\eta2$ = 0).

Finally, an analysis was performed to find out whether those who reported said they would be more likely to report again, in agencies with higher capacity. This is perhaps the most meaningful analysis, given that it tests for an association using the views of respondents who are known to have had firsthand experience of the investigatory capacity of the organisation. On a scale of 1 to 5, the mean response in agencies with 'slightly better than average' capacity (mean = 4.22) was significantly higher than in the agencies with 'average' investigatory capacity (mean = 4.01; F (1650) = 6.85, p = 0.009). In other words, those with experience of 'slightly better than average' investigatory processes indicated that they would be more likely to report again. For the same reason that these data were seen as important in Chapter 5, these results were an indicator of how a higher level of capacity was likely to flow back into attitudes to reporting held more widely across the organisation.

Each part of the process of encouraging staff to report and then managing reports of alleged wrongdoing must work well. Not only do staff members need to feel comfortable about reporting, their reports need to be dealt with properly by managers and others to whom they report. Analysis in earlier chapters showed that staff members find it difficult to accurately assess what the real management response will be, even when they have high trust that it will be positive. Their likely knowledge of investigation practices and standards, before the event, is more limited again. Fundamentally, even if 'first-time' reporting behaviour is likely to be based more on trust than experience, the confidence of employees that an effective organisational response will follow does appear to be impacted on by the capacity to conduct investigations objectively, competently and professionally. Exactly how the benefits of stronger investigatory capacity flow through to the awareness of staff and their increased propensity to report is a matter for further research. This analysis has nevertheless indicated that stronger investigatory capacity can make a difference—not simply in terms of correct substantive outcomes, but in terms of the broader reporting climate within the organisation.

## Discussion and conclusions

A properly investigated report is the only sound basis for taking institutional action with regard to an individual found to be responsible for wrongdoing or for effecting organisational change where systems, governance and processes are found to be at fault. The manner in which employee disclosures about wrongdoing are investigated will, from the outset, have an impact on whether there is a satisfactory result. Poor investigations can lead to protracted and expensive cases, give cause for further complaint and conflict, contribute to the many stresses on individuals and the organisation and bring about a loss of public confidence in the agency's ability to 'investigate its own'. Debate often arises about whether investigations of misconduct or wrongdoing can be conducted appropriately by individuals or units within the agency that is the subject of the complaint.

Notwithstanding this debate, by far the majority of investigations into reports are conducted internally—and often with success. The aim of this chapter has been to explore in greater detail whether there is scope for investigative practice to be improved, so as to help build more robust, well-recognised systems for dealing more effectively with whistleblowing reports in a higher number of cases.

The chapter has examined who conducts investigations of reports of wrongdoing and what training they have, across a wide pool of public agencies. It has also compared their level of training with other measures such as internal witnesses' satisfaction with the progress and outcome of the investigation of their report. A notable result was the inconsistency in the level and type of training of investigators, with very low levels of training in circumstances in which a much higher level should reasonably be expected, and an awareness of these inadequacies on the part of many of the staff involved.

It is possible that these results can be explained partially by the wide variation in roles and responsibilities included under the broad grouping of 'case-handlers and managers' and others who conduct investigations. It is also clear that decisions about who should conduct an investigation, and how, are grounded in a range of agency-specific issues, including the size of the agency and the number and nature of reports it deals with. The current state of affairs, however, could also be explained by the fact that development of practice and procedure in administrative investigations is still in relative infancy. The recognition of the need for coherent, comprehensive and professional investigation approaches has, until relatively recently, been limited to a range of specific, segmented fields. Reliance on former police as criminal investigators might not necessarily translate into quality investigations of non-criminal issues. Human resource officers familiar with investigations of personnel and workplace grievances, equal opportunity, bullying or harassment might not recognise the public interest components of disclosures about defective administration or professional negligence. Specialist accounting and auditing consultants might have expertise in cases of fraud or breach of security, but be ill equipped to identify, substantiate or suggest answers to internal policy breakdowns. Generalist managers tasked with guiding the organisational response might have any of these areas of expertise, or none of them.

For these reasons, a new model of investigation is emerging distinct from criminal investigations. Manuals are being developed—for example, by the NSW Ombudsman (2004b)—that provide guidance for how administrative investigations should be conducted. The results presented in this chapter contribute substantially to the developing literature on these types of investigations. As suggested in the body of the chapter, there is a need for a thorough audit of investigatory expertise, training and experience to complement this information about the investigation of whistleblower reports. Irrespective of the fact that this is a developing field, however, it is clear that to improve practice, attaining certain levels of training is essential—particularly given the evidence that the significance of professional training lies not only in technical skills but in improved understanding of whistleblowing as a total process.

In considering the scope for the improvement of investigatory expertise, it should be recognised that many public sector organisations require this sort of capacity for reasons other than for investigations arising from a whistleblowing incident. Indeed, they could already possess it. For example, most large public sector agencies regularly investigate breaches of codes of conduct and other workplace matters, while any agencies whose functions include licensing need to investigate breaches as a part of their statutory function. Organisations that have other areas of investigatory capacity should be able to swing that capacity across to the effective investigation of whistleblower reports.

While this chapter's finding about low levels of investigatory expertise, training and experience have wider ramifications than just whistleblowing, the need to deal well with employee disclosures can, and should, nevertheless provide a catalyst for the development of more expertise. Internal reporting of wrongdoing occurs in a more fraught social context than many other subjects of criminal and administrative investigation, such as non-compliance. Investigation skills must be addressed to the permeability of the boundaries between personal grievances and matters of broader organisational or public integrity. Distinguishing between the elements of disclosures that raise public interest elements and those that spring from an unhappy workplace, and ensuring all are dealt with appropriately, is a challenge for any agency. These challenges must be met head on, recognising that in many whistleblowing situations, the workplace has become a contested space in which there are differences of opinion, work standards, power relationships, professional judgment and ethical standards. Whistleblowing also imposes obligations on agencies to conduct and manage investigations in ways that recognise their special duty of care towards their informants and witnesses, being also their own employees—as will be discussed further in the next chapter.

Finally, the chapter showed a number of relationships between the existing 'investigatory capacity' of agencies and other outcomes, including general attitudes of managers and case-handlers to whistleblowing, confidence in the ability to prevent or contain management mistreatment of whistleblowers and the willingness of employees to report. While more study is needed into the role of investigatory capacity in encouraging employees to feel more comfortable about reporting, these results confirm that addressing weaknesses in capacity is a fundamental element of ensuring that staff members speak up about their concerns.

As discussed in Chapters 1 and 2, and again in the previous chapter, an overall conclusion from this research is the finding of a high level of staff and management commitment to professional management of whistleblowing reports. The question remains how this commitment can be more routinely translated into practice. There is a clear need to close the gaps between broad principles and practical realities.

The results from this chapter reinforce the pivotal importance of approaches taken by public sector managers to prevent and remedy problems on the ground. The need for better systems and procedures begins with efforts to ensure any investigation can be carried out competently by the organisation or passed appropriately outside the organisation for investigation. There is special need for effective resources to be devoted to investigation by the organisations involved. Areas shown as requiring more attention include the training of investigators, the professionalisation of investigation practices, clearer differentiation between investigation roles and other institutional roles and mechanisms for ensuring that complainants are dealt with sensitively and kept informed of the progress and outcome of the investigation. The data also indicate a need for a better relationship between frontline managers and specialist units in the way reports of wrongdoing are notified and referred; and a better relationship between agencies and integrity agencies to overcome the problems of distance and time that, on this evidence, can hamper the usefulness of the latter. These reforms will provide the foundation for developing excellent practice in the investigation of employee reports and a basis for reflection on the developing practice of internal investigations more generally.

## ENDNOTES

[1] The author thanks James Herbert and Peter Cassematis for conducting the analyses in this chapter, and acknowledges Gary Manison and Edith Cowan University for access to teaching materials, co-written by the author, on the general conduct of administrative investigations, and Shayne Sherman for productive discussions.

# 9. Internal witness support: the unmet challenge

## A. J. Brown and Jane Olsen

## Introduction

In recent decades, the protection of public interest whistleblowers from reprisals has become a major goal in Australian public administration. Practical theories for how this is to be achieved have, however, been slow to emerge. Much of the commitment to protecting whistleblowers has been confounded by the complexity of the issues that internal reporting provokes in the workplace, as well as by a range of conflicting stereotypes and assumptions about what whistleblowing involves, without the benefit of any detailed understanding of what really occurs.

At the same time, concepts of whistleblower protection have often been focused on the 'back end' of the problem. These include affording legal protection, such as relief from criminal or civil liability, and other responses such as the criminalisation of reprisals themselves. While important for their facilitating and deterrent effects, these responses serve only a likely minority of cases, in which whistleblowers have persevered to the point of attracting heavier risks or have cases fitting tight criteria for prosecution. Most importantly, these remedies are tailored to circumstances in which damage has already been done and in which the whistleblower has already become the victim of reprisals or other conflicts. Once experienced, these are likely to be problems from which an individual public officer's career and wellbeing might never fully recover, irrespective of legal protection and remedies. Little guidance has been available on how to minimise the number of public interest whistleblowers who find themselves in this position in the first place.

This chapter describes the extent to which Australian public sector agencies are making progress in pursuing this last, complementary approach to the risks faced by whistleblowers: the development of systems and procedures to help support and guide employees who report wrongdoing, as well as other employees, through the complex issues that inevitably accompany many whistleblowing cases. It therefore addresses the second of the two most crucial responses to whistleblowing in any agency—Chapters 5 and 8 having already addressed investigatory outcomes and capacity. How well are agencies addressing the risks of reprisal and other internal conflicts, managing the welfare of whistleblowers and remedying such problems that their best efforts have been unable to successfully prevent? To what extent is internal witness management becoming less of a secret 'art' and more of a 'science' (Brown 2001)?

The first part of this chapter examines the evidence provided by participating agencies about their internal witness support strategies—in response to the agency survey and, in the case study agencies, through the reported experiences of respondents to the internal witness, case-handler and manager surveys. The analysis outlines how many public sector agencies have procedures and organised systems for internal witness support and the scale of these systems, in terms of how many people they assist and how those people come to be supported.

The results show that organised systems for supporting and protecting internal witnesses are in relative infancy. Only 54 per cent of all agencies surveyed had relevant procedures and only 11 per cent of all agencies surveyed had a formal internal witness support system. Moreover, even within the group of case study agencies that did have a higher level of informal and formal systems, only a very small proportion of public interest whistleblowers were estimated as having ever come into contact with those systems. For these agencies, the number of employees who received organised internal witness support of this kind equated to perhaps 1.3 per cent of all public interest whistleblowers in those agencies and 6.5 per cent of all public interest whistleblowers who indicated via the research that they were treated badly by management or colleagues.

The reasons for this low take-up of organised or dedicated support services, even in the case study agencies, are likely to include:

- the low level of resources dedicated to such programs
- a previous shortage of data regarding the overall level of whistleblowing
- uncertainty or confusion about the types of employees intended to be targeted by programs
- an absence or inadequacy of procedural guidance on how employees should access the support, including an over-reliance on whistleblowers' self-identifying as such for the purposes of gaining support
- lack of management information systems for ensuring that all deserving whistleblowing cases can be identified and assessed for support
- inadequate or misapplied statutory definitions.

The second part of the chapter documents the sources of support experienced by public interest whistleblowers and the types of strategies or methods used. These analyses draw on data from the case study agencies. Not surprisingly, given the first results, the main sources of support that currently prevent more whistleblowers from suffering more than they do are not organised support programs, but informal social and professional networks, including family, friends, colleagues, union officials and supervisors. For those whistleblowers whose experience becomes more difficult, some sources of support, including professional counsellors and more formalised assistance programs, become more important, but supervisors, managers and investigation agencies become increasingly less so.

These analyses confirm the low uptake to date of more formalised support programs. They also reveal that case-handlers and managers—while not excessively optimistic about their own success—nevertheless continue to overestimate the extent to which organised or official sources of support are helping prevent worse outcomes. In other words, the extent to which whistleblower support is currently reliant on informal, social and professional networks does not appear to be properly appreciated. This creates a high risk that support will fail in any of the many circumstances in which the dual role of direct supervisors and line managers, described in Chapter 7, can turn from positive to negative. There are also signs that most support strategies can be somewhat reactive and attuned to bolstering the coping skills of whistleblowers in order to help them 'tough out' any difficult situations, rather than geared to management intervention against the sources of workplace conflict.

Third, the chapter examines the measures taken by agencies to assess the risks of reprisal and other major problems in whistleblowing cases and to respond to those risks should they be realised. These results provide like evidence that agency systems are currently largely reactive. In the majority of agencies, there is insufficient focus on thorough assessment of cases for the risks of what might go wrong, as opposed to providing support in the hope that nothing will. The reasons for this include a lack of prior data about the nature of the risks, such as would enable a more coherent approach to assessment. They also include, again, a lack of the internal management information systems needed to enable case-handlers to engage supervisors and other managers in an effective risk-management approach, by knowing more about more cases earlier, rather than waiting for problems to arise.

Finally, the analyses also show that when reprisal risks are realised, agency case-handlers and managers do not currently regard themselves as very well equipped or well placed to deal with them. Their evidence confirms the indications from Chapter 5 that, generally, allegations that whistleblowers have suffered reprisals or other management lapses are not currently handled well. The most common reasons for the fact such allegations are only rarely substantiated are not that reprisals have not occurred, but a range of difficulties in investigation, especially relevant to the fact that most reprisals are not acts for which individuals can be held culpable to a criminal standard of proof, but rather management reprisals and institutional reactions. Overall, the evidence indicates the need for a fresh approach to the handling of whistleblowing cases in which questions arise about the adequacy of the management response, including a new or different relationship between line and integrity agencies.

A major aim of internal witness support strategies is to reduce the need for whistleblowers to take on an adversarial role when they disclose information about public interest wrongdoing—either in the course of the investigation or as instigators of their own support or as prosecutors of their own cause should they suffer detriment as a result of reporting. Instead, the aim is to enable public officials to play a more 'instrumental role' in the public sector's integrity systems (Whitton 1996) in which their duty is done, wrongdoing is addressed and rectified and they are able to emerge from their reporting role without undue stress and without having experienced, or caused, undue conflict. The term 'internal witness' itself, introduced in Chapter 1, is intended to connote this more instrumental role. The corollary of this role is that public sector agencies and the wider integrity system must accept a greater responsibility for ensuring the welfare of those who report and face up more rapidly to circumstances in which internal witness support requires more active intervention, or, should this fail, other remedies. These analyses suggest that while the prospects for greater success are good, the public sectors studied have a long way to go.

## Internal witness support programs

### Agency procedures and systems

The reasons for internal systems for supporting public interest whistleblowers and other internal witnesses are already well demonstrated. Chapter 5 reviewed the extent of the problems that can befall those who report wrongdoing, whether in the form of mistreatment, either from management or from colleagues, or other indirect impacts including those associated with natural tension and stress. In the case study agencies, whistleblowers' evidence of reprisals was confirmed largely by case-handlers and managers. Further, Chapter 6 demonstrated that as soon as a report of wrongdoing becomes more complex—for example, as soon as a case involves more serious wrongdoing, more alleged wrongdoers and more senior people—the risks of mistreatment rise exponentially.

The data presented in Part 1 nevertheless also demonstrate why these are not problems of which agencies can afford to wash their hands, and hence they demonstrate why internal support strategies represent a logical response. Contrary to many assumptions, the basic value of whistleblowing to organisational and public integrity is widely appreciated in public sector organisations, by fellow employees and managers alike. Notwithstanding the known incidence of reprisals and other conflicts, the principle is widely accepted that employees who report wrongdoing should not be made to suffer as a result. Contrary to many assumptions, the bulk of public interest whistleblowing begins and ends as an internal process, for which no-one other than the agency is currently responsible. In common law, employers already have a duty of care to employees to provide support and guidance through these processes. Finally, agencies know that it is in their own interests to facilitate internal reporting, as an alternative to external whistleblowing—and that this goal is made difficult if they have made no allowance for the protection of those who come forward. For all these reasons, how to support and protect whistleblowers is already a 'live' internal issue in most agencies.

How many agencies currently meet these needs with explicit policies, procedures and programs? The answer is: only a limited number. Of the 304 agencies who responded to the agency survey, 76 per cent (231 agencies) said that they had 'internal disclosure procedures' of some kind. These procedures are, however, often focused only on encouraging staff to make disclosures and dealing with how they should be investigated—as will be confirmed in more detail in Chapter 10. Tables 9.1 and 9.2 show that fewer agencies currently have procedures or systems that extend to the identification of employees needing 'active management support' as a result of their report or disclosure. Table 9.1 shows that only 54 per cent (162) of all agencies surveyed, including 61 per cent (70) of the agencies that participated in the employee survey, indicated that they had such procedures or systems. All 15 case study agencies indicated that they had such systems.

Moreover, when agencies indicated that they had relevant systems, these were often acknowledged to be only 'informal'. Only 34 per cent of all agencies surveyed had formal procedures for the provision of support, while Table 9.2 shows that only 20 per cent of agencies with procedures—11 per cent of all agencies surveyed—supported these procedures with a formal program.

While the ability to provide a dedicated program is undoubtedly often constrained by issues of agency size, these figures indicate that the development of such programs is still only in its early stages in the Australian public sector. In the meantime, as also shown by Table 9.2, in the majority of agencies, the only available strategies for support lie with generalised employee welfare services (not tailored for whistleblowing) or support services that agencies believe are available from external or central government agencies. In fact, at the time of the survey, few if any external agencies provided any such support services in the jurisdictions studied, beyond general advice in relation to reporting and investigation processes. While there is a recognised need for support programs, there is also uncertainty—if not confusion—about what is available and how it should be provided.

**Table 9.1 Presence of agency systems for providing internal witness support (per cent)**

| Does your agency have procedures or systems for identifying internal witnesses who may need active management support as a result of their report or disclosure? | All agencies (n = 304) | Employee survey agencies (n = 118) | Case study agencies (n = 15) |
|---|---|---|---|
| No | 46 (136) | 40 (46) | - |
| Yes, formal procedures | 34 (101) | 41 (47) | 87 (13) |
| Yes, informal procedures or systems | 20 (61) | 20 (23) | 13 (2) |
| Total | 100 (298) | 100 (116) | 100 (15) |
| (Missing) | (6) | (2) | - |

Source: Agency survey: Q25.

**Table 9.2 Source of internal witness support in agencies (per cent)[a]**

| Who does your agency rely on to support or manage internal witnesses? | All agencies (n = 162) | Employee survey agencies (n = 70) | Case study agencies (n = 15) |
|---|---|---|---|
| General assistance or counselling services available to all employees | 83 (135) | 81 (57) | 87 (13) |
| Our own informal internal witness support systems | 46 (74) | 57 (40) | 47 (7) |
| External/central government agencies | 24 (39) | 17 (12) | 13 (2) |
| Our own, formal internal witness support program | 20 (33) | 29 (20) | 60 (9) |

[a] Total does not add to 100 per cent because multiple responses were permitted.
Source: Agency survey: Q27.

Overall, these results show a cup that is more empty than full. The fact that many agencies do have systems and procedures for supporting internal witnesses confirms that the provision of support is recognised by many as important. The high proportion of agencies admitting to having no organised approach, however, indicates that many agencies are yet to scratch the surface in this direction. These results show that across the public sector, there could be considerable untapped potential for reducing the number of internal witnesses who feel mistreated, if only for the reason that many agencies are yet to make an organised effort.

The question becomes, what effort should be made? In some jurisdictions, as discussed in Chapter 11, all agencies are in theory under a legislative obligation to have such procedures and systems and their failure to do so already represents a technical statutory breach. The low take-up of procedures and systems indicates, however, a deeper problem than simply lack of organisational will and commitment. Even where statutory obligations exist, these are short on useful detail. Until this research, there have been little data on the nature of more formal programs and, most crucially, on whether they have any effect. The remainder of this chapter begins to broach these questions.

## Scale and uptake of internal witness support programs

When agencies do have more formalised internal witness support programs, what is the size of these programs? Most importantly, how many internal witnesses do they reach? The answers confirm that even where they exist, more formal programs are currently relatively weak in terms of scale and—most importantly—accessibility.

Table 9.3 shows that whether formal or informal, most internal witness support programs currently function without any dedicated staff. Only 21 per cent (65) of all agencies could provide an estimate of having expended any staff resources on internal witness support, including contracted support, with the overall number of full-time equivalents (FTEs) very low. The case study agencies, all of which had procedures but only 10 of which provided staff support to a program, expended the highest number of staff resources, averaging 3.2 FTE per agency.

**Table 9.3 Agencies with staff resources for internal witness support (FTE and mean)**

| Estimated number of staff (FTE) involved in internal witness support and management | All agencies n = 65 Total (mean) | Employee survey agencies n = 32 Total (mean) | Case study agencies n = 10 Total (mean) |
|---|---|---|---|
| Central support unit/services | 65.0 (1.0) | 40.0 (1.2) | 12.0 (1.2) |
| Other nominated support people | 67.1 (1.0) | 16.1 (0.5) | 6.0 (0.6) |
| Contracted/external support people | 33.1 (0.5) | 17.1 (0.5) | 9.0 (0.9) |
| Other | 17.0 (0.3) | 9.0 (0.3) | 5.0 (0.5) |
| Total | 182 (2.8) | 82 (2.5) | 32 (3.2) |

Source: Agency survey: Q30.

**Table 9.4 Internal witnesses in receipt of active management support (number and means)**

| Number of internal witnesses who received active management support under agency procedures or systems | | All agencies (n = 136) | Employee survey agencies (n = 54) | Case study agencies (n = 14) |
|---|---|---|---|---|
| a. | 2002–03 | 408 (3.0) | 378 (7.0) | 168 (12.0) |
| b. | 2003–04 | 392 (2.9) | 356 (6.6) | 144 (10.3) |
| c. | 2004–05 | 427 (3.1) | 388 (7.2) | 192 (13.7) |
| | Three-year period | 1 227 (9.0) | 1 122 (20.8) | 504 (36.0 |

Source: Agency survey: Q36.

Table 9.4 sets out the number of individual employees who accessed agency support services in the three years before the survey, according to responses to the agency survey. These data are not limited to agencies with formal programs or dedicated staffing, but include all agencies. Slightly less than half of all agencies, and 84 per cent of all agencies with procedures for providing 'active management support', were able to estimate the number of employees assisted—totalling more than 1200 in the period. Across the 14 case study agencies that supplied data, all of which had procedures and most of which had programs, the estimated total of employees assisted was 504, averaging 36 employees per agency in the three years.

These figures are not insignificant and confirm that, where programs exist, they do have a real workload. The scale of these programs is, however, placed in perspective by the employee survey data from earlier chapters. The 14 case study agencies had a combined total of approximately 330 000 employees at the time of the research. Applying the averaged data for reporting rates arrived at in Chapter 2, which also held for the group of case study agencies, these agencies can be estimated as having had in the order of 38 400 whistleblowers within their ranks in the two-year period (12 per cent of employees, 97 per cent of whom reported internally in the first instance). The total of 504 individuals estimated to have been provided with organised support by these agencies, in the three years, represents about 1.3 per cent of the estimated total whistleblower population.

Clearly, a large proportion of the whistleblowing described in Chapter 2 involves low-level reporting, with reduced risk of major conflict or management reprisal. Therefore, a more meaningful way of gauging the extent to which support programs are reaching their target audience is with reference to the number of whistleblowers who go on to report mistreatment. Across the case study agencies, on average, 20 per cent of whistleblowers went on to report having been treated badly by management or colleagues—giving an estimate in the order of 7700 individuals. On this measure, the total individuals estimated as being provided with organised support (in three years) still represents only 6.5 per cent of the population that can be estimated in retrospect as having been of potential need (in two years). The estimated size of the 'at-risk' population could be further refined in various ways, based on Chapter 6. On any analysis, however, the gap between the number of employees provided with organised support and the likely number of whistleblowers in need is very large.

Why are such a small minority of at-risk whistleblowing cases—probably less than 6 per cent—making it onto the 'radar' of organised internal witness support programs? There is a range of possible explanations.

A first explanation is that the programs themselves, based on the levels of resources involved, have never been designed to operate at a large scale—even if agency resources would permit this. In part, this limited scale can be explained by the fact that, until now, little comprehensive evidence has existed to indicate how much whistleblowing goes on or what the size of the at-risk population might be. Further, it is logical for agencies to have designed any centrally organised and monitored program to meet perceived need—that is, to have planned to service only a limited proportion of those at risk, in order to focus on the worst types of known cases.

A second explanation is that there could be low staff awareness of the existence of the support program; while a third explanation is that even if they are aware of it, staff might be unwilling to access this support.

All these explanations, however, beg the question of exactly what 'gateway' procedures are used to make support services available to employees who report. Tables 9.5 and 9.6 set out evidence for how internal witnesses currently access the available support and the types of individuals at which support programs are aimed.

**Table 9.5 How internal witnesses access available support (per cent)**

| | All agencies (n = 162) | Employee survey agencies (n = 70) | Case study agencies (n = 15) |
|---|---|---|---|
| The internal witness must approach a designated person in the agency | 27 (43) | 30 (21) | 27 (4) |
| The internal witness is approached by a designated person in the agency | 23 (38) | 27 (19) | 27 (4) |
| Combination of the above | 15 (24) | 17 (12) | 33 (5) |
| Our agency's procedures do not specify | 19 (31) | 20 (14) | 7 (1) |
| Other | 27 (44) | 20 (14) | 20 (3) |

Source: Agency survey: Q28.

**Table 9.6 Types of internal witnesses recognised as potentially needing support (per cent)**

| Which best describes the type(s) of internal witnesses recognised by agency procedures or systems as potentially needing active management and support? | Case-handlers and managers combined (n = 464) | Integrity case-handlers (n = 40) |
|---|---|---|
| Any internal witness/employee who provides information about wrongdoing | 41 (192) | 11 (9) |
| Any internal complainant/employee who reports | 30 (138) | 10 (4) |
| Those whose case becomes or is likely to become difficult to manage | 14 (63) | 8 (3) |
| Those identified as making a formal public interest disclosure, protected disclosure or whistleblowing report under legislation | 11 (50) | 33 (13) |
| Those who ask to be, or consent to being, identified as a 'whistleblower' | 5 (21) | 28 (11) |

Sources: Case-handler and manager surveys: Q46; integrity case-handler survey: Q43.

These data reveal some uncertainty about the best methods for identifying those employees who are in need of organised support and for admitting them to the program. As shown in Table 9.5, about 20 per cent of all agencies surveyed did not have any specified procedure for how employees should be identified. In these agencies, it is little wonder that the result is hit-and-miss. The same results also show a divergence between agencies that rely simply on whistleblower self identification and agencies that rely on designated people approaching individual whistleblowers for inclusion. Less than 20 per cent of all agencies (but one-third of the case study agencies) use both methods.

In either case, however, a range of problems arises. If agencies are entirely reliant on employee self-identification, they face the problems of ensuring high staff awareness of the fact that support is available and persuading the more deserving staff to self-identify—not simply as a 'whistleblower', but as one unable to self-manage the situation. Given the evidence in Chapter 6 of the difficulties faced by whistleblowers in accurately assessing reactions and risks, self-identification alone is unlikely to be a reliable strategy, even if staff know of and are prepared to trust the program. Anecdotally, there is evidence that many deserving staff prefer not to access specialised support, at least initially, for fear of the possible negative effects of being tagged as a whistleblower. Conversely, any staff who see whistleblowing processes as possible alternative means for pursuing a personnel or private grievance could be very ready to enlist in such a program.

For all these reasons, best practice is more likely to be found among the 42 per cent of agencies (and 60 per cent of case study agencies) in which at-risk employees are identified and approached by designated people—whether as a sole method or in addition to self-identification. The data show, however, the significant challenges that still stand in the way of agencies extending organised support in this way. First, this relies on an overall understanding of the level of whistleblowing in the organisation, of the kind that is only now becoming available through research such as that outlined in this book. Second, Chapter 4 showed that the bulk of employee disclosures were made to supervisors and other managers in the first instance, being also where many of the most significant reprisal risks could lie. Just as this raises important issues for how investigations are triggered and carried out (Chapter 8), it also raises important issues about effective methods for early identification of those in need of support. In many agencies, the necessary management information systems might not exist that would enable monitoring of incoming cases for assessment as to likely need for intervention—or such systems might not exist in relation to complaints and internal workplace issues. The creation of effective systems for the receipt and notification of all such disclosures, to ensure that appropriate responses can include intervention for the purposes of internal witness support, is an important priority.

Table 9.6 also shows a diversity of opinions, within agencies, as to what types of employees are eligible for support. These data come from case-handlers and managers in the case study agencies, as well as from case-handlers from those integrity agencies from which more than one response was received. There was significant variation in who case-handlers and managers thought were the intended focus of protection, indicating some differences between agencies, but also conflicting assumptions within agencies since, in any one agency, at most only two-thirds of respondents selected the same response. While overall the largest single group of respondents chose the least restrictive definition, and the group sizes reduced in line with increasing restrictiveness, the fact remains that they could not all be right.

Similarly, in integrity agencies in which more than one case-handler responded, at most, only three-quarters of the respondents selected the same answer. Most concerning was the fact that, unlike the case study agency case-handlers, 61 per cent of integrity agency case-handlers selected one of the two most restrictive definitions. This could suggest that integrity agency case-handlers tend only to see cases that fit these definitions. Their assessment could, however, also reflect the reality—as indicated by the data already outlined—that only a very narrow band of employees who report wrongdoing are in fact coming into contact with agency support systems.

Finally, these analyses point to problems in the relationship between legislative requirements and agency practice, in the extent to which statutory definitions of 'public interest disclosures' are helping or hindering the provision of internal support. As outlined in Chapters 1 and 2, the amount of public interest whistleblowing that occurs, which should logically trigger the basic statutory provisions for whistleblower protection that exist in most jurisdictions, is much higher than is currently being reported under that legislation (where reporting obligations exist). This could be explained by the restrictive nature of some statutory definitions; by misunderstanding or misapplication of the definitions within agencies; or, again, by simple lack of management information about the true number of internal disclosures that satisfy those definitions. The key problem is that very little purpose exists for such definitions, if not to ensure that as many at-risk whistleblowers as possible (potentially, almost any) can be identified, assessed and, where necessary, provided with an appropriate level of internal witness support. The fact that current statutory frameworks are providing only limited assistance—and some barriers—to the meeting of this goal becomes an important issue for discussions of legislative reform, taken up in Chapter 11.

## Sources and methods of internal witness support

## Who does provide support?

Given that relatively few agencies have formal support programs, and that few internal witnesses come into contact with them, how is that more whistleblowers do not report mistreatment or reprisals? While the previous section analysed mainly evidence about organised and formalised systems for providing support, it was always presumed that the functions of supporting and managing whistleblowers were likely to involve a wide variety of organisational actors and that these could—and often should—include the direct supervisors and managers of internal witnesses themselves (Brown et al. 2004). In the case study agencies, whistleblowers, case-handlers and managers alike were surveyed about who played important roles in providing assistance and support and offered a range of options in addition to organised support programs. Integrity agency case-handlers were asked the same questions.

The internal witness survey asked who provided the greatest help and support—after the respondent provided their original information about wrongdoing and then after they experienced any 'bad treatment or harm'. Table 9.7 shows the results, ranked in order of the people or unit recorded by the greatest number of whistleblowers as providing support after their initial report (AR = 'after report'), with the second percentage indicating the proportion of those who nominated the same people or unit as having provided support, after they had experienced any bad treatment or harm (AH = 'after harm'). Bold figures highlight a decrease in the proportion of respondents who nominated that source as providing support after experiencing harm. Both sets of results are broken down according to how respondents said they were treated overall by management and co-workers, to indicate how the pattern of support fell, depending on the source of the perceived bad treatment.

The small group who reported being treated badly only by co-workers drew on the least number of sources. Those who were treated well or the same by management and co-workers drew on more sources of support. The largest number of sources was accessed by those treated badly by management. The overall pattern is one of greatest reliance on the existing personal, social and professional networks that surround the employee, at least in the first instance. This was especially true of those claiming bad treatment by management, who relied especially heavily on their own work colleagues for support, as well as on union support. Those who said that they were not treated badly nevertheless found the greatest support among other work colleagues, and also their supervisor, when the going got tough.

One respondent wrote: '[T]he best support is psychological and comes from colleagues with previous similar experiences.' Another respondent, however, highlighted the difficulty of maintaining collegial support in the longer-term:

> Many work colleagues supported me initially. This included phone calls and providing information to me about what was happening in the workplace (because I was suspended). I made a list of these supporters so that I could thank them when it was all over. However, about a year onwards when the matter finally concluded—I had crossed off most of the supporters on my list. Fearful of losing their jobs (some reported being threatened with this) they simply felt the risk of being aligned with me was too great.

## Table 9.7 Sources of help, assistance and support to whistleblowers (per cent)[a]

| Sources of help and support | | How treated by management and/or co-workers | | | | |
|---|---|---|---|---|---|---|
| | | Well/same by both | Badly only byco-workers | Badly only by management | Badly by both | Total |
| | AR | (n = 78) | (n = 8) | (n = 73) | (n = 49) | (n = 213) |
| | AH | (n = 19) | (n = 7) | (n = 60) | (n = 49) | (n = 139) |
| Other work colleagues at my level | AR | 44 (34) | 50 (4) | 66 (48) | 40 (19) | 50 (106) |
| | AH | 63 (12) | 43 (3) | 67 (40) | 31 (15) | 52 (72) |
| My family | AR | 31 (24) | 63 (5) | 51 (37) | 53 (26) | 44 (94) |
| | AH | 37 (7) | 71 (5) | 53 (32) | 57 (28) | 52 (72) |
| Other work colleagues below my level | AR | 22 (17) | -- | 27 (20) | 18 (9) | 22 (47) |
| | AH | 47 (9) | -- | 32 (19) | 14 (7) | 25 (35) |
| A union or professional association | AR | 5 (4) | -- | 22 (16) | 25 (12) | 16 (34) |
| | AH | 10 (2) | 14 (1) | 30 (18) | 12 (6) | 19 (27) |
| My supervisor | AR | 22 (17) | 75 (6) | 12 (9) | 6 (3) | 16 (35) |
| | AH | 21 (4) | **43 (3)** | **7 (4)** | 6 (3) | **10 (14)** |
| A counsellor or counsellors | AR | 4 (3) | 43 (3) | 19 (14) | 18 (9) | 14 (29) |
| | AH | 21 (4) | 29 (2) | 23 (14) | 20 10) | 22 (30) |
| Senior managers | AR | 22 (17) | 25 (2) | 6 (4) | 8 (4) | 13 (27) |
| | AH | **5 (1)** | **14 (1)** | 10 (6) | **6 (3)** | **8 (11)** |
| Internal ethics, audit, investigation unit | AR | 21 (16) | 13 (1) | 7 (5) | 6 (3) | 12 (25) |
| | AH | **5 (1)** | -- | **3 (2)** | 8 (4) | **5 (7)** |
| Human resources/ EEO unit | AR | 10 (8) | -- | 7 (5) | 4 (2) | 7 (15) |
| | AH | **5 (1)** | -- | 8 (5) | -- | **4 (6)** |
| External government watchdog agencies | AR | 1 (1) | -- | 7 (5) | 6 (3) | 4 (9) |
| | AH | 5 (1) | -- | **3 (2)** | -- | **2 (3)** |
| Member(s) of parliament | AR | 1 (1) | -- | 3 (2) | 4 (2) | 3 (6) |
| | AH | -- | -- | 7 (4) | 4 (2) | 4 (6) |
| Internal support program for employees | AR | 5 (4) | -- | 1 (1) | -- | 2 (5) |
| | AH | 5 (1) | -- | 5 (3) | 6 (3) | 5 (7) |
| Whistleblower support group | AR | -- | -- | 1 (1) | 6 (3) | 2 (5) |
| | AH | 5 (1) | -- | 2 (1) | 6 (3) | 4 (5) |
| The media | AR | -- | -- | 4 (3) | -- | 2 (4) |
| | AH | -- | -- | 3 (2) | 2 (1) | 3 (4) |
| Other community-based support | AR | -- | -- | 3 (2) | 2 (1) | 2 (4) |
| | AH | -- | -- | 2 (1) | 2 (1) | 1 (2) |
| Other specialist officers or units | AR | -- | -- | 3 (2) | -- | 1 (3) |
| | AH | -- | -- | 3 (2) | -- | 1 (2) |

[a] Total does not add to 100 per cent because multiple responses were permitted.

**Note:** Bold highlights decreases in the percentage of respondents indicating support from this source after bad treatment or harm (AR).

**Source:** Internal witness survey: Q47 ('Which of the following assisted or supported you after you reported?' [AR]); Q57 ('Which gave you good help and support after you experienced bad treatment or harm?' [AH]).

Table 9.7 also shows that whistleblowers who were treated badly by colleagues fell back heavily on their own family for support. Importantly, they also drew heavily on their supervisor and management and were likely to be the first to access professional counselling support. Counsellors became increasingly important for all groups once problems emerged. For those treated badly only by colleagues, however, the fact that they did not go on to seek other forms of support suggests that they were able to 'ride out' the storm using these basic resources.

Apart from the diffuse and informal nature of support, four results are particularly noteworthy. First, as expected, internal witness support programs featured only weakly as a source of support, nominated by only 2 per cent of all respondents and by only 5 per cent of those respondents who experienced bad treatment or harm. While the different modes of data collection meant no similarity was likely, it was a notable coincidence that those proportions aligned closely with the results from the agency and employee survey comparisons in the previous section. The clearest explanation for this result is that few respondents had ever come into contact with these programs, even though most of these agencies said they had them and agreed to encourage all known beneficiaries of these programs to participate in the survey. It is also possible that respondents did not necessarily see the 'program' as having provided support, even though it was in fact responsible for the support they received from others, such as counsellors, managers or peer support officers.

Any direct evidence as to the real performance of these programs is mixed. As indicated in Chapter 5, while these programs did become more important as a source of support for those who experienced bad treatment, 4 per cent of public interest whistleblowers also indicated that the internal program was responsible for that bad treatment. This is a sure sign that even when it was accessed, the program fails to meet expectations; and both results could indicate that the program is accessed only too late, after problems have become intractable. Further analysis of the performance of these programs will await the second report from this project, and further research.

The second notable result is that internal investigators did not feature strongly as support mechanisms, other than in the first instance by those who did not go on to report being treated badly. This suggests that internal investigators could have been very valuable as sources of support in the first instance and helped whistleblowers prevent a range of problems. The results also show, however, that as problems arose—often no doubt linked to an adverse investigation outcome—the ability and/or willingness of investigators to provide support fell away. This tends to confirm the problem discussed earlier, and in the preceding chapter, that while investigators are crucial, their institutional role is not compatible with continuing support.

The third result was that this pattern was broadly repeated in relation to external watchdog agencies, which had a minimal support role throughout and one that reduced rather than became stronger. This result confirms that, even though a large number of agencies cite external agencies as an important source of support, in fact, this does not occur. As with internal support programs, it could be that this happens partly for the reasons suggested in Chapters 4 and 5: few whistleblowers persist with a disclosure to an external agency unless they are already experiencing bad treatment or reprisals, by which time it is already too late for the external agency to positively assist. Reprisal responses are also discussed further in the next section.

Finally, the results highlight the crucial role of managers, including direct supervisors. Chapter 7 highlighted their dual roles as the biggest potential source of official support for whistleblowers and also, potentially, as the biggest source of their problems. This duality is demonstrated clearly by the data. One respondent to the internal witness survey wrote that 'managers were very understanding and supportive of the need to properly and thoroughly investigate [the] wrongdoing'—again highlighting the connection between investigation process, outcome and perceived support. Even without feeling he or she had been positively mistreated, however, another respondent 'generally felt a lack of support by supervisor (senior manager), and [the] organisation [in] general', writing that 'two new senior managers viewed my action in a negative light and questioned my course of action, suggesting it would put the organisation in a negative light'.

While this duality of roles means that first and second-level managers could be the most significant source of reprisal risk or exposure in any given situation, there is clearly no wisdom in excluding them from the overall process of internal witness management—even if this were possible. This is because they could also be the most crucial source of support and protection. The evidence from case-handlers and from managers themselves reinforces this complex problem.

## Who do case-handlers and managers see as providing support?

Table 9.8 sets out the responses of case-handlers and managers, from the same case study agencies, showing the relative importance of a similar range of people and units in managing the welfare of employees who report wrongdoing. Again, these are ranked in order of most to least important, according to the combined sample of case-handlers and managers, with most options rating as at least somewhat important. Bold results indicate variations from the rank order. The low variation between the rankings given by case study agency case-handlers and managers provides significant validation of the results, since these groups can bring quite different perspectives. Integrity agency case-handlers had quite different views to others.

While there are many similarities with the relative importance of different sources as indicated by whistleblowers, there are also some striking differences. None of the aggregated assessments of the internal case-handler, manager or integrity case-handler groups proved fully accurate in respect of the relative importance of the major sources, when compared with the internal witnesses. A large proportion of the internal witness sample had experienced mistreatment and, by definition, could have had less experience of good support sources that helped prevent any perceived mistreatment at all. Even taking this into account, however, the first striking difference is that all of these groups tended to overestimate the importance of official sources of support, especially supervisors and managers, relative to the more informal sources. The partial exception was the integrity case-handler group, which rated 'supervisors' as somewhat less important and instead rated 'senior managers' and 'the CEO' as very important.

This result is not surprising from respondents whose institutional roles require some faith in the working of their own management systems—for example, integrity case-handlers also rated their own agencies as much more important than any other group, including the internal witnesses. Nevertheless, just as Chapters 5 and 6 revealed significant mismatches in understanding between internal witnesses and these groups, these results suggest that those responsible for managing whistleblowing currently see support arrangements more as they hope them to be than as they probably are. In this complex field, any overconfidence about the relative effectiveness of the official support systems clearly carries a number of dangers.

Particularly important is that internal witness support programs were rated as playing the fourth most important role overall and both groups of case-handlers rated them third. These results highlight that while those responsible for whistleblowing might place great stock in these schemes, and might even be rightly optimistic about their potential, their weak relevance in the actual experience of whistleblowers is not something that has yet been grasped at official levels (at least until now). Based on the evidence set out so far, the assumption that these programs can provide the cornerstone of support—especially in those circumstances in which a whistleblower's supervisors or other managers are compromised—is a potentially dangerous one, at least given the current state of these programs and associated agency systems.

In contrast, emphasising the preference for official support over informal sources, all groups underestimated unions as a source of support compared with their real importance in the experience of many whistleblowers.

**Table 9.8 People with an important role in managing employee welfare (mean)**

| Which of the following people have an important role in managing the welfare of an employee/public employee who has reported wrongdoing?<br>1 = not important<br>2 = somewhat important<br>3 = very important | Case-handlers<br>(n = 254) | Managers<br>(n = 374) | Case-handlers and managers combined<br>(n = 628) | Integrity case-handlers<br>(n = 64) |
|---|---|---|---|---|
| The employee's supervisor | 2.81 | 2.87 | 2.85 | 2.67 |
| The employee's family and/or friends | 2.78 | 2.79 | 2.78 | **2.80** |
| Senior managers | 2.64 | 2.68 | 2.66 | **2.88** |
| Internal support program for employees who report wrongdoing | **2.65** | 2.56 | 2.60 | **2.78** |
| Internal staff counselling or welfare service | 2.48 | 2.42 | 2.44 | 2.48 |
| Peer-support person for employees who report | 2.45 | 2.41 | 2.43 | **2.63** |
| Human resources/equity and merit unit | 2.31 | 2.37 | 2.35 | 2.45 |
| External staff counselling or welfare service | **2.34** | 2.29 | 2.31 | 2.45 |
| The CEO (or equivalent) | 2.16 | 2.27 | 2.22 | **2.72** |
| Internal audit, fraud, investigation or ethics unit | 2.15 | 2.11 | 2.13 | 2.33 |
| Unions or professional associations | 2.15 | 2.07 | 2.10 | 2.17 |
| Whistleblower support group(s) | 2.02 | 1.95 | 1.98 | 2.08 |
| External government watchdog agencies | 1.67 | 1.53 | 1.59 | **2.20** |
| Other community-based support services | 1.61 | 1.54 | 1.57 | 1.80 |
| Lawyers | 1.45 | 1.40 | 1.42 | 1.53 |
| Member(s) of parliament | 1.21 | 1.21 | 1.21 | 1.39 |
| Journalists | 1.16 | 1.10 | 1.12 | 1.31 |

Note: Bold results highlight mean ratings that differ from the combined case-handler and manager rank order.
Sources: Case-handler and manager surveys: Q43; integrity case-handler survey: Q50.

While the aggregate views of case-handlers and managers demonstrate this general overconfidence in official support, some particular results show an important counter-trend. The fact that integrity case-handlers rated supervisors as comparatively less important suggests a recognition of the duality of their role and the need for stronger oversight of managerial responses to whistleblowing in the experience of integrity agencies. Contrary to much of the evidence from the agency survey in Chapter 8, none of these groups (including case-handlers themselves) rated internal investigation staff as very important. This could represent something of an underestimate of their importance, but it accords with whistleblowers' overall experiences and an operational recognition of the risk of conflict between investigation and support roles.

Overall, these data again provide no evidence that increased investment in organised strategies of internal witness support is ineffective. Rather, they suggest there is a danger in any assumptions that the current level of investment, or the adequacy of associated information and management systems, is sufficient. In those circumstances in which supervisors and other senior managers recognise that wrongdoing has been reported and do not feel compromised by the information disclosed, in accordance with the risk factors revealed in Chapter 6, there is a good chance that the combination of formal and informal sources of support can carry many whistleblowers through. The primary challenge is that as soon as there is a risk of conflict with supervisors and other managers, and the normal management chain becomes less reliable as a source of support, alternative internal witness support programs and systems are clearly not yet filling the breach.

## What are the strategies for support?

This chapter has so far discussed 'support' as a general concept. Indeed, the research has generally confirmed that support to whistleblowers facing a range of complex processes and conflicts is more important as a primary organisational response than a focus on 'protection' from direct reprisals. As shown in Chapter 5, direct personal reprisals are relatively rare, compared with the more indirect forms of stress, conflict and managerial mistreatment that represent more common outcomes for many whistleblowers and from which the risks of more direct reprisals then arise.

'Support, support, support' was a simple, yet common sentiment expressed by respondents to the internal witness survey when asked how they could be better provided with assistance. One internal witness survey respondent was able to summarise, with some detachment, some of the key forms of support involved:

> I think the main components in supporting these people are: keeping them informed; praising them for their co-operation; ensuring confidentiality; providing them with counselling if the wrongdoing is extremely serious; always provide a listening ear for when they need to express concerns or just discuss the matter.

These comments also reflect a little-recognised fact: when an employee has been working in close proximity with serious wrongdoing—potentially for some time and potentially in a manner in which they themselves feel compromised or responsible for its continuation—such circumstances can be sufficient to constitute a traumatic level of stress. In other words, in serious cases, many whistleblowers might not need to experience any active or passive mistreatment from managers or colleagues before entering a state in which they need intensive personal and professional support.

What methods do those involved with whistleblowing regard as the most effective for managing the welfare of those who report?

Table 9.9 sets out the opinions of those case study agency case-handlers and managers and integrity agency case-handlers who indicated direct knowledge of the available strategies for providing active support. All of the support methods offered were rated as at least fairly effective, with only 'workers' compensation' tending towards a rating of 'fairly ineffective'. Of the 521 case study agency respondents who completed this question, only one indicated any knowledge of any other method used, beyond the items offered by the survey.

**Table 9.9 Methods for managing employee welfare (mean)**

| How effective are the following methods for managing and ensuring the welfare of staff/public employees who report wrongdoing?<br><br>1 = very effective;<br>2 = fairly effective;<br>3 = fairly ineffective;<br>4 = very ineffective | Case-handlers<br>(n = 209) | Managers<br>(n = 312) | Case-handlers and managers combined<br>(n = 521) | Integrity case-handlers<br>(n = 45) |
|---|---|---|---|---|
| Maintaining confidentiality of the employee's identity | 1.53 | 1.42 | 1.46 | 1.68 |
| Advice and counselling | 1.51 | 1.62 | 1.58 | 1.71 |
| Provision of information about the investigation | 1.75 | 1.76 | 1.76 | 1.85 |
| Special access to senior management | 1.98 | 1.89 | 1.93 | 1.93 |
| Support for the family of the staff member | 1.93 | 1.94 | 1.93 | **1.90** |
| Advice and counselling to co-workers and other staff | 2.03 | 2.01 | 2.01 | **1.81** |
| Special leave/transfer arrangements | 2.04 | 2.03 | 2.04 | 2.15 |
| Physical protection | 2.15 | 2.15 | 2.15 | **1.80** |
| Workers' compensation | 2.51 | 2.50 | 2.51 | 2.53 |

Sources: Case-handler and manager surveys: Q47; integrity case-handler survey: Q44.

While the recognition given to these methods is largely self-explanatory, further issues are raised if any of these methods—however effective—is simply not available. This is clearly the case in respect of the strategy identified above as most effective: confidentiality. Indeed, as is seen in the review of agency procedures provided in the next chapter, and in many statutory provisions, many organisations place a premium on trying to maintain confidentiality to the maximum possible extent. Elsewhere, 85 per cent of all respondents to the case-handler and manager surveys (Q56) rated the protection of an internal witness's identity as either very or extremely important.

Certainly, for as long as it can be preserved, confidentiality provides whistleblowers, case-handlers and managers with crucial time to assess risks and plan options. Even once a whistleblower's identity becomes known or suspected, confidentiality requirements can assist as a strategy for suppressing workplace conflict, by helping contain workplace gossip and reminding staff that the individual personalities involved are less important than the real issues (Brown et al. 2004). A question arises, however, as to what support remains available when confidentiality ceases to be possible. That this is usually the case, sooner or later, is reflected in the results in Chapter 6, in which the number of people who knew that the whistleblower had reported was not a risk factor for identifying whether, ultimately, they were likely to suffer mistreatment.

It is notable in Table 9.9 that once confidentiality ceases to be an option, the next four methods are all aimed at assisting whistleblowers to better self-manage their role in the process, rather than addressing objective risks such as potential action from and reactions of affected managers or staff. That 'advice and counselling to co-workers and other staff' was rated as the fifth most effective method and as only 'fairly effective' overall is an indicator that many strategies remain relatively passive in their approach to managing the risks that follow whistleblowing. If a major perceived source of stress or conflict is the reaction from co-workers, this result suggests relatively low success to date in efforts to confront such risks head-on. If a major perceived source of problems is the reaction of a supervisor or other managers—as Chapters 5 and 6 indicate—the result is even more worrying, again suggesting a strategy of helping the whistleblower to 'tough it out' rather than workplace intervention. The data suggest a continuing need for the development of more effective intervention strategies once confidentiality ceases to be practical (see, for example, NSW Ombudsman 2005).

The relatively low rating given to 'workers' compensation' suggests that rather than being ineffective, measures to compensate internal witnesses for problems endured might simply be less available. As discussed in Chapter 11, while most public interest disclosure legislation is predicated on ensuring that employees who suffer detriment as a result of whistleblowing are able to seek compensation, the legal procedures are typically onerous. There are no known cases in which such applications have been attempted under this legislation, let alone successful.

How effective, overall, are agencies' strategies for managing the welfare of internal witnesses in the view of case-handlers and managers? Table 9.10 shows that case-handlers and managers have a relatively sober view of their agencies' success. On average, case-handlers rate their own organisations as only 'somewhat' effective. Managers had only a slightly more positive view. In contrast, case-handlers in integrity agencies had a very negative view of how well organisations in their jurisdiction were managing whistleblowers' welfare, with 89 per cent also indicating that they believed that the proportion of organisations that were effective was about half or less (integrity case-handler survey: Q58). Like the agency case-handlers, the respondents from the integrity agencies also viewed the performance of their own agency's systems as only 'somewhat' effective (Q60; mean = 3.07, n = 75).

**Table 9.10 Perceived effectiveness in managing whistleblower welfare (mean)**

| Overall, how effective do you believe your organisation is/public sector organisations in your jurisdiction are at managing the welfare of employees who report wrongdoing? | Case-handlers (n = 295) | Managers (n = 430) | Case-handlers and managers combined (n = 725) | Integrity case-handlers (n = 76) |
|---|---|---|---|---|
| 1 = not at all; 2 = not very; 3 = somewhat; 4 = very; 5 = extremely | 3.00 | 3.18 | 3.10 | 2.41 |

Sources: Case-handler and manager surveys: Q60; integrity case-handler survey: Q57.

A better understanding of the precise methods and strategies used to provide effective support is a priority for further research. The project's second report will probe these more deeply. While there is evidence that strategies for managing the workplace effects of wrongdoing and whistleblowing are in rapid development, it is clear that they remain less 'a science' than 'an art' (Brown 2001; Brown et al. 2004). Many outcomes depend on the varying ethical and professional standards of individual managers, the personal coping capacities of whistleblowers, the strength of their personal relationships and a range of other random influences, including luck. For these reasons, the strategies used and their relative effectiveness are also important subjects for more rigorous evaluation by agencies themselves. When asked about exit and follow-up procedures involving internal witnesses, only one-fifth of all case-handlers and manager respondents from the case study agencies (21 per cent) indicated an awareness of such procedures and only 3 per cent indicated that they included any 'follow-up evaluation'. There is much that agencies can do to improve their own knowledge about what works and what doesn't within their own organisation.

## Reprisals, risk assessment and responses

The final analyses in this chapter concern how agencies respond to reprisals and reprisal risks. As shown in Chapters 5 and 6, and noted again above, the anticipation and management of reprisal risks are central tasks in the process of internal witness support. Contrary to the expectations of many case-handlers and managers, the major source of risks of mistreatment against whistleblowers (real and perceived) is management itself, with direct reprisals and mistreatment by colleagues arising in only a relatively small proportion of cases.

By their nature, most of the types of reprisal described in Chapter 5 also do not relate to 'cleanly' identifiable risks and events, for which particular individuals can be easily held directly responsible. Instead, risks of mistreatment are often interwoven with failures in management support—for example, when no attempt is made to manage workplace tensions and conflicts, or these attempts fail or are withdrawn at a critical stage. While direct 'payback' actions are a risk, mistreatment can take other forms—for example, actions to discipline or marginalise an employee due to failures in their work performance, when these failures could be real but have also been exacerbated by the organisation's own failures in managing the whistleblowing incident.

The present research therefore collected evidence not only about agencies' positive approaches to assisting internal witnesses, but their readiness to deal with negative possibilities—in other words, their strategies for anticipating, managing and dealing with things that could go wrong. The results indicate these to be areas of particular procedural weakness in many agencies.

## Reprisal risk assessment

Earlier, it was seen that only about half of all agencies surveyed in the project had procedures for supporting internal witnesses. Only about one-third of all agencies surveyed had formal procedures. The agency and case-handler and manager surveys also asked if agencies had any routine procedures for assessing the risks of reprisals being taken against internal witnesses.

The agency survey revealed this to be an area of particular weakness. Seventy per cent of the 304 agencies said plainly that they did not carry out any assessments of reprisal risk. Moreover, the bulk of the remainder claimed to have only 'informal/unwritten' procedures for risk assessment, with only 46 agencies (15 per cent of all agencies) able to nominate who had responsibility to 'undertake or coordinate' these risk assessments and only six agencies (2 per cent) indicated that any of their risk-assessment procedures were formal.

Across those agencies able to indicate who was responsible for assessing reprisal risk, this role was shared between a range of officers: designated disclosure officers, internal audit and investigations staff, CEOs and senior managers and staff involved in internal witness support. In the same way that support roles are shared between these different actors, this tends to suggest, to differing extents, that the assessment of reprisal risk occurs on an 'as needed' basis in the normal, ad hoc handling of cases.

The agency survey, however, also showed it is not safe to assume that the assessment of reprisal risks simply forms an automatic part of the management of whistleblowing cases and therefore does not need specific procedures. As set out in Table 9.11, agencies were also asked whether, irrespective of whether they had other procedures or staff for providing internal witness support, they had any staff responsible for ensuring that internal witnesses were protected from reprisals.

**Table 9.11 Agencies with staff for protecting employees from reprisals (per cent)**

| Does your agency have staff responsible for ensuring that internal witnesses are protected from reprisals? | All agencies (n = 294) | Employee survey agencies (n = 115) | Case study agencies (n = 15) |
|---|---|---|---|
| No | 30 (89) | 23 (26) | 0 |
| Yes | 70 (205) | 77 (89) | 100 (15) |
| *Investigation staff* [a] | 45 (93) | 55 (49) | 60 (9) |
| *The internal witness's supervisor and/or line managers* [a] | 48 (99) | 34 (39) | 60 (9) |
| *Support staff* [a] | 30 (62) | 49 (44) | 33 (5) |
| *Other* [a] | 36 (73) | 34 (30) | 40 (6) |

[a] Total below line does not add to 100 per cent as multiple responses were permitted.
**Source:** Agency survey: Q38.

Thirty per cent of all agencies responded that they had no such staff. This was a startling admission of weakness, given the options included their own investigation staff, discussed above, and the whistleblower's own supervisor and line managers, who are present in all agencies and have many legal responsibilities to protect their employees. If no-one is considered responsible for protecting whistleblowers from reprisals in these agencies, it is safe to assume that no-one is considered responsible for assessing the risk of reprisals or doing anything to prevent or minimise them.

A more detailed picture can be seen from the 15 case study agencies, all of which said they had staff responsible for protecting internal witnesses from reprisals. Ten of these agencies responded in the agency survey that they had risk-assessment procedures, eight of which could also nominate who was responsible, but only agency whose procedures were formalised.

Even this picture might be optimistic, however, as an indicator of agency practice. Across the case study agencies, 80 per cent of all respondents to this item in the case-handler and manager surveys said either that no-one carried out any reprisal risk assessments in their organisation (32 per cent) or they did not know whether anyone did (48 per cent). This result was not significantly different for case-handlers who were more likely to know and came notwithstanding that the bulk of these respondents were from agencies that claimed to have risk-assessment procedures.

The case-handler and manager surveys also revealed uncertainty about when any conscious assessment of reprisal risks did, or should, occur. Of the 147 respondents who indicated knowledge of risk assessments, 8 per cent did not know at what point they usually occurred. A substantial proportion (49 per cent) indicated that it was most usual for risk to be assessed either when the employee first expressed fears (37 per cent) or only after they reported real detriment from a reprisal (12 per cent); 40 per cent indicated that it was when the employee first provided the original information about wrongdoing. A similar pattern was found among integrity agency case-handlers.

These results confirm that even if it does occur, conscious assessment of the risks of reprisal can often follow only when whistleblowers start to experience stress or problems, or might be triggered by those cases in which whistleblowers themselves anticipate risks. Together, the results highlight the extent to which the support strategies described in the earlier parts of the chapter could be predicated on luck—that is, hoping for the best that problems will not arise—rather than proactive assessment of the risks before they emerge. Chapter 6 highlighted that it could also be those whistleblowers who appeared to see no risks, and who were therefore by definition more 'naive' or trusting, who were least well served by this reactive approach and were in most need of support systems that included more routine, objective assessment from the outset. Chapter

6 also highlighted some of the key risk factors that can now be more readily used to frame a more proactive approach, based on the present research.

## Responses to reprisals

Finally, the most crucial form of support that a whistleblower can come to expect from their organisation is effective action if problems unravel to the stage of a direct reprisal or other inappropriate workplace reaction—including management reactions—to the circumstances provoked by a report. As with reprisal risk assessment, there is evidence that many agencies have made little or no provision for this worst-case scenario. Just as an alarming number of agencies responded to the agency survey that they had no staff responsible for protecting internal witnesses from reprisals, more than half of all agencies surveyed (n = 158, or 54 per cent) had no procedures for responding to reprisals and only 20 per cent of all agencies (n = 60) reported having any specific practices and procedures for the investigation of reprisals if they occurred.

The evidence from the case-handler and manager surveys suggests that even in the case study agencies, where most respondents felt the agency was at least fairly effective in supporting whistleblowers, there is much lower confidence in agencies' ability to provide support when the 'going gets tough'.

As shown in Chapter 5, many respondents to these surveys had direct experience of reprisal allegations: 50 per cent of the case study agency case-handlers (n = 149), 38 per cent of the managers (n = 165) and 72 per cent of the integrity agency case-handlers (n = 53). The majority of these respondents indicated that in at least some cases, they believed the alleged reprisal had in fact occurred, with a considerable degree of congruence between the types of reprisals, or bad treatment, that were considered most common by case-handlers, managers and whistleblowers alike.

When asked how well they thought their organisation dealt with allegations of reprisals on a scale from 1 ('not at all well') to 5 ('extremely well'), the mean for all case-handlers fell below the midpoint of 'somewhat' (2.82; n = 288), while the mean for all managers was the midpoint (3; n = 413). For the case-handlers and managers with direct experience of reprisal cases, the results were even less positive (for case-handlers, a mean of 2.60, n = 148; for managers, a mean of 2.75, n = 160). Integrity case-handlers had an even more negative opinion of public sector organisations in their jurisdictions, perceiving that, on average, agencies dealt with allegations of reprisals 'not very well' (mean = 2.11, n=73; or, for those with direct experience, mean = 1.98, n = 53). In fact, asked what proportion of agencies they believed had successfully dealt with alleged reprisals, 82 per cent of all integrity agency case-handlers estimated the proportion to be 'about one-quarter' or less (Q39).

This low level of confidence in current responses to reprisals does not stem from any substantial view that the outcomes for whistleblowers are too favourable. While some respondents (notably, some managers) might believe this, the responses from all groups indicate that the majority are aware that presently, in the agencies studied, allegations of reprisal are only very occasionally substantiated. Instead, it is clear that most case-handlers, and even managers, agree that fewer allegations are currently substantiated than should be. Contrary to a stereotype of whistleblowers as prodigious complainants, a majority of case-handlers and managers (71 per cent) and integrity agency case-handlers (81 per cent) indicated a belief that at least 'sometimes' whistleblowers experienced reprisals but did not go on to report them.

Table 9.12 confirms that case-handlers and managers believe that the fact that few allegations are substantiated does not necessarily mean that no reprisal occurred. The table shows the reasons selected by case-handlers and managers with direct experience of reprisal cases, ranked in order of the perceived frequency with which the reason arises. Lack of real reprisal (that is, the allegation was wrong) was ranked as only the third most frequent reason by managers and integrity case-handlers and the fifth most frequent reason by case study case-handlers (arguably, those in the best position to form an objective view). The most common reason was lack of evidence, and several other reasons were also common, including inability to identify who was responsible and, for integrity case-handlers, inability to distinguish between legitimate and illegitimate actions against the whistleblower (presumably by management).

**Table 9.12 Reasons for unsubstantiated allegations of reprisal (mean)**

| When allegations of reprisal have not been substantiated, what are the most common reasons for this finding?<br><br>1 = never;<br>2 = rarely;<br>3 = sometimes;<br>4 = often;<br>5 = always | Case-handlers<br>(n = 136) | Managers<br>(n = 149) | Case-handlers and managers combined<br>(n = 285) | Integrity case-handlers<br>(n = 49) |
|---|---|---|---|---|
| There was insufficient evidence | 3.42 | 3.33 | 3.37 | 3.67 |
| The employee subject to the reprisal did not want it investigated | 3.29 | 3.13 | 3.21 | 2.43 |
| There was no reprisal | 2.97 | 3.08 | 3.03 | 3.12 |
| There was evidence of a reprisal, but not enough to identify or prosecute any individual(s) | 3.07 | 2.91 | 2.99 | 2.96 |
| Passage of time prevented proper investigation | 3.07 | 2.89 | 2.98 | 2.92 |
| There was evidence of a reprisal, but also that the same action could be reasonable or lawful | 2.76 | 2.62 | 2.69 | 3.18 |

**Sources:** Case-handler and manager surveys: Q40; integrity case-handler survey: Q37.

Given the frequency with which management was identified as being responsible for the bad treatment reported in Chapter 5, the responses to this last item in Table 9.12 are particularly important. Unreasonable or inappropriate management action against a whistleblower can be a direct reprisal, or can represent simply the final stages in the unravelling of a whistleblowing case that is not, and perhaps cannot be, well handled. In any case, it will usually have bases that readily appear legitimate even if, overall, it is really the product of a state of affairs for which the agency should accept responsibility. Integrity case-handlers identified this problem as the second most frequent reason why allegations were not substantiated, and even though agency case-handlers and managers perceived it to be the least frequent reason, a majority (63 per cent) nevertheless agreed that it at least 'sometimes' happened.

Many case-handlers and managers went further and confirmed that they had experienced cases in which managers used disciplinary or personnel action as a 'cover' for a reprisal. In response to additional questions, 45 per cent of experienced case-handlers and managers indicated that it 'sometimes' or 'often' occurred that reprisals were alleged that were in fact legitimate disciplinary or personnel actions, but a large number (38 per cent) also saw the reverse as similarly common: disciplinary or personnel action was sometimes or often used 'as a cover for what is really just a reprisal' (Q39). Integrity case-handlers report an even more prevalent experience of both types of cases, with 91 per cent of experienced respondents agreeing that the former scenario sometimes or often arises and 75 per cent reporting the 'cover' scenario is similarly common (Q35; n = 52).

These results highlight a number of challenges that could help explain why public sector organisations are—on their own account—struggling to provide more effective resolutions to these difficult problems. As with other forms of internal witness support, there are questions about the degree of effort and the adequacy of resources indicated by the current state of systems and procedures. As discussed in Chapter 5, there has been a misplaced assumption as to the most likely sources of reprisal risk that need to be addressed by agencies. The focus on the criminalisation of reprisals might not have helped their effective investigation by agencies, focusing as this does on establishing the responsibility of culpable individuals for deliberate acts, proven beyond a reasonable doubt. The more frequent problems are more complex, and sometimes simply negligent, management actions that are unlikely to ever be provable in that manner or to that standard, even when it is clear that a whistleblower has suffered undue detrimental outcomes as an overall result of management action, or inaction, in the course of the handling of the disclosure.

Some of these difficult issues can be addressed by agencies making more effort, filling gaps in their procedures, engaging in capacity building in the specialist area of reprisal investigation and taking a more flexible approach to investigations. The development of more effective support systems, as suggested in the first part of the chapter, should also relieve the opportunity and the need for individual managers to make some of the poor decisions that lead to justifiable allegations of reprisal. When the organisation is prepared to take more effective responsibility as a whole for the outcomes from the process—bad as well as good—there is less need for individual managers to feel that their inability to properly manage an individual case is their own responsibility.

The results also highlight the point at which internal agency systems often begin to be poorly placed to resolve issues on their own. Many agencies are clearly capable of receiving, investigating and resolving primary disclosures about internal wrongdoing. When issues arise about the adequacy of their management of the whistleblower, however, unless the case is relatively simple (that is, individual direct reprisals or obvious management lapses can be identified), internal processes are clearly less well placed to independently judge the extent to which things went wrong, for which the organisation itself should accept responsibility. The problem is that external integrity agencies are not currently well positioned, or perhaps well enough skilled, to fill this gap. While integrity case-handlers were highly critical of agencies' responses to reprisals, we saw in Chapter 8 that internal case-handlers were also highly critical of the contribution of the integrity agencies. Perhaps most importantly, while integrity case-handlers were naturally less sceptical of their own capacity than those in the agencies, they were still quite sceptical—like the internal case-handlers themselves in respect of their own role (integrity case-handler survey, Q41: mean = 3.11, n = 73; for experienced, mean = 3.06, n = 53).

As suggested also in Chapter 8, these data point to the need for a new relationship between agencies and integrity agencies in the way in which whistleblowing cases are managed—particularly when questions arise about the propriety of management reactions. While integrity agencies can and should continue to rely on line agencies to conduct their own investigations where appropriate, the evidence suggests a differentiated strategy is needed when issues arise about the adequacy of management responses in whistleblowing cases. At present, even if integrity agencies have the capacity, their involvement can simply come too late to help constructively resolve the true level of organisational responsibility for a whistleblower's problems. In cases in which conflict is well developed and bridges have already been burned between a whistleblower and their organisation, it can be that there are few remedies that an external investigation can realistically offer the whistleblower (as opposed to the agency and the public interest), with access needed instead to a different last line of 'appeal', such as a compensation umpire. These issues raise questions of statutory reform for discussion in Chapter 11.

## Discussion and conclusions

This chapter has shown the large field of opportunity that exists for the development of more effective internal witness and whistleblower support programs, in public sector agencies in the jurisdictions studied.

The first part of the chapter showed that organised systems for supporting and protecting internal witnesses are in relative infancy. Only 54 per cent of all agencies surveyed had relevant procedures and only 11 per cent of all agencies surveyed had a formal internal witness support system. Moreover, even in the case study agencies, only a very small proportion of public interest whistleblowers—perhaps 1.3 per cent, or 6.5 per cent of all whistleblowers treated badly by management or colleagues—are estimated as having ever come into contact with those systems. The reasons for this low take-up of organised support services can include:

- the low level of resources dedicated to such programs
- a prior shortage of data regarding the overall level of whistleblowing
- uncertainty or confusion about the types of employees intended to be targeted by programs
- an absence or inadequacy of procedural guidance on how employees should access the support, including an over-reliance on whistleblowers' self-identifying as such for the purposes of gaining support
- lack of management information systems for ensuring that all deserving whistleblowing cases can be identified and assessed for support
- inadequate or misapplied statutory definitions.

The second part of the chapter documented the sources of support experienced by public interest whistleblowers and the types of strategies or methods used. Not surprisingly, given the first results, the main sources of support that currently prevent more whistleblowers from suffering are not organised support programs, but informal social and professional networks, including family, friends, colleagues, union officials and supervisors. These analyses also revealed that case-handlers and managers—while not excessively optimistic about their own success—nevertheless continue to overestimate the extent to which organised or official sources of support are helping prevent worse outcomes. This creates a high risk that support will fail in any of the many circumstances in which the dual role of direct supervisors and line managers, described in Chapter 7, can turn from positive to negative. There are also signs that strategies can be somewhat reactive and attuned to bolstering the coping skills of whistleblowers in order to help them 'tough out' difficult situations, rather than to management intervention against sources of conflict.

The third part of the chapter examined the measures taken to assess the risks of reprisal and other major problems and to respond to those threats. These results provided like evidence that agency systems are currently largely reactive. In the majority of agencies, there is little focus on thorough assessment of cases for the risks of what might go wrong, as opposed to providing support in the hope that nothing will.

Finally, the analyses show that when reprisal risks are realised, agency case-handlers and managers do not see themselves as very well equipped or well placed to deal with them. Their evidence confirms indications from Chapter 5 that, generally, allegations that whistleblowers have suffered reprisals or other management lapses are not currently handled well. The most common reasons why such allegations are only rarely substantiated are not that reprisals do not occur, but because of a range of difficulties in investigation, especially relating to the fact that most reprisals involve management reprisals and institutional reactions, not acts for which individuals can be held culpable to a criminal standard of proof.

This somewhat negative overall picture does not detract from the reality that in many agencies considerable efforts are taking place to develop more effective strategies of internal witness support. Nor does it suggest these efforts are not achieving success. Rather, it highlights the extent of the challenges faced by agencies and governments if such systems are to be properly developed and made to work. The second report from this project will examine in more detail the strategies and resources currently being used by many agencies to support and manage internal witnesses, with a view to better understanding current best practice. The analysis here has highlighted the importance of this approach, by demonstrating that many agencies are yet to even scratch the surface in this effort.

Overall, the results also suggest there are ready gains to be made by more public sector agencies in reducing the proportion of public interest whistleblowers who complain of mistreatment and in improving the reporting climate in organisations by developing more sophisticated support strategies. The results also suggest, however, that a new level of commitment is needed for this to occur.

The research now available confirms that the potential catchment of employees for which such strategies need to work is much larger and more diffuse through most organisations than previously believed. In addition to simply expanding the scale and scope of support programs in resource terms, there is a clear need for more effective management information systems, to support a new relationship between internal coordination points for investigations and support, and supervisors and line managers, who currently receive most disclosures and are the most crucial players in determining whether an internal witness will receive support or suffer reprisals.

Similarly, the evidence suggests that some key developments in internal witness support are likely to hinge on regulatory and legislative reform. The low take-up of formal systems appears to be related to either restrictive statutory definitions of public interest disclosures, misapplication of those definitions or inadequate requirements for agencies to recognise, monitor and track disclosures. The patchy state of agency procedures and systems suggests a need for greater statutory guidance on agencies' employee support obligations and mechanisms for more effective external policy support and oversight. More effective handling of individual cases appears to rely on a new, differentiated relationship between agencies and integrity agencies, to lift the burden on the former by enabling the latter to provide more timely and useful assistance in difficult cases. These issues are further explored in the next two chapters.

Consistent with the aim of enabling more whistleblowers to accept an 'instrumental role' in the progress, support strategies need to be more proactive, involve more organised approaches to risk assessment and develop a new range of options for active intervention in the management of whistleblowing cases. Currently, it is likely because a large number of whistleblowing cases are easy to manage, or largely 'self-managing', that they do not lead to worse outcomes. By learning to supplement current support strategies with additional options for intervention, there is good reason to believe that agencies with higher proportions of problem cases can better encourage reporting and achieve greater workplace harmony. The feasibility of these objectives is explored further in the next chapter, in which further analysis shows that, statistically, those taking more effort to develop stronger whistleblowing procedures are indeed achieving better outcomes.

# 10. Evaluating agency responses: the comprehensiveness and impact of whistleblowing procedures

## Peter Roberts[1]

## Introduction

What does the empirical evidence about whistleblowing in Australian public sector agencies, described in Part 1 of this book, say about the quality of their systems and procedures? So far in this part, analysis has focused on the attitudes and knowledge of managers, internal investigation systems and systems for protecting and managing whistleblowers (Chapters 7, 8 and 9). This chapter present an overall picture of how the reporting of wrongdoing is formally dealt with from an organisational perspective, examining and comparing the totality of agencies' procedures using the empirical evidence of key whistleblowing outcomes in the agencies studied.

As is already clear, many public sector organisations have accepted the challenge of encouraging staff to disclose perceived wrongdoing and have committed themselves to protecting staff from reprisals—but some have not, and most are finding at least some parts of the challenge to be substantial. From the outset, it is worth noting the three broad (and overlapping) themes, encountered by the researchers to date, which appear to drive organisational approaches to the management of whistleblowing. These themes demonstrate that the same challenges can be viewed differently by different managers and can help explain differences in agency approaches.

The first theme is compliance: many senior managers are aware that they are required to establish procedures and implement policies for the purpose of complying with applicable legislation, such as 'public interest disclosure' or 'whistleblower protection' legislation. Chapter 7 highlighted, however, that when it comes to basic management knowledge of statutory obligations and therefore their effective implementation, challenges begin to arise.

The second theme is utilitarian: many senior managers in organisations recognise that good governance requires that wrongdoing be identified and dealt with. A second dimension of this response is that managers might also recognise that when reporting wrongdoing results in individual staff members suffering mistreatment or reprisals, the potentially devastating effects on individuals, along with impacts on the productivity of others, can put large resource burdens on the organisation.

Finally, senior managers in organisations often also take an ethical stance, viewing reporting of wrongdoing as a fundamental part of maintaining the integrity of the organisation. Those managers will work to establish whistleblowing systems and procedures for the reason that these promote integrity within the organisation as a whole, maintain public integrity more generally and perhaps also provide for fairer outcomes for individuals through the type of organisational justice described in Chapter 3.

This chapter analyses the contents and apparent effectiveness of agency procedures, in their legislative and jurisdictional context, in light of these three themes. The first part of the chapter looks for evidence from the employee survey of whether the existence of whistleblowing legislation is associated with desired outcomes from whistleblowing, at any agency level. These analyses provide some measure of the impacts when agencies rely simply on the existence of legislation to provide guidance to their staff about responses to whistleblowing or limit their approach to minimal compliance. The existence of legislation is measured subjectively, in terms of the level of staff awareness and confidence in that legislation within individual agencies. The outcomes measured are the reporting and inaction rates in those agencies (the proportion of employees who observe wrongdoing but do and do not report it) and the proportion of reporters who complain of mistreatment.

The results show that in those agencies in which more staff are aware of and confident about whistleblowing legislation, there are more positive attitudes to whistleblowing, higher whistleblowing 'propensity' on the part of staff, higher trust in the anticipated management response to whistleblowing and a higher likelihood that serious wrongdoing will be exposed or 'flushed out' (lower inaction rates). While these results suggest that even a 'mere compliance' approach can have positive effects, they also reveal some of its limitations. Despite these outcomes, the same agencies did not record any lower rates of mistreatment of reporters than other agencies. This suggests that while increased awareness of legislation encourages staff to report and to trust their management, more is needed for agencies to meet these raised expectations.

The second part of the chapter examines the comprehensiveness of procedures across the 175 agencies that provided written procedures to the study and the 102 of these agencies that also participated in the employee survey. These procedures provide the main framework within which organisations deal with, and respond to, reports of wrongdoing, at a level below or even irrespective of the framework provided by the legislation. The comprehensiveness of the procedures is assessed against the basic requirements of the relevant Australian Standard and also an extended set of requirements developed for the public sector by this project.

The results show that while some areas in current procedures have some strength, there are systemic weaknesses in all jurisdictions in how agencies currently formally respond to whistleblowing. Only five of the 175 agencies were rated as having procedures that would reasonably satisfy all the requirements set out in the current Australian Standard. The substantial variability in the comprehensiveness of procedures found across all jurisdictions, together with their patchiness and generally low comprehensiveness, confirm the need for the development of new best-practice or model procedures. Consistent with the results from Chapter 9, the analysis reveals that agencies' formal procedures appear to be skewed towards encouraging reporting and setting in place the investigative responses to those reports, more than management of the welfare of those involved. The results also suggest a need for clearer statutory requirements and oversight of the quality of procedures. Even when agencies have moved beyond a mere compliance approach and have taken up a more utilitarian approach, this appears to remain limited in its focus.

The third part of the chapter examines the effectiveness of current procedures and establishes that more comprehensive procedures are indeed associated with a higher incidence of positive outcomes from whistleblowing. These results indicate that a more comprehensive approach is likely to deliver results for agencies—not only in terms of heightened support for whistleblowing and trust in management, but in substantive outcomes such as reporting rates and reduced rates of whistleblower mistreatment. The general weakness of most procedures for the protection of whistleblowers means that these outcomes cannot be traced directly to better whistleblower support programs. Nevertheless, the evidence suggests that more comprehensive approaches do yield better outcomes, providing significant encouragement for those agencies prepared to make an effort to develop better whistleblowing management systems.

## Awareness of, and confidence in, legislation

As reviewed throughout this book, and discussed in more detail in Chapter 11, in each jurisdiction the management of whistleblowing takes place in a specific legislative context. In each case, whistleblowing or 'public interest disclosure' legislation sets in place different requirements for agency-level procedures and different frameworks for ensuring or increasing the likelihood of agency compliance. The adequacy of these legislative frameworks is assessed in the next chapter, in light of all the evidence.

An important issue is whether the existence of whistleblowing legislation has any direct impact on reporting behaviour and other outcomes in the agencies studied. This is especially salient given the importance of legislative obligations to those agencies taking simply a compliance approach to their whistleblowing procedures and systems. Despite the differences in the legislative frameworks, they share the objectives of facilitating disclosures about wrongdoing by public employees, ensuring that disclosures are properly dealt with and ensuring whistleblowers are protected from reprisals or mistreatment. At a general or symbolic level, therefore, the impacts of these regimes on public officials' behaviour should be broadly comparable.

The following sections examine first the levels of awareness of legislation within agencies and second the differing levels of confidence in that legislation. The focus of this analysis is not the accuracy of employees' beliefs, but how their beliefs might influence attitudes, behaviour and outcomes.

## Awareness of legislation

In Chapter 7 (Table 7.5), it was seen that 44 per cent of all employee survey respondents believed they were subject to legislation covering their 'rights and responsibilities associated with reporting alleged wrongdoing', while very few (2 per cent) believed they were not covered and a very large proportion (54 per cent) did not know. Earlier, in Chapter 3, it was seen that awareness of and opinions about the relevant legislation did not differ significantly between the employees who reported wrongdoing and those who observed wrongdoing but did not report it. This could suggest that the presence of legislation or employees' views of its contents make no difference; however, further analysis shows that the picture is more complex.

Table 10.1 sets out the relationship between whether or not respondents to the employee survey believed they were covered by legislation and how they answered the questions designed to establish their attitudes to whistleblowing, or their level of whistleblowing propensity. The table shows the relationship for all respondents divided into four groups according to their reporting behaviour. The table shows a very strong correlation between the belief that an employee is covered by relevant legislation and the likelihood that they will blow the whistle according to the whistleblowing-propensity scale. This correlation was present for all groups—including, as seen in Chapter 3, those who observed wrongdoing but did not report the most serious instance.

These results suggest either that the (perceived) presence of legislative obligations and protection is a strong contributing factor to employees' positive attitude to blowing the whistle or that those who have a positive attitude to blowing the whistle assume that they are subject to legislative obligations and protection. In either case, irrespective of how their beliefs influence their real reporting behaviour, there is an important relationship between the presence of legislation and employees' expectations about what should happen if they disclose wrongdoing.

**Table 10.1 Relationship between awareness of legislation and whistleblowing propensity**

| Group of employees (by reporting behaviour) | Correlation between awareness of legislation and whistleblowing propensity |
|---|---|
| Non-observers of wrongdoing (n = 2 074) | Pearson correlation = −0.39* |
| Observers but non-reporters (n = 3 198) | Pearson correlation = −0.35** |
| Role reporters (n = 583) | Pearson correlation = −0.37** |
| Non-role reporters (n = 1 427) | Pearson correlation = −0.35** |
| All respondents (n = 7 310) | Pearson correlation = −0.38** |

* correlation is significant at the 0.05 level
** correlation is significant at the 0.01 level
**Notes:** Correlations are negative because the awareness rating specifies awareness as scoring low and a lack of awareness as scoring high. The whistleblowing-propensity scale ranges from low propensity scoring lowest to high propensity scoring highest.
**Source:** Employee survey: Q15, Q16.

To better examine whether awareness of legislation also translates into real whistleblowing behaviour, analysis was conducted comparing the results between different agencies. As shown in Chapter 7 in relation to managers, there were significant jurisdictional differences in the proportion of respondents who believed they were covered by legislation. Figure 10.1 shows the number of agencies in each jurisdiction according to the differing proportions of their employees who believed they were covered. There is even greater variation at an agency level. Some of the variation is probably explained by variations in the legal reality—for example, many Commonwealth Government agencies operate outside the framework of the *Public Service Act 1999* (Cth), which provides the only legislative provision relevant to whistleblowing. This could explain why some Commonwealth agencies showed lower percentages of employees believing they were covered by legislation; the fact is that many were not. It does not, however, explain the large number of state agencies in the same category, since almost all were covered by legislation at the time.

Table 10.2 shows whether, at an agency level, there was any relationship between the proportion of employees who believed they were covered by legislation and a number of the key outcomes discussed earlier in Chapters 2 and 5. These are: the overall trust of employees in how management would respond to whistleblowing in that agency; the proportion of employees who did not report or take other action (inaction rate); the proportion of employees who reported the most serious wrongdoing they saw (reporting rate); and the proportion of those who reported who indicated they were then treated badly, either by management or by co-workers.

## Figure 10.1 Awareness of legislation by agency and jurisdiction

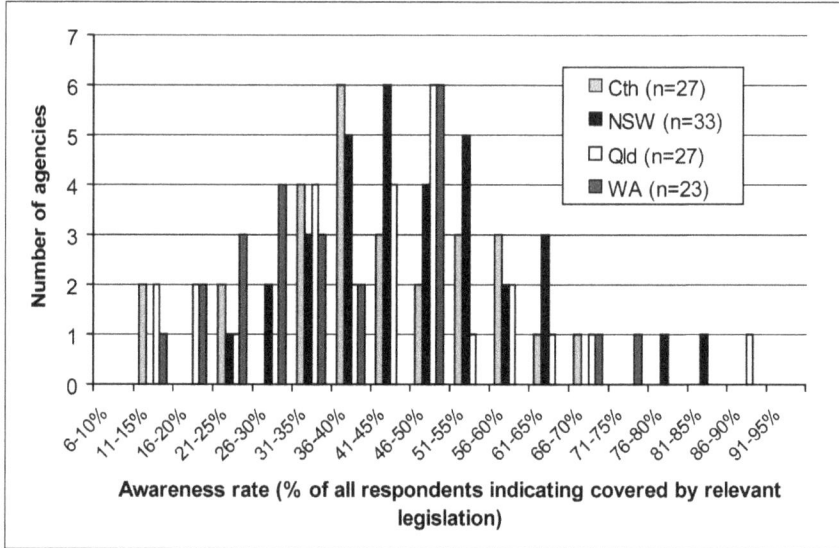

Source: Employee survey: Q16.

## Table 10.2 Relationship between legislation awareness and reporting and outcome measures (agencies)

| Measures from employee survey | Correlation with legislation awareness rate (Q16) |
|---|---|
| 1) Mean agency rating for how management would respond to report of wrongdoing (Q18 as a 13-item scale) 1 = poor and 5 = well | Pearson correlation = 0.25 *<br>Significance (two-tailed) = 0.008<br>(n = 110) |
| 2) Inaction rate: proportion of respondents who observed wrongdoing they believed to be very/extremely serious but did not report, did not deal with by self and it was not reported by someone else (Q26, Q35)[a] | Pearson correlation = –0.05<br>Significance (two-tailed) = 0.640<br>(n = 86) |
| 3) Reporting rate: proportion of respondents who observed wrongdoing they believed to be very/extremely serious and reported it (Q26) | Pearson correlation = 0.16<br>Significance (two-tailed) = 0.142<br>(n = 86) |
| 4) Proportion of all non-role reporters who rated treatment by management as 'bad' or 'extremely bad' (Q30)[a] | Pearson correlation = 0.17<br>Significance (two-tailed) = 0.222<br>(n = 52) |
| 5) Proportion of all non-role reporters who rated treatment by co-workers as 'bad' or 'extremely bad' (Q31)[a] | Pearson correlation = 0.08<br>Significance (two-tailed) = 0.556<br>(n = 51) |

* correlation significant at the 0.01 level
[a] It was anticipated that these correlations would be negative because these outcome scales run from a good outcome scoring lowest to a poor outcome scoring highest.

A significant relationship was found only on the first measure. Similar to the result for whistleblowing propensity, agencies that had higher proportions of employees who believed they were covered by legislation also had higher proportions of staff who believed that management's response to whistleblowing would be positive, including protection of their rights if they suffered reprisals. In other words, while there is no evidence that the simple belief that legislation applies has any direct influence on reporting behaviour, this belief does go hand-in-hand with employees' confidence in management reaction and support. Whistleblowing legislation appears to do at least one thing for which it was intended: it increases employees' expectations that they will be taken seriously and will be protected if they blow the whistle. This has immediate implications for agencies that seek to discharge their whistleblowing management obligations simply by telling their employees about the legislation that applies.

## Confidence in legislation

Even if they are aware of the legislative protections and obligations they think apply, how confident are employees in them? Confidence in legislation was gauged using four items in the employee survey already introduced in Chapter 7, in which the confidence of managers and non-managers was compared. These items are shown in Table 10.3, with results according to jurisdiction. For those who believed they were covered by legislation, confidence in it was highest among Commonwealth respondents and lowest among Queensland respondents. This is an interesting result, since Queensland has been assessed as having the most comprehensive legislation and the Commonwealth the least comprehensive (Brown 2006).

For contrast, Table 10.4 shows how case-handlers and managers in the case study agencies answered when asked a similar question about their confidence in the legislation. Given that this survey was targeted towards participants who had experience of the issues, it would be expected that their understanding of the legislation would be deeper than the random sample of employees. Here again, as in Table 10.3, the Commonwealth participants reported higher levels of confidence, even though the Commonwealth had the least comprehensive legislative cover. The average opinions of NSW and West Australian case-handlers and managers closely or exactly match the level of confidence held by the average employee in these jurisdictions. The Queensland results are again divergent, with case-handlers and managers having a significantly higher level of confidence than the average employee.

## Table 10.3 Confidence in legislation by jurisdiction (means)

| 1 = strongly disagree<br>5 = strongly agree | Cth<br>(n = 1 085) | NSW<br>(n = 1 319) | Qld<br>(n = 925) | WA<br>(n = 418) |
|---|---|---|---|---|
| The existence of the legislation makes it easier for me to consider reporting corruption | 3.64 | 3.66 | 3.56 | 3.53 |
| I am confident that the legislation has the power to protect me from any negative consequences if I were to report corruption | 3.13 | 3.05 | 2.96 | 3.10 |
| I believe that the legislation is ineffective[a] | 2.69 | 2.78 | 2.84 | 2.80 |
| The legislation is in need of major change to improve employee reporting of wrongdoing[a] | 2.86 | 2.95 | 3.06 | 2.94 |
| **Overall mean** | **3.30** | **3.24** | **3.15** | **3.22** |
| 1 = low, 5 = high | (n = 1 103) | (n = 1 352) | (n = 942) | (n = 425) |

[a] Items reverse scored
Source: Employee survey: Q17.

## Table 10.4 Confidence in legislation: case-handlers and managers, by jurisdiction

| Overall means<br>1 = low, 5 = high | Cth | NSW | Qld | WA |
|---|---|---|---|---|
| **Case-handlers** | 3.26 (n = 94) | 3.07 (n = 45) | 3.18 (n = 29) | 3.05 (n = 36) |
| **Managers** | 3.26 (n = 71) | 3.36 (n = 64) | 3.39 (n = 48) | 3.22 (n = 66) |
| **Total** | **3.26**<br>(n = 165) | **3.24**<br>(n = 109) | **3.31**<br>(n = 77) | **3.16**<br>(n = 102) |

Sources: Case-handler and manager surveys: Q21.

## Table 10.5 Trust in management response, and whistleblower treatment (means, by jurisdiction)

| Measures from employee survey | Cth | NSW | Qld | WA | Total |
|---|---|---|---|---|---|
| How management would respond to report of wrongdoing (Q18 as a 13-item scale)<br>1 = poor, 5 = well | 3.30<br>(n = 2 261) | 3.31<br>(n = 2 517) | 3.23<br>(n = 1 687) | 3.30<br>(n = 950) | 3.30<br>(n = 7 473) |
| For all non-role reporters, treatment by management 1 = well, 5 = poor | 2.99<br>(n = 379) | 2.83<br>(n = 456) | 2.99<br>(n = 339) | 2.87<br>(n = 144) | 2.92<br>(n = 1 325) |
| For all non-role reporters, treatment by co-workers<br>1 = well, 5 = poor | 2.77<br>(n = 373) | 2.59<br>(n = 444) | 2.68<br>(n = 336) | 2.70<br>(n = 1 445) | 2.68<br>(n = 1304) |

Source: Employee survey: Q18, Q30, Q31.

## Table 10.6 Confidence in legislation by salary range (means)

| 1 = strongly disagree<br>5 = strongly agree | < $20,000<br>(n = 56) | $20,000–39,999<br>(n = 298) | $40,000–59,999<br>(n = 1 297) | $60,000–79,999<br>(n = 1 155) | $80,000–99,999<br>(n = 548) | $100,000–120,000<br>(n = 234) | > $120,000<br>(n = 159) |
|---|---|---|---|---|---|---|---|
| The existence of the legislation makes it easier for me to consider reporting corruption. | 3.68 | 3.59 | 3.58 | 3.61 | 3.67 | 3.67 | 3.67 |
| I am confident that the legislation has the power to protect me from any negative consequences if I were to report corruption.[a] | 3.46 | 3.22 | 3.10 | 2.94 | 3.04 | 3.06 | 3.16 |
| I believe that the legislation is ineffective.[a] | 2.71 | 2.75 | 2.79 | 2.81 | 2.71 | 2.72 | 2.67 |
| The legislation is in need of major change to improve employee reporting of wrongdoing.[a] | 3.05 | 3.03 | 3.00 | 2.98 | 2.88 | 2.82 | 2.68 |

[a] significant at $p = 0.01$ level using Chi-square test
**Source:** Employee survey: Q15.

Before examining the possible effects of confidence in legislation, it is worth noting two further features of this evidence. First, the differences between the mean results, while still statistically significant, are nevertheless objectively small. The confidence means of all groups—in every jurisdiction and in most agencies—tend to hover around the midpoint of the scales, indicating large numbers of respondents who did not know or were unwilling to state a view about the content or effectiveness of the legislation. Thirty-eight per cent of all employee survey respondents could neither agree nor disagree that they were confident that the legislation had power to protect them, 52 per cent could not state a view about whether they thought it was effective and 57 per cent could not or would not say whether it needed major change. As seen in Chapter 7, respondents were generally very likely to agree they needed more information and training about the legislation.

It is also worth noting where confidence is lowest and highest. Table 10.6 shows the distribution of confidence according to salary range. As indicated in Chapter 7, managers tend to be more confident in the legislation than non-managers, but this table also shows that junior and/or part-time staff members are also likely to be more confident. The least confident employees are likely to be those in middle salary brackets ($40,000–79,000 per annum).

Overall, there is good reason to believe that confidence in legislation does correlate with some of the outcomes considered earlier. Even if simply being aware of legislation does not influence behaviour, differences emerge if employees are both aware and hold the legislation in either high or low regard. On the surface, Table 10.5 suggested a possible relationship, given basic results by jurisdiction. In at least one case in which confidence in the legislation ranked low—Queensland, as shown in Table 10.3—there is also lower overall trust in the likely management response and some higher levels of reported mistreatment by managers.

Do these patterns hold statistically or at an agency level? Table 10.7 tests this by again looking for correlations at the agency level, comparing the level of confidence in legislation within specific agencies with their outcomes on the same five measures used earlier in relation to awareness.

## Table 10.7 Relationship between employee confidence in legislation and reporting and outcome measures (agencies)

| Measures from employee survey | Correlation with confidence in legislation |
|---|---|
| 1) Mean agency rating for how management would respond to report of wrongdoing (Q18 as a 13-item scale) <br> 1 = poor and 5 = well | Pearson correlation = 0.62** <br> Significance (two-tailed) = 0.0005 <br> (n = 92) |
| 2) Inaction rate: proportion of respondents who observed wrongdoing they believed to be very/extremely serious but did not report, did not deal with by self and it was not reported by someone else (Q26, Q35)[a] | Pearson correlation = −0.23* <br> Significance (two-tailed) = 0.041 <br> (n = 83) |
| 3) Reporting rate: proportion of respondents who observed wrongdoing they believed to be very/extremely serious and reported it (Q26) | Pearson correlation = 0.15 <br> Significance (two-tailed) = 0.165 <br> (n = 83) |
| 4) Proportion of all non-role reporters who rated treatment by management as 'bad' or 'extremely bad' (Q30)[a] | Pearson correlation = −0.19 <br> Significance (two-tailed) = 0.209 <br> (n = 51) |
| 5) Proportion of all non-role reporters who rated treatment by co-workers as 'bad' or 'extremely bad' (Q31)[a] | Pearson correlation = −0.14 <br> Significance (two-tailed) = 0.313 <br> (n = 51) |

* correlation is significant at the 0.05 level
** correlation is significant at the 0.01 level
[a] It was anticipated that these correlations would be negative because these outcome scales run from a good outcome scoring lowest to a poor outcome scoring highest.

A strong relationship was found only on the first measure (higher trust in management response to whistleblowing), with a somewhat lesser relationship on the second measure (lower inaction rate in response to serious wrongdoing). No significant relationship was found between the proportion of employees who were confident in the legislation and the reporting rate or the outcomes in terms of treatment in those agencies.

These nil results could nevertheless be important since they suggest that confidence in legislation is based primarily on its symbolic intent, rather than on any observable pattern in better (or worse) outcomes for whistleblowers. This reinforces the extent to which employees simply do not know what happens under the legislation. The results mean that while a high incidence of whistleblower mistreatment is not flowing through into negative views about the legislation, nor is good treatment of whistleblowers flowing through to bolster confidence.

The mixed results on reporting and inaction rates make it difficult to conclude that confidence in the legislation increases the level of reporting, at the agency level. Across the 83 agencies for which sufficient data exist to permit this analysis, however, the significant correlation between confidence and lower inaction rates suggests there is something about agencies in which this confidence is higher that does lead to wrongdoing being more likely to be dealt with or 'flushed out'. As levels of confidence in the legislation increased in an agency, the proportion of observers of serious wrongdoing who did nothing went down. As explained in Chapter 2, this is perhaps a better result than an increased reporting rate, since even if many people observe the same wrongdoing, all it takes is one or a few people to report or otherwise deal with it for action to be taken. It is plausible that in agencies with higher confidence in legislation, the perceived higher likelihood of someone reporting the wrongdoing is enough to induce action from those in positions of responsibility.

These results indicate that even at the current low level of knowledge of whistleblowing legislation among employees, awareness of and belief in that legislation can be associated with positive effects. The results clearly suggest that higher awareness of and confidence in whistleblowing legislation, at the agency level, help convince employees that their own management's response to whistleblowing can be trusted, including protection of their rights. In other words, the results point to the conclusion that employees who are confident they will be taken seriously and protected by management appear to assume that this is either required or reinforced by effective legislation—or vice versa. In organisations in which awareness and confidence of the legislation are higher, it is also generally more likely that serious wrongdoing will be brought to light.

These results indicate that even a mere compliance approach to whistleblowing by agency management, relying only on the simple existence and symbolic value of the applicable legislation, can yield some positive outcomes. These results also confirm, however, that, as yet, there is no evidence that legislation is helping deliver improved outcomes for whistleblowers themselves or reduced levels of conflict within organisations about the management of the process. Given that whistleblowing legislation appears to do at least one thing for which it was intended—increasing employees' expectations that they will be taken seriously and protected—the lack of evidence that it has the latter effect raises a serious challenge for agencies relying simply on compliance. Irrespective of the precise procedural requirements imposed on agencies by the legislation, even its simple existence—if known to staff—creates an obligation to develop effective procedures for managing the individuals involved. The alternative is that legislative frameworks will function simply as a 'trap', achieving their goals in encouraging employees to report but not meeting reasonable expectations regarding support and protection as a consequence of having done so.

The importance of agencies taking active measures to fill the gap between legislative requirements and their own needs is also reflected elsewhere in these results. It is notable that differences in the reality of legislative arrangements do not appear to impact on key results, such as the level of trust in management to handle reports among Commonwealth agencies, as shown in Table 10.5. The indications of how Commonwealth whistleblowers feel they were treated by management and co-workers similarly does not appear to have any direct relationship to the objectively weak legislative framework. In relation to treatment by management, the Commonwealth average is the same for one jurisdiction that does have comprehensive whistleblowing legislation. A similar pattern will emerge in relation to procedures. This confirms that, at an agency level, the relationship between legislation and procedures is not direct. Jurisdictions with relatively good legislation are not necessarily currently getting the desired results at an agency level, while even in jurisdictions with weaker legislation, some agencies can achieve—and are achieving—relatively good systems and results.

In thinking about the relationship between the procedures and the legislation, it is useful to keep in mind that organisations have available general employment powers that can fulfil many of the objectives of an effective whistleblower scheme. Clearly, specific legislation is necessary to provide a high level of protection against reprisals and the capacity for individuals to seek compensation. Having said that, there is still a considerable amount of discretion for organisations to develop procedures that go beyond legislative requirements.

This is particularly the case when it comes to the listing of concerns that can be brought forward in a whistleblowing procedure. As will be demonstrated below, some Commonwealth organisations effectively go beyond the very limited whistleblower regime in that jurisdiction and use general employment powers to encourage and protect staff reporting on a broader range of issues. Attempting to overlay specific legislative protections with a general employment authority is, however, quite complex. Care needs to be taken not to mislead staff into thinking that they have legislative protection against reprisal when their protection is based only on a general employment power.

## Comprehensiveness of policies and procedures

If the comprehensiveness of legislation has been the subject of debate, what of the comprehensiveness of agency procedures for managing whistleblowing? To arrive at a better picture of the state of agency procedures, data were collected from 304 public sector agencies on their whistleblowing-related practices and procedures, via the agency survey. Seventy-three of these were Commonwealth agencies, including a mix of APS and non-APS agencies; while 85 were from New South Wales, 83 from Queensland and 63 were agencies of the West Australian Government. The aim was to collect comprehensive data on:

- policies and procedures relating to wrongdoing
- the investigation and assessment of disclosures (reviewed in Chapter 8)
- support and management of internal witnesses (reviewed in Chapter 9)
- reprisals against internal witnesses (reviewed in Chapter 9).

## Table 10.8 Agency whistleblowing procedures: contents and mean score (maximum 3)

| Assessment item/topic | Mean |
|---|---|
| 1. Ease of comprehension of document[a] | 1.79 |
| 2. To whom and how whistleblowing concerns can be directed (internally) | 1.70 |
| 3. **Reporting will be kept confidential and secure within the law** [a] | **1.68** |
| 4. Types of concerns for which it is appropriate to use the whistleblowing mechanism | 1.62 |
| 5. Information about legislation[a] | 1.62 |
| 6. Investigation process to follow on receipt of a whistleblowing report | 1.57 |
| 7. To whom and how whistleblowing concerns can be directed (externally) and in what circumstances[a] | 1.51 |
| 8. Organisation's opinion of reporting wrongdoing through appropriate channels | 1.49 |
| 9. **Commitment to protect and respect internal witnesses** [b] | **1.48** |
| 10. Roles and responsibilities of the key players in the organisation | 1.43 |
| 11. Commitment to principle of whistleblowing | 1.21 |
| 12. A description of the protection of the rights of people against whom allegations have been made[a] | 1.26 |
| 13. Internal witnesses will receive feedback | 1.21 |
| 14. Who may invoke the whistleblowing mechanism (that is, employees, contractors, the general public, and so on) | 1.15 |
| 15. **Staff who report wrongdoing not to suffer disciplinary action** [ab] | **0.96** |
| 16. How sure the internal witness should be of the truth of their concerns before invoking the whistleblowing mechanism | 0.72 |
| 17. **Active management and support of internal witnesses** [ab] | **0.72** |
| 18. Benefits and importance to the entity of having a whistleblowing mechanism | 0.70 |
| 19. Anonymous reports will be acted on | 0.67 |
| 20. **Procedures for responding to reprisal action against internal witnesses** [ab] | **0.54** |
| 21. Sanctions for making a false or frivolous allegation[a] | 0.47 |
| 22. **Rights of the internal witness to request positive action by the entity to protect them** [b] | **0.22** |
| 23. **Procedures for the investigation of reprisal action against internal witnesses** [ab] | **0.22** |
| 24. **Procedures for the assessment of risk of reprisal against individual whistleblowers** [ab] | **0.12** |

[a] Criterion added by the research team.
[b] Criterion relating directly or indirectly to whistleblower management and protection.

As outlined in Chapter 9, 76 per cent (231) of the 304 agencies indicated that they had formal internal disclosure procedures. This figure was itself somewhat low, given that some non-APS Commonwealth agencies had procedures even when under no legislative obligation; many agencies that were under such an obligation provided responses clearly indicating that they were not fulfilling them. In all, 186 of the agencies surveyed indicated they had attached copies of their formal internal disclosure procedures. In fact, written procedures were received for only 175 agencies.

To allow a comparative assessment of the contents and the comprehensiveness of agencies' procedures, an instrument was developed by which their contents could be coded and rated. This procedures assessment involved examining the written procedures for their coverage of 24 items, or topics, listed in Table 10.8.

Fourteen of the items were drawn directly from the Australian Standard *Whistleblower Protection Programs for Entities* (AS 8004-2003). Ten items were added by the research team in light of issues of known importance in public sector agencies and the results of an initial project symposium held in July 2005. The identification of the essential criteria that go to make up effective whistleblowing procedures also followed the lead of a study of 57 private and 57 public sector organisations in the United Kingdom (Lewis 2002). In that study, 14 essential elements were identified, all of which were present in the procedures-assessment instrument developed in the present study. In a study for the European Parliament, Bjorn-Liebenau (2006) identified 18 key elements and these also closely matched the criteria used in this study.

Table 10.8 also sets out the mean score for each item across all 175 agencies, ranked in order of the overall strength or comprehensiveness of the criteria. Each mean reflects a rating of between 0 and 3, with the contents of procedures having been rated in one of two ways: statements of commitment or principle were rated according to strength (0 = no mention, 1 = brief mention, 2 = reasonably strong, 3 = extremely strong), while actual procedures were rated according to comprehensiveness (0 = no mention, 1 = brief mention, 2 = reasonably comprehensive, 3 = extremely comprehensive). Detailed guidance was given to the researchers involved in order to ensure consistency and to minimise variations in assessment approaches.

As seen in the table, there was great variation in the content of procedures, without any items being consistently strong right across all agencies. The overall weakness of the procedures, even on more frequent topics, is reflected in the fact that none of the strongest items even reached a score of 2 (reasonably strong/comprehensive). There was also great variation between those aspects that were treated well in procedures, on average, and those treated poorly. Many key issues were often either entirely omitted or dealt with far more scantily than others. In some cases, stronger items reflected the fact that many public sector agencies have procedures in place dealing with other issues, such as internal investigations, which are not focused on the management of whistleblowing but can be applied to that process. While investigatory capacity remains open to debate, as discussed in Chapter 8, the fact is that procedures exist. Similarly, most agencies responded to the imperative for procedures by setting out the process to be followed by people who came forward with reports (for example, who they should report to and what the recipient of the report should do).

The weaker items in Table 10.8 confirm the results presented in Chapter 9 regarding the absence and weakness of mechanisms for the protection and support of internal witnesses. The eight items relating directly or indirectly to management and protection of whistleblowers are also highlighted in the table. The weakness of many of these items confirms that active measures to support and protect internal witnesses remain the single greatest unmet challenge in the operational practices of agencies.

How do individual agencies compare in the comprehensiveness of their procedures?

The mean scores for all agencies in each jurisdiction are shown in Table 10.9. The results are shown, first, using simply the 14 items contained in the Australian Standard. Given 14 items, the maximum score for any agency on this measure was 42, but the average score for all agencies was only 15.9. This low average score is of obvious concern, given that, if an assumption is made that a score of 2 (reasonably strong/comprehensive) is needed to meet a reasonable standard on any topic, the minimum score needed to meet the Australian Standard would be 28 out of 42. Only five of the 175 agencies provided procedures that met or exceeded this standard.

The same table also shows the results using all 24 items in the more comprehensive assessment developed in this research. The outcome is similar. Given the 24 items, the potential maximum score for any agency was 72, but the average score across all agencies was only 24.4. Of course, there was significant variation between agencies, across the entire group and within each jurisdiction. The average score for the 15 case study agencies was substantially higher, at 36.2, reflecting the stronger organisational emphasis that many of these agencies have given to these issues. Nevertheless, the lowness of the scores is striking, confirming that, overall, few of the whistleblowing procedures submitted by agencies can be regarded as comprehensive.

**Table 10.9 Comprehensiveness of agency procedures (average scores)**

| Jurisdiction | Number of agencies assessed | Mean score out of 42 Australian Standard (standard deviation) | Mean score out of 72 WWTW (standard deviation) |
|---|---|---|---|
| Commonwealth | 56 | 14.5 (8.23) | 24.5 (11.08) |
| New South Wales | 60 | 18.3 (4.96) | 27.4 (7.61) |
| Queensland | 31 | 11.2 (6.18) | 18.9 (10.67) |
| Western Australia | 28 | 15.9 (6.78) | 24.3 (11.04) |
| Overall | 175 | 15.9 (6.68) | 24.4 (10.27) |

Figure 10.2 shows the distribution of the individual scores of all agencies—again, for each jurisdiction. There is considerable range in the comprehensiveness of agency whistleblowing procedures. A wide range can be found in every jurisdiction, indicating that even those jurisdictions with more detailed legislative frameworks in relation to procedures are not achieving a consistently comprehensive approach.

There are, however, also some notable features. The higher average scores for NSW agencies can be seen in the cluster of NSW agencies at the upper end of the scale. The pattern of the Commonwealth results is also different from the pattern of other jurisdictions, being most widely spread. A significant number is clustered towards the low end of the scale, but there is also a significant number at the high end. Keeping in mind that the Commonwealth agencies included a number outside the APS, with no standard whistleblowing provisions in law, a number of Commonwealth agencies have taken it on themselves to develop procedures that go well beyond legal requirements. Queensland has the largest number of agencies with low scores, notwithstanding—as mentioned earlier—that it has quite comprehensive legislation.

A comparison of the scores for procedures and the size of the organisation, based on information provided in the agency survey, indicates a significant correlation (0.38, n = 64, $p < 0.05$). This confirms that, across the jurisdictions, more comprehensive whistleblowing procedures are likely to be found in larger organisations.

**Figure 10.2 Comprehensiveness of procedures: distribution of (total) scores by jurisdiction**

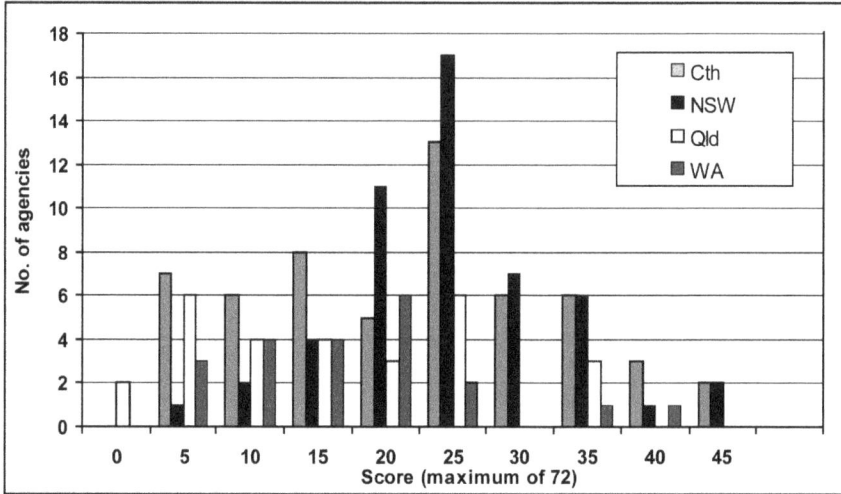

The variability, patchiness and general low comprehensiveness of whistleblowing procedures—on these basic measures—indicates that many agencies have much to learn in relation to the content of their procedures and systems. As outlined in Chapter 1, further analysis as part of the present research is intended to set out lessons for best-practice or model procedures based on the collective experience of Australian public sector agencies so far. A new framework for Internal Witness Management Systems derived from the research so far, reflecting all the items used in the procedures assessment, is provided in Appendix 3.

Two general conclusions can nevertheless be drawn from the current state of whistleblowing procedures in most agencies and jurisdictions. First, where they exist, agencies' formal procedures are skewed towards encouraging reporting and setting in place the investigative responses to those reports, much more than towards the management of the welfare of those involved. In other words, procedures tend to be geared towards meeting the interests of the organisation rather than the needs of the employees who come forward with reports. This bias in the content of procedures suggests that, even when agencies move beyond a mere compliance approach to whistleblowing processes and take up a more utilitarian approach, this can be limited in its focus. Agencies often appear to recognise the practical benefits of reporting from a management perspective without addressing the importance of whistleblower welfare—whether for its practical value in sustaining a positive reporting climate and reducing the costs of conflict or in recognition of other legal and ethical responsibilities towards employees. In the majority of agencies, procedures need substantial review to achieve a more effective balance of approaches.

Second, the great variability in procedures—such as demonstrated in particular by the clusters of low Queensland and Commonwealth scores—suggests a need for clearer statutory requirements and oversight. Currently, even when legislation provides frameworks aimed at ensuring agencies put in place quality procedures, this is frequently not having its intended effects. Chapter 11 further discusses the need for a new approach to minimum statutory requirements for the content of procedures and for more routine external monitoring of their quality and implementation.

## Impact and effectiveness of procedures

The previous discussion has assumed that comprehensive whistleblowing procedures are desirable because they can and should lead to better outcomes for organisations and whistleblowers. Is there empirical evidence that this is the case?

To answer this question, the results from the employee survey were further analysed for the 102 agencies that had participated in that survey and provided written whistleblowing procedures for assessment. First, the degree of awareness about the existence of the procedures was examined, along with how this awareness appeared to have been achieved and the degree of association between comprehensiveness of procedures, awareness of them and employees' attitudes to whistleblowing and the likely management response. Second, the effectiveness of the procedures was tested for in terms of the same key outcomes identified earlier, including reporting rates and the proportion of employees who said they were treated well or badly as a result. Third, further analysis was conducted to see whether the relationship between procedures and outcomes could be explained with reference to any specific items in the procedures.

## Awareness of, and confidence in, procedures

Across the board, public officials are more aware of the fact that their organisations have procedures relating to whistleblowing than they are of any relevant legislation. When asked whether their organisation had formal policies covering the reporting of wrongdoing, 74 per cent of all employee survey respondents said 'yes', 3 per cent said 'no' and only 22 per cent did not know (n = 7663, 118 agencies). Generally, reported knowledge of procedures is widespread in agencies.

It is also clear that higher employee awareness of procedures results directly from management action and the efforts of agencies to embed procedures in their organisation. Of the 231 agencies that responded to the agency survey that they had formal internal disclosure procedures, almost all (229 agencies) indicated they had arrangements in place for informing staff about their policies. The employee survey also asked officials within agencies about the mechanisms by which they had been made aware of the reporting policy of their organisation, including via the code of conduct, general training, induction programs and a range of other mechanisms.

The first, though unsurprising, conclusion is that the agencies in which staff awareness of procedures is highest are also those with the most comprehensive procedures rated above. The data reveal a strong and direct correlation between professed knowledge of the existence of procedures and their comprehensiveness in practice (0.30, n = 101, p < 0.01). This result is reassuring in that it shows that more comprehensive procedures are not just fatter documents that then become less likely to have any effect. The reasons for this higher awareness are clear: agencies that have gone to the effort of developing comprehensive procedures also appear to have been most likely to expend resources in making staff aware of them. Organisations with more comprehensive procedures were likely to have used more mechanisms for promoting their contents, with, again, a correlation between larger agency size and greater reported use of different promotional mechanisms (agency survey, 0.26, n = 79, p < 0.05).

As shown in Table 10.10, there was also a strong association between the comprehensiveness of an agency's awareness-raising approach, in terms of the number of mechanisms used, and two indicators of employee confidence in the procedures: more positive attitudes towards the reporting of wrongdoing generally and greater confidence that management would respond well to reporting if it occurred. Respondents to the internal witness survey also confirmed that the formal internal policies of their organisation played important roles in forming their view of the wrongdoing they went on to report, rating key internal policies second and third (after legislation) out of a list of 10 factors (internal witness survey: Q7).

**Table 10.10 Relationship between promotion of procedures and attitudes/expectations about reporting**

| Measure from employee survey | Correlation with total number of awareness mechanisms used to promote procedures [a] |
| --- | --- |
| Attitudes held by staff to reporting of wrongdoing<br>1 = bad and 5 = good | Pearson correlation = 0.36*<br>Significance (two-tailed) = 0.000<br>(n = 7 436) |
| View of staff on how management would respond to reporting of wrongdoing (Q18 scale)<br>1 = poor and 5 = well | Pearson correlation = 0.23*<br>Significance (two-tailed) = 0.000<br>(n = 7 544) |

* Correlation is significant at the 0.01 level
[a] The awareness mechanism measure runs from 0 (no mechanism nominated) to 16 (all mechanisms nominated).

**Table 10.11 Relationship between comprehensiveness of procedures and employee confidence**

| Measure from employee survey | Correlation with comprehensiveness of agency procedures |
| --- | --- |
| 1) Attitudes held by staff to the reporting of wrongdoing<br><br>1 = bad and 5 = good | Pearson correlation = 0.23*<br>Significance (two-tailed) = 0.020<br>(n = 102) |
| 2) View of less senior staff on how management would respond to reporting of wrongdoing (Q18 as a 13-item scale); respondents earning less than $80,000 per annum<br><br>1 = poor and 5 = well | Pearson correlation = 0.12<br>Significance (two-tailed) = 0.213<br>(n = 102) |
| 3) View of more senior staff on how management would respond to reporting of wrongdoing (Q18 as a 13-item scale); respondents earning more than $80,000 per annum<br><br>1 = poor and 5 = well | Pearson correlation = −0.29**<br>Significance (two-tailed) = 0.004<br>(n = 102) |

\* correlation is significant at the 0.05 level
\*\* correlation is significant at the 0.01 level

Table 10.11 confirms these results by also showing the direct correlation between more comprehensive procedures and more positive general attitudes to whistleblowing, across the 102 agencies.

The remaining two analyses in Table 10.11, however, show that while awareness might be higher and general attitudes more positive, more comprehensive procedures are not necessarily translating into specific trust on the part of employees about how management will respond if wrongdoing is reported. These analyses provide, in effect, a measure of the level of respondents' confidence that management will deal fairly with reports of whistleblowing and protect employees from reprisals. The third analysis examines the relationship between comprehensiveness of procedures and trust in the management response to whistleblowing for less senior employees (earning less than $80,000 per annum); there was no significant relationship. In other words, even if more comprehensive procedures improve the general outlook of employees towards whistleblowing, they do not appear to lead to higher employee confidence in the management response. One reason could be that employees do not become fully aware of the procedures until such time as they are contemplating reporting. It could, however, also be that staff members are aware of the relative weakness of most procedures in areas of real, effective protection and support. Certainly, staff members are not yet convinced about these elements, even if they are otherwise predisposed to report.

The fourth analysis shows a particularly troubling result. It shows the same analysis for more senior employees (earning $80,000 or more per annum). Consistent with the results in Chapter 7, more senior staff showed greater overall confidence in the management of their organisations to deal fairly with reports of whistleblowing (mean 3.35, n = 3619) compared with the less senior staff (mean 3.25, n = 3838). This difference was significant at the 0.001 level. The higher confidence of more senior staff in their agencies' procedures did not, however, tend to be a feature of agencies with comprehensive procedures, but rather of agencies with weaker procedures. In other words, there was a strong negative correlation between comprehensiveness of procedures and the confidence of more senior staff in the likely management response. Senior staff members were more confident about the management response in agencies with less comprehensive procedures and less confident about the response in those agencies with stronger procedures. In some circumstances, managers even reported high levels of confidence in the organisation's capacity to deal with reporting of wrongdoing when the organisation had no whistleblowing procedures at all.

What might explain this perverse result? Comments received on this result, when initially published, suggested as one explanation (called an 'ill-intentioned agency' hypothesis) that managers might be confident in their procedures specifically because they knew them to be weak. In other words, managers were aware that the procedures did not provide proper systems for reporting or effective protection to employees—and believed this was the right way for management to handle whistleblowing. This hypothesis was not, however, consistent with the nature of the 13 survey items making up the relevant scale (employee survey: Q18), which meant that these respondents were explicitly professing confidence that the responses would be favourable to whistleblowers, even when no procedures were in place for this.

Consequently, the more logical explanations—while still troubling—are that senior staff have low knowledge of the real contents of their own systems and procedures and/or do not know whether what they contain is valuable or not. In other words, their confidence is simply misplaced. Evidence of this mismatch between the content of procedures and perceptions of their adequacy was also present among managers and case-handlers in the case study agencies. Case-handlers and managers were surveyed about whether they believed their agencies' whistleblowing policies gave employees 'a reasonable idea about what is going to happen' when they reported wrongdoing. The results for 10 of these agencies are presented in Table 10.12, alongside their score for the comprehensiveness of their real procedures. The data show that case-handlers and managers are generally positive about the usefulness of their procedures. In some cases, however, they appeared to be concerned about their procedures when they were really relatively comprehensive; and, in other cases (especially NSW agency C, bolded), the procedures were poor but case-handlers and managers thought they were useful.

**Table 10.12 Usefulness of procedures for employees contemplating reporting**

| Case-study agency | Comprehensiveness score for agency procedures (max. 72) | Percentage of case-handlers agreeing on usefulness | Percentage of managers agreeing on usefulness |
|---|---|---|---|
| **Commonwealth** | | | |
| A | 45 | 80.8 (n = 26) | 81.3 (n = 32) |
| B | 37 | 60.9 (n = 23) | 50.0 (n = 28) |
| C | 46 | 89.1 (n = 55) | 83.8 (n = 43) |
| **New South Wales** | | | |
| A | 46 | 87.5 (n = 24) | 96.4 (n = 28) |
| B | 41 | 87.5 (n = 16) | 64.3 (n = 14) |
| **C** | **25** | **80.0 (n = 5)** | **90.0 (n = 30)** |
| **Queensland** | | | |
| A | 30 | 50.0 (n = 24) | 80.0 (n = 40) |
| B | 26 | 75.0 (n = 4) | 70.0 (n = 10) |
| **Western Australia** | | | |
| A | 45 | 81.0 (n = 21) | 84.9 (n = 53) |
| B | 41 | 76.9 (n = 26) | 70.6 (n = 34) |

Sources: Case-handler and manager surveys: Q17.

In the same agencies, the internal witnesses were less positive about the usefulness of the written procedures when it came to the process thereafter. Although 79 per cent of case-handlers and managers believed that their procedures gave employees a reasonable idea about what was going to happen, only 50 per cent of internal witnesses said this was really the case (internal witness survey: Q12; n = 193). This is a further sign that while comprehensive procedures do make a difference, there are contradictory assessments within agencies about their current adequacy.

In summary, in some agencies, more senior staff members appear to be excessively optimistic about how well the organisation's procedures are likely to deal with the reporting of wrongdoing. This finding brings further light to bear on the gap between broad principles and practical realities in relation to managerial awareness of legislative obligations, identified in Chapter 7, in the context of the broadly positive outlook of managers. It reinforces the need for systematic review and greater statutory guidance, since it suggests that even if procedural approaches are having discernable effects—positive or negative—more senior staff members currently have only a very limited grasp of their relative quality or what these effects might be.

## Impact and effectiveness

The most crucial issue is whether more comprehensive procedures are positively associated with better substantive outcomes, in terms of the level of actual reporting behaviour and the treatment of whistleblowers. The relationships between the comprehensiveness of procedures and these outcomes are shown in Table 10.13.

The first analysis shows a positive relationship, although not necessarily strong, between comprehensive procedures and a higher level of reporting. Earlier, there was no evidence that awareness of or confidence in legislation directly increased reporting behaviour, but there was evidence that it reduced the incidence of employees observing serious wrongdoing and doing nothing. Here, there is a modest positive relationship between the comprehensiveness of an agency's procedures and the proportion of staff members who report the serious wrongdoing they observe. Given the evidence in Chapter 3 about the complexity of reporting behaviour, it would be unlikely that the comprehensiveness of agency procedures was the sole or direct determinant of whether an employee blew the whistle. Large proportions of employees still report wrongdoing in agencies with no or poor procedures. Nevertheless, this result provides an indication that comprehensive procedures provide positive reinforcement for reporting and it is particularly likely that they also shape how employees report.

**Table 10.13 Relationship between comprehensiveness of procedures and key outcomes (agencies)**

| Measure from employee survey | Correlation with comprehensiveness of agency procedures |
| --- | --- |
| 1) Reporting rate: proportion of respondents who observed wrongdoing they believed to be very/extremely serious and reported it (Q26) | Pearson correlation = 0.20* <br> Significance (two-tailed) = 0.043 <br> (n = 102) |
| 2) Proportion of all non-role reporters who rated treatment by management as 'bad' or 'extremely bad' (Q30)[a] | Pearson correlation = −0.39** <br> Significance (two-tailed) = 0.008 <br> (n = 45) |
| 3) Proportion of all non-role reporters who rated treatment by co-workers as 'bad' or 'extremely bad' (Q31)[a] | Pearson correlation = −0.34* <br> Significance (two-tailed) = 0.026 <br> (n = 44) |

\* correlation is significant at the 0.05 level
\*\* correlation is significant at the 0.01 level
[a] It was anticipated that these correlations would be negative because these outcome scales run from a good outcome scoring lowest to a poor outcome scoring highest.

The second and third analyses in Table 10.13 also show positive results. Respectively, they show the relationship between comprehensiveness of an agency's procedures and the proportion of non-role reporters (whistleblowers) in the agency who indicated they were treated badly by management or by co-workers. As with other analyses, organisations in which fewer than 10 participants responded to the relevant measures were omitted from the calculations, meaning the presence of any relationship could be tested in only 45 and 44 agencies respectively.

The analysis shows a strong relationship between the comprehensiveness of procedures and better treatment by management and a weaker, but still statistically significant, relationship between the comprehensiveness of procedures and better treatment by co-workers. This is a major finding, supporting the conclusion that when an organisation has comprehensive procedures, there is more likely to be a positive outcome in terms of treatment and protection for the person who reported. The remaining question is why this is the case, given that, across the board, procedures are weak in the area of whistleblower protection and support.

## Evaluating specific areas of the procedures

Up to this stage, relationships have been examined in relation to the comprehensiveness of the procedures in their totality. The comprehensiveness of the procedures was, however, assessed on 24 individual items, as described in Table 10.8. The weakest areas were those associated with whistleblower protection and support. Depending on the specific areas of relative strength, an agency's procedures could still show as relatively comprehensive overall without necessarily indicating any particular strength on issues relating to protection and support. In other words, the procedures themselves might not explain why more comprehensive procedures correlated with better treatment outcomes.

The analysis was therefore taken to a further stage, looking for correlations between the various outcome measures above and specific items in the procedures. Table 10.14 identifies the nine items in the written procedures that were more likely to be present when better treatment by managers, better treatment by co-workers or more positive attitudes to reporting were indicated by the employee survey respondents from the agency concerned. Notably, three of the items (bolded) relate directly to the protection of internal witnesses, even though these were the items least commonly present in most agency procedures, as indicated in Table 10.8.

The correlations with these particular items were not, however, strong. This tends to reinforce that in addition to being weakly represented across the board—at least in so far as they are described in written procedures—systems for actively protecting and managing internal witnesses do not currently seem to explain why some agencies achieve better outcomes. There is a correlation with comprehensive procedures, but the better outcomes experienced by whistleblowers in these agencies could have more to do with other factors also consistent with the attempt to be more comprehensive, such as overall management commitment to fairness and equity, than to specific systems and policies for managing whistleblowers. Agencies that manage to protect more whistleblowers could even be doing so despite a lack of effective systems, rather than because of them.

**Table 10.14 Relationship between content of procedures and key outcomes (correlations)**

| Procedure assessment item/topic (numbers indicate rank order in Table 10.8) | Treatment by management | Treatment by co-workers | Attitude to reporting |
|---|---|---|---|
| 4. Types of concerns for which it is appropriate to use the whistleblowing mechanism | −0.48** | −0.30* | 0.08 |
| 11. Commitment to principle of whistleblowing | −0.40** | −0.33* | 0.22 |
| 5. Information about legislation | −0.37* | −0.42** | 0.02 |
| 10. Roles and responsibilities of the key players in the organisation's whistleblowing arrangements | −0.28 | −0.38* | 0.08 |
| 2. To whom and how whistleblowing concerns can be directed internally | −0.37* | −0.23 | 0.14 |
| 17. Active management and support of internal witnesses | −0.19 | −0.33* | 0.29** |
| 7. To whom and how whistleblowing concerns can be directed (externally) and in what circumstances | −0.30* | −0.29 | 0.00 |
| 22. Rights of the internal witness to request positive action by the entity to protect them | −0.01 | 0.01 | 0.31** |
| 24. Procedures for the assessment of risk of reprisal against individual whistleblowers | −0.11 | −0.11 | 0.25* |

* correlation is significant at the 0.05 level
** correlation is significant at the 0.01 level
Notes: Correlations on the outcome analyses are negative because the outcome scales run from a good outcome scoring lowest to a poor outcome scoring highest. The procedural analysis ratings run from poor procedures scoring lowest to good procedures scoring highest.
Sources: Procedures assessment and employee survey.

## Discussion and conclusions

Public sector organisations almost universally react to difficult workplace issues by developing and implementing sets of procedures. Every public sector organisation has many volumes of these procedures. It is not surprising that these will usually include procedures for the sensitive and difficult area of the reporting of wrongdoing. It is also not surprising that the difficulty of the area will lead to widespread uncertainty regarding the appropriate content for procedures and doubts regarding their effectiveness.

This analysis has, however, demonstrated empirically that the effort put into developing and implementing more comprehensive whistleblowing procedures is worthwhile. There are strong indications that comprehensive procedures help raise confidence that the organisation will deal with reports effectively and sensitively and will encourage reporting. Comprehensive procedures are also associated with better outcomes for those staff who do report. In particular, comprehensive procedures for the reporting of wrongdoing and the protection of whistleblowers are associated with good outcomes, as indicated by the measures of how internal witnesses are treated by management and their co-workers. Besides engendering good outcomes, comprehensive procedures are strongly associated with the encouragement of staff to come forward. Legislation itself also appears to have clear positive effects, although these could also relate to elevated expectations of good treatment by management, which might or might not necessarily pan out in practice.

This chapter has nevertheless also shown some serious weaknesses in procedures and conflicting assessments of the adequacy of procedures at different levels in agencies. A surprising and troubling result was a negative relationship between the comprehensiveness of the procedures and the confidence of more senior staff in the likely response of management to whistleblowing. More-senior staff (such as managers) often appeared to have either overly optimistic or pessimistic views of their own procedures, depending on the case. In either case, their views appeared to be somewhat disconnected from the reality, particularly since the views of less-senior staff tended to correlate more directly with the real quality of the procedures.

The analysis of which procedural items were most commonly present when the outcomes were positive, and when the attitude to reporting wrongdoing was positive, enables a tentative conclusion about which elements of the procedures were most important to staff. Some of those elements relate to the way in which organisations handle reprisals. The analysis of procedures indicated that, overall, this was the weakest area in reporting procedures and one in which organisations could make significant improvements. While more comprehensive procedures correlated with better outcomes, these were not necessarily explained by the contents of the procedures themselves on the relevant issues.

This evaluation of the whistleblowing procedures of individual organisations has essentially been a measure of the completeness of written documents. While the evaluation in this chapter has attempted to include all relevant procedural elements relating to whistleblowing, there are many other issues involved in the effective handling of wrongdoing besides the completeness of written procedures. Clearly, procedures alone do not guarantee a good outcome; this is likely to hinge on management commitment, promulgation of the procedures and effective resources devoted to investigation and to supporting staff. Nevertheless, the evidence suggests that these factors are also more likely to be present in those organisations that take the trouble to develop more comprehensive whistleblowing procedures, which appear to reflect at least some aspects of organisational practices.

The second report from the present research will describe, in greater qualitative detail, the direct relationships between agencies' procedures, operational systems and outcomes from whistleblowing. Using the framework already developed and provided in Appendix 3, this further research will support a clearer picture of current and potential best practice in systems for managing the reporting of wrongdoing. As it stands, while most agencies in most jurisdictions are yet to move beyond a mere compliance approach to whistleblowing procedures, there is clear evidence that such movement is necessary and potentially rewarding.

As more senior managers move to recognise the utility of good whistleblowing systems, as well as their legal and ethical responsibilities to ensure the welfare of their own employees, the value of a more comprehensive approach to whistleblowing is likely to be immense.

## ENDNOTES

[1] The author thanks Jane Olsen for conducting some of the analyses in this chapter, and A. J. Brown for editorial guidance and direction. Particular thanks also to the other members of the research team who participated in the task of coding the procedures for assessment, as described in the third part of the chapter: Lindy Annakin, Marika Donkin, Dr Michael Carrel and Dr Yasmine Fauzee.

# 11. Best-practice whistleblowing legislation for the public sector: the key principles

## A. J. Brown, Paul Latimer, John McMillan and Chris Wheeler

## Introduction

In Australia, legislative frameworks have long been considered fundamental to encouraging and managing public interest disclosures. Since 1993, almost all Australian jurisdictions have put in place relevant legislation for the public sector, as shown in Table 11.1. In practice, the content of whistleblowing legislation has nevertheless been a vexed issue. Several jurisdictions, including New South Wales, Western Australia and Victoria, have conducted or are conducting major reviews of their legislation, at least partly in response to public doubts about its effectiveness. Bills for new or replacement legislation have been introduced in the Northern Territory and the Australian Capital Territory. At the Commonwealth level, where comprehensive legislation has long been recommended (Senate Select Committee on Public Interest Whistleblowing 1994; McMillan 1994), private member's bills were introduced, but lapsed, in 2001 and 2007. Most recently, the new Commonwealth Government has committed itself to 'provide best-practice legislation to encourage and protect public interest disclosure within government' (ALP 2007).

**Table 11.1 Australian public sector whistleblowing legislation, in date order**

| No. | Act/bill | Jurisdiction |
|---|---|---|
| 1 | *Whistleblowers Protection Act 1993* | South Australia |
| 2 | *Whistleblowers Protection Act 1994* | Queensland |
| 3 | *Protected Disclosures Act 1994* | New South Wales |
| 4 | *Public Interest Disclosure Act 1994* | Australian Capital Territory |
| 5 | *Public Service Act 1999*, section 16 | Commonwealth |
| 6 | *Whistleblowers Protection Act 2001* | Victoria |
| 7 | *Public Interest Disclosures Act 2002* | Tasmania |
| 8 | *Public Interest Disclosure Act 2003* | Western Australia |

This chapter distils the major lessons of the present research for current debate about best practice in legislative design. A core reason for the research described throughout this book was to help fill the substantial gap in knowledge as to what a best-practice legislative approach might really be.

In line with this objective, the extensive differences in approach in the existing Australian legislation have already been detailed and compared in an issues paper, *Public interest disclosure legislation in Australia: towards the next generation*

(Brown 2006). That analysis showed that while each existing legislative approach contained at least some elements of current best practice, none contained all such elements, and many approaches were clearly deficient by comparative standards. Since then, the pressure for legislative reform has only increased, while some lessons from international reforms have also become clearer. Endorsing the conclusions reached in that paper, an audit by Irene Moss (2007:57), commissioned by Australia's Right to Know Committee, also made a case for greater national uniformity. Positively, the feasibility of adopting a simplified, more targeted legislative approach in Australia has been demonstrated by the second of the above Commonwealth bills, the Public Interest Disclosures Bill 2007, introduced by the Australian Democrats, for which the present research and the 2006 issues paper from this project provided 'the prompt' (Murray 2007).

To assist the search for best practice, this chapter sets out a new basic guide for the minimum content of Australian public sector whistleblowing legislation, in the form of 13 key principles for best-practice legislation. Much of the logic of these principles is set out in the earlier issues paper and not all will be detailed here. Building on the research from the Whistling While They Work project, this chapter identifies three areas in which there is a need for a significant departure from, or extension of, the approaches contained in current legislation.

First, there is a need for legislation to require the implementation of more effective operational systems for the management of whistleblowing. Historically, the Australian legislative focus has been on legal protection of whistleblowers. Important though that is, the research in this book demonstrates that it is equally important to have effective operational systems for managing whistleblowing as and when it occurs. That requires legislative reform in three areas:

- defining the coverage of the act—that is, subject matter and jurisdiction—in a more comprehensive or 'inclusive' manner, to support an 'if in doubt, report' approach to managing disclosures within agencies
- establishing minimum standards for internal disclosure procedures in agencies, particularly for managing the welfare of employees who report
- introducing a new statutory framework for coordinating the management of public interest disclosures, through an external oversight agency and a new relationship between that agency and public sector organisations.

Second, there is a need for legislative reform to address the current lack of practical remedies for public officials whose lives and careers suffer as the result of having made a public interest disclosure. Inevitably, some whistleblowers experience adverse outcomes for which governments should accept responsibility—for reasons of individual and organisational justice and in recognition of the practical need to demonstrate that public interest reporting of wrongdoing is valued. The data indicate that current legislative settings are insufficiently focused on restitution (including financial compensation) as a response to adverse outcomes, as opposed to criminal remedies that are, in any event, inappropriate for the bulk of cases. There is also a need for legislation to better define the legal responsibilities of employers for the welfare of employees, including by providing incentives for public sector managers to be more diligent in exercising their duty of care to prevent and minimise adverse outcomes.

Third, legislative reform is needed to provide better protection for public officials who justifiably go public with their concerns. While the research has confirmed that public whistleblowing is statistically infrequent in comparison with internal whistleblowing, it nevertheless does arise and is widely recognised as healthy and sometimes necessary in a mature democracy. Only New South Wales currently has legislative provisions dealing with such circumstances, and then inadequately. The imperative for reopening this aspect of current legislation has been boosted by the Commonwealth Government's commitment to do so. This chapter sets out principles for how a workable formula might be achieved.

The final part of the chapter sets out the key principles for best-practice whistleblowing legislation as a whole, including those issues dealt with in greater detail in earlier parts. These principles reflect feedback on the most important issues identified in the issues paper, the lessons of the empirical research and previous reviews from the academic literature (for example, Latimer 2002a). As with the remainder of this research, these principles have been developed with the public sector in mind, also recognising that in Australia it is the public sector that has had greatest experience to date with statutory public interest disclosure regimes. It could be, however, that these principles can be readily adapted to the private and civil society sectors.

## Organisational systems for encouraging and managing whistleblowing

As outlined in Chapter 1, despite frequent controversy about policy and legislative responses to whistleblowing, the objectives of current public sector whistleblowing laws are relatively consistent and clear (NSW Ombudsman 2004a; Brown 2006:5). As set out in the key principles below, they are:

- to support public interest whistleblowing by facilitating disclosure of wrongdoing
- to ensure that public interest disclosures are properly assessed and, where necessary, investigated and actioned
- to ensure that a person making a public interest disclosure is protected against detriment and reprisal.

There is reason to doubt whether existing legislation is carrying these objectives into practice. Chapter 10 has indicated that the 'symbolic' or communicative purposes of the legislation are having their desired effect. Where awareness of the legislation is higher, attitudes to public interest whistleblowing are more positive within organisations and inaction rates in response to wrongdoing tend to be lower. There remains, however, a great deal of uncertainty as to whether legislative protection does or will flow through to measures for the management of whistleblowers. Chapters 4 to 6 reinforce the heavy responsibilities that lie on public sector managers to deliver the third of the above objectives; Chapters 9 and 10, however, show the weak state of current systems and procedures for fulfilling this obligation.

From these analyses, it is apparent that legislative regimes can and should be strengthened to provide more robust systems for managing whistleblowing. Three issues stand out as important, practical foci for reform.

## Comprehensive definitions and application

As set out in the issues paper and elsewhere (NSW Ombudsman 2004a; Brown 2006:8–13, 16–99; Latimer and Brown 2007), some of the most obvious differences between current legislative regimes relate to technical differences in the coverage and jurisdiction of the legislation. These differences affect which public officials—and others, such as family, friends or innocent bystanders—are eligible for protection, to whom they may make a disclosure, the types and seriousness of the wrongdoing that can give rise to protected disclosures and the people and bodies about which disclosures may be made.

While some diversity could be necessary or desirable, the current differences on these issues indicate uncertainty and confusion about the right approach, more than well-informed design. The impacts of these differences can be quite heavy. In general, the distinctions that define coverage and jurisdiction tend to dictate that an unnecessarily fine degree of technical knowledge is needed to calculate whether or not the legislation applies to a given case. At best, these difficulties work against the ability of managers to easily recognise that they have received or are dealing with a disclosure to which the legislation applies. This could explain why the protective measures intended to be triggered by disclosures are triggered only in a small minority of cases—as discussed in Chapter 9.

At worst, however, the technical nature of the coverage given by the legislation can also be helping defeat its purpose, in an operational sense, by causing the number of disclosures that are formally recognised to be minimised. Chapter 2 explained that a conservative estimate of the proportion of all respondents to the employee survey who fitted the definition of public interest whistleblowing was approximately 12 per cent. While this inevitably includes a proportion of less serious wrongdoing, Chapters 5 and 6 demonstrate that the type of wrongdoing involved is not in itself a factor that currently indicates whether there is a risk of mistreatment or conflict, while perceived seriousness is only one of a number of risk factors. If it is to help ensure that public interest whistleblowing is appropriately managed, the legislation should operate to maximise—not minimise—the number of whistleblowers whose disclosures trigger official attention.

The data nevertheless indicate that, in practice, the bulk of public interest whistleblowing is occurring without being recorded, monitored or reported under public interest disclosure legislation. The agency survey asked agencies how many internal reports of wrongdoing they had formally identified as public interest disclosures, protected disclosures or whistleblowing reports under the legislation relevant to their jurisdiction in the period 2002–04. Table 11.2 sets out the results, against the estimated incidence of public interest whistleblowing from the employee survey.

### Table 11.2 Numbers of formally recognised disclosures compared with estimated whistleblowing levels

| | Agency survey results | | | Employee survey (ES) results | | |
|---|---|---|---|---|---|---|
| | No. of agencies reporting no PIDs[a] | No. of agencies reporting PIDs | Total number of PIDs reported (2002–04) | Estimated total employees of these agencies | Proportion of ES respondents who were public interest whistleblowers (2004–06) | Estimated total public interest whistleblowers |
| Cth | 13 | 11 | 377 | 103 314 | 11.1% | 11 468 |
| NSW | 23 | 11 | 4 631 | 232 221 | 12.4% | 28 795 |
| Qld | 18 | 13 | 294 | 168 039 | 12.7% | 21 341 |
| WA | 22 | 3 | 6 | 55 402 | 11.0% | 6 094 |
| | 76 | 38 | 5 308 | 559 076 | 12.1% | 67 698 |

[a] PID = public interest disclosure
Sources: Agency survey: Q24; employee survey: Q26.

Given the similarity between jurisdictions in terms of the proportion of employees observing and reporting wrongdoing, there are few possible explanations for the low and very different rates of formally recognised disclosures. Some difference is explained by jurisdiction-specific factors. For example, only some Commonwealth agencies are covered by the limited whistleblower protection provided by Section 16 of the *Public Service Act 1999*; while the West Australian legislation began only halfway through the relevant period, in 2003–04. The Australian Public Service Commission (APSC 2004:112) has, however, previously recorded that a 'significant level of confusion' exists around the Commonwealth framework; and, in Western Australia, even in 2006–07, only 14 disclosures by 13 people were formally recognised as having been made under the legislation, for all state agencies (OPSSC 2007:18).

The likely explanation is that even in jurisdictions recording a higher number of disclosures, the majority are still being managed outside the legislation and hence are underreported. The reasons could be because technical definitions are excluding them; because restrictive procedures have been put in place (for example, dealing with disclosures only if they are lodged on a specific form, as occurs in Western Australia); or because there is a lack of understanding among agencies and managers, as indicated in Chapter 7, about how the legislation is intended to apply.

A paradox also exists in some jurisdictions where a low proportion of public interest whistleblowing is being formally recognised, but there are liberal definitions of who can be a whistleblower. In Western Australia, Victoria, the Australian Capital Territory and South Australia, literally 'anyone' may make a public interest disclosure, even if they are not a whistleblower in the sense used throughout this book—that is, even if they are not internal to the public sector organisation concerned. In other words, any member of the public may make a public interest disclosure and seek special protective measures, in addition to normal avenues of complaint under other legislation (such as ombudsman legislation).

In these jurisdictions, it appears that this 'open standing' approach has led to the insertion of other restrictions, either in the legislation or in its implementation, in order to limit the potentially huge number of cases that come within the legislation. This appears to explain why it was decided, in Section 3 of the *Whistleblowers Protection Act 2001* (Victoria), that the legislation should apply only to disclosures that would, if proved, constitute a criminal offence or reasonable grounds for dismissing a public officer—even though, in other jurisdictions, such high thresholds only apply to, at most, a limited category of disclosures (see Brown 2006:16–18, 65). It also provides the most logical explanation for why disclosures by Victorian public employees about maladministration are not covered by the Act—that is, to prevent the Act also being used by non-internal complainants, such as prisoners, ratepayers and consumers, as an alternative to existing complaint avenues. Nor does the act then provide coverage for public officials who disclose information about defective administration, no matter how serious.

In other jurisdictions, such as New South Wales, there is a related problem that to escape restrictive eligibility criteria, public officials may make disclosures in the form of complaints under other legislation, directly to external integrity agencies such as the Ombudsman or the Independent Commission Against Corruption. These complaints may qualify more easily for similar legal protections. In these contexts, the overly technical approach has again failed, for two reasons: it has encouraged officials to make their disclosures externally even in circumstances in which the agency could be equipped and best placed to act on the disclosure; and, while the alternative legislation could provide legal protection, it is not geared to trigger the vital, internal management protections on which the welfare of most whistleblowers depends.

All these issues combine to suggest that the jurisdiction and coverage of the legislation need to be stripped back to first principles. The principles set out in the conclusion take it as a given that the focus of whistleblowing legislation is to detail the special measures required for protecting and managing people internal to an organisation who possess crucial information about internal wrongdoing, but who face great disincentives against revealing it. The criteria for determining when those protective measures are triggered should be no more onerous than the threshold for a person to make a complaint under other legislation. There should be consistency in the basic principles that apply to protect external complainants, whistleblowers and staff involved simply in the handling or referral complaints, so as to minimise the potential for technical barriers to arise that frustrate agencies' ability to extend this protection. Different legislation may be needed, however, to put in place the different requirements for how this protection is to be achieved. In the case of whistleblowing, the legislative threshold should be calibrated to encourage a philosophy of 'if in doubt, report'. This will occur only if those making a disclosure receive appropriate official encouragement.

## Minimum standards for agency obligations and procedures

Further reasons for the underreporting of the bulk of disclosures covered by existing legislation relate to the weak state of procedures and systems within most agencies, in all jurisdictions, for how disclosures should be managed. Even where the legislative approach is comprehensive, it is unlikely to be implemented in a reliable and consistent manner in the absence of clear procedures. Moreover, where procedures are weak, uncertainties prevail as to the implications of recognising an employee's disclosure as being one to which the legislation applies—for example, there can be an erroneous belief that the administrative burden of managing an employee will increase when, in fact, the medium to long-term effects should be that the burden is simplified.

The evidence reviewed in Chapter 10 suggests that when agency procedures are more comprehensive, the response to whistleblowing is likely to be more effective and achieve better overall results. The present standard of procedures, however, remains generally low. This is especially the case in Queensland and Western Australia, notwithstanding that these jurisdictions have the most comprehensive legislation. Across all the agencies studied, only relatively few internal disclosure procedures satisfy the relevant Australian Standard for whistleblower protection (AS 8004-2003) (Standards Australia 2003).

What can be done to lift the standard of agency procedures and systems? Many of the practical lessons emerging from existing experience will be set out in the second report from this project. It is, however, already clear that legislative action is necessary. Table 11.3 provides an outline of the current legislative requirements with respect to agency procedures. Consistent with the analyses in Chapters 9 and 10, even when there are legislative requirements for procedures, these currently often do not extend to procedures for discharging all the basic objectives of the legislation, including protection and management of whistleblowers. Of the four instruments that explicitly require agencies to develop procedures for how whistleblowers are to be protected, none specifies any particular guidance or minimum content for these procedures.

**Table 11.3 Legislative requirements for internal disclosure procedures**

| Legislation | Agency procedures for | | | Agency procedures must follow model code/guidelines |
|---|---|---|---|---|
| | How disclosures can and should be made | Investigation of and action on disclosures | Protection of people as a result of disclosures | |
| 1. SA 1993 | Nil | | | |
| 2. Qld 1994 | Contemplated, but not required | Nil | Required | Nil |
| 3. NSW 1994 | Contemplated, but not required | Nil | Nil | Nil |
| 4. ACT 1994 | Required | Required | Required | Nil |
| 5. Cth 1999 | Required | Required | Nil | Nil |
| 6. Vic 2001 | Required | Required | Required | Ombudsman guidelines |
| 7. Tas 2002 | Contemplated | Nil | Nil | Nil |
| 8. WA 2003 | Required | | Required | Commissioner guidelines |

Source: Brown, A. J. 2006, *Public interest disclosure legislation in Australia: towards the next generation*, Issues paper, Commonwealth Ombudsman, NSW Ombudsman and Queensland Ombudsman, p. 46.

While Western Australia's approach remains operationally problematic, its legislation does provide the benchmark for making clear that the protection of public interest whistleblowers represents a basic test of management. Section 23(1)(b) of the *Public Interest Disclosure Act 2003* (WA) places a positive obligation on the principal executive officer of all public authorities to 'provide protection from detrimental action or the threat of detrimental action for any employee…who makes an appropriate disclosure of public interest information'.

In other jurisdictions, positive obligations regarding implementation of the legislation are inserted into other parts of the public sector management framework. In New South Wales, for example, the Model Contracts for Chief Executives and Senior Executives stipulate that their responsibilities include to 'ensure employees are aware of the procedures for making protected disclosures and of the protection provided by the *Protected Disclosures Act 1994*' (in respect of chief and senior executives) and to 'ensure satisfactory introduction and operation of…reporting systems (including protected disclosures)' (in respect of chief executives). In line with the evidence in Chapter 7, however, it is unclear whether senior executives are presently sufficiently aware of how to fulfil these obligations.

Several of the principles below—especially Principles 5, 6, 11 and 12—spell out the ways in which best-practice legislation can more clearly identify the key responsibilities of all public sector agencies, which can be implemented through agency systems and procedures. These include systems for ensuring that employee reports of wrongdoing, including all possible public interest disclosures, are comprehensively recorded, tracked and reported, so that accurate management information is available to support an early intervention approach to problems. For the reasons set out in Chapters 6 and 9, there is also a need for more comprehensive agency procedures for assessment of reprisal risk, at the outset of matters, as well as closer coordination between line managers and internal specialist integrity units in how risks are to be managed.

Much of the current legislation was drafted at a time when it was assumed that the welfare of public employees was best left to the chief executives of individual agencies to manage, unassisted by statutory guidance or external oversight. The findings from this research demonstrate that while that is generally desirable, the risks of conflict and reprisal inherent in whistleblowing require a more structured understanding of the responsibilities of all managers, even if there still can and should be flexibility in how these responsibilities are discharged in practice.

## Central clearing house, monitoring and oversight role

The third operational development needed is improved coordination and monitoring of the management of whistleblowing on a sector-wide basis. Chapters 4 to 6 demonstrate the heavy responsibility that lies on agencies to deal productively with the bulk of current public interest disclosures. While this responsibility is often being met, this is typically in simpler cases, and often due to informal systems and procedures rather than through the planned programs of agencies. The variability in outcomes and in the quality of agency procedures further mitigate in favour of a more consistent and coordinated approach, in which public employees and the general public can have greater confidence that disclosures are being managed in a fair and professional manner.

In general, it might be expected that these quality-assurance roles will be naturally fulfilled as a result of the fact that employees may have recourse to external integrity agencies if dissatisfied with their agency's handling of the matter. The data in Chapters 4, 5, 6, 8 and 9 indicate, however, the need to revisit this assumption. In particular, it appears clear that the majority of employees have a natural tendency to blow the whistle internally, to their line managers, rather than using other avenues—even when, in hindsight, they might recognise this to have been unwise. It is also clear that many employees will let a disclosure drop rather than pursue it outside and that, when reprisals or other mistreatment do cause them to pursue it with an external integrity agency, the level of conflict has often already become such that any opportunity for the external agency to usefully intervene has passed.

These indications were supported by other results from the integrity case-handlers survey. While 53 per cent of case study agency case-handlers and managers indicated that it was 'often' or 'always' the case that employees who reported wrongdoing experienced 'emotional, social, physical or financial' problems, this figure rose to 72 per cent among the integrity agency case-handlers. While it could be that case-handlers in integrity agencies have a greater awareness of the problems experienced by whistleblowers, an alternative explanation is that by the time cases reach the integrity agencies, they have indeed become more problematic. A majority of integrity case-handlers also estimated that at least half of all reporters were treated badly by their management (20 per cent estimated 'about half', 23 per cent estimated 'about three-quarters' and 17 per cent estimated 'all or almost all'). While Chapter 5 shows this to be a pessimistic assessment of average outcomes at an agency level, it could be an accurate indicator of the state of cases by the time they reach integrity agencies.

The issues paper canvassed some of the basic areas in which greater coordination might be fruitful (Brown 2006:51–4). At present, legislation supports a coordinated approach in only two of the jurisdictions participating in the project. In Western Australia, as seen earlier, the Public Sector Standards Commissioner is responsible for setting the standards for agency procedures and also monitors but does not intervene in individual cases. In Victoria, the ombudsman sets the standard for agency procedures and acts as a clearing house for individual cases, while also having the power to take over or advise on investigations or the management of the individuals involved.

While there are a number of ways in which the Victorian arrangement can be improved (Brown 2006:28–30), it provides the logical departure point for a more systematic approach. Under such an approach, an efficient regime of 'mandatory reporting' would be adopted—akin to the regimes operating successfully in respect of much of the other business of key integrity agencies—in which agencies bring the details of their internal case load to the attention of an external oversight agency on a routine basis, before problems emerge, rather than waiting for problems to emerge *ex post facto*.

In the most recent review of the NSW legislation, the relevant NSW Legislative Assembly Committee (NSW Legislative Assembly 2006:10–11, 36–7) similarly recommended the creation of a Public Interest Disclosures Unit within the Office of the Ombudsman, 'funded by an appropriate additional budgetary allocation', to:

a.   provide advice to people who intend to make, or have made, a disclosure
b.   provide advice to public authorities on matters such as the conduct of investigations, protection for staff and general advice
c.   provide advice and assistance to public authorities on the development or improvement of internal reporting systems
d.   audit the internal reporting policies and procedures of public authorities
e.   monitor the operational response of public authorities, including a requirement for all public authorities including other integrity agencies to notify the unit of all disclosures received that appear to be protected under the act
f.   act as a central coordinator for the collection and collation of statistics on disclosures
g.   publish an annual report containing statistics on disclosures and identifying any systemic issues or other problems with the operation of the act
h.   coordinate education and training programs and provide advice to public authorities seeking assistance in developing internal education programs
i.   publish guidelines on the act
j.   develop proposals for reform.

It is important that an independent agency with existing expertise in investigations and case-handling takes on these coordination roles. It is clear that, in addition to compliance, reporting and advisory roles, this oversight agency must be empowered to act in the shoes of line agencies in circumstances in which action is needed—for example, to ensure effective investigations or effective responses in cases of reprisal or breakdown in the ability of agencies to support and protect their employees.

The importance of building a more effective, operational relationship between public agencies and the relevant integrity agencies is reflected below in Principles 7, 12 and 13. The development of such arrangements is not necessarily a simple process. As recognised by the NSW review, it requires resources and the building of capacity within the oversight agency on many of the practical and human resource management issues relevant to the prevention and minimisation of reprisals and other internal conflicts. It also requires the support and participation of all integrity agencies through a coordination steering committee. Despite these challenges, the development of such a role and its entrenchment in legislation provides a further important key to achieving more effective operational systems for the management of whistleblowing.

## Realistic compensation mechanisms

A primary objective of whistleblowing legislation is to provide legal protection to officials who make public interest disclosures. In Australia, legal protection frequently takes four forms:

- relief from criminal liability for breach of statutory secrecy provisions, as just discussed
- relief from civil liability for, for example, defamation or breach of confidence
- protection from disciplinary or other workplace sanctions, such as reduction in salary or position or termination of employment, resulting from the disclosure
- legal redress for any detriment suffered as a result of making the disclosure.

This last form of protection, legal redress, itself takes two forms. In every jurisdiction other than the Commonwealth and South Australia, it is a criminal offence for any person (in Queensland, any public officer) to undertake a reprisal as a result of the making of a public interest disclosure (Brown 2006:37). In all jurisdictions other than the Commonwealth and New South Wales, a person who suffers detriment is also entitled to sue a person or body responsible for detriment in the Supreme or District Court. This can be by way of a tort action under personal injuries law or (in South Australia and Western Australia) as an action for victimisation under equal opportunity legislation (Brown 2006:40). Table 11.4 sets out the availability of these different civil remedies.

## Table 11.4 Current civil, industrial and equitable remedies

| Legislation | Civil action (tort) | Equal opportunity/ anti-discrimination | Workplace relations law | Injunctive relief |
|---|---|---|---|---|
| 1. SA 1993 | Yes | *Equal Opportunity Act 1984* | No | No |
| 2. Qld 1994 | Yes | *Unfair treatment of office* | *Industrial Relations Act 1998*, unfair dismissal | Yes |
| 3. NSW 1994 | No (common law only) | | | |
| 4. ACT 1994 | Yes | No | No | Yes |
| 5. Cth 1999 | No | Victimisation or discrimination | No | No |
| 6. Vic 2001 | Yes | No | No | Yes |
| 7. Tas 2002 | Yes | No | No | Yes |
| 8. WA 2003 | Yes | *Equal Opportunity Act 1984* | No | No |

Source:Brown, A. J. 2006, *Public interest disclosure legislation in Australia: towards the next generation*, Issues paper, Commonwealth Ombudsman, NSW Ombudsman and Queensland Ombudsman, p. 40.

A second major issue for legislative action, arising from this research, is the need to develop a more effective mechanism for providing such remedies—including ensuring that appropriate compensation flows to those public employees whose lives and careers do suffer as a result of disclosures. Chapter 5 demonstrated that adverse career and life outcomes from whistleblowing were a significant issue, even for purely internal whistleblowers. Chapter 3 demonstrated the powerful effect that anticipated reprisals had in dissuading officials from speaking up about wrongdoing. Chapters 6, 9 and 10 also showed that currently, many agencies are doing little—in any organised way—to ensure that employees who report wrongdoing are supported and protected. The data from the case study agencies confirm that many case-handlers and managers believe their agencies are not currently achieving a great deal of success in their handling of the problems experienced by whistleblowers.

The data from the case study agencies also point to some clear explanations for this relative lack of success. In Chapter 5, it was seen that the bulk of mistreatment experienced by public interest whistleblowers resulted from the acts and omissions of management, rather than individual co-workers and colleagues, as once widely believed. The most frequent types of detriment or harm are also not discrete acts to which criminal liability is readily attached, even if the responsible people can be identified. Rather, the most frequent and problematic forms of detriment involve adverse outcomes related to deteriorations in the workplace environment and in employment conditions and prospects. These are likely compounded by subjective factors such as unmanaged stress, especially when there is failure in active support. Wherever there is a history of dysfunction in the immediate workplace, or a whistleblower's work performance suffers as a result of their involvement in the process, it can be difficult to distinguish between management actions against a whistleblower that would (in other circumstances) be reasonable and management responses that are not acceptable. The unacceptable response can take the form of a deliberate reprisal, an attempt to dispose of a troublesome case or a de facto cover-up of the manager's own failure to deal with matters effectively in the first instance.

In many circumstances, a compensatory approach to the problems experienced by a whistleblower will provide the only effective remedy. In contrast, the attempt to investigate and prosecute an individual manager for having undertaken a deliberate reprisal—especially to a criminal standard of proof—is only occasionally likely to be a feasible or fruitful exercise. Criminal prosecutions for reprisal are known to have been attempted only against individual colleagues and, even so, have been few in number and are yet to lead to any convictions.

Given these realities, it is crucial that there be effective avenues for providing restitution to aggrieved employees, including financial compensation where necessary. It is clear that public sector agencies, as employers, do have a legally enforceable duty of care to support and protect those employees who fulfil obligations to report wrongdoing within the organisation. Damages might be payable for a failure to take reasonable steps to meet that duty. This duty exists in common law, irrespective of public interest disclosure legislation; this much is demonstrated in New South Wales, where, as seen in Table 11.4, there is no legislative avenue for compensation. Nevertheless, in 2001, the District Court of New South Wales found in *Wheadon v. State of New South Wales*[1] that the NSW Police Service was liable for damages of $664 270 for having breached its duty of care to one officer, who had reported suspected corrupt conduct. The officer experienced harassment and victimisation resulting in serious stress culminating in psychiatric illness. The breaches for which the agency was held liable included:

- failure to give support and guidance to the plaintiff
- failure to provide the plaintiff with a system of protection (including active steps to prevent or stop harassment and persecution)
- failure to properly investigate the plaintiff's allegation
- failure to properly investigate allegations against the plaintiff
- failure to assure the plaintiff that he had done the right thing by reporting corruption.

In contrast with this common-law duty, no whistleblower in a jurisdiction with a statutory compensation mechanism is known to have ever succeeded in gaining compensation. Comparative analysis and case law provide some indication of the reasons why. A general problem is that these statutory mechanisms do not locate the avenue for enforceable legal compensation within the employment relationship, where the duty of care is most obvious, as shown by *Wheadon v. State of New South Wales*. Rather, as seen in Table 11.4, the statutory mechanisms equate the damage suffered by a whistleblower to a personal injury suffered by the individual as the result of negligence by another individual (for example, as if in a car accident). The burden of establishing the nature of the duties involved, combined with the costs of taking legal action in an intermediate or superior court, combined with the risk of a costs order should the action fail, are all enough to explain why whistleblowers would seek to live with adverse outcomes rather than seek compensation.

As also seen in Table 11.4, when an alternative compensation mechanism is provided, such as under equal opportunity legislation, it is usually no more appropriate. While providing a lower cost and potentially more flexible forum, equal opportunity tribunals are geared to mediating and remedying discrimination against employees based on identified characteristics (gender, race, age, disability, sexual orientation). They are less well placed to find responsibility for failures in an employer's duty of care to protect an employee, who could be any employee depending on the circumstances.

It is conspicuous that only one jurisdiction, Queensland, provides a direct statutory link between whistleblower protection and workplace relations law, by providing that an employee may challenge their dismissal as unfair when that action has been taken as a result of their having made a public interest disclosure (*Industrial Relations Act 1998* (Qld), s. 73(2)(f)(i)). This remedy is, however, limited to dismissal and does not provide a mechanism for compensation in respect of any detriment short of dismissal, nor for any acts or omissions of agency management constituting a failure to support or protect the employee.

Also in Queensland, two cases demonstrate the inadequacy of the current personal injury-based compensation provisions, in their juxtaposition with the criminalisation of reprisals. In 2000, the Queensland Court of Appeal found in *Howard v. State of Queensland* that a whistleblower's entitlement to seek damages under section 43 of the *Whistleblower Protection Act 1994* did not extend to an entitlement to establish that their employer was vicariously liable for the detriment that they had suffered. The primary reason given by the court was that Section 42(2) of the act also made the detrimental action a criminal offence, triggering the problem that '[i]llegal acts committed by an employee which are inimical to the purposes of the employment are regarded as falling outside the course of employment and no vicarious liability falls upon the employer for them'.[2] According to Thomas, J. A., the 'direct liability of a public sector entity for its own acts' marked the limits of the civil law liability that the act envisaged on the part of a public sector entity, meaning that the tort identified in section 43 could 'be committed only by the direct acts of a person or corporation', with 'vicarious liability for the acts of others…excluded'.

Ironically, the Court of Appeal also found this situation to have been reinforced, rather than ameliorated, by the fact that section 44 of the act cast a duty on a public sector entity to establish reasonable procedures to protect its officers from reprisals. The net effect of the decision was to limit the extent to which the compensation provisions of the act could extend to breaches of an employer's duty of care to prevent, minimise or remedy the detrimental actions of its employees and managers. Instead, the compensation provisions become little more than a 'victim compensation' mechanism in the so-far unlikely event that a criminal prosecution for reprisal ever succeeds.

A second Queensland case confirms the confused relationship that exists between the law of whistleblower compensation and general workplace relations law. In *Reeves-Board v. Queensland University of Technology*, the Supreme Court of Queensland found that since the tort of reprisal under the *Whistleblower Protection Act 1994* provided for 'damages for personal injury by an employee from an employer to which the employment was a significant contributing factor', any action for compensation must also comply with the requirements of the subsequent *WorkCover Queensland Act 1996*—leading the court to strike out those parts of the whistleblower's claim seeking damages for personal injury.[3] The decision confirms that the correct basis for whistleblowing compensation claims lies in the employment relationship, but reduces this to a subset of existing, traditional compensation mechanisms for injury.

Significantly, the opposite result was recently obtained in Victoria, where, in *Owens v. University of Melbourne and Anor* (2008), the Supreme Court found that nothing in the *Accident Compensation Act 1985* (Vic.) limited the right of a whistleblower to seek damages from her employer under section 19 of the

*Whistleblowers Protection Act 2001* (Vic.).[4] This was partly because, unlike in Queensland, in Victoria, the whistleblowing legislation had come after the relevant workers' compensation legislation. More importantly, the court also recognised the different purposes and nature of the legislation, with the existing workers' compensation legislation addressed to 'serious injury' meaning 'any physical or mental injury', including such things as industrial deafness and workplace-triggered diseases—while the whistleblowing legislation was aimed at a broader conception of employers' responsibilities:

> Detrimental action [under the *Whistleblowers Protection Act 2001*] includes injury but importantly, extends to what may be described as collateral damage to a person's career, profession or trade, all of which may be apt to describe aspects of loss and damage suffered by employees as well as other classes of person. The breadth of the compensable loss and damage under the Act defines the cause of action within an entirely different category to claims under the *Accident Compensation Act*, notwithstanding an overlap that might occur in the case of injury...In my opinion s 19 creates a new, novel and additional class of rights and remedies to those which already existed...for work related injury...
>
> The purpose of the Act would be frustrated if those who suffered detrimental action in the workplace were denied the full range of remedies available under the Act merely because any injury they suffer arose out of or in the course of their employment.[5]

While the Victorian case reached a more beneficial result, the fact that this last statement was needed further underscores the extent to which the right to compensation under public interest disclosure legislation has been dislocated, in general in Australia, from the basic responsibilities of public agencies as employers.

The Australian confusion suggests a need to strip back current legislative provision to first principles—or create them, in the case of the Commonwealth—in two ways. First, it should be made express in the legislation that the criminal offence of reprisal, provable beyond reasonable doubt, does not limit the entitlement of a whistleblower to seek compensation for detriment suffered, whether criminal or non-criminal. In other words, to escape the consequence experienced in Queensland in *Howard*, but consistent with *Wheadon*, it should be clear that employers can indeed by held vicariously liable for the acts and omissions of individual staff, direct or indirect, whenever detriment follows and there has been a breach of an individual or organisational duty of care. It should also be made clear that normal evidentiary principles apply—that is, that a claim for compensation may be satisfied based on a balance of probabilities, irrespective of the criminal standard. Consequently, it should be made possible to conclude, on a balance of probabilities, that detriment occurred and that the organisation may therefore owe remedial action, even if individuals cannot be identified as criminally liable.

Second, a more appropriate compensation avenue should be found than those presently existing under Australian legislation. In particular, as set out in Principle 12 below, the assumption should be revisited that the appropriate compensation mechanism is by way of application to a superior court, in a manner analogous with personal injuries. The guiding principle should be that an employer's workplace responsibilities include a duty to ensure that detrimental acts and omissions do not occur and to protect and support employees in the face of risks of detrimental action.

This alternative approach is taken in the United Kingdom; other jurisdictions such as South Africa and Japan follow a similar model. The *Public Interest Disclosure Act 1998* (United Kingdom) created neither criminal offences of reprisal nor compensation mechanisms based on tort law. Instead, it simply amended the *Employment Rights Act 1996* (United Kingdom) so as to entitle employees to compensation from their employers for detriment suffered as a result of the making of a disclosure (see Gobert and Punch 2000; Calland and Dehn 2004; generally, <www.pcaw.co.uk>). The location of the mechanism within workplace relations law makes clear that this entitlement exists alongside, rather than as a subset of, existing workers' compensation schemes. The forum for determination of compensation applications is the British system of Employment Appeals Tribunals, akin to Australian industrial relations commissions, rather than courts of law. Damages may be pursued for actions short of dismissal, they are uncapped and are assessed according to what is 'just and equitable in all the circumstances', having regard to the infringement complained of and any loss suffered by the worker (*Employment Rights Act 1996* (United Kingdom), s. 49(2)).

The British scheme applies to most public sector and all private sector employers—as is possible under a unitary workplace relations system. Nevertheless, irrespective of how Australia's workplace relations might evolve (see Brown and Latimer forthcoming), the principles of this approach have clear application to all Australian jurisdictions in respect of protection of government employees. It is meaningless to offer a legislative avenue for compensation if the avenue offered is unnecessarily difficult and carries undue risks of further stress and detriment in the form of exposure to costs. An efficient compensation mechanism, on the other hand, will not only deliver justice more easily in deserving cases, it will provide a powerful incentive for agencies to limit their potential exposure by taking more effective action to prevent employees from suffering detrimental responses in the first place. The research has shown not only that the original intent of Australian legislatures in respect of compensation has not been achieved, but that such incentives for prevention of reprisals and other conflict are badly needed.

# Recognising public whistleblowing

## The case for reform

In statistical terms, as shown by Chapter 4, the bulk of whistleblowing in relation to Australian public sector agencies occurs internally. Very little involves disclosure to the media or other third parties, other than in circumstances in which agencies and external integrity agencies have failed to act—at least in the view of the public employee blowing the whistle.

For a range of reasons, it is appropriate that public interest disclosure legislation should continue to be framed around the principle that public officials should first disclose suspected wrongdoing to internal authorities, or to relevant integrity agencies. In many cases, the managers in public sector agencies are the best placed to act on a problem in a timely manner. The results in Chapter 5 indicate that this often occurs. The prevalence of internal whistleblowing also suggests that most employees who make a disclosure do not wish to pit themselves against the organisation, embarrass their agency or colleagues unnecessarily or seek celebrity.

Nevertheless, the focus on encouraging disclosures to management and to integrity agencies should not be limited, as it presently usually is, to the exclusion of public whistleblowing. Internal, regulatory and public whistleblowing should not be mutually exclusive options. Rather, the last avenue needs to be recognised as available should either of the first two avenues fail. It is clear that the successful management of whistleblowing as a process hinges in part on the confidence of employees and the understanding of agencies that if authorities fail to act, a further disclosure could be justified and, if so, will still attract legal protection. It is well documented that when agency systems break down and wrongdoing cannot be reported internally with safety, or authorities do not act in a timely manner, public whistleblowing may be the only way in which effective action is triggered (for example, Gibbs 1991; Senate Select Committee on Public Interest Whistleblowing 1994; Davies 2005).

At present, in Australia, only the NSW legislation reflects this reality (s 19). While the NSW provisions are far from best practice (Brown 2006:43–4; Brown 2007), it is noteworthy from Chapter 10 that NSW government agencies currently have, on average, the most comprehensive procedures for managing whistleblowing and, on average, a range of outcomes that is at least as good as any other jurisdiction. These results come notwithstanding that the remainder of the NSW legislation is weak in many areas, including no statutory framework for agency procedures and no mechanisms for compensation. While there could be several explanations for the relative quality of NSW agency procedures, the presence of the risk that a public disclosure will be recognised is, on anecdotal evidence, a significant part of the explanation. Even the mere risk that a whistleblower will legitimately repeat their disclosure to the media is a motivating factor in convincing agencies to deal with internal disclosures seriously.

Since the present research began, public and official opinion has fortunately moved significantly towards recognition of the importance of extending legal recognition to justified public whistleblowing. In part, this has been prompted by a number of prosecutions of Commonwealth officials for breaching criminal prohibitions on the release of official information to third parties, including at least one instance in which the prosecution was widely seen as contrary to the public interest (the case of Australian Customs official Alan Kessing; see Brown 2007). Such cases have made clear that without legislative reform through public interest disclosure legislation, it is questionable whether an official will ever claim any kind of public interest immunity from criminal prosecution, no matter what the circumstances. In October 2007, an audit of government secrecy laws by Irene Moss, conducted for Australia's Right to Know Committee, concluded that public interest disclosure legislation 'should at least protect whistleblowers who disclose to the media after a reasonable attempt to have the matter dealt with internally or where such a course was impractical' (Moss 2007:73). At the same time, recognising that much of the media operates across more than one jurisdiction, the Moss audit concluded in favour of a uniform national legislative approach, led by a 'new model Commonwealth law'.

While these recommendations are welcome, it is important to note that different philosophical approaches can inform these desired outcomes. From a news media perspective, restrictions on officials' ability to disclose official information are often seen as restrictions on free speech, given that in practical terms they operate as a restriction on the ability of the media to receive and report on matters of potential public interest. In Canada, the legal principles have also been traditionally seen as involving a balance between a public servant's freedom of expression and their duty of loyalty.[6] In Australia, the notion that public officials possess a 'right' to blow the whistle on matters they consider important has also gained encouragement from the *Bennett* case, in which the Federal Court ruled that APS regulations prohibiting disclosure of information by a union official transgressed the implied constitutional freedom of political communication.[7] At the Prime Minister's Australia 2020 Summit, held in April 2008, the imperative for 'whistleblower protection to be respected and strengthened' was also bracketed as one item for a new 'Charter of Free Speech' (Commonwealth of Australia 2008:310).

Protection of public whistleblowing should be understood as something more than the protection of freedom of speech. Its underpinnings lie as much in the duty of loyalty that is owed by public officials to their employing organisation, and ultimately to the community. All employees, and especially public officials, have a duty to report perceived wrongdoing of which they are aware. As seen in Chapters 3 and 4, a willingness to report wrongdoing is consistent with high standards of organisational citizenship, including loyalty, for most employees in most organisations. An official who blows the whistle to an integrity agency is also seen as upholding the public interest, even if this act places them in tension with their own management. Protection should be given to employees who engage in public whistleblowing arising from their sense of duty to report wrongdoing, when the public disclosure is the only avenue reasonably available for ensuring that the matter is addressed.

An incidental benefit of recognising public whistleblowing is that it could relieve public confusion about the differences between whistleblowing and 'leaking' or other forms of unauthorised disclosure (such as selling state secrets). The media often treats these different forms of disclosure as essentially similar. There can be a fine line between anonymous public whistleblowing and mere 'leaking', but there is a difference that should be reflected in workable legal formulae. There is a need for rules that can be applied in individual cases by public employees, governments, prosecuting authorities, courts and tribunals to determine whether a disclosure is a reasonable attempt by an official to discharge their duty of loyalty to the public interest, to have perceived wrongdoing rectified or is an act driven purely by other motives, whether personal, political or financial.

When governments prosecute or discipline their own employees for disclosing official information, this inevitably has a major dampening effect on the willingness of employees to speak up about wrongdoing, via any channel. Workable rules for recognising public whistleblowing will help encourage disclosures via appropriate channels and will make it easier for authorities to establish when action against an official who discloses information is justified.

## The nature of reform

Principle 10, below, includes the recognition of public whistleblowing as a key and necessary element of best-practice legislation. How this principle is best implemented remains an issue for analysis and debate; this much is demonstrated by the new Commonwealth Government's important commitment in this area, modelled on the existing NSW precedent. The Commonwealth commitment foreshadows two tests:

> In situations where there may be compelling reason requiring disclosure [to third parties such as journalists], a court will be able to weigh up all the relevant factors and balance the public interest in disclosure against any breach of confidentiality which may have occurred.

> In these cases, there will be two key tests to determine when public interest disclosure will attract legal protection. Firstly, where the whistleblower has gone through the available official channels, but has

not had success within a reasonable timeframe and, secondly, where the whistleblower is clearly vindicated by their disclosure. (ALP 2007)

It is not clear from that summary whether a person must satisfy either or both tests in order to gain legal protection. If both tests must be satisfied, and particularly the second test, the scope of protection could be very narrow. The first test reflects the principles embodied in sub-section 19(3) of the *Protected Disclosures Act 1994* (NSW), which provides that before a disclosure to a parliamentarian or journalist can attract protection, it must first have been made to an official person who either did not investigate, did not tell the person within six months whether or not it was to be investigated, did not complete the investigation within six months or did not recommend any action. This first test is broadly reasonable, although a question arises about the time limits, discussed further below.

The second test is more difficult to satisfy. It reflects the principles in sub-sections 19(4) and (5) of the NSW legislation that a whistleblower must also have reasonable grounds for believing the disclosure is 'substantially true' and that the disclosure must indeed be substantially true. This 'substantially true' requirement is a blunt and difficult method for gauging whether public disclosure is justified. A disclosure may be reasonable even if authorities still refuse to act after public pressure. Proving that an allegation of wrongdoing was 'substantially true' may also be a difficult challenge, particularly if the whistleblower has to satisfy a court or tribunal of this matter when seeking compensation or resisting criminal prosecution or civil action. The court or tribunal may also be placed in the position of having to determine the truth of the whistleblower's public allegation, possibly on the basis of evidence led primarily by the whistleblower. In the worst of all worlds, the court or tribunal could rule that the whistleblower acted reasonably, based on a reasonably held belief or suspicion regarding the wrongdoing, but that the truth of the allegation cannot be substantiated. In summary, it could be invidious and impractical to require both tests to be satisfied in order for a person to gain legal protection.

Consideration should also be given to using other criteria as a test for legal protection. Another circumstance in which public disclosure might be reasonable is when investigation is occurring, but too slowly, and there is a 'serious, specific and immediate danger' to public health or safety (Solomon 2006:157, 163). As that suggests, strict time limits should not apply in the test for legal protection: these can be incompatible with a genuine emergency. Recent Canadian legislation provides for public disclosure in such circumstances in section 14 of the *Public Interest Disclosure (Whistleblower Protection) Act 2007* (Manitoba), the *Public Interest Disclosure Act 2007* (New Brunswick) and section 16 of the Canadian *Public Servants Disclosure Protection Act 2005*.

The UK *Public Interest Disclosure Act 1998* provides for further disclosure beyond the whistleblower's employer or a regulatory agency, if the disclosure is reasonable in all the circumstances, is not made for personal gain and meets one of four preconditions, either that: 1) the whistleblower reasonably believed he or she would be victimised; 2) there was no prescribed regulator and he or she reasonably believed the evidence was likely to be concealed or destroyed; 3) the concern had already been raised with the employer or a prescribed regulator; or 4) the concern was of an exceptionally serious nature.[8] A refined formulation was suggested in Australia in Senator Andrew Murray's private member's bill of June 2007.

These alternative formulations show that there is a range of more flexible options for legal protection of public whistleblowing than currently applies in Australia. The key principle is not whether the whistleblower has been vindicated, but whether the public disclosure is reasonable in all the circumstances. It is well established that if authorities fail to act on an initial disclosure through proper channels, a further disclosure could be reasonable. Other circumstances, however, could also need to be allowed for, including those in which it is not reasonably open to the official to make a disclosure internally or to an integrity agency.

No existing law provides a best-practice model for managing the complex issues that confront public officials who possess information about official wrongdoing or incompetence, in circumstances in which action can reasonably depend on disclosures made outside official channels. This situation has been brought into sharp relief at a Commonwealth level, but, in fact, state whistleblower protection laws also currently provide no better solution. There is, however, real potential for a new legislative response that can deliver a workable balance on this inherently complex issue. How to best allow for such circumstances requires careful consideration.

## Best-practice legislation: the key principles

### Overview

These 13 principles outline the essential features of effective public interest disclosure legislation. The principles are framed to apply to public sector agencies because of the research focus of the Whistling While They Work project. The principles can nevertheless apply, with some modification, to the private sector and to non-government agencies. The unifying theme of the principles—that a person has a right to protection if they complain or disclose information about unacceptable activity occurring in an organisation—imposes like obligations on all organisations in society.

The principles are designed to apply to any employee, contractor or other person working in a public sector agency. The principles are not designed to apply to disclosures or complaints made by members of the public, such as clients and customers of an agency. Members of the public warrant comparable protection, but when it does not already exist, separate legislation may be required for that purpose. Equally, there are specific situations for which a tailored scheme may be required to protect people against reprisal or detriment by reason of making a complaint, such as patients or aged persons in a nursing home.

## Principles

### 1. Objectives and title

The stated objectives of public interest disclosure legislation should be:

- to support public interest whistleblowing by facilitating disclosure of wrongdoing
- to ensure that public interest disclosures are properly assessed and, where necessary, investigated and actioned
- to ensure that a person making a public interest disclosure is protected against detriment and reprisal.

These objectives should be captured in the short and long title of the legislation. The *Public Interest Disclosure Act* is a preferred title to 'Whistleblower Protection Act' or 'Protected Disclosures Act'.

### 2. Subject matter of disclosure

Legislation should specify the topics or types of proscribed wrongdoing about which a public interest disclosure may be made. The topics should cover all significant wrongdoing or inaction within government that is contrary to the public interest. The topics should include:

- an alleged crime or breach of the law
- official corruption, including abuse of power, breach of trust and conflict of interest
- official misconduct
- defective administration, including:
  - negligence or incompetence
  - improper financial management that constitutes a significant waste of public money or time
  - any failure to perform a duty that could result in injury to the public, such as an unacceptable risk to public health, public safety or the environment.

### 3. Person making disclosure

A disclosure should qualify as a 'public interest disclosure' if either of two tests is satisfied:

a. the person making the disclosure holds an honest and reasonable belief that the disclosure shows proscribed wrongdoing (the subjective test)

b. the disclosure does show, or tends to show, proscribed wrongdoing, irrespective of the person's belief (the objective test).

The motivation or intention of the person making the disclosure should not be relevant. Nor should a person be required to use a special form or declare that it is a public interest disclosure.

## 4. Receipt of disclosure

Legislation should allow a public interest disclosure to be made to a variety of different people or agencies, including:

- the immediate or any higher supervisor of the person making the disclosure
- the CEO of the agency
- any designated unit or person in an agency
- any dedicated hotline, including external hotlines contracted by an agency
- any external agency with jurisdiction over the matter (for example, ombudsman, corruption commission, auditor-general or public sector standards commissioner).

## 5. Recording and reporting

All public interest disclosures to an organisation should be formally recorded, noting the time of receipt, general subject matter and how the disclosure was handled. Recording systems, including required levels of detail, will vary according to agencies' circumstances, but should be consistent with minimum standards across the public sector (see Principle 7).

## 6. Acting on a disclosure

An agency receiving a disclosure should be obliged:

- to assess that disclosure and take prompt and appropriate action, which can include investigating the disclosure or referring it to an external agency
- to the extent practicable and reasonable, to keep the person who made the disclosure informed of action proposed to be taken, the progress of any action and the outcomes of any action
- to include in its annual report a summary of the numbers of public interest disclosures received and the action taken.

## 7. Oversight agency

One of the external agencies with responsibility for public interest disclosures should be designated as the oversight agency for the administration of the legislation. The responsibilities of the oversight agency should include:

- being notified by agencies of all disclosures and recording those disclosures and how they were dealt with and resolved
- having the option to decide, on being notified of a disclosure, to provide advice or direction to an agency on how the disclosure should be handled, to manage the investigation of the disclosure by the agency or to take over the investigation of the disclosure
- providing advice or direction to agencies on the steps that should be taken to protect people who have made disclosures, or to provide remedial action for a person who has suffered detriment as a result of making a disclosure
- promoting the objectives of the legislation, within government and publicly, and conducting training and public education
- publishing model procedures for the administration of the legislation, with which agencies' internal procedures must be consistent
- conducting a public review of the operation of the legislation at least once every five years.

## 8. Confidentiality

Disclosures should be received and investigated in private, so as to safeguard the identity of a person making a disclosure to the maximum extent possible within the agency's control. Avenues should be available for disclosures to be made confidentially and, where practical, individual disclosures should be dealt with in ways that do not disclose the identity of the person making the disclosure, and preferably even that a disclosure has in fact been made. This principle is subject to the need to disclose a person's identity to other parties—for example, when this is absolutely necessary to facilitate the effective investigation of a disclosure, provide procedural fairness, protect a person who has made a disclosure or make a public report on how a disclosure was dealt with.

## 9. Protection of person making a disclosure

A person who has made a disclosure to which the legislation applies should be protected against criminal or civil liability, or other detriment, for making the disclosure. For example, the person:

- should not be liable to prosecution for breach of a statutory secrecy provision
- should not incur civil liability, for example, for defamation or breach of confidence
- should not be subject to discipline or other workplace sanction, such as reduction in salary or position or termination of employment
- should be entitled to legal redress if they suffer detriment as a result of making the disclosure.

## 10. Disclosure outside an agency

A disclosure made to a person or body that is not designated by the legislation to receive disclosures (for example, the media) should be protected in exceptional circumstances as defined in the legislation. The protection should apply only if it is reasonable in all the circumstances for the disclosure to be made to some other person or body to ensure that it is effectively investigated. As a general guide, the protection should apply when a person has first made the disclosure to a designated person or body and there has been a failure by that person or body to take reasonable and timely action.

## 11. Agency responsibility to ensure protection

The responsibilities of an agency under the legislation should include:

- establishing proper internal procedures in the agency for receiving, recording and investigating disclosures, for protecting people who make disclosures and for safeguarding the privacy of those who make disclosures
- ensuring that staff of the agency are made aware of their responsibilities under the legislation, including the responsibility to support and protect any person making a disclosure
- on receipt of a disclosure, assessing whether the person who made the disclosure—or any other person—faces any risk of detriment or requires special protection as a result
- where necessary, taking all reasonable measures to protect a person who has made a disclosure against direct or indirect detriment, actual or foreseeable
- taking remedial action in the event that a person suffers detriment as a result of making a disclosure.

It should be the duty of the senior executives of an agency to ensure that these responsibilities are met by the agency.

## 12. Remedial action

When a person suffers detriment as a result of a disclosure having been made, remedial action of the following kind should be taken by the agency or, failing that, the oversight agency, to the extent necessary to prevent or remedy the detriment:

- stopping the detrimental action and preventing its recurrence, including by way of injunction
- placing the person in the situation they would have been in but for the detrimental action, including if necessary the transfer of the person (with their informed consent) to another equivalent position
- an apology

- compensation (pecuniary and/or non-pecuniary) for the detriment suffered, if the detriment could have been prevented, avoided or minimised
- disciplinary or criminal action against any person responsible for the detriment.

Jurisdiction to deal with compensation applications should be conferred on a low-cost tribunal with expertise in determining the rights and responsibilities of employers and employees. Consideration should also be given to reducing or reversing the onus of proof in cases of detrimental action, so that where a public interest disclosure has been made and detriment is suffered, it falls to those allegedly responsible to explain why the detriment did not result from the making of the disclosure.

## 13. Continuing assessment and protection

To the extent practicable, an assessment should be undertaken into the impact on a person of having made a disclosure under the legislation. This assessment should be undertaken at an appropriate time or times (for example, at intervals of two, five or 10 years). This assessment can be conducted by the agency to which the disclosure was made or by the oversight agency.

## Discussion and conclusions

This chapter has presented 13 key principles for the design or review of public interest disclosure legislation in the public sector. While there could be different options for implementing these principles, no legislation can be considered to be adequately comprehensive unless all these issues are addressed. Fortunately, the research in this book is already showing that if this occurs, the results are likely to be positive.

The reform of existing whistleblowing legislation is already an important issue for many Australian governments. In particular, the Commonwealth Government—for whom the existing legislative framework is weakest—has committed to substantial reform by introducing best-practice legislation. Previous analysis has shown that best practice does not lie in any existing law, but requires something of a 'second-generation' approach, including reconsideration of many of the fundamental principles rather than ad hoc tinkering with existing laws. The principles set out in this chapter are intended to provide a basic guide for this second-generation approach. In the interests of the increasing number of public officials who transfer between different governments within the Australian public sector, there are benefits to be gained from uniform public interest disclosure legislation if a new best-practice approach emerges.

The present research has also demonstrated that while current best practice can be found on different issues in different existing laws, there are major deficiencies that all legislative approaches to date tend to share. This chapter has focused on several of these issues—in particular, operational systems, compensation avenues and protection of public whistleblowing. The extent of the problems confirms there is presently a divide between the important intentions or 'symbolism' of these frameworks and their substantive effectiveness. The symbolism of whistleblower protection is a powerful force, frequently reaffirmed at the highest levels of government. Until legislative frameworks more effectively fulfil these practical needs, however, the full benefits will not be achieved. Fortunately, it is now increasingly clear that reform is not only needed, but possible.

## ENDNOTES

[1] *Wheadon v. State of New South Wales*, unreported, District Court of New South Wales, No. 7322 of 1998 (2 February 2001) per Cooper J.; see NSW Ombudsman (2004, 2005).

[2] *Howard v. State of Queensland*, [2000] QCA 223 (9 June 2000), per Thomas, JA (with whom the rest of the court agreed).

[3] *Reeves-Board v. Queensland University of Technology*, [2001] QSC 314 (28 August 2001), [2002] 2 Qd R 85, per Mullins J.

[4] *Owens v. University of Melbourne & Anor*, [2008] VSC 174 (27 May 2008), per Judd J.

[5] Ibid.

[6] *Fraser v. Public Service Staff Relations Board*, [1985] 2 SCR 455 at 470, per Dickson CJ (Supreme Court of Canada), cited in, for example, *Alberta Union of Provincial Employees v. Alberta*, 2000 ABQB 600; see Carson (2006); Brown and Latimer (forthcoming).

[7] *Bennett v. President, Human Rights and Equal Opportunity Commission*, (2003) 204 ALR 119, per Finn J. The case concerned the validity of Public Service Regulation 7(13), prohibiting an Australian Public Service employee from disclosing 'directly or indirectly, to any person any information about public business or anything of which the employee has official knowledge'.

[8] *Employment Rights Act 1996* (UK), s 43G and 43H, as inserted by *Public Interest Disclosure Act 1998* (UK); see explanatory guide by Public Concern at Work, <www.pcaw.co.uk>

# 12. Project findings: an agenda for action

## A. J. Brown and Chris Wheeler

## A new picture of whistleblowing

In this book, new research has revealed that far from being rare, whistleblowing is a relatively common and routine activity in a majority of public sector agencies. Part 1 of the book showed that in the four jurisdictions studied, on a conservative estimate, 12 per cent of employee survey respondents had acted as public interest whistleblowers in their organisation over two years. Even if often problematic, whistleblowing is a natural feature of public sector life.

The research also showed that, contrary to the bleak picture of whistleblowing as a crisis in which every whistleblower is destined to suffer for their experience, a majority of officials who reported public interest concerns—on average, at least 70 per cent—regarded management and colleagues as having treated them either the same or well as a result. There remains another side to both these stories. In some agencies and circumstances, the incidence and seriousness of reprisals are very much greater than this average and, even when direct reprisals are not involved, whistleblowing often involves stresses, tensions and problems for individuals and organisations alike. At least as many public officials who observe wrongdoing also continue to choose not to report, citing lack of confidence in the management response and in management support.

Nevertheless, the research shows that it is far from inevitable that whistleblowers need suffer for their experience or that, when employees make disclosures, nothing will be done. The organisational and social importance of whistleblowing is well recognised in many public agencies. This new picture of whistleblowing provides public sector managers with good reason to invest in strategies for encouraging staff to blow the whistle on perceived wrongdoing within their organisation, in ways that will enable them to be better managed and will help lead to more positive outcomes.

Part 2 of the book has shown the need for this greater institutional investment. In the jurisdictions studied, major challenges remain to be overcome before it can be said that all that can reasonably be done, is being done to manage whistleblowing productively. Many public agencies have actively grappled with the issue of how to encourage staff to disclose perceived wrongdoing and even the difficult issue of how to protect staff from reprisals should they do so. There remain, however, substantial differences in outcomes depending on the circumstances in which wrongdoing is seen and whistleblowing occurs. Some organisations are encouraging and managing whistleblowing more successfully than others. Agencies that make more credible efforts are achieving more positive results and are therefore showing the way for the development of best practice; but their relative success confirms that many more systems are patchy and are missing out on achieving more positive outcomes.

This chapter draws together the major lessons of the research, for what can and should be done to improve current approaches to whistleblowing in the Australian public sector—within individual agencies and at a whole-of-government level in the jurisdictions studied. As outlined in Chapter 1, these conclusions are drawn from the research to date as a whole—including the results of the empirical surveys conducted across the participating agencies, assessment of the comprehensiveness of agency procedures, comparative analysis of the different legislative regimes in place and the researchers' assessments of the relationships between these different elements of governments' overall responses to whistleblowing. While there are variations between jurisdictions and agencies in the extent of some challenges, there are also major challenges that exist right across the board. This chapter focuses on action to address these major challenges.

The first part of the chapter summarises some main lessons and challenges from the research to date, for those ultimately responsible for the management of whistleblowing. These include case-handlers and other managers responsible for the internal integrity systems of agencies, chief executives and senior management and governments as a whole. The discussion highlights the importance of the internal processes by which agencies respond to and encourage whistleblowing and the important role of individuals within these processes. It also highlights the evidence that many agencies are currently making insufficient institutional efforts to actively address the management of whistleblowing, even when subject to statutory requirements.

The second part of the chapter draws on these lessons to state 10 key findings from the research, identifying priority areas for action. In summary, the research shows a particular need for:

1.  more comprehensive agency systems for recording and tracking employee reports of wrongdoing
2.  agency procedures for assessing and monitoring the risk of reprisals or other conflict for those who report
3.  clearer and better advice for employees on the range of avenues available for reporting wrongdoing
4.  basic training for public sector managers in how to recognise and respond to possible public interest disclosures
5.  a program of training for internal investigators in basic techniques, with special attention given to issues of internal witness management

6.  adoption and expansion of structured support programs for employees who report wrongdoing
7.  improved mechanisms for monitoring the welfare of employees who report wrongdoing, from the point of first report
8.  more detailed and flexible agency procedures for the investigation and remediation of reprisals and breaches of duty of care
9.  a dedicated oversight agency or unit for the coordination of responses to employee-reported wrongdoing
10. legislative action to provide more effective organisational systems and realistic compensation mechanisms and to recognise public whistleblowing.

More detailed recommendations regarding current and prospective best practice in agencies are the subject of a further, second report from this project. The final part of this chapter briefly outlines some of this continuing analysis, along with areas for future research.

## Lessons and challenges

The purpose of recognising and facilitating public interest whistleblowing—and the research in this book—is to help create environments in which individual public officials are willing and able to speak up when concerned about possible wrongdoing. Fortunately, the new evidence from earlier chapters confirms that in the Australian public sector today, it is often possible for public officials to blow the whistle, have their concerns acted on and not suffer reprisals. In many organisations, speaking up about serious concerns is accepted as a natural part, if not duty, of the life of a public servant. The research also shows that when officials are able to report wrongdoing internally with confidence that action will be taken, the outcomes are often positive. Many of the data confirm that when an official's concern is to stop or prevent wrongdoing, the fastest and safest way to achieve this, in the bulk of instances, is by speaking up and reporting through official channels.

At the same time, the research has confirmed that reporting wrongdoing is rarely an easy experience. In any situation, it is inherently difficult for employees to draw attention to suspected wrongdoing or organisational failures without the risk of personal or organisational conflict. The challenge for many, if not most, employees who report their concerns lies in the management of these risks. Employees who assess the risks accurately, have good coping skills and good personal support networks are those best placed to manage the process to a reasonable conclusion and to exit their role as a whistleblower having served the public interest and survived. Employees who are less good at anticipating and managing conflict, or who exacerbate it, are inevitably at higher risk of negative outcomes, even if their primary concerns are correct. These outcomes can reverberate not only for the individual, but for colleagues, managers and the entire workplace.

In every jurisdiction studied, employees are entitled by law to rely on the support and protection of the management of their agency if or when they report concerns about wrongdoing through appropriate channels. The crucial questions become, how safe is it currently for employees to rely on that support and protection and what can be done to increase the extent to which the trust of employees and the wider public are justified in respect of institutional responses? The research holds several key lessons for integrity managers, chief executives, senior management and governments as a whole.

## Case-handlers and integrity managers

The most important overall lesson for those responsible for integrity matters within agencies is the crucial importance of their own role. Chapter 4 showed in detail that the majority of public employees who reported wrongdoing did so internally—in the first instance and even if they went on to make a subsequent disclosure. Only a small minority of public employees are prepared to make disclosures outside their organisation, and then principally only after first having made one or more internal disclosures. These results indicate that the first, internal responses to public interest disclosures are the most crucial and could be the only opportunities for concerns about wrongdoing to be brought to light at a point when the problems remain manageable. In this context, the research results translate into six key lessons for those with responsibility for the internal integrity systems of agencies.

### 1. Quality internal investigations are crucial

First, the quality, conduct and outcomes of internal assessments and investigations are vital factors on which rest many of the results of any whistleblowing process. As demonstrated by Chapters 5 and 6, the professionalism of an agency's systems for assessing and investigating possible wrongdoing will determine not only whether the primary issues are identified and problems rectified; they will bear directly on whistleblowers' experiences of reporting, their level of stress, the risk that they will suffer reprisals or become engaged in organisational conflict and on the messages that pass to other employees about whether the organisation is a safe environment in which to speak up.

While following through on internal investigation outcomes is the responsibility of management, those responsible for investigations typically have the best and often the only opportunity to help the agency resolve difficult issues without them becoming unnecessarily damaging to individuals and the organisation. The data in Chapters 4–6 show that once the whistle is blown, the investigation outcome becomes crucial to many employees' chances of survival and is perceived by them as such. Especially until other support strategies for whistleblowers are strengthened, in what can become an unexpectedly stressful process for many individuals, the investigation is often all that whistleblowers have on which to pin their hopes. At the same time, if doubts arise about what action is being taken, or if initial investigations do not deal with all the key issues, the potential for disputation, delay, internal organisational conflict and further investigations increases. Apart from the quality of the primary outcome, those assessing disclosures and undertaking and overseeing internal investigations have special responsibility for:

- ensuring that whistleblowers' expectations of and understandings about internal processes are as realistic as possible
- regularly communicating with whistleblowers as to what action is being taken in relation to their disclosure
- regularly meeting or communicating with whistleblowers to identify continuing issues or issues that have arisen since an original disclosure, so that these can be appropriately addressed or answered.

## 2. Recognise the gatekeeper roles of managers

The second challenge for integrity managers is recognising the full extent to which first and second-level line managers currently act as the gatekeepers for receipt of the bulk of possible public interest disclosures. Previously, and in legislation in some jurisdictions, it has often been assumed that managers simply manage and if an official needs to make a disclosure, they will use separate internal processes to do so—such as an internal hotline or by reporting to an auditor or internal investigation staff. The reality is different. The bulk of disclosures first come to the knowledge of direct supervisors or, if they are not trusted by employees, another higher or similar manager. Integrity managers need to frankly assess and frankly advise senior management as to how well line managers are equipped in their agencies to handle this role.

Integrity managers also need to recognise the dual roles that line managers play in such circumstances, as described in Chapters 6, 7 and 9. Direct supervisors could be the best people to provide support and protection to a whistleblower—or they could be the greatest source of any risk of conflict and reprisals. It can no longer be assumed that the role of integrity-related staff will not cut across the traditional responsibilities of line managers for issues raised by or with their staff, because it is now clear that line managers are handling a much more important and sensitive range of internal integrity matters than might have been previously realised.

## 3. Stronger alternative reporting avenues

A further particular lesson arising from the large proportion of disclosures received by supervisors is the need for integrity managers to revisit their strategies for educating employees about the different avenues available for reporting. In line with the findings below, this may require some reconception of the roles of integrity practitioners within the organisation and particularly their visibility and accessibility. The research strongly suggests that employees will most often make disclosures to people they already know. Unless integrity-related staff are widely known and perceived as trustworthy and approachable in an organisation, attempts to encourage disclosures to be made directly to points other than the normal management chain—where this is desirable—could have limited effect. For some agencies, however, making integrity staff more visible (for example, through training and internal outreach) is not a priority strategy.

## 4. Recognise and develop whistleblower support roles

It is now clearer than before that integrity practitioners play different roles in the welfare of employees who report. When agencies have dedicated support programs, with staff other than investigators and line managers tasked with helping oversee the welfare of whistleblowers, this is an emerging new specialist role in its own right. As discussed below, however, as a challenge for senior management, such programs are currently relatively few and far between, and organisationally weak. The research in Chapters 5, 8 and 9 also confirms that investigators should not be relied on to provide internal witness support, for the simple fact that their investigation role often directly conflicts with the role of a trusted source of personal guidance and support. This reinforces the need for agencies to invest in more organised, alternative support strategies.

In the absence of these stronger programs, internal integrity staff members currently continue to play vital support roles, in conjunction with their traditional core business (investigation, risk assessment, standard setting, complaint handling, workplace education). Chapter 9 shows that these support roles do not rate as strongly as might have been expected. At present, however, whistleblowers are also most likely to survive largely on their own personal resources and with the support of personal and professional networks (including friends, family, colleagues and unions). Only in a minority of cases is there evidence that an 'anti-dobber' mentality in workplaces results in withdrawal of this crucial collegiate support. Survival is often largely thanks to the support of line managers, where this is possible. Chapter 9 showed that when the support of line managers is not likely, not possible or not forthcoming, or is withdrawn, internal integrity staff again become the first port of call in terms of institutional support. This situation needs to be addressed.

## 5. Develop investigators' roles in reprisal risk assessment

The fifth lesson is that, while integrity staff with investigation roles should not be relied on for support, integrity managers can develop clearer strategies for the roles that investigators can play, consistent with their core business, in helping ensure the welfare of whistleblowers. One crucial role, at the outset of cases, lies in the field of the assessment of reprisal risk. Another associated role lies in the provision of 'pre-emptive' investigation of the whistleblower's work environment in order to put support staff and management in a better position to establish—should issues arise later—whether reprisals or mismanagement of a whistleblower have occurred. Chapter 6 sets out a comprehensive new picture of the risk factors associated with whistleblowing cases in which mistreatment is later alleged. Chapters 5, 6 and 9 demonstrate the difficulties that agencies have in resolving whether mistreatment has occurred. In the last part of this chapter, Findings 2, 7 and 8 point to some key actions to enable internal integrity staff to play more structured and strategic roles in the prevention and resolution of adverse outcomes.

## 6. Work with integrity agencies

The final lesson is that internal integrity systems cannot be expected to resolve all issues satisfactorily, all of the time, without external help. Many whistleblowing cases can be resolved internally, to the satisfaction of all concerned, with the public interest served. By their nature, however, there will always be whistleblowing cases in which internal integrity systems cannot resolve conflicts between individual employees and the organisation as a whole, either because the internal investigation outcome is not favourable to the whistleblower or because it has not been possible to satisfactorily manage the welfare of the whistleblower. Agencies do sometimes get it wrong and public employees might even go on to blow the whistle publicly, and be justified in doing so—an issue for legislative recognition, as discussed in Chapter 11.

In between internal and public whistleblowing, however, lie the crucial roles that external integrity agencies can play in better assisting agencies to manage more cases to positive conclusions and to deal more expeditiously with those cases that should not or cannot be resolved internally. Without abrogating their own responsibility for these cases, integrity managers need to look to a new partnership with external agencies in the management of whistleblowing and help identify those roles that they think external integrity agencies can usefully play, as well as the resources and skills needed to enable them to do so. Similarly, external integrity agencies need to help build this partnership and be ready and able to assist in ways that have not previously been possible. The need for legislative and institutional reform in support of this new partnership is discussed further below.

# Chief executives and senior management

## 1. Whistleblowing is a positive resource for management

The same research provides eight major lessons for the senior management of the agencies studied. A first important lesson is that whistleblowing is, for the most part, a positive force for the good management of public sector organisations. Whistleblowing is valuable. Even if employee disclosures often involve other personal and workplace issues, the information they hold has been proven to be vital in the detection and remediation of wrongdoing, ranging from the minor to the most serious cases. In Chapter 2, the surveys of the case study agencies' own managers and case-handlers confirm that in their assessment, the information provided by whistleblowers is generally significant and valuable and represents the single most important source of information for the purposes of uncovering wrongdoing. As shown in Chapters 2 and 5, a large proportion of whistleblower reports are substantiated and lead to necessary management action—a larger proportion than is often the case in respect of allegations or complaints from all sources.

Whistleblowing therefore has proven organisational value. The likelihood is also increased that, when it is not heeded, or it is mismanaged, the same accurate information will eventually surface among external integrity agencies or the wider public. It is in the interests of chief executives to shift from seeing whistleblowing and whistleblowers as a problem—should they hold that view—to instead invest in systems to enable employees to report perceived wrongdoing more easily, and earlier. This includes more integrated systems for recognising the different public and private interest elements that are frequently caught up in disclosures, for the purposes of ensuring that these are all professionally dealt with, as reflected in Finding 1.

## 2. All staff members are, and should be, potential whistleblowers

It is often easy for senior managers to assume that there are particular personal characteristics that drive particular employees to blow the whistle. Anecdotally, it is also common for chief executives and senior managers to assume that most whistleblowers are difficult and disgruntled individuals predisposed to conflict, who represent more of a hindrance than a help to the smooth functioning of a busy agency. Any such view is, however, likely to be biased by the fact that it is cases like this that are the most likely to become intractable problems and therefore come to senior management attention—whether because of the nature of the individuals or the case or because it has already been mismanaged. Statistically, a far higher number of whistleblowing cases involve internal disclosures that, even when made for mixed motives or associated with a history of conflict, are successfully investigated and resolved, often to the benefit of the agency. Because of this simple fact, especially in large agencies, senior managers are less likely to ever be troubled by the details of this larger number of cases, or ever know the identity of the whistleblowers involved.

On a more general scale, the evidence that personal characteristics can predict whistleblowing—for example, that whistleblowers are slightly more likely to be female and to have spent longer time in their organisations—pales against the evidence that, depending on the issue and context, almost any employee can eventually be driven to blow the whistle on perceived wrongdoing. As demonstrated in Chapter 3, employees who report are difficult to distinguish from those who do not, on basic measures such as job satisfaction and organisational citizenship. Indeed, there is good reason to surmise that most conventional employees do not rush to blow the whistle, but rather persist for some time in workplaces in which they perceive there to be problems. What is most clear, from Chapter 3, is that staff will typically blow the whistle when matters become sufficiently serious and if they believe their disclosure will make a difference or serve some good purpose. The responsibility of agencies is to ensure that the value of disclosures is realised in a way that further inspires the trust of others.

## 3. Equipping managers to be reliable gatekeepers

While these basic results provide good reason for senior managers to take the management of whistleblowing more seriously, a challenge arises from the evidence of where and how the bulk of employees are currently first disclosing their concerns. The fact that the bulk of whistleblowing currently occurs within agencies, rather than to outside agencies or the public, places a heavy responsibility on agencies to manage reporting well. This responsibility is increased by the fact that within agencies, the bulk of reporting takes place directly to supervisors and other line managers, rather than other points in the organisation. The extent of the reporting that first occurs this way means every manager must be equipped to recognise and deal appropriately with a wide range of disclosures, many of which trigger particular statutory obligations as well as responsibilities of the agency as an employer. These results reinforce the need for more comprehensive systems of recording and tracking the handling of alleged wrongdoing cases. As will be discussed, the same results confirm that junior managers are often not the ideal people to first receive disclosures or to be the only ones to receive them—increasing the need for review and education about the different available reporting avenues for staff, as discussed in Finding 3.

To the extent that first and second-level managers also often are appropriate first recipients, and are likely to retain that role, the research also identifies that most managers are not familiar with their obligations and perceive themselves to be in need of greater training. In addition to the broad evidence in Chapter 7, Chapter 10 showed the problem to be sometimes acute. In some agencies, the confidence of managers in the quality of internal whistleblowing procedures was high, when the agency really had no such procedures at all. Meeting the need for basic managerial training is the challenge reflected in Finding 4.

## 4. Whistleblowers continue to be treated unjustly

A fourth challenge lies in the fact that, while a majority of whistleblowers indicate that they are treated well or the same in their organisations, on average, a sizeable minority do continue to suffer. Moreover, the data in Chapter 5 showed that in some agencies, the proportion of public interest whistleblowers who reported mistreatment ranged towards 50 per cent. The risk factors for reported mistreatment, described in Chapter 6, show that the cases with better outcomes tend to be simpler, easier and lower level in terms of the number and seniority of the people involved. In more complex cases, many agencies continue to struggle to prevent damaging conflicts from arising or to control the risk of real reprisals being taken against reporters. This active mistreatment comes on top of some of the often natural, unavoidable negative impacts of reporting processes, such as increased stress.

The need for more comprehensive management and reporting systems (above) as well as more active support strategies (below) is reinforced by the fact that it is not colleagues or co-workers who represent the most important sources of perceived mistreatment. Contrary to many impressions and the design of much whistleblowing legislation, the major sources of perceived mistreatment are managers. This is especially the case in circumstances in which managers are themselves implicated in or compromised by the alleged wrongdoing, but it also reflects the failure of managers to provide support and guidance to employees, to control the risks of reprisals being taken by others or to recognise when problems affecting an employee's work performance or workplace relationships are related to the difficult experience of having reported wrongdoing. These data confirm the complex dual role of line managers as potentially the most important source of support for employees who report, but alternatively also the people most likely to 'shoot the messenger' or leave a whistleblower exposed to preventable and controllable conflicts, as a means of trying to end a troublesome incident or exit a troublesome process.

## 5. Management responses are crucial to ensuring reporting

The fact that managers appear to represent the major source of the problems experienced by whistleblowers is not something that senior management can afford to ignore. Chapter 3 demonstrated two overwhelming reasons why many staff currently did not report wrongdoing: because they assessed that nothing would be done or because they believed they would be exposed to, and not protected by management from, reprisals. As shown in Chapter 2, an average of 29 per cent of public employees who observed very or extremely serious wrongdoing neither reported it nor took any action, even when no-one else had reported it. This 'inaction rate' rises to more than 60 per cent in some agencies. Chief executives can ill afford to preside over organisations in which confidence in the management response to reporting is low. Poor or negligent treatment of whistleblowers has direct impacts on whether other members of staff are prepared to report or take other action in response to perceived wrongdoing. It therefore impacts on the ability of management to ensure that wrongdoing is identified and addressed early, rather than being allowed to fester or emerge first in the public domain.

Clearly, a positive reporting climate cannot be fostered in organisations in which managers' own mistreatment or mishandling of whistleblowers goes unaddressed. While the dual roles of line managers as both custodians of and threats to the welfare of whistleblowers raise complex problems, managerial reprisals and mishandling of reporting processes have too many far-reaching implications to be simply written off as inevitable and unavoidable problems. Chief executives and senior managers face legal responsibilities, as employers, for the welfare of staff members who fulfil their duty to report. They can be held responsible for allowing a workplace environment to develop in which more junior managers fail to properly manage reprisal risks, let alone feel they can undertake direct reprisals. An agency's public reputation, including its reputation as a preferred employer, can suffer severely if it becomes known as one that fails to provide systems and procedures that deliver organisational justice.

## 6. Current whistleblowing procedures are weak, especially on issues of support

The sixth challenge for senior managers lies in the fact that, objectively assessed, the typical quality of agency procedures and systems for the management of whistleblowing is not strong. Despite statutory requirements in many cases, some agencies continue to have, in effect, no specific systems or procedures for encouraging and managing whistleblowing. While some agencies do have more comprehensive procedures, it is not a large number. In most cases, such procedures are not comprehensive and they are particularly weak on mechanisms for supporting and protecting those employees who report. Chapter 10 assessed only five of 175 agencies nationally as having developed reasonably strong procedures for the management of whistleblowing, measured against the current Australian Standard.

At present, whistleblowers who survived the experience were most likely to have done so thanks to their own personal skills and support networks, the fact that their disclosure was able to be substantiated and because they happened by chance to have a manager who was willing and able to support them. The formal management systems of the majority of organisations currently do little to ensure or increase the likelihood of such outcomes. As a default, senior managers instead tend to extend support only in those cases that appear to involve the 'perfect' whistleblower—but these are not the cases in which intervention is most likely to be needed. The data suggest that, logically, institutional investment is most needed in those cases with the highest risk of conflict, which are likely to be the more 'murky' and complex cases.

This project's second report will deal further with new, best-practice models for effective internal witness management systems. However as reflected in Finding 6,. As reflected in Finding 6, it is already clear that the bulk of agencies, in most jurisdictions, need to give active and urgent consideration to strategies for providing whistleblower support. In particular, agencies need to develop programs, commensurate with their own size and needs, for ensuring that support strategies are directed and, where necessary, directly delivered, by people with an institutional role that conflicts as little as possible with the challenges often implicit in providing that support. As seen above, an employee's line managers can be crucial sources of support—but this cannot be relied on and in some situations the reverse will be true. Similarly, internal investigation and other integrity staff can be crucial, but their role can also involve direct conflicts. In most cases, and all higher-risk ones, chief executives must ensure that someone with institutional independence from both the whistleblower's chain of command and the investigation response is tasked to monitor and direct the provision of support.

## 7. Support programs must be properly resourced

The research has also shown that for whistleblower support programs to be effective, they must be more than a token. Such programs must be given resources and organisational status commensurate with the level of need in individual agencies, given their size and likely desirable incidence of reporting. They also need to be embedded in management systems that ensure the support program can be triggered early in all the most needy cases. The evidence shows, in Chapter 9, that so far, even in large agencies, such programs are functioning at a fraction of the scale at which they need to operate to make a real difference. Only perhaps 1.3 per cent of all likely public interest whistleblowers are currently appearing on the 'radar' of active support programs, even in the project's case study agencies—or about 6.5 per cent of all public interest whistleblowers who reported being mistreated. Findings 1 and 6 summarise the actions needed to address these issues.

## 8. Management support must be active

As also shown in Chapter 9, and underscored by Chapter 6, management strategies for actively protecting whistleblowers are in need of development. The research has generally confirmed that agencies have the option of three broad responses when employees report wrongdoing: trusting in the confidentiality of the matter, to prevent anyone from knowing the whistle has been blown; doing nothing and hoping that problems do not arise or will dissipate naturally; and intervening actively in the workplace to ensure that relevant employees know that an employee has management's support. Currently, agencies rely heavily on the first response, even though confidentiality is likely to work only as medium to long-term protection in a limited number of cases. If agencies wish to address the problem of staff confidence in the likely or known response of management to reporting, and really protect those who report, procedures and systems must be in place to support active intervention when needed. Such strategies also require strong commitment from the leaders of any organisation, to the highest level.

## 9. Leadership

Finally, the research confirms that the tone of an organisation's responses to issues of integrity and wrongdoing is set from the top. As shown throughout the book, and particularly in Chapters 2, 5 and 10, the extensive differences in performance and outcome between agencies are not easily explained by jurisdictional or legislative differences nor by the differing nature of the core business of agencies. Instead, the differences point to the individualised nature of agency responses to the challenges of whistleblowing. In some cases, chief executives and their management teams are overseeing systems that, even if capable of improvement, are delivering good outcomes. In many more agencies, the management team has either given low priority to the issue or is struggling to find a workable formula.

The importance of management leadership carries through into the question of how, even if whistleblower support is extended, its effectiveness is ultimately to be judged. The evidence in Chapters 5, 6 and 9 suggests that in most agencies, most managers know that more can be done to positively manage whistleblowing cases and that, when poor outcomes occur, this is because not enough has been done to prevent reprisals and other adverse consequences. The confidence of employees that senior management will support staff who fulfil their responsibility to report depends less on what management says than on what it does in response to notable cases—including cases that could have been better managed. Having better equipped all managers to discharge the agency's duty of care to its employees in such circumstances, chief executives must be seen to ensure that justice is done and to admit responsibility when, for whatever reason, agencies fail to meet the necessary high standards.

# Lessons for government

## 1. Whole-of-government responsibility

The research holds four major lessons for Australian governments. First, it is clearly in the interests of governments at all levels to get the management of public interest disclosures right. History shows that when disclosures are not properly dealt with and whistleblowers are not treated appropriately, this can have a detrimental, long-term impact, not only on individuals and individual agencies, but on the reputation of the government of the day and on levels of trust in government as a whole.

Until now, governments have attempted to address the management of public interest disclosures largely through important but symbolic statements of policy through legislation, with individual public sector agencies left to implement the detail, largely unassisted and often unsupervised. Until now, there has also been a relative dearth of information regarding even the simple extent of whistleblowing, let alone how it might be better managed. With that gap now smaller, it is important for governments to adjust—or, in the case of the Commonwealth Government, to introduce—their legislative framework to work in practical ways to achieve the desired outcomes.

## 2. Lifting the standard of agency systems and procedures

Second, as part of this reform process, it is clear that governments have a responsibility to ensure that their agencies bring their approaches to whistleblowing up to a more comprehensive and consistent standard. There is some way to go before this occurs. The broad policy setting of requiring individual agencies to shoulder the primary burden of managing employee disclosures productively, as public employers, has been shown by the research to be valid. The similarity of overall outcomes between jurisdictions, notwithstanding very different legislative settings, contrasts sharply with the great diversity of outcomes obtained by agencies within all the jurisdictions studied. This confirms that it is at the agency level that the major decisions matter—and at which most attention needs to be directed.

Nevertheless, it is clear that there is a long way to go before a majority of individual public sector agencies are maximising their chances of gaining improved outcomes for themselves and their staff. While the research indicates that current whistleblowing legislation has positive effects in building the expectations of public employees that they can safely report, this promise is not necessarily being effectively met by agencies. Governments must now shoulder their responsibility for ensuring that agencies are equipped, empowered and required to do so.

The primary actions needed to do so are laid out in Chapter 11 and summarised by Findings 9 and 10 below. They include the need to extend new resources to integrity agencies to let them undertake the vital coordination and oversight roles on which effective implementation partly depends.

## 3. Legislating from first principles

Governments need to particularly recognise that effective whole-of-government frameworks for the management of public interest whistleblowing cannot realistically operate at their current level of abstraction. They need to be underpinned by clearer first principles and more detailed operational arrangements. These include clearer standards and processes by which the whistleblowing procedures of agencies can be developed, implemented and judged. The fact that a large proportion of public interest whistleblowing is probably going unreported and therefore effectively unmanaged under present laws is just the first sign of the need for a more comprehensive approach. The second major sign is the evidence, discussed earlier, of the even smaller proportion of public interest whistleblowers coming into contact with the types of internal witness support strategies contemplated by most legislation.

While the next steps in a second generation of legislative frameworks include more detailed operational and oversight frameworks for agencies, there are also important issues of principle involved in effective legislative reform. Perhaps in order to avoid an anticipated flood of disclosures, most Australian public interest disclosure legislation has been relatively complicated, technical and restrictive in its application. As argued in Chapter 11, the consequence has been laws that are difficult to administer—when in fact they should err on the side of catching more, rather than less, public officials within their ambit if they are to support public employees and agencies taking an 'if in doubt, report' approach. Addressing these issues, in the face of misplaced concerns that a less technical approach might somehow encourage more whistleblowing than currently occurs, requires political will and clarity of legislative purpose.

## 4. Effective legislative support for basic outcomes

Finally, legislative reform needs to reapproach, from first principles, two of the major objectives of whistleblowing legislation that have never been properly delivered, despite up to 15 years' experience in some jurisdictions. Most Australians would be relatively astounded to know that despite the evidence of the importance of whistleblowing, and the knowledge that whistleblowers have suffered, no public official is believed to have yet been able to secure formal compensation for damage to their career under whistleblower protection legislation. Similarly, most Australians would find it nonsensical that no whistleblower protection law extends adequately to the regulation of public whistleblowing, even though this is the most obvious and legally risky example of the phenomenon. As outlined in Chapter 11, and in the findings below, government action to reform existing whistleblowing regimes is unlikely to be judged to be credible by the broader public, whose interests are intended to be protected by such disclosures, unless such basic issues are meaningfully addressed.

## Key findings: an agenda for action

What are the areas in which action is most clearly needed and in which it can most clearly lead to better outcomes? The research to date has found 10 key areas warranting particular attention and action. The first eight of these findings specify areas in which action can be taken on an agency and a whole-of-government basis, while, as outlined above, the final two findings involve legislative change and whole-of-government action.

## 1. More comprehensive agency systems for recording and tracking employee reports of wrongdoing

Most agencies currently lack sufficiently comprehensive systems for recording and tracking employee reports of wrongdoing. Some agencies still have no such systems. As shown by Chapters 2, 8, 9, 10 and 11, these systems are a basic prerequisite for effective monitoring of how many public interest disclosures are being made, what investigation or other action is being taken and how those involved in the disclosures are being managed, at an agency and a whole-of-government level.

Even more importantly, such systems are basic to enabling the senior management of agencies to know what disclosures are being received at junior and middle-management levels—which is where the bulk of disclosures are currently received (Chapter 4) and where the key risks of mismanagement, mistreatment or reprisal currently arise (Chapters 5 and 6). For all these reasons, integrated systems need to be put in place that:

- allow senior management to track reports and report-related issues wherever they are being dealt with throughout the organisation, including informally by lower-level managers
- record and track wrongdoing reports in a coordinated way, together with other forms of complaints, grievances and conflicts
- record and track all reports that could possibly be classified as public interest disclosures (PIDs) under legislation, not just reports that staff have requested be treated as PIDs or that evolve into more serious cases
- require all reports to be assessed at the outset for the level of reprisal risk or other conflict associated with the making of the report, classified according to risk, and routinely monitored for any change in risk level (see also Finding 2).

## 2. Agency procedures for assessing and monitoring the risk of reprisals (or other conflict) for those who report

The research found that a majority of agencies had no systematic methods in place for ensuring that when employees reported wrongdoing, assessments were made as to what if any risks of reprisal or mistreatment surrounded that report (Chapters 6, 9 and 10). Such procedures are basic prerequisites for the effective management of disclosures if agencies are to anticipate and minimise problems rather than trying to deal with them only in an *ex post facto* fashion. Without the information afforded by early assessment of risk, agencies also leave themselves unable to properly defend themselves against later allegations of having mismanaged employees who make disclosures.

While further recommendations about effective risk-assessment procedures are also the subject of the project's second report, it is clear that standard procedures for risk assessment should:

- be triggered by all initial reports, rather than only in response to employee requests or after problems arise (see also Finding 1)
- be simple and flexible, so as to be efficiently administered by all first and second-level managers, with more detailed assessment requirements triggered only on an as-needs basis
- take a broad view of possible sources of problems (that is, identify and assess indirect sources of conflict or difficulties as well as direct reprisal risks)
- involve the employee(s) making the disclosure (that is, reflect and address their self-assessment of risk as well as objective assessment)
- include a third party, trusted by the employee(s) making the disclosure, who will be involved in helping them manage their own responses to risks
- ensure that the risk assessment is recorded
- ensure that the risk assessment is updated as necessary
- trigger meaningful support arrangements, protection measures or other management action.

## 3. Clearer and better advice for employees on the range of avenues available for reporting wrongdoing

Agencies need to actively review their strategies for informing staff about the range of reporting avenues that are open to them and which avenues might be most appropriate in different circumstances. Chapter 4 showed that the bulk of disclosures were made directly to supervisors or managers in the normal management chain, rather than to internal specialist areas, hotlines or integrity agencies. While reporting to supervisors and line managers is not to be discouraged, the research demonstrates the importance of the initial responses made to disclosures—in terms of investigation action and control of reprisals or other conflicts—and therefore who it is who first receives a disclosure (Chapters 5, 6, 8 and 9).

Employees who are considering reporting need to know it is also possible—and could be preferable—to not make their disclosure directly to a supervisor or line manager and that they may also make their disclosure directly and confidentially to other points in the organisation or to an external integrity agency (and, if so, which points and which agency). While further recommendations about reporting paths and workplace education are also the subject of the project's second report, the precise arrangements and strategies needed are likely to be specific to individual agencies. The research indicates that agencies need to do more to ensure that, in as many cases as possible, employees direct their concerns about wrongdoing to the most appropriate place, in the first instance.

## 4. Basic training for public sector managers in how to recognise and respond to possible public interest disclosures

Chapters 7 and 8 demonstrated that most managers in the agencies studied did not have a practical understanding of their responsibilities under public interest disclosure legislation and considered themselves in need of more training about their obligations and how to fulfil them. With first and second-level managers currently receiving the bulk of wrongdoing reports (Chapter 4), this lack of understanding can do much to explain why more reports are not being accurately identified as possible public interest disclosures (Chapters 2 and 11), why major reprisal risks are not being identified and addressed (Chapter 6) and why available support mechanisms are not being triggered in more cases (Chapter 9).

These results make it clear that agencies should not be giving supervisory responsibilities to first and second-level managers without first providing basic training to managers about how to recognise and respond to employees' concerns regarding wrongdoing in the organisation. The basic training should be:

- simple
- comprehensive (that is, including the different ways to respond to a range of information or allegations about wrongdoing, not simply the technical requirements of public interest disclosure legislation)
- geared towards an 'if in doubt, report' approach to employee concerns, by ensuring that managers trigger the agency's procedures in respect of all possible public interest disclosures, not simply those that they consider especially serious or doubt their own ability to handle.

## 5. A program of training for internal investigators in basic techniques, with special attention to issues of internal witness management

Chapter 8 identified the need for a higher level of available expertise and consistency of approach and performance in the way in which agencies investigated employee reports of wrongdoing. There is a clear need for agencies to ensure that they have available to them staff with sufficient training in all relevant types of investigation, including 'evidence-based' investigations (for example, those that could result in disciplinary or criminal action) and 'outcome-focused' investigations (for example, investigations into administrative action or inaction, failures to follow procedures or inadequate procedures and policies). Chapters 5, 6 and 9 also showed that while internal investigators should not carry responsibility for supporting and protecting agency whistleblowers, they played vital roles in the process that required a higher level of training.

Only limited professional training is currently available in Australia that meets all these needs and is suitable for the bulk of agencies. The need to develop new training is also taken up below in relation to Finding 9. As part of the process of developing the appropriate training approaches, agencies need to:

- evaluate existing performance and conduct more comprehensive assessments of their training needs in these areas
- maximise those training opportunities currently available in the tertiary and commercial sectors
- where resources permit (that is, in larger agencies), dedicate new resources to the development of agency-specific training
- when using external investigation resources, such as consultants, take responsibility for ensuring they have the necessary expertise
- work more closely with external integrity agencies to ensure they are using appropriately trained investigators, including consultants, and ensure the development of new training packages to help meet their needs.

## 6. Adoption and expansion of structured support programs for employees who report wrongdoing

As discussed earlier, Chapters 9 and 10 showed that only a limited number of agencies had active programs for supporting and protecting employees who reported wrongdoing. Only about half of all agencies surveyed had procedures for supporting employees in these circumstances, with many of these only informal procedures, and only 11 per cent of all agencies had a formalised program for the provision of internal witness support.

Further, even when programs are more formal, agency systems are not ensuring these are accessed by a large proportion of those employees who could benefit from support. In the agencies and the period studied, perhaps only 1.3 per cent of all public interest whistleblowers—or 6.5 per cent of those who reported mistreatment—received the benefit of such a program.

The description of current and prospective best practice in internal witness management programs is the subject of the project's second report. The existing identified elements of an internal witness management system, developed in collaboration with the project's case study agencies, are set out in Appendix 3. The precise requirements will vary greatly between different agencies. It is, however, already clear that most agencies do not have any such program at all, often notwithstanding statutory requirements, and that even when agencies do have formalised programs, these need to be extended. In particular, there is a widespread need for agencies to put in place official support strategies that:

- are accessible to all employees who might potentially need them, triggered proactively rather than only reactively (see also Finding 1)
- are based on an active risk-assessment and management approach (see also Finding 2)
- recognise and maximise the role of informal networks as well as formal supervision and professional services in the provision of support (Chapter 6)
- are resourced to deal with the likely real need within the agency and not just selected cases (as suggested by Chapters 2, 5 and 6)
- provide formal recognition to employees who report, as appropriate in individual cases, as well as evaluation of their treatment and follow-up monitoring of their welfare.

## 7. Improved mechanisms for monitoring the welfare of employees who report wrongdoing, from the point of first report

Chapters 5, 6 and 9 demonstrated the need for more effective strategies for responding to alleged and suspected reprisals or other mistreatment of internal witnesses. The research indicates that the most common sources of perceived mistreatment are management-related and involve workplace-based harassment and negative personnel action against whistleblowers taken either directly or indirectly as a result of the whistleblowing incident. Chapters 2 and 5, however, also confirm that public interest whistleblowing frequently arises in conjunction with other conflicts; and Chapter 9 confirms that even when it is clear that adverse actions have been taken, agencies often have difficulty separating justified management actions from those that represent an unjust or inappropriate reprisal against a whistleblower.

These results indicate a need in most agencies for a procedure that allows independent verification of the organisational position (for example, work performance) of employees who report wrongdoing, as close as possible to the exact point at which they first report it. It is clear that part of the difficulty in establishing whether the treatment of a whistleblower is or is not justified lies in evidentiary difficulties as to whether particular problems associated with an employee's relationships with colleagues or supervisors began before, simultaneously with or subsequent to a disclosure issue arising.

While the nature of a best-practice procedure will be further explored in the second report, elements of such a procedure include:

- clear documentation as to when and how concerns about wrongdoing were first aired
- collection by the relevant investigator of the evidence existing at the time of the report regarding the reporter's work performance and workplace relationships, undertaken with the knowledge and participation of the reporter
- when the fact of a report is still confidential, alternative strategies such as a general audit of the work histories of all employees in the relevant section to establish the relative position of the employee, in parallel with the primary investigation.

This procedure is above and beyond procedures for the investigation of real allegations regarding reprisals or failures in duty of care, discussed below—because the above actions would be taken as a matter of routine, as a proactive measure to help resolve later issues in case they arise and as a preventive measure against unjustified actions being taken.

## 8. More detailed and flexible agency procedures for the investigation and remediation of reprisals and breaches of duty of care

As discussed in Chapters 8, 9 and 10, a majority of agencies have no specific procedures for the investigation and remediation of alleged or suspected reprisals against whistleblowers. In these circumstances, the default procedure is to investigate such an allegation as if it were the same as any other allegation of wrongdoing, notwithstanding its much greater complexity. Further, as shown in Chapter 11, in most jurisdictions, a reprisal is a criminal offence, requiring proof beyond reasonable doubt that an identifiable individual has taken detrimental action, not otherwise justified, and taken it in response to the act of whistleblowing. As a consequence, unless someone is first found criminally liable, it becomes difficult for agencies to establish that an employee has suffered unjustly in less direct ways—let alone admit any vicarious liability for the actions or inactions of individual managers, and take steps to remediate the injustice.

Resolving the inconsistencies caused by the conjunction of criminal and civil remedies for detrimental action is partly an issue for law reform, as discussed in Chapter 11. These results, however, also show the need for most agencies to:

- develop specific procedures for dealing with alleged reprisals, where they do not already exist
- frame their procedures more broadly than simply the identification of specific acts of reprisal for which individuals might be held culpable (in a criminal or disciplinary sense), and also recognise more generalised causes and sources of detrimental impacts for which the agency should take responsibility (including impacts that were reasonably foreseeable by individuals but not prevented—that is, negligent; and impacts that were preventable in hindsight, if the agency had had better procedures or had been exercising a higher standard of care).

## 9. A dedicated oversight agency or unit for the coordination of responses to employee-reported wrongdoing

As discussed in Chapter 11, there is a clear need for legislative reform to task an appropriate agency or unit in each jurisdiction with the role of coordinating and overseeing the responses of agencies to public interest whistleblowing. Given the extent of the challenges confirmed by the research, and the state of systems and procedures in most agencies, a more coordinated approach is required, capable of delivering greater consistency and quality in agency-level responses and allowing earlier intervention in investigations or specific problems of internal witness management where needed.

As outlined in Chapter 11, the responsibilities of the oversight agency should include:

- being notified by agencies of all possible public interest disclosures and recording those disclosures and how they were dealt with and resolved
- having the option to decide, on being notified of a disclosure, to provide advice or direction to an agency on how the disclosure should be handled, to manage the investigation of the disclosure by the agency or to take over the investigation of the disclosure
- providing advice or direction to agencies on the steps that should be taken to protect people who have made disclosures or to provide remedial action for a person who has suffered detriment as a result of making a disclosure
- promoting the objectives of the legislation, within government and publicly, and conducting training (see Findings 4 and 5) and public education
- publishing model procedures for the administration of the legislation, with which agencies' internal procedures must be consistent
- conducting a public review of the operation of the legislation at least once every five years.

Given that these resource-intensive responsibilities involve reviewing, assessing and assisting with individual cases, the most appropriate existing agencies to undertake this oversight role would be ones with experience and roles in investigations and case-handling, rather than agencies whose roles primarily involve policy and broad standard setting.

Care needs to be taken to ensure that, if an oversight body is created, agencies are still encouraged to manage disclosures at the local level. The research consistently points to the need for a new, coordinated partnership between line managers, agencies' central units and senior management and external integrity agencies. Any oversight agency also needs to be properly resourced and skilled to play the necessary guidance and support roles in relation to primary investigations, reprisal investigations and the handling of complex issues of employee welfare and whistleblower management.

## 10. Legislative action to provide more effective organisational systems and realistic compensation mechanisms and to recognise public whistleblowing

Chapter 11 sets out the key principles for the design of best-practice public interest disclosure legislation resulting from the research. The effective management of public interest whistleblowing in all jurisdictions now hinges, at least in part, on the quality of the legislative approach. In particular, as discussed in the previous chapter, there is need for legislative reform to:

- implement more effective operational systems for the management of whistleblowing—including a more comprehensive 'if in doubt, report' approach to the management of disclosures; minimum standards for internal disclosure procedures in agencies (to be further informed by the second report); and a new framework for coordination and oversight
- address the current lack of practical remedies for public officials whose lives and careers suffer for having made a public interest disclosure
- better protection for public officials who justifiably go public with their concerns.

## Future research

As already noted, the second report from this project will supplement the above findings with a more detailed guide to current and prospective best practice for the management of whistleblowing at an organisational level. This research focuses on the 15 case study agencies and includes further comparative analysis of the quantitative data relating to those agencies, interviews with individual whistleblowers, case-handlers and managers, review of written procedures and operational systems and workshops with agency representatives.

From the studies undertaken so far, six priority areas for future research can also be identified:

- longitudinal research on how agencies are handling whistleblowing matters, including reporting, inaction and mistreatment rates, in order to measure whether legislative and procedural reforms are having an effect
- longer-term tracking of the life and career outcomes of a wide cross-section of public interest whistleblowers, recognising that participants in the present studies were restricted to those who had reported wrongdoing within the previous two years
- further research into options for practical internal witness support and management intervention as an alternative or adjunct to strategies based primarily on confidentiality
- closer study of the handling of reprisal allegations in whistleblowing cases, to identify with even greater precision why such cases are so complex, and how and by whom they can be best handled and resolved
- closer study of the forms of compensation available to employees who suffer adverse outcomes from reporting, including informal compensation and the positive action taken by agencies to extend justice, and how these efforts might be more effectively supported by the broader legal and management frameworks surrounding workplace relations in the public sector
- more detailed analysis of the training needs of agencies.

While the conclusions reached in this chapter show that institutional responses to whistleblowing have a long way to go, this new picture of public sector whistleblowing shows it will be worth the effort to travel the necessary distance. These data show that, in a field of policy and public management that previously looked wholly bleak, many more of these complex conflicts are being, and can be, resolved in a positive manner. By managing whistleblowing better, outcomes can be found that are just to individuals, serve the long-term interests of organisations and better discharge our institutions' wider obligations to transparency and public integrity.

# Select bibliography

Acquino, K., Tripp, T. M. and Bies, R. J. 2006, 'Getting even or moving on? Power, procedural justice, and types of offence as predictors of revenge, forgiveness, reconciliation, and avoidance in organisations', *Journal of Applied Psychology*, vol. 91, pp. 653–68.

Agho, A. O., Price, J. L. and Mueller, C. W. 1992, 'Discriminant validity of measures of job satisfaction, positive affectivity and negative affectivity', *Journal of Occupational and Organisational Psychology*, vol. 65, pp. 185–96.

Ambrose, M. L. and Arnaud, A. 2005, 'Are procedural justice and distributive justice conceptually distinct?', in J. Greenberg, and J. A. Colquitt (eds), *Handbook of Organisational Justice*, Lawrence Erlbaum Associates, London, pp. 59–84.

Anderson, P. 1996, Controlling and managing the risk of whistleblower reprisal, Paper presented at the Australian National Occupational Stress Conference, March 1996, Brisbane, Australia.

Appelbaum, S. H., Deguire, K. J. and Lay, M. 2005, 'The relationship of ethical climate to deviant workplace behaviour', *Corporate Governance*, vol. 5, pp. 43–55.

Ashforth, B. E. and Anand, V. 2003, 'The normalisation of corruption in organisations', in R. M. Kramer and B. M. Staw (eds), *Research in Organisational Behaviour*, Elsevier, Amsterdam, pp. 1–52.

Australian Bureau of Statistics (ABS) 2007, *Wage and Salary Earners, Public Sector, Australia, June 2007*, cat. no. 6248.0.55.001, Australian Bureau of Statistics, Canberra.

Australian Labor Party (ALP) 2007, *Government information: restoring trust and integrity*, Australian Labor Party Election 2007 Policy Document, October 2007, Canberra.

Australian Public Service Commission (APSC) 2004, *State of the Service Report 2003–04*, Commonwealth of Australia, Canberra.

— 2005, *State of the Service Employee Survey Results 2004–05*, Commonwealth of Australia, Barton, Australian Capital Territory.

Berry, B. 2004, 'Organisational culture: a framework and strategies for facilitating employee whistleblowing', *Employee Responsibilities and Rights Journal*, vol. 16, no. 1, pp. 1–11.

Bies, R. J. 2005, 'Are procedural and interactional justice conceptually distinct?', in J. Greenberg and J. A. Colquitt (eds), *Handbook of Organisational Justice*, Lawrence Erlbaum Associates, London, pp. 85–112.

Bies, R. J. and Tripp, T. M. 2005, 'The study of revenge in the workplace: conceptual, ideological and empirical issues', in S. Fox and P. Spector (eds), *Counterproductive Work Behaviour: Investigations of actors and targets*, American Psychological Association, Washington, DC, pp. 65–82.

Bjorn-Liebenau, R. A. 2006, *Whistleblowing rules: best practice; assessment and revision of rules existing in EU institutions*, Study for the European Parliament, vol. 14, viewed 31 December 2007, <http://www.europarl.europa.eu/comparl/cont/site/calendrier/documents/3mai06/etude.pdf>

Brennan, N. and Kelly, J. 2007, 'A study of whistleblowing among trainee auditors', *The British Accounting Review*, vol. 39, pp. 61–87.

Brewer, G. A. and Selden, S. C. 1998, 'Whistle-blowers in the federal civil service: new evidence of the public service ethic', *Journal of Public Administration Research and Theory*, vol. 8, no. 3, pp. 413–39.

Brief, A. P. and Motowidlo, S. J. 1986, 'Prosocial organisational behaviours', *Academy of Management Review*, vol. 11, no. 4, pp. 710–25.

Brockner, J. and Wiesenfeld, B. 2005, 'How, when, and why does outcome favourability interact with procedural fairness', in J. Greenberg and J. A. Colquitt (eds), *Handbook of Organisational Justice*, Lawrence Erlbaum Associates, London, pp. 525–53.

Brockner, J., Fishman, A.Y., Reb, J., Goldman, B., Spiegel, S. and Garden, C. 2007, 'Procedural fairness, outcome favourability, and judgements of an authority's responsibility', *Journal of Applied Psychology*, vol. 92, pp. 1657–71.

Brown, A. J. 2001, 'Internal witness management: an art or a science?', *Ethics and Justice*, vol. 3, no. 2, pp. 45–61.

—— 2006, *Public interest disclosure legislation in Australia: towards the next generation*, Issues paper, Commonwealth Ombudsman, NSW Ombudsman and Queensland Ombudsman.

—— 2007, 'Privacy and public interest disclosures—when is it reasonable to protect whistleblowing to the media?', *Privacy Law Bulletin*, vol. 4, no. 2, pp. 19–28.

Brown, A. J. and Latimer, P. (forthcoming), 'Symbols or substance? Priorities for the reform of Australian public interest disclosure legislation', *Griffith Law Review*; <http://papers.ssrn.com/sol3/papers.cfm?abstract_id=991710>

Brown, A. J., Adair, D., Baker, G., Connors, C., Gilligan, G., Head, B. et al. 2005, *Chaos or coherence? Strengths, opportunities and challenges for Australia's integrity systems*, Final Report of the National Integrity Systems Assessment (NISA), Griffith University and Transparency International.

Brown, A. J., Magendanz, D. and Leary, C. 2004, 'Speaking up: building positive reporting climates in the Queensland public sector', *Building Capacity Series*, vol. 6, Crime and Misconduct Commission, Brisbane, Queensland.

Byrne, Z. S. 2005, 'Fairness reduces the negative effects of organisational politics on turnover intentions, citizenship behaviour and job performance', *Journal of Business and Psychology*, vol. 20, pp. 175–200.

Calland, R. and Dehn, G. 2004, 'Introduction—whistleblowing around the world: the state of the art', in R. Calland and G. Dehn (eds), *Whistleblowing Around the World—Law, Culture and Practice*, Public Concern at Work, London.

Carson, J. 2006, The need for whistleblowing legislation in Canada: a critical defence, Paper presented to the Canadian Political Science Association Conference, June 2006, <http://www.cpsa-acsp.ca/papers-2006/Carson.pdf>

Colquitt, J. A., Conlon, D. E., Wesson, M. J., Porter, C. and Ng, K. Y. 2001, 'Justice at the turn of the millennium: a meta-analytic review of 25 years of organisational justice research', *Journal of Applied Psychology*, vol. 86, pp. 425–45.

Colquitt, J. A., Greenberg, J. and Scott, B. A. 2005, 'Organisational justice: where do we stand?', in J. Greenberg and J. A. Colquitt (eds), *Handbook of Organisational Justice*, Lawrence Erlbaum Associates, New Jersey, pp. 589–620.

Colquitt, J. A., Scott, B. A. and LePine, J. A. 2007, 'Trust, trustworthiness and trust propensity: a meta-analytic test of their unique relationships with risk taking and job performance', *Journal of Applied Psychology*, vol. 92, pp. 909–27.

Colquitt, J. A., Scott, B. A., Judge, T. A. and Shaw, J. C. 2006, 'Justice and personality: using integrative theories to derive moderators of justice effects', *Organisational Behaviour and Human Decision Processes*, vol. 100, pp. 110–27.

Commonwealth of Australia 2008, *Australia 2020 Summit: Final report*, Department of Prime Minister and Cabinet, Canberra.

Commonwealth Ombudsman 1997, *Professional Reporting and Internal Witness Protection in the Australian Federal Police: A review of practices and procedures*, Commonwealth Ombudsman, Canberra.

Cropanzo, R., Byrne, Z. S., Bobocel, D. R. and Rupp, D. E. 2001, 'Moral virtues, fairness heuristics, social entities, and other denizens of organisational justice', *Journal of Vocational Behaviour*, vol. 58, pp. 164–209.

Davies, G., 2005, *Report of Queensland Public Hospitals Commission of Inquiry*, Queensland Government, Brisbane.

Dawson, S. 2000, Whistleblowing and public policy, Paper presented at the Australasian Political Studies Association Conference, October 2000, Canberra, Australia.

De Cremer, D. and Tyler, T. R. 2007, 'The effects of trust in authority and procedural fairness on cooperation', *Journal of Applied Psychology*, vol. 92, pp. 639–49.

de Maria, W. 1994, Unshielding the shadow culture: Queensland whistleblower study, Result release one, University of Queensland, Brisbane.

—— 1999, *Deadly Disclosures: Whistleblowing and the ethical meltdown of Australia*, Wakefield Press, Adelaide.

de Maria, W. and Jan, C. 1994, Wounded workers: Queensland whistleblower study, Result release two, University of Queensland, Brisbane.

Dempster, Q., 1997, *Whistleblowers*, ABC Books, Sydney.

Dobel, J. P. 1999, *Public Integrity*, Johns Hopkins University Press, Baltimore.

Dozier, J. B. and Miceli, M. P. 1985, 'Potential predictors of whistle-blowing: a prosocial behaviour perspective', *The Academy of Management Review*, vol. 18, pp. 823–36.

Dworkin, T. M. and Baucus, M. S. 1998, 'Internal vs external whistleblowers: a comparison of whistleblowing processes', *Journal of Business Ethics*, vol. 17, no. 12, pp. 1281–98.

Ellis, S. and Arieli, S. 1999, 'Predicting intentions to report administrative and disciplinary infractions: applying the reasoned action model', *Human Relations*, vol. 52, pp. 947–67.

Elliston, F. 1985, *Whistleblowing Research: Methodological and moral issues*, Praeger, New York.

Fassina, N. E., Jones, J. D. and Uggerslev, K. L. 2007, 'Meta-analytic tests of relationships between organisational justice and citizenship behaviour: testing agent-system and shared-variance models', *Journal of Organisational Behaviour*, viewed 10 October, 2007, <http://www3.interscience.wiley.com>

Ferraro, E. F. and Spain, N. M. 2006, *Investigations in the Workplace*, Auerbach Publications/Taylor & Francis, Florida.

Foote, D. and Robinson, I. 1999, 'The role of the human resources manager: strategist or conscience of the organisation?', *Business Ethics: A European Review*, vol. 8, pp. 88–98.

Freeman, P. 1998, Law enforcement agencies in North America and their management of internal complainants, Report to NSW Police Service/Churchill Fellowship.

Freeman, P. and Garnett, B. 1996, *The physical, psychological and social effects of becoming an internal witness in the NSW Police Service*, NSW Police Service Internal Witness Support Unit, Sydney.

Gibbs, H. 1991, *Review of Commonwealth Criminal Law—Final report*, Sir Harry Gibbs, Chairman, December, Australian Government Publishing Service, Canberra.

Glazer, M. and Glazer, P. M. 1989, *The Whistleblowers: Exposing corruption in government and industry*, Basic Books, New York.

Gobert, J. and Punch, M. 2000, 'Whistleblowers, the public interest and the *Public Interest Disclosure Act 1998*', *Modern Law Review*, vol. 63, pp. 25–54.

Goyder, J. C. 1987, 'The silent minority', *Public Opinion Quarterly*, vol. 51, pp. 156–72.

Grace, D. and Cohen, S. 1998, 'Whistleblowing', in D. Grace and S. Cohen, *Business Ethics: Australian problems and cases*, Oxford University Press, Melbourne, pp. 148–61.

Graham, J. W. 1989, Whistleblowing as organisational citizenship behaviour and/or civic duty, Annual Meeting of the American Society of Criminology, Reno, Nevada.

Grant, C. 2002, 'Whistle blowers: saints of secular culture', *Journal of Business Ethics*, vol. 39, no. 4, pp. 391–9.

Harlos, K. P. 2001, 'When organisational systems fail: more on the deaf-ear syndrome and frustration effects', *The Journal of Applied Behavioural Science*, vol. 37, pp. 324–42.

Jubb, P. 1999, 'Whistleblowing: a restrictive definition and interpretation', *Journal of Business Ethics*, vol. 21, pp. 77–94.

Keenan, J. P. 2000, 'Blowing the whistle on less serious forms of fraud: a study of executives and managers', *Employee Responsibilities and Rights Journal*, vol. 12, no. 4, pp. 199–217.

—— 2002, 'Whistleblowing: a study of managerial differences', *Employee Responsibilities and Rights Journal*, vol. 14, no. 1, pp. 17–31.

Kramer, R. M. 1999, 'Trust and distrust in organizations: emerging perspectives, enduring questions', *Annual Review of Psychology*, vol. 50, pp. 569–98.

Kray, L. J. and Lind, E. A. 2002, 'The injustices of others: social reports and the integration of others' experiences in organisational justice judgements', *Organisational Behaviour and Human Decision Processes*, vol. 89, pp. 906–24.

Latané, B. and Darley, J. M. 1970, *The Unresponsive Bystander: Why doesn't he help?*, Appleton-Century-Crofts, New York.

Latimer, P. 2002a, 'Whistleblowing in the financial services sector', *University of Tasmania Law Review*, vol. 21, no. 1, pp. 39–61.

—— 2002b, 'Reporting suspicions of money laundering and "whistleblowing": the legal and other implications for intermediaries and their advisers', *Journal of Financial Crime*, vol. 10, no. 1, pp. 23–9.

Latimer, P. and Brown, A. J. 2007, 'In whose interest? The need for consistency in to whom, and about whom, Australian public interest whistleblowers can make protected disclosures', *Deakin Law Review*, vol. 12, pp. 1–21.

Lewis, D. B. 2001, 'Introduction', in D. B. Lewis (ed.), *Whistleblowing at Work*, The Athlone Press, London, pp. 1–9.

—— 2002, 'Whistleblowing procedures at work: what are the implications for human resource practitioners?', *Business Ethics: A European Review*, vol. 11, no. 3, pp. 202–9.

McLain, D. L. and Keenan, J. P. 1999, 'Risk, information, and the decision about response to wrongdoing in an organisation', *Journal of Business Ethics*, vol. 19, no. 3, pp. 255–71.

McMillan, J. 1994, 'Whistleblowing initiatives: an overview', in N. Preston (ed.), *Ethics for the Public Sector: Education and training*, Federation Press, Sydney, pp. 115–32.

MacNab, B. R. and Worthley, R. 2007, 'Self-efficacy as an intrapersonal predictor for internal whistleblowing: a US and Canada examination', *Journal of Business Ethics*, viewed 9 October 2007, <http://www.springerlink.com>

Martin, B. 1997, *Suppression Stories*, Fund for Intellectual Dissent, Wollongong, New South Wales.

Masser, B. and Brown, R. 1996, '"When would you do it?" An investigation into the effects of retaliation, seriousness of malpractice and occupation on willingness to blow the whistle', *Journal of Community & Applied Social Psychology*, vol. 6, pp. 127–30.

Mesmer-Magnus, J. R. and Viswevaran, C. 2005, 'Whistleblowing in organisations: an examination of correlates of whistleblowing intentions, actions, and retaliation', *Journal of Business Ethics*, vol. 62, pp. 277–97.

Miceli, M. P. and Near, J. P. 1984, 'The relationships among beliefs, organisational position, and whistle-blowing status: a discriminant analysis', *Academy of Management Journal*, vol. 27, no. 4, pp. 687–705.

—— 1988, 'Individual and situational correlates of whistle-blowing', *Personnel Psychology*, vol. 41, no. 2, pp. 267–81.

—— 2005, 'Standing up or standing by: what predicts blowing the whistle on organisational wrongdoing?', *Research in Personnel and Human Resource Management*, vol. 24, pp. 95–136.

—— 2006, Whistle-blowing as constructive deviance: an integration of the prosocial and social information processing models, Manuscript submitted for publication.

Miceli, M. P., Near, J. P. and Schwenk, C. R. 1991, 'Who blows the whistle and why?', *Industrial & Labor Relations Review*, vol. 45, no. 1, pp. 113–30.

Miceli, M. P., Rehg, M., Near, J. P. and Ryan, K. C. 1999, 'Can laws protect whistle-blowers? Results of a naturally occurring field experiment', *Work and Occupations*, vol. 26, no. 1, pp. 129–51.

Miceli, M. P., Van Scotter, J. R., Near, J. P. and Rehg, M. 2001, 'Responses to perceived organisational wrongdoing: do perceiver characteristics matter?', in J. M. Darley, D. M. Messick and T. R. Tyler (eds), *Social Influences on Ethical Behaviour*, Lawrence Erlbaum Associates, Mahwah, NJ, pp. 119–35.

Miethe, T. D. and Rothschild, J. 1994, 'Whistleblowing and the control of organisational misconduct', *Sociological Inquiry*, vol. 64, pp. 322–47.

Moorman, R. H. and Blakely, G. L. 1995, 'Individualism–collectivism as an individual difference predictor of organisational citizenship behaviour', *Journal of Organisational Behaviour*, vol. 16, no. 2, pp. 127–42.

Moss, I. 2007, *Report on the independent audit into the state of free speech in Australia*, 31 October 2007, Australia's Right to Know Committee, Sydney.

Murray, A. 2007, 'Second reading speech', *Public Interest Disclosures Bill 2007 (Cth)*, Commonwealth Parliamentary Debates, Senate, 14 June 2007.

Near, J. P. and Miceli, M. P. 1996, 'Whistle-blowing: myth and reality', *Journal of Management*, vol. 22, no. 3, pp. 507–26.

Near, J. P., Rehg, M. T., Van Scotter, J. R. and Miceli, M. P. 2004, 'Does type of wrongdoing affect the whistleblowing process?', *Business Ethics Quarterly*, vol. 14, no. 2, pp. 219–42.

NSW Legislative Assembly 2006, *Review of the Protected Disclosures Act 1994*, November 2006, Committee on the Independent Commission Against Corruption, Parliament, New South Wales Legislative Assembly, Sydney.

NSW Ombudsman 2004a, *The adequacy of the* Protected Disclosure Act [NSW] *to achieve its objectives*, Issues paper, Sydney.

—— 2004b, *Protected Disclosure Guidelines*, Fifth Edition, Sydney, pp. E5–6.

—— 2005a, *Protecting whistleblowers: practical alternatives to confidentiality*, Information sheet, <http://www.ombo.nsw.gov.au>

—— 2005b, *Whistleblowing*, Public Sector Agencies Fact Sheet No. 23, December 2005, Sydney.

Oakes, L. 2005, 'Pillars of democracy depend on leaks', *The Bulletin/National Nine News*, 24 August 2005, <http://news.ninemsn.com.au>

Office of the Public Sector Standards Commissioner (OPSSC) 2007, *Compliance Report: Public interest disclosures 2006–2007*, Office of the Public Sector Standards Commissioner, West Australian Government, Perth.

Organ, D. W. 1988, 'A restatement of the satisfaction-performance hypothesis', *Journal of Management*, vol. 14, no. 4, pp. 547–57.

Padraic, S. 2005, *Sympathy for the Devil*, ABC Books, Sydney.

Penner, L. A., Dovidio, J. F., Piliavin, J. A. and Schroeder, D. A. 2005, 'Prosocial behaviour: multilevel perspectives', *Annual Review of Psychology*, vol. 56, pp. 365–92.

Pershing, J. L. 2003, 'To snitch or not to snitch? Applying the concept of neutralization techniques to the enforcement of occupational misconduct', *Sociological Perspectives*, vol. 46, no. 2, pp. 149–78.

Podsakoff, P. M., MacKenzie, S. B., Paine, J. and Bachrach, D. G. 2000, 'Organisational citizenship behaviours: a critical review of the theoretical and empirical literature and suggestions for future research', *Journal of Management*, vol. 26, no. 3, pp. 513–63.

Queensland Electoral and Administrative Review Commission 1991, *Report on protection of whistleblowers*, Queensland Electoral and Administrative Review Commission, Brisbane, Australia.

Robinson, S. L. and Rousseau, D. M. 1994, 'Violating the psychological contract: not the exception but the norm', *Journal of Organisational Behaviour*, vol. 15, pp. 245–59.

Rothschild, J. and Miethe, T. D., 1999, 'Whistle-blower disclosures and management retaliation: the battle to control information about organization corruption', *Work and Occupations*, vol. 26, no. 1, pp. 107–28.

Senate Select Committee on Public Interest Whistleblowing 1994, *In the Public Interest: Report of the Senate Select Committee on Public Interest Whistleblowing*, The Parliament of the Commonwealth of Australia, Canberra.

Sennewald, C. A. 1991, *The Process of Investigation*, Butterworth-Heinemann, Boston.

Sims, R. L. and Keenan, J. P. 1998, 'Predictors of external whistleblowing: organisational and intrapersonal variables', *Journal of Business Ethics*, vol. 17, no. 4, pp. 411–21.

Skarlicki, D. P. and Folger, R. 1997, 'Retaliation in the workplace: the roles of distributive, procedural and interactional justice', *Journal of Applied Psychology*, vol. 82, pp. 434–43.

Smith, C. 1996, Development and management of the Internal Witness Support Program in the NSW Police Service, RIPAA Investigation Techniques Conference.

Solomon, D. 2006, 'Whistleblowers and Governments Need More Protection', in *Proceedings of the 2nd National Conference of Parliamentary Oversight Committees of Anti-Corruption/Crime Bodies*, NSW Parliament House, Sydney, 22-23 February 2006, Report 7/53.

Somers, M. J. and Casal, J. C. 1994, 'Organisational commitment and whistle-blowing', *Group & Organization Management*, vol. 19, no. 3, pp. 270–84.

Spigelman, J. J. 2004, '"The integrity branch of government": First 2004 National Lecture, Australian Institute of Administrative Law, Sydney, 29 April 2004', *Australian Law Journal*, vol. 78, no. 11, pp. 724–37.

Standards Australia 2003, *Whistleblower Protection Programs for Entities (AS 8004-2003)*, Standards Australia International, Sydney.

Steiger, J. J. 1980, 'Tests for comparing elements of a correlation matrix', *Psychological Bulletin*, vol. 87, no. 2, pp. 245–51.

Strandmark, M. and Hallberg, L. R. M. 2007, 'The origin of workplace bullying: experiences from the perspective of bully victims in the public sector', *Journal of Nursing Management*, vol. 15, pp. 332–41.

Tavakoli, A. A., Keenan, J. P. and Crnjak-Karanovic, B. 2003, 'Culture and whistleblowing: an empirical study of Croatian and United States managers utilizing Hofstede's cultural dimensions', *Journal of Business Ethics*, vol. 43, pp. 49–64.

Thau, S., Bennett, R. J., Stahlberg, D. and Werner, J. M. 2004, 'Why should I be generous when I have valued and accessible alternatives? Alternative exchange partners and OCB', *Journal of Organisational Behaviour*, vol. 25, pp. 607–26.

Trevino, L. K. and Victor, B. 1992, 'Peer reporting of unethical behaviour', *Academy of Management Journal*, vol. 35, pp. 38–65.

Trevino, L. K., Weaver, G. R. and Reynolds, S. J. 2006, 'Behavioural ethics in organisations: a review', *Journal of Management*, vol. 32, pp. 951–90.

Truelson, J. A. 2001, 'Whistleblower protection and the judiciary', in T. L. Cooper (ed.), *Handbook of Administrative Ethics*, Marcel Dekker, New York, pp. 407–28.

Tschannen-Moran, M. and Hoy, W. K. 2000, 'A multidisciplinary analysis of the nature, meaning, and measurement of trust', *Review of Educational Research*, vol. 70, no. 4, pp. 547–93.

US Merit Systems Protection Board 1981, *Whistleblowing and the Federal Employee: Blowing the whistle on fraud, waste, and mismanagement—who does it and what happens*, Office of Policy and Evaluation, US Merit Systems Protection Board, Washington, DC.

—— 1993, *Whistleblowing in the Federal Government: An update*, Office of Policy and Evaluation, US Merit Systems Protection Board, Washington, DC.

—— 2003. *The Federal Workforce for the 21st Century: Results of the Merit Principles Survey 2000*, Office of Policy and Evaluation, US Merit Systems Protection Board, Washington, DC, pp. 1–67.

Uhr, J. 2005, *Terms of Trust: Arguments over ethics in Australian government*, University of New South Wales Press, Sydney.

Vandekerckhove, W. 2006, *Whistle-Blowing and Organisational Social Responsibility: A global assessment*, Aldershot, Hampshire, England.

Vinten, G. (ed.) 1994, *Whistleblowing—Subversion or corporate citizenship?*, St Martin's Press, New York.

Weber, M. 1978, 'Economy and Society', in G. Roth and C. Wittich (eds), University of California Press, Berkeley.

Weinstein, D. 1979, *Bureaucratic Opposition*, Pergamon Press, New York.

Whitton, H. 1996, Whistleblowers and whistleblower protection: troublemakers or open government?, Paper presented to AIC Conference: Achieving Quality Decision-Making at Administrative Law, 21–22 November 1996.

Williams, L. J. and Anderson, S. E. 1991, 'Job satisfaction and organisational commitment as predictors of organisational citizenship and in-role behaviours', *Journal of Management*, vol. 17, no. 3, pp. 601–17.

Wood, J., Hon. Justice 1997, *Royal Commission into NSW Police Service Final Report. Volume III*, Appendices, 29.

Zellars, K. L., Tepper, B. J. and Duffy, M. K. 2002, 'Abusive supervision and the subordinates' organisational citizenship behaviour', *Journal of Applied Psychology*, vol. 87, pp. 1068–76.

Zhuang, J., Thomas, S. and Miller, D. L. 2005, 'Examining culture's effect on whistleblowing and peer reporting', *Business & Society*, vol. 44, pp. 462–86.

Zipparo, L. 1999a, 'Factors which deter public officials from reporting corruption', *Crime Law and Social Change*, vol. 30, no. 3, pp. 273–87.

—— 1999b, 'Encouraging public sector employees to report workplace corruption', *Australian Journal of Public Administration*, vol. 58, no. 2, pp. 83–93.

# Appendix A. Research questions

| Primary questions | Subsidiary questions |
|---|---|
| **A. The incidence and significance of public sector whistleblowing (and other internal witness roles)** | |
| 1. How common is whistleblowing (and other internal witness roles) in public sector organisations? | 1. How common is whistleblowing according to agency statistics?<br>2. How common is whistleblowing according to staff in general?<br>3. How common is whistleblowing *perceived* to be by specific target groups (internal witnesses/case-handlers/management at different levels)?<br>4. How common are different *types* of whistleblowing and other internal witness roles? |
| 2. How important is whistleblowing (and other internal witness roles) in public sector organisations? | 1. What proportion of public sector wrongdoing comes to light through whistleblowing?<br>2. What types of wrongdoing come to light through whistleblowing?<br>3. How serious are the types of wrongdoing that come to light through whistleblowing?<br>4. How important is whistleblowing according to official (including legislative) policies?<br>5. How important is whistleblowing according to staff in general?<br>6. How important is whistleblowing according to specific target groups (internal witnesses/case-handlers/management at different levels)? |
| 3. What factors and circumstances give rise to whistleblowing (and other internal witness roles) in public sector organisations? | 1. What factors and circumstances are *perceived* as giving rise to whistleblowing according to staff in general?<br>2. What factors and circumstances are *perceived* as giving rise to whistleblowing according to specific target groups (internal witnesses/case-handlers/ management at different levels)?<br>3. What factors and circumstances appear to give rise to whistleblowing based on *all* the evidence? |

| Primary questions | Subsidiary questions |
|---|---|
| **B. The experiences and perceived experiences of public sector whistleblowers (and other internal witnesses)** | |
| 4. What do whistleblowers and other internal witnesses experience in the course of this role? | 1. What do internal witnesses expect to happen to them *before* they become internal witnesses?<br>2. What do internal witnesses perceive as happening to them *when* they become internal witnesses?<br>3. How do internal witnesses think they are perceived and treated by others in their organisations?<br>4. Do internal witnesses' self-perceptions affect their treatment in organisations, or result from their treatment, or neither?<br>5. Do internal witnesses' experiences affect their judgments about future whistleblowing?<br>6. Are differences in outcomes of a) investigations or b) internal witness management associated with differences in internal witnesses' *self-perceptions* of their experience?<br>7. Are differences in outcomes of a) investigations or b) internal witness management associated with differences in *staff/management perceptions* of whistleblowing? |
| 5. How common are reprisals against whistleblowers and what forms do they take? | 1. What frequencies and types of reprisals are reported by internal witnesses?<br>2. What frequencies and types of reprisals are experienced by internal witnesses or observed by others (for example, case-handlers), but not reported?<br>3. What proportion of reported reprisals are short, medium and long term?<br>4. What proportion of reported reprisals are a) deliberate/negligent or b) unofficial/official?<br>5. What proportion of internal witnesses does *not* experience or report reprisals?<br>6. What proportion of reported reprisals occurs against people *other* than whistleblowers or internal witnesses (for example, mistaken identity)?<br>7. Are differences in frequency or type of reported reprisals (including no reprisals) associated with differences in organisations' internal witness management programs?<br>8. How are reported reprisals investigated—including by whom, according to what standards of proof?<br>9. What are the outcomes of reprisal investigations and are differences in outcome associated with differences in frequency, type, internal witnesses' perceptions of their experience, staff/management perceptions of whistleblowing, different types or manner of investigations? |

| Primary questions | Subsidiary questions |
|---|---|
| **C. The incidence, nature and influence of internal witness management/whistleblower protection programs within and across the public sector** | |
| 6. What is the range of internal witness management policies and programs within and across the public sector? | 1. How many agencies are required to have internal witness management/ whistleblower protection programs?<br>2. How many agencies do have programs?<br>3. What are the elements of agencies' internal programs?<br>4. How many agencies have active (as opposed to simply reactive) programs?<br>5. What roles do external integrity agencies play in respect of internal witnesses; how many have internal witness management/whistleblower protection programs; what are the elements of their programs? |
| 7. Are different outcomes of the whistleblowing process associated with differences in a) legislation, b) procedures/ programs and/or c) CEO/senior management commitment and culture, in respect of internal witnesses? | 1. Are differences in wrongdoing reporting rates associated with differences in legislation, procedures and/or management commitment?<br>2. Are differences in reporting climate (culture)/expressed willingness to report associated with differences in legislation, procedures and/or management commitment?<br>3. Are differences in whistleblower/internal witness experiences associated with differences in legislation, procedures and/or management commitment?<br>4. Are differences in perceptions towards whistleblowing associated with differences in legislation, procedures and/or management commitment?<br>5. What is the relative impact/importance of legislation, procedures and management commitment in the above? |
| 8. Which external factors have effects (positive or negative) on internal witness management? | 1. Is the legislative framework an important influence on the success or failure of internal witness management programs?<br>2. Which features of different legislative frameworks are associated with different levels of success or failure of programs?<br>3. What effects do external integrity agency activities have on the internal witness management practices and programs of organisations, including success or failure? |
| 9. What policies can organisations pursue to most effectively manage and maximise whistleblowing? | Drawn from all of the above. |
| 10. What reforms can governments pursue to most effectively manage and maximise whistleblowing? | Drawn from all of the above. |

# Appendix B. Wrongdoing categories and types

## Employee survey, internal witness survey and case-handler and manager surveys

| Category | | Wrongdoing type |
|---|---|---|
| 1. Misconduct for material gain | a. | Theft of money |
| | b. | Theft of property |
| | c. | Bribes or kickbacks |
| | d. | Using official position to get personal services or favours |
| | e. | Giving unfair advantage to a contractor, consultant or supplier |
| | f. | Improper use of agency facilities or resources for private purposes |
| | g. | Rorting overtime or leave provisions |
| | h. | Making false or inflated claims for reimbursement |
| 9. Conflict of interest | i. | Failing to declare a financial interest in an agency venture |
| | j. | Intervening in a decision on behalf of a friend or relative |
| | k. | Improper involvement of a family business |
| 12. Improper or unprofessional behaviour | l. | Downloading pornography on a work computer |
| | m. | Being drunk or under the influence of illegal drugs at work |
| | n. | Sexual assault |
| | o. | Stalking (unwanted following or intrusion into personal life) |
| | p. | Sexual harassment |
| | r. | Racial discrimination against a member of the public |
| | s. | Misuse of confidential information |
| 19. Defective administration | t. | Incompetent or negligent decision making |
| | u. | Failure to correct serious mistakes |
| | v. | Endangering public health or safety |
| | w. | Producing or using unsafe products |
| | bb. | Acting against organisational policy, regulations or laws |
| 24. Waste or mismanagement of resources | y. | Waste of work funds |
| | z. | Inadequate record keeping |
| | aa. | Negligent purchases or leases |
| 27. Perverting justice or accountability | cc. | Covering up poor performance |
| | dd. | Misleading or false reporting of agency activity |
| | ee. | Covering up corruption |
| | ff. | Hindering an official investigation |
| | gg. | Unlawfully altering or destroying official records |
| 32. Personnel and workplace grievances | q. | Racial discrimination against a staff member |
| | x. | Allowing dangerous or harmful working conditions |
| | hh. | Unfair dismissal |
| | ii. | Failure to follow correct staff-selection procedures |
| | jj. | Favouritism in selection or promotion |
| | ll. | Bullying of staff |
| 38. Reprisals against whistleblowers | kk. | Reprisal against whistleblowers |
| 39. Other | mm. | Other |

## Agency survey categories and examples

### a. Misconduct for material gain

For example: theft, fraud, bribery, private use of agency resources.

### b. Conflict of interest

For example: failure to declare financial interest, improper involvement of family business.

### c. Improper/unprofessional behaviour

For example: rudeness or mistreatment of public, inappropriate sexual relations, misuse of confidential information, personal misconduct.

### d. Defective administration

For example: failures in duty, negligence, incompetence, delay, uncorrected mistakes, breach of administrative law or procedures, dangers to public health or safety.

### e. Waste or mismanagement of resources

For example: bad grants or purchases, poor budget control, inadequate record keeping.

### f. Perverting justice or accountability

For example: making false statements, misleading the public, fabricating evidence, hindering investigation, cover-ups.

### g. Poor personnel practices

For example: unfair dismissal, breaches of merit and equity, favouritism, breaches of workplace health or safety, workplace discrimination.

# Appendix C. A new framework for internal witness management systems

This document sets out a framework of the 'dimensions' of internal witness management systems that are currently found and/or might be desirable in public sector agencies. The ultimate aim of the research is to fully understand what makes a comprehensive and viable whistleblowing system within an organisation.

These seven dimensions and 39 sub-dimensions were drawn from a variety of sources: background literature; a July 2005 symposium held by the project in Canberra; issues emerging from empirical data collected by the project (including the agency survey); an analysis of the written whistleblowing procedures supplied to the project by 175 agencies; workshops with the project's case study agencies in July 2007 and July 2008; and revised findings from and comments on the draft report of October 2007.

The framework provides a consistent approach for description and comparison of the different approaches to whistleblower management and support found among different agencies. It also provides a structure for the analyses to be presented in the second project report, outlining current and prospective best practice across a diverse range of organisations.

# The dimensions of an internal witness management system

**Dimension and sub-dimensions**

1. **Organisational commitment**

    1.1. Management commitment to the principle of whistleblowing and statements of the organisation's support for the reporting of wrongdoing through appropriate channels.

    1.2. Understanding of the benefits and importance to the entity of having a whistleblowing mechanism.

    1.3. Commitment that a credible investigation process will follow the receipt of a whistleblowing report and that any confirmed wrongdoing will be remedied.

    1.4. Commitment to protect and respect internal witnesses.

    1.5. Positive organisational engagement on whistleblowing issues with external integrity agencies, staff associations and client groups.

2. **Reporting pathways**

    2.1. Clear *internal* pathways setting out how, to whom and about whom whistleblowing reports may be made, including guidance on the most appropriate pathways for different types of reports.

    2.2. Clear *external* pathways setting out how, to whom and about whom whistleblowing reports may be made, including guidance on the most appropriate pathways for different types of reports.

    2.3. Clear and understood relationships between internal and external reporting.

    2.4. Clear advice to employees on who may invoke the whistleblowing mechanism (that is, employees, contractors, and so on).

    2.5. Clear advice to employees on the types of concerns about which it is appropriate to use the whistleblowing mechanism, including levels of proof required (for example, certainty versus suspicion regarding the truth of concerns).

    2.6. Organisational capacity for differentiating, where appropriate, between employment-related grievances and public interest disclosures.

    2.7. Mechanisms for ensuring responses to whistleblowing are undertaken with the appropriate informality/formality, as the case requires.

    2.8. Commitment that anonymous reports will be acted on.

3. **Management obligation to employees**

    3.1. Realistic assurance of the confidentiality of reports.

    3.2. Assessment of the risk of reprisal against internal witnesses.

    3.3. Procedures and resources for responding to reprisal risks against internal witnesses.

    3.4. Commitment that staff who report wrongdoing will not suffer any disciplinary or similar action as a result.

    3.5. Mechanisms to ensure positive action by the entity to protect internal witnesses, including restitution/compensation when protective action becomes unsuccessful or impossible.

    3.6. Continuing monitoring of the welfare of whistleblowers.

    3.7. Clear procedures for the protection of the rights of people against whom allegations have been made.

    3.8. Appropriate sanctions against false or vexatious allegations.

4. **Organisational support for internal witnesses**

    4.1. Systems and/or services for providing active management and support of internal witnesses.

    4.2. Procedures and resources for the investigation of reprisal action against internal witnesses, including action against any people found responsible.

    4.3. Provision of information, advice and feedback to internal witnesses on actions being taken in response to disclosure.

    4.4. Exit strategies for finalising whistleblowing cases.

    4.5. Regular evaluation of the effectiveness of the program.

**Dimension and sub-dimensions**

5.    **Institutional arrangements**

5.1. Clear understanding of the whistleblowing-related roles and responsibilities of key players—internal and external to the organisation.

5.2. Effective sharing of responsibility for the support and management of whistleblowers between line managers, corporate management and external agencies.

5.3. Effective separation of investigation and support functions.

5.4. Proactive (not reactive) operation of the whistleblower support program.

5.5. Embedding of policies and procedures in existing management systems and corporate governance arrangements, including mechanisms for recording, tracking and reporting all whistleblowing reports.

6.    **Skills and resources**

6.1. Financial resources dedicated to the whistleblower program.

6.2. Investigation competencies and training.

6.3. Reprisal investigation competencies and training.

6.4. Support, counselling and management competencies and training.

7.    **Promulgation of procedures**

7.1. Multiple strategies for ensuring staff awareness of the whistleblowing program.

7.2. Clear information about legislative protection.

7.3. Easy-to-comprehend procedures, including relationship with other procedures.

7.4. High level of employee awareness and comprehension of and confidence in procedures.

www.ingramcontent.com/pod-product-compliance
Lightning Source LLC
Chambersburg PA
CBHW061241270326

41928CB00041B/3357